SUSTAINABLE INFRASTRUCTURE

SUSTAINABLE INFRASTRUCTURE

The Guide to Green Engineering and Design

S. Bry Sarté

WILEY

JOHN WILEY & SONS, INC.

For general information about our other products and services, please contact our Customer Care Department within the United States at (800) 762-2974, outside the United States at (317) 572-3993 or fax (317) 572-4002.

Wiley also publishes its books in a variety of electronic formats. Some content that appears in print may not be available in electronic books. For more information about Wiley products, visit our web site at www.wiley.com.

Library of Congress Cataloging-in-Publication Data:

Sarte, S. Bry, 1972-

   The green infrastructure guide : innovative water resource, site design, and land planning strategies for design professionals / S. Bry Sarte.

        p. cm.

Summary: "As more factors, perspectives, and metrics are incorporated into the planning and building process, the roles of engineers and designers are increasingly being fused together. The Art of Eco-Engineering explores this trend with in-depth look at sustainable engineering practices in an urban design as it involves watershed master-planning, green building, optimizing water reuse, reclaiming urban spaces, green streets initiatives, and sustainable master-planning. This complete guide provides guidance on the role creative thinking and collaborative team-building play in meeting solutions needed to effect a sustainable transformation of the built environment"—Provided by publisher.

Summary: "In-depth look at sustainable engineering practices in an urban design context, this book offers guidance on developing strategies for implementing the complex solutions needed to effect a sustainable transformation of the built environment. With coverage of watershed master-planning, green building, optimizing water reuse, reclaiming urban spaces, green streets initiatives, and sustainable master-planning, the book supplements the core reference material with international examples and case studies" —Provided by publisher.

   Includes bibliographical references and index.

   ISBN 978-0-470-45361-2 (hardback); ISBN 978-0-470-91295-9 (ebk); ISBN 978-0-470-91294-2 (ebk); ISBN 978-0-470-91293-5 (ebk)

   1. Sustainable engineering. 2. Sustainable design. I. Title.

   TA170.S24 2010

   710--dc22

                                    2010013928

10 9 8 7 6 5 4 3 2 1

FOR SIMONE AND SCARLETT SARTÉ
AND ALL THE OTHER CHILDREN
INHERITING THIS PLANET

CONTENTS

FOREWORD
Cliff Garten

Since World War II, questions as to how we build our infrastructure have largely been left to the engineering community. For the most part, engineers have done a remarkable job of answering our needs with buildings, pipes, bridges, and tunnels that maximize service and efficiency. But in the new millennium, the social, economic, and ecological issues surrounding infrastructure are increasingly becoming too complex to be left to the engineering community alone. In a time of exploding urban populations, dwindling natural resources, and the threat of climate change, creating sustainable systems for water and energy is no longer a question solely for engineers. Ecologists, landscape architects, artists, and architects must become involved as well.

By necessity, we are now moving toward an interdisciplinary, collaborative approach to solving these problems. Multidisciplinary design teams are using sustainable infrastructure projects as an opportunity to take a broader view of the intrinsic relationships between humanity and the planet. By celebrating infrastructure itself, we also recognize our dependency on the natural systems that we mediate with our infrastructure.

Infrastructure delivers the resources that feed us and our cities—resources in ever-shorter supply. The professional design community knows that the ways we use water and the systems we depend on to grow our food—to name just two examples—are unsustainable. But if infrastructure is hidden from view, the public is much less likely to contemplate the interrelationships between themselves and the greater ecological world. A new, revitalized approach to environmental engineering is proceeding from the recognition that sustainable infrastructure is as much about shifting the values we hold as a culture as it is about science and design.

The infrastructure projects of the Works Progress Administration are some of the best known and loved public works in American history in part because of the values they reflect and express: a shared belief in progress and a consensus that the works were important. Today we are undergoing a paradigm shift comparable to that of the Great Depression, one also necessitated by financial and environmental crisis. And the excitement and innovation that presently drive sustainable development and green design indicate that there is again a growing consensus that we have important work to do.

The word *sustainable* is really one we use to speak about our own survival. And to be sustainable, we must change our intention toward the earth and its resources. If our survival depends on a conscious shift in the ways we use our resources, then what better place to start than the infrastructures that support our cities, towns, and agriculture? And what better way to engage the public in the issues surrounding our most precious resources than by putting a renewed emphasis on the very structures that move and manage these resources?

In the context of these new sensibilities, engineering can function in two innovative ways. The way a bridge looks and its public presence is as important as its physical functionality. We can build water systems that deliver clean water efficiently, but we must also bring the hidden workings of this and other infrastructure above ground. Engineering thus deals with our most precious resources in a way that the public understands and connects with in every encounter with a detention basin, a bridge, or a water system. Although this is seldom discussed, infrastructure must be visually and aesthetically sustainable, so as to solicit long-term cultural support.

This book is addressed to a broad audience of designers, planners, architects, and engineers and advocates for projects that integrate all of these professions. It provides numerous examples from all over the world, from greener streets in San Francisco to greener cities in China, of projects that engage the public in a new relationship with natural systems. It demonstrates how to create more livable communities by blending ecologically functional and reliable design with an artistic sensibility to make infrastructure that is both green and good-looking. It shows designers how to reconnect the public to vital resources like open space, clean energy, running water, and biodiversity by creating infrastructure that is beautiful to look at as well as a source of knowledge and pride about our relationship to where we live.

The way we rebuild infrastructure in the twenty-first century will be a measure of our respect for our Earth and ourselves, and it will surely determine the quality of our existence and our children's. In the end, it becomes a question of how important to the culture are the infrastructures that mediate our most precious resources. Can we design systems that are as beautiful as they are useful, and that the public can connect with, value, and understand? We think the answer is yes.

In *Sustainable Infrastructure: The Guide to Green Engineering and Design*, Bry Sarté and his team offer the paradigms, strategies, and technical tools that designers need to understand not only why this work is critical to our survival but also how it is possible for cities and communities around the world.

PREFACE

"Let us go," we said, "into the Sea of Cortez, realizing that we become forever part of it; that our rubber boots slogging through a flat of eel-grass, that the rocks we turn over in a tide pool, make us truly and permanently a factor in the ecology of the region. We shall take something away from it, but we shall leave something too." And if we seem a small factor in a huge pattern, nevertheless it is of relative importance. We take a tiny colony of soft corals from a rock in a little water world. And that isn't terribly important to the tide pool. Fifty miles away the Japanese shrimp boats are dredging with overlapping scoops, bringing up tons of shrimps, rapidly destroying the species so that it may never come back, and with the species destroying the ecological balance of the whole region. That isn't very important in the world. And thousands of miles away the great bombs are falling and the stars are not moved thereby. None of it is important or all of it is.

—John Steinbeck, *The Log from the Sea of Cortez*

I read this passage from Steinbeck on my second trip to the Sea of Cortez. We had been hired to put development controls in place for a newly formed marine preserve to protect the very coral colonies and marine ecosystems that Steinbeck mentions. Both an artist and a scientist, Steinbeck expresses in his work the idea that our impacts cannot be disconnected from the natural world, and that it is our responsibility to consider those impacts, whether large or small, immediate or remote, present or future. As an engineer, environmental scientist, and artist, I share this perspective.

Steinbeck reminds us that all of the details of a place are important. Likewise, all of the individuals that comprise our project teams are invaluable because their input and ideas create the larger patterns of our design. Each perspective and design decision builds an interconnected fabric that shapes our project outcome. This deeply collaborative approach allows us to find solutions that protect individual species as well as entire coastlines and to regenerate individual sites as well as communities and whole cities. This book would not have been possible without the dedication to pursuing sustainable design of our clients, collaborators, and design partners on projects around the world.

Writing this book has also been a very collaborative project, and it would not have been possible without the tireless efforts and vision of my lifelong friend and our lead writer, Andy Mannle. Andy's inspiration, dedication, and expertise were invaluable in championing this project through many drafts, interviews, edits, and late-night meetings to a finished manuscript.

Like every project we work on at Sherwood Design Engineers and at the Sherwood Institute, this book has been shaped by the efforts and input of our remarkable staff. John Leys, thanks for your leadership and tireless nights and weekends dedicated to this project. Colin Piper and Mike Thornton, the project would not have succeeded without your numerous weekends and quick sprints in times of need. I offer my immense gratitude to those who put in personal time from our San Francisco team, including Robert Dusenbury, Eric Zickler, Ken Kortkamp, Drew Norton, Michael Amodeo, Josh Andresen, Cheryl Bailey, Bryce Wilson, Shauna Dunton, Miwa Ng,

Marlene Lopez, and Whitney Lee, as well as from our New York staff—Dahlia Thompson, Jason Loiselle, Jim Remlin, and Manon Terrell. Your assistance, advice, and contributions were invaluable. Thanks as well to Adrienne Eberhardt for inspiring this project by helping us with our first self-published book, and to Blake Robin for identifying the opportunity and helping to kick off the project with John Wiley & Sons. Thanks also to Ike Red for the fantastic drawings that stitch the book together.

This book has also been shaped by the many voices of our contributors, and we are grateful to them for their perspectives on architecture, planning, sustainability, green building, and public art. Special thanks to Erin Cubbison at Gensler; Robert Devine, managing director, Great Wall Resort; Jim Heid, founder of UrbanGreen; Rosey Jencks at the Urban Watershed Management Program of the San Francisco Public Utilities Commission; Clark Wilson, U.S. Environmental Protection Agency Smart Growth Division; Jane Martin, founding director of Plant*SF; Cliff Garten, public artist and founder of Cliff Garten Studio; Chi Hsin from CHS for his contributions to our transportation discussion; David Howerton, Eron Ashley, Jim Tinson, and Paul Milton at Hart Howerton; Mark J. Spalding, president of the Ocean Foundation; Jacob Petersen and Alan Lewis at Hargreaves Associates; Brett Terpeluk of Studio Terpeluk; Douglas Atkins, principal of Chartwell School; Kevin Perry and Ben Ngan of Nevue/Ngan Associates; Brad Jacobson at EHDD Architecture; Gene Schnair, Ellen Lou, and Michael Powell of Skidmore, Owings & Merrill–San Francisco; Roger Frechette and Ruth Kurz of Skidmore, Owings & Merrill–Chicago; David Bushnell at 450 Architects; Willett Moss at Conger Moss Guillard Landscape Architecture; Matt Fabry from the San Mateo Countywide Water Pollution Prevention Program; and Ben Shepherd from Atelier Ten. Demonstrating the collaborative nature of sustainable design was an important goal of this project, and without these contributions this story would not be complete.

Composing the pieces of a book into a coherent whole is like creating a complex piece of artwork, and in a very real sense my approach to engineering has grown out of my work as a sculptor and artist. I can only begin to thank my mentors in both art and design, TomX Johnson, Fred Hunnicutt, Jack Zajack, David Howerton and Richard Shaw, for their guidance and encouragement over the years. Engineering would have been a brief exploration if it had not been for the encouragements of Jack Van Zander, who showed me how the tools of engineering could be used to create large-scale artistic installations.

Many thanks to our editors at Wiley, Margaret Cummins and David Sassian, and their staff, for the invitation to write this book and the support and guidance needed to make it happen. Special thanks to Marilyn Levine and her colleagues at the Massachusetts Institute of Technology's Writing and Communication Center for their edits and key insights as we wrapped up the manuscript. Thanks as well to Sandy Mendler, Dan Parolek, Doug Farr, and the other Wiley-published authors who reviewed and provided feedback over the course of the manuscript's development.

Lastly, I offer heartfelt thanks for the love and support of my family. To my brothers Max and Jesse, who gave me the courage and support to pioneer this new field; to my parents for their enduring support of new ideas; to my daughters, Simone and Scarlett, who inspire my vision of the future; and above all to my wife, Ciela, who inspires me every day.

It is an honor to author this book in the company of so many fine individuals and inspirations.

INTRODUCTION

This book offers an in-depth look at sustainable engineering practices in an urban design context.

The global challenge of meeting expanding human needs in the face of dwindling resources and a changing world climate are major drivers of both design and engineering. But as more issues, perspectives, and metrics are incorporated into the planning and building process, the roles of engineers and designers are increasingly being fused. Designers are being asked to account for and incorporate systems thinking, material flows, and environmental performance into their work. Engineers are being asked to apply their technical and infrastructural expertise earlier and more comprehensively as an integral part of a holistic design process. Together, we are all trying to address critical questions: how can we plan, design, and build healthy cities, homes, and communities for a burgeoning population? How can we provide food, energy, and transportation in ecologically sustainable ways?

This book addresses these challenges by first exploring the need for creative, integrated engineering approaches to redesigning the built environment. It then elucidates the engineer's role in the collaborative design process necessary for developing effective, integrated solutions.

Why is this kind of exploration so timely? Today's integrated design teams are incorporating ecological infrastructure into buildings by using stormwater to create more beautiful communities and by designing urban environments that respect and engage natural systems. On every project, our infrastructure solutions emerge from a process of on- and off-site collaborative thinking involving a wide array of stakeholders.

Through this collaborative thinking process, we move beyond the engineer's traditional domain toward achieving a truly sustainable transformation of our infrastructure systems. More than a technical challenge, this kind of transformation requires a softer approach that continually seeks opportunities to celebrate the human experience of making greener, healthier, more beautiful and more efficient communities. This in turn calls for a new, more inventive approach to engineering—one that responds to the ideas of ecologists, architects, planners, and community groups while also respecting the requirements of clients, developers, and regulators.

With this challenge in mind, this book is offered as a way to shed more light on the technical solutions that have emerged as a direct result of an ongoing, rich dialogue, demonstrating how creative design teams can weave together the different priorities and approaches of their collaborators to achieve design synergies and cost savings.

Implicit in this multidimensional approach is the recognition that, over the past forty years, public pressure on environmental issues has strengthened the argument for environmental remediation, water treatment, alternative energy, and green building. Not only is there greater public awareness of the need to protect our planet, but in the same way many in the professional communities of architects, planners, and builders have adopted this challenge as their own. Organizations like Architecture for Humanity, Architecture 2030, the American Institute of Architects' Committee on the Environment, and the U.S. Green Building Council have all been enormously influential in promoting green design. While engineers may have been slower to take up these challenges, many more engineers are now coming to the field.

It is in this light that a unique manual of solutions is offered, bringing together three diverse components:

1. The technical requirements of site design and civil engineering
2. The sustainability priorities of ecologists, biologists, urban planners, landscape architects, and regulators
3. The aesthetic and human aspects of a project central to the work of architects, landscape architects, designers, community members, and artists

The book is divided into three sections. Part I: The Process and Systems of Sustainable Design introduces the integrative design process that is essential to truly green design. Part II: Sustainable Resource Systems offers a technical guide to our work in a common language that all design professionals share—a systematic discussion of approaches and strategies to working with water, wastewater, energy, and site design. Finally, Part III: Design Applications shows how to combine these systems on projects at the city, community, and site scale.

Part I is devoted to process, and chapter 1 outlines the collaborative design process from an engineer's perspective, showing readers what we bring to the design team and how we participate in the process of finding collaborative solutions. Chapter 2 discusses four sustainable infrastructure frameworks used to develop clear design goals and criteria, understand the ecological context of a project, and identify opportunities for better design.

Part II offers a system-by-system analysis of the major infrastructure resources society depends on and the strategies we're using to sustainably manage them. Chapter 3 begins with water supply systems, which are fundamental to the growth, health, and survival of societies around the world. The engineer's role in improving the stewardship of existing water supplies, optimizing water use, and harvesting new sources of water is discussed in detail. But water supply is only half of the water equation: the other half is the wastewater produced by millions of municipal users, industrial and agricultural pollution, and storm runoff in urban areas. Chapter 4 discusses how integrated water management is allowing engineers to reclaim and reuse that water, harvest stormwater to turn our streets green, treat and reuse graywater, and combine natural technologies with advanced design to improve our blackwater treatment systems.

Chapter 5 covers the energy needed to power all our infrastructure systems and cities. The need to remove carbon from our energy cycle is driving the whole design profession to rethink what we build, the way we operate, and how we move, and this chapter provides a strategic design process for finding better sources of power and a design approach that will reduce a project's energy demand and carbon footprint. Chapter 6 deals with sustainable site design, the art of creating, expanding, and connecting the places we inhabit. It explores how to understand a site as a living system, methods for conducting baseline analyses of local ecosystems, better ways to integrate development into the landscape, tips for improving the materials we use to build, and how good site design is the key to building greener streets and better transportation systems.

Part III brings all these resource systems together and shows how to integrate them into sustainable project designs. Because both design processes and solutions are scale specific, designers must consider solutions in the context of their scale. Chapters 7, 8, and 9 cover design applications at the three scales most commonly used to define our projects: city, community, and building. Yet scale alone is not a primary driver of design decisions. For example, as the density of a project increases, we exchange passive systems that require time and space to operate for active systems that rely on technology or energy. Finding a mix of strategies that strikes the appropriate balance for a particular project and its environment is what makes it sustainable. Green roofs may work better in Chicago than Los Angeles; bioswales may be better in Portland, Oregon, than in Manhattan; a solar thermal farm may be more cost-effective for a community than adding individual solar panels to every home.

Every project is unique, and this book is not intended as a cookbook with precise recipes for sustainability. On the contrary, it is conceived as a way to help engineers work more creatively and to help others work more creatively with engineers.

To coincide with the release of this book, the Sherwood Institute has created a new section on its Web site at www.sherwoodinstitute.org to support and enhance the written material using online resources. Throughout the text are notes with URLs that look like this:

🖱 For more information on this subject please see www.sherwoodinstitute.org

Follow these links to find more in-depth information, original source material, and additional resources regarding many of the topics touched on in the book. The online content will be updated frequently, staying current with many of the ever-changing issues involved in sustainable engineering.

Hopefully, *Sustainable Infrastructure: The Guide to Green Engineering and Design* will encourage more conversations between design professionals of different backgrounds on the common ground of sustainability. As a resource guide to sustainable site engineering, the book is designed to help architects, landscape architects, and planners better communicate with engineers. As a book about the practice and possibility of green design, it provides engineers with the tools to collaborate more effectively with other disciplines, integrating the kind of green design work that is in such high demand all over the world.

We stand at the threshold of a very exciting time of renewal and recovery, and yet the challenge to identify ecologically sound, affordable, inventive, aesthetic, socially responsible solutions is enormous. Many of the strategies described in this book are built on the creative reapplication of similar methods used or tried in the past. In a very real sense, we are bringing together ecology, creativity, and engineering—drawing on existing designs and concepts for inspiration and integrating them in new ways. Readers are invited to do the same: to take what we are doing and build on it.

As a society, we have only just begun to understand how to create sustainable communities, and our work designing them is now in full swing. Similarly, this book serves as both a valuable reference tool for approaching projects with a new way of thinking, and as a guide to working with others toward our shared goal of positive change for future generations.

PART I

THE PROCESS AND SYSTEMS OF SUSTAINABLE DESIGN

As designers of sustainable infrastructure, we are concerned with both bringing an ecological awareness to engineering technology and fostering an integrative design process that addresses evolving global challenges. From aging infrastructure and failing ecosystems to drought, pollution, and rising sea levels, designers can have a meaningful impact on some of the world's most significant environmental problems, and this is indeed a primary responsibility of our work.

The ecological imperatives are clear: we need to bring natural systems back into balance. Equally clear are the human requirements for healthy food, water, shelter, and energy. Our primary design challenge is to knit together gray infrastructure and green infrastructure; our goal is to design systems that harness natural technologies and meet human needs by working *with* nature, instead of solving our problems at nature's expense. Creating green infrastructure is about designing regenerative systems and establishing new ecologies that thrive in their own right.

Ours is not a new field; it is, however, rapidly evolving. In fact, the primary challenges for green design have shifted over the years. The obstacles used to be technical: discovering better ways to treat water and provide clean power. As technologies are developed, the challenges shift toward changing social and regulatory environments. Now that green design has become more common, clients are demanding sustainability. Support for these projects is coming by way of governmental policy, green building codes, and climate action plans around the world. The initiative is now with implementing solutions in an integrated way and applying them globally.

Every building retrofit, urban master plan, and streetscape redesign can be implemented more sustainably. There is more work than could possibly be done by one company—or even one country. And this is precisely the point: we face a global challenge. While this book does not have an answer for every sustainable design challenge, it does offer the tools and strategies to get you started. It is not a blueprint for changing the world as much as an approach: a way of thinking to address the most pressing challenges. We are on the verge of a paradigm shift—engineering that moves beyond ameliorating the negatives of conventional design and instead seeks to create a host of new positive outcomes. This book offers a method for implementing new tools and integrating existing ones into a holistic approach to sustainable design.

In chapter 1 we present an engineer's perspective on the integrated design process, and a detailed look at the role engineers play on integrated design teams. We cover the various drivers of project design, and the expanded criteria for sustainability on design projects. We also discuss how to define project goals and metrics with examples from San Francisco, Brazil, China, and Florida, to give readers a concrete sense of how systems are applied.

Chapter 2 provides an overview of four sustainable infrastructure frameworks used in integrative design. Establishing an overarching framework is critical to understanding the interrelationships between the different systems including energy, water, land use, and waste products. Accounting for system overlaps is critical for understanding the full potential of these systems, while system synergies can be powerful levers for transformative design. In this chapter we discuss the "5 Pillars" framework for integrating and prioritizing different systems on a project. We discuss the scale-density framework, used to understand the intersection of these two critical variables of development; and the transect system developed by New Urbanists to understand different land use patterns on a project. Finally, we cover the built form-ecology framework to address the intersection of natural ecologies and the built environment, and how sustainable design works to integrate the two.

In the standard design process, sustainable frameworks are not used. This has resulted in fragmented infrastructure that is highly unsustainable and vulnerable. Centralized power systems are prone to rolling brownouts, peaking failures, and power losses during transmission. Channelized rivers and extensive stormwater systems are characterized by complex, expensive infrastructure systems that are prone to dangerous, unhygienic failures. Sustainable design, on the other hand, seeks to work in accordance with nature's flows and cycles, using natural materials when possible to establish localized, resilient, diverse infrastructure systems modeled on natural principles.

CHAPTER 1

The Process
of Sustainable
Engineering Design

CREATING A NEW PARADIGM FOR DESIGN

Traditional site engineering design concentrated solely on building infrastructure. Today, engineers are an integral part of complex design teams. Our role has expanded to include the strategies that help determine a project's design concepts at the outset. Such strategies include adopting and adapting the ideas and priorities of others

INTEGRATING DISCIPLINES: ARCHITECTS AND ENGINEERS

ERIN CUBBISON, GENSLER

In the last several years, architects and planners have increasingly delved into topics outside their typical skill sets. Now that design projects must meet specific energy reductions or water savings, for example, there is greater collaboration between designers and other disciplines—especially engineering. As engineers move upstream in the design process, they can offer more design options at lower costs.

The American Institute of Architects (AIA) has solidified this shift toward performance-based design and the increased integration of disciplines early in the design process through its proposal for integrated design and delivery (see Figure 1-1). Integrated design and delivery typically refers to the collaborative, information-sharing process of project design and delivery carried out by a team

of owners, designers, consultants, builders, fabricators, and users. Figure 1-1 shows how current practices place the emphasis (time, effort, and fee) on the construction phase but should instead emphasize the design phase in order for collaboration to take place. In addition to improving the project's level of sustainability, this can also increase overall project quality and value, while reducing risk.

The architects and planners at Gensler have taken the idea a step further by adding two phases for consideration by the project team: a strategy phase and a use phase. This addresses the entire real estate life cycle, from business and real estate strategy through the occupancy and use of completed buildings and facilities. Strategy and use involve activities such as portfolio analysis, commissioning, and post-occupancy evaluation. By extending the

Figure 1-1 AIA integrated design model. Gensler.

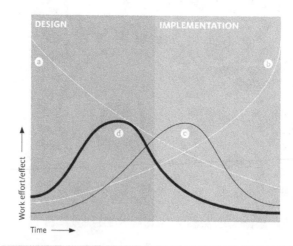

during the design process as well as developing maintenance guidelines for keeping an integrated, "living" design operating properly throughout its life span.

An engineer's ability to make the biggest impact on a project comes at its beginning, when assumptions are laid out, goals are established, and limitations are imposed. Working within an integrative design process is the most effective way to meet a project's many (often competing) objectives while helping to ensure the most sustainable project possible. Engineers are much better equipped to succeed in their

focus of integrated delivery, the teams responsible for dispatching specific projects understand the need to ensure that the knowledge gained at each stage is captured for the future, not only for individual projects but also for the broader initiatives of the organization whose strategic goals and plans they serve. The strategy phase is particularly important because it allows for critical evaluations

and decisions to be fully integrated with design work. As illustrated by Figure 1-2, if the project team can begin the design process in the strategy phase, then it can reduce risk even further. This provides the opportunity for even deeper sustainability efforts and a higher quality of work.

⏚ For more information on this subject please see www.sherwoodinstitute.org/resources.

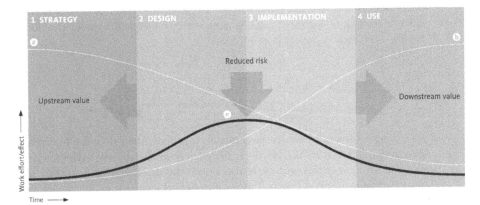

KEY
ⓐ Ability to impact cost and functional value
ⓑ Cost of design changes
ⓒ Traditional project delivery
ⓓ AIA Integrated Project Delivery
ⓔ Gensler Integrated Delivery

Figure 1-2 Gensler integrated design model. The Gensler integrated design model includes the use of a strategy phase and a use phase within the AIA integrated design model. This diagram shows how the ability to have the largest impact on value for the lowest cost (a) is in the strategy and design phases of a project. Once a project is under construction, the situation is reversed, and the cost of design changes (b) is much higher relative to their potential impacts. In Figure 1-1, (c) represents traditional project delivery while (d) demonstrates how integrated project delivery improves by moving the bulk of the work upstream into the design phase of the project. The Gensler integrated design model (e) shows a gentler curve that reduces risk and improves benefits by beginning in the strategy phase and continuing through occupancy. This allows critical decisions to be fully integrated with design, bridging the gap between strategy and implementation while ensuring that those strategies are put successfully to use by a site's occupants. Gensler.

areas of specialty when they have the opportunity to help shape such factors, be they increased water savings, decreased materials usage, or earthwork balancing. Without the chance to create integrated solutions, engineers are essentially left to solve technical problems created by the design.

A successful design process has a much greater chance of yielding an integrated design that creates synergies between the various elements and design disciplines. This synergy—creating a whole that is greater than the sum of its parts—is a cornerstone of sustainable design. Without a site engineer at the table from the outset to coordinate with the architect, landscape architect, and engineers from other disciplines, many of the sustainable elements that engineers help realize become more difficult to achieve.

The environmental and energy performance of our buildings and built environment is of increasing concern in the design process; it is therefore critical that engineers offer their technical expertise in the early phases. While this occasionally creates a longer, more complex design process, it reduces a project's overall costs by providing significant improvements in design. In a successful integrative design process, the higher up-front costs of design will be offset by savings on construction, reduced maintenance, and improved operations and performance over the lifetime of the project. However, such benefits must be clearly demonstrated to the client from the outset. Throughout this book, successful engineering strategies are described in order to show how incorporating engineers early on—and throughout the design process—can make a project more successful.

THE SUSTAINABLE DESIGN TEAM: AN ENGINEER'S PERSPECTIVE

As a project advances, different professionals contribute their expertise in different ways and at different times. Effectively integrating the members of a design team is essential for a successful process. It also creates an atmosphere of familiarity that allows for more collaboration and higher levels of achievement in design each time professional teams reconvene. Figure 1-3 illustrates the consultant team's structure on a master planning project in Brazil and how its members interacted throughout the process.

Each of these design team members interfaces in unique ways. A list of the typical team members and how each interacts with the site engineer follows:

Sustainability consultant: Often in-house at one of the design team members. Helps design clear priorities for the whole project and encourages synergies to engender success in reaching sustainability metrics. Works with engineers to reduce demand for water, energy, and source materials; integrate green space; and reduce carbon footprint.

Ecologist: Conducts baseline surveys of existing ecosystems and partners with site engineer and design team members to determine areas of constraints and opportunities for development. Helps establish development priorities that promote ecological benefits and diminish environmental impact.

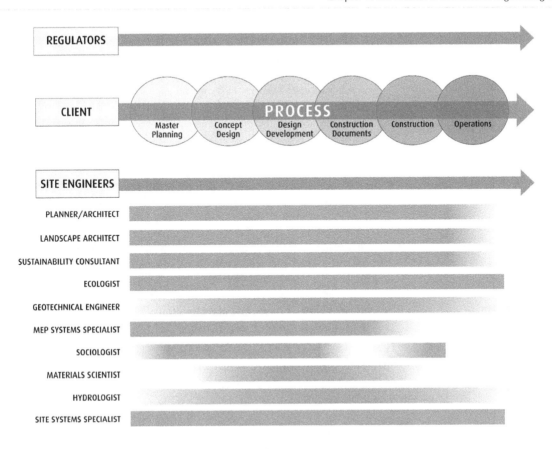

REGULATORS

CLIENT

PROCESS

Master Planning | Concept Design | Design Development | Construction Documents | Construction | Operations

SITE ENGINEERS

PLANNER/ARCHITECT

LANDSCAPE ARCHITECT

SUSTAINABILITY CONSULTANT

ECOLOGIST

GEOTECHNICAL ENGINEER

MEP SYSTEMS SPECIALIST

SOCIOLOGIST

MATERIALS SCIENTIST

HYDROLOGIST

SITE SYSTEMS SPECIALIST

Planner/architect: Designs site master plan and/or buildings. Works with engineer on site design to determine optimal placement, sizing, and integration of buildings at the site. Works with engineers on water and energy balance models to develop appropriate strategies for meeting project demands. Coordinates design between disciplines among all designers and ensures that built infrastructure will perform as designed. Oversees the development of a sustainability plan to ensure the project meets ongoing goals of energy savings, water reuse, sustainable waste practices, and so on.

Landscape architect: Helps engineers improve site aesthetics by incorporating an overarching design philosophy into the site that manifests in physical form through hardscape and softscape organization, vegetation management, stormwater facility placement, and so on. Assists engineers in minimizing damage to soils, trees, and native plants during construction. Chooses appropriate site plantings and landscaping. Works with engineers to integrate landscaping with on-site water systems. Coordinates landscaping maintenance of green infrastructure on-site (swales, green parking lots, rain gardens, wetlands, etc.).

Figure 1-3 The design team through the life of a sustainable planning project in northeast Brazil. For this project, Sherwood Design Engineers acted as both sustainability consultant and site engineer. © Sherwood Design Engineers.

Geotechnical engineer: Analyzes underground rock and/or soil characteristics to provide recommendations for subsurface engineering related to planned roads, buildings, and site infrastructure. Determines soil types that will support infiltration and various types of landscaping. Consults with engineers on land-forming strategies.

Mechanical, electrical, and plumbing (MEP) systems specialist: Designs energy and electrical systems, including heating, ventilation, and air-conditioning (HVAC). Works with engineer and architect to integrate energy systems into the building design and perform accurate energy modeling to ensure systems are sized and placed correctly. Coordinates with site designer and engineer to minimize infrastructure, including piping, trenching, and wiring, when placing utility corridors on-site.

Hydrologist: Often a part of the site engineering team, works with engineers to determine local groundwater levels and qualities, determine potential stormwater runoff and stream flow, develop watershed master plans, establish water balance models, and review strategies for capture and reuse of water on-site. Helps engineer develop water treatment and delivery strategies that minimize piping, culverts, and other hardscape in favor of swales, rain gardens, infiltration basins, and/or wetlands.

DESIGN DRIVERS FOR SUSTAINABLE INFRASTRUCTURE SYSTEMS

Although the specifics of the design process Sherwood Design Engineers employs vary from project to project, there are a number of components that tend to remain central to our work. Typically, this process includes some, if not all, of the following elements:

- Identifying and understanding the project drivers
- Setting goals
- Establishing desired outcomes and metrics for success
- Creating frameworks and action plans that organize the approach
- Identifying concrete, measurable design strategies to achieve the above items

For more information on related topics please see www.sherwoodinstitute.org/ideas.

Project Drivers

Project drivers define the fundamental requirements of a project (such as budget or timeline) that in turn help to establish the design criteria. Conventional project drivers continue to be supplemented or replaced by additional, more integrated drivers, often defined by environmental and infrastructure constraints, increased regulatory controls, or the desire to conform to a green rating system.

For the development project mentioned above located in a very dry part of Brazil, this included a detailed look at the interrelationship between the site's hydrology and vegetation to inform an ecological succession strategy that phased with the project's horizontal infrastructure development. The project driver in this case was its role in a larger reforestation and protection strategy of the much deteriorated Atlantic Forest.

Another common set of drivers include those related to increased regulatory controls. From water and energy efficiency requirements to stormwater quantity and quality requirements, we have seen much stricter controls placed on our design solutions. "Business as usual" for designers is changing rapidly. In recent years there have been shifts in the planning process to account for new requirements from municipalities. Building codes, water policies, emissions standards, labor laws, material use, and carbon accounting are all being revised—and designers must keep pace.

An increasingly important set of drivers involve meeting the requirements of rating systems. Whether these are green rating systems such as Leadership in Energy and Environmental Design (LEED) or the Building Research Establishment Environmental Assessment Method (BREEAM), goal-based systems such as One Planet Living and the Living Building Challenge, performance-based systems such as SmartCode and the benchmarks established by the American Society of Landscape Architects' (ASLA) Sustainable Sites Initiative, or education-based systems such as the Energy Star program, designers are being called upon to integrate them into their design solutions. This has led many design firms to either bring this additional expertise in-house or add sustainability consultants or other specialists to their team.

Often, decisions must be made that improve one aspect of a project but impact another negatively; for such situations, a clear understanding of a project's key values is important so the decisions will favor the project's highest priorities. Developing a framework for sustainable design can help designers prioritize a project's core values in order to make the hard choices so often required.

Establishing Project Values and Setting Goals

Every project starts with a vision and a set of objectives. It is the design team's responsibility, in coordination with the client, to establish project values that can be used to define clear goals for the design effort. These values are sometimes lofty and hard to interpret. At the headquarters of a nonprofit, Sherwood was recently asked to create a "replicable" project—one that had elements that could be re-created on green buildings throughout the world. The project value established was the creation of a model coming from a desire to contribute to the advancement of green building.

Project values get translated into goals that are more tangible and can be used to drive the design process. Quantitative goals are advantageous because they allow a project to measure its success in various ways. This is not always easy to do and, if these goals are not clearly formulated, a design team can be left scrambling, trying to figure out the best way to then measure progress. (A goal of "conservation of biodiversity," for example, might prove elusive and difficult to measure.) Projects often implement a variety of goals, some of which are qualitative and others that are quantitative. For quantitative goals, it is important to define the metric that will be used to determine achievement.

Project goals can be met in different ways. For instance, on an urban project, the goal of reducing vehicle trips may be met by increasing the number of residential units in the urban core so fewer people have to commute, or by expanding access to public transportation so fewer commuters have to drive. Project goals can be as detailed as the achievement of a certain LEED credit, or as general as a positive impact on global warming. For a recent green streets project in Florida, the project stakeholders identified the following goals to support the widely held triple bottom-line values related to project achievement:

- Community
  - Improve site aesthetics.
  - Increase pedestrian connectivity.
  - Expand multiuse functionality.
- Environment
  - Improve energy efficiency.
  - Reduce carbon emissions.
  - Increase water efficiency.
  - Reduce stormwater runoff.
  - Improve stormwater quality.
  - Expand local material use.
- Economics
  - Increase marketability.
  - Stay within budget limits.
  - Optimize maintenance requirements.
  - Increase systems durability.

Defining Desired Outcomes and Metrics

Various industry standards have been developed to help designers reach measurable outcomes for all scales of projects. Some systems use predefined, widely accepted metrics. Others are narrow in focus and are not all-encompassing when it comes to analyzing a project's commitment to sustainability. These systems often provide a defined format for projects to compare to a baseline to determine how they measure up against other projects. One of the most widely used standards in the United States is the U.S. Green Building Council's (USGBC) LEED rating system. There are many other standards in use internationally.

The benefits of pursuing LEED (or another similar rating system) are that it provides third-party verification, brand recognition, marketing cachet, and even investment opportunity. Whether utilizing a rating system or not, resource-efficiency analysis is a great way to measure progress and show results. For many projects, this may mean analyzing the key site resources in the following ways:

- *Water:* Compare the site's expected water demands with a baseline case and strive for a water balance that focuses on low-use and renewable sources.

Goal: Triple Bottom Line

Environmental   Social

Economic

Expected Outcomes

Restoration of
Natural Systems

Celebrate
Lingnan Culture

Balanced
Water Cycle

Health &
Prosperity

Reduce
Energy Dependence

Improved
Air Quality

Regenerative
Materials

Figure 1-4 Design drivers for the Baietan master plan in Guangzhou, China. In this project, the major goals of environmental, social, and economic improvement to the city were connected to a variety of outcomes. The anticipated outcomes exist on a scale from the more quantitative, like water and energy use, to others that are more qualitative in nature, like health and prosperity or celebrating local culture. Each of these outcomes is then supported by a variety of action plans. These action plans usually support several of the desired project outcomes. © Skidmore, Owings & Merrill LLP 2009 with Sherwood Design Engineers. All rights reserved.

- *Energy:* Compare the project's final energy requirements with a baseline case and strive for net zero energy use.
- *Carbon:* Compare the project's carbon footprint through the design, construction, and occupancy phases with a baseline case and strive to be carbon negative.
- *Materials:* Complete a life-cycle analysis for the project and specify materials with long life cycles. Local resources should also be evaluated.

While working on the sustainability plan for a recent park project, Sherwood developed the following sustainable infrastructure systems metrics:

- Ecology
  - ○ Annual aquifer recharge of 55 acre-feet
  - ○ Water quality treatment of all runoff
  - ○ 25 acres of habitat restoration

- Water
  - 75 percent water reuse for irrigation
  - 95 percent recycled water for fountains
  - 35 percent water reuse for restrooms

- Energy
  - Carbon neutrality for park operations
  - 75 percent on-site renewable power generation
  - 50 percent energy reduction from baseline for parking garage

Every project will have specific needs and require a customized approach to establishing the proper metrics for evaluating the progress and success of the project goals.

Creating Frameworks and Action Plans

Frameworks and action plans are methods by which the designer can organize the various strategies and means of achievement. These systems are not requirements of most projects but can be imperative when trying to tackle complex objectives with many interwoven parts and integrated strategies.

For the project mentioned in Brazil, Sherwood developed a comprehensive sustainability plan using the pillars of sustainability framework, which is explained more fully in chapter 2. Briefly, the five pillars of water, energy, community, ecology, and materials are all important to a project's success. But it may not be possible to address all of them equally. For this project, "community" was given a high priority because the analysis, which used the United Nations Human Development Index, revealed that the local community scored below some of the poorest and most war-torn countries in Africa. It became clear to the client that investments in renewable energy or decreasing carbon would not be sustainable without first improving conditions in the local community.

As part of the sustainability plan, Sherwood coordinated with local leaders to develop programs that would offer immediate educational and job-training opportunities to the community in order to lay a foundation for future community development. It was decided that additional money spent up front in this sector was a better investment in sustainability than alternative options, such as expanding wind power generation capacity to decrease the carbon footprint.

Design Strategies

Once the structure driving a project has been defined and agreed upon, the next step is to establish appropriate design strategies to meet those goals.

In order to establish design strategies, it is important to respond to a project's context. The same goal will be met in different ways depending on whether the project is in a dense urban area, a rural development, or a delicate ecosystem. Managing stormwater through passive means in an urban area might involve developing a network of rain gardens above underground cisterns. In a rural development, the same goal might be met with bioswales and wetlands, while a reforestation program might be called for in an undeveloped area.

Design strategies become integrated when the entire design team is aware of the criteria and works toward a complementary set of solutions. On the LEED Platinum Chartwell School in Monterey, California, one desired outcome was a reduction in embodied energy for the materials involved. This resulted in a variety of strategies: the use of salvaged materials from nearby sites, the specification of materials with recycled content throughout the project, and a building system that allows for the planned deconstruction of the buildings many years in the future. From the architect to the structural engineer and site designer, the consultant team worked to incorporate strategies in support of the desired outcome.

IMPLEMENTING THE PROCESS

The collaborative process is rooted in a belief in teamwork, in developing a solid understanding of project goals, and in all parties doing their best to realize those goals. Meeting with the other design team members as often as is practical and staying coordinated through regular communication allows the team to achieve these

Figure 1-5 Vertical bars in this process diagram indicate where the sustainability drivers are introduced during a specific project. In this case, most critical is the introduction and calibration of metrics. © Sherwood Design Engineers.

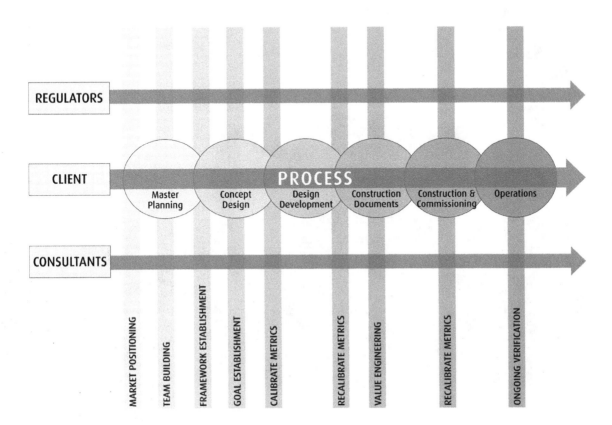

goals while staying on schedule and on budget. Sherwood's process, of course, varies slightly from project to project; below are two detailed examples (see pages 16–18) of that process, including a green streets project in San Francisco, California, and a green community project on Florida's Gulf Coast.

The overall process that design teams go through during the course of a project is standard across the industry. It begins with defining the concept, developing designs, and preparing construction documents. What makes the collaborative process unique are the design steps taken within each of these phases.

As part of the sustainability plan for the project in Brazil mentioned earlier, Sherwood laid out the following project schedule and key milestones for the client. Determining the market position and the framework was critical to establishing our goals. Once goals were set, they were tracked using metrics through the life of the project. Below is an outline of some of the steps of the engineering process:

Figure 1-6 This concept sketch from a charrette for a sustainable technology park captures a combination of design strategies and shows their integration through graphic expression. EHDD Architecture.

1. Project planning
   - Perform initial research to identify climate conditions; energy source and costs; water source and costs; and environmental constraints and opportunities.

- Identify key components (at a charrette) of sustainable opportunities specific to site and region.
- Provide case studies relevant to the site.

2. Concept design
   - Establish a framework.
   - Conduct a design/client team sustainable systems workshop, including all designers and client representatives, to present opportunities, understand site-specific limitations and opportunities, and gain consensus on project goals and design criteria.
   - Provide and quantify comprehensive strategies for achieving established goals.
   - Develop metrics and benchmarks to determine whether goals are being met.

3. Design development
   - Integrate and track goals with the master plan program; as the plan changes, identify when goals are being compromised and recommend alternatives to preserve them.
   - Revise design to meet priorities through collaborative iteration with other stakeholders.
   - Recalibrate metrics, if necessary, to accommodate any design changes as the project develops.
   - Create sustainability guidelines that fully integrate with the project design guidelines, moving from design to operations.

4. Construction documentation
   - Recalibrate metrics, if necessary, to accommodate design changes associated with value engineering.
   - Collaborate with the project team on the detailing of unique elements critical to project goals and/or integrated systems.

5. Construction and commissioning
   - Develop a sustainable systems construction manual.
   - Use project specifications as a means to require sustainable construction practices.
   - Develop a materials use plan to minimize construction waste.
   - Commission site infrastructure, including drainage systems.

6. Operations
   - Develop an operations and maintenance manual for new or innovative design solutions.
   - Develop a plan for ongoing carbon management and greening project operations.

APPLYING INTEGRATIVE DESIGN ON OLD MINT PLAZA

Our work on San Francisco streetscapes ranges from residential streets to thoroughfares to urban plazas. Though each of our projects varies slightly, they all have consistent components: overarching goals, design strategies, and targeted outcomes. As part of an interdisciplinary team led by CMG Landscape Architecture, Sherwood was responsible for the reconstruction of an existing streetscape adjacent to the historic Old Mint building in downtown San Francisco. Conversion of the 19,000-square-foot block into a flagship stormwater park and public plaza has set future development standards for urban stormwater management techniques, infiltration best management practices (BMPs), and green street design on projects throughout the San Francisco Bay Area. Central to the project were the goals of creating a community amenity and having a net positive impact on San Francisco's combined sewer overflows. Figure 1-7 summarizes the results of this process for the Old Mint Plaza and outlines the project's key design goals, the strategies chosen, and the resulting benefits.

Figure 1-7 Applying integrative design at Old Mint Plaza, San Francisco. The Old Mint Plaza was able to achieve the city's overarching design goals and their associated synergistic benefits through the implementation of design strategies that were integrated within the consultant team's final design. © Sherwood Design Engineers.

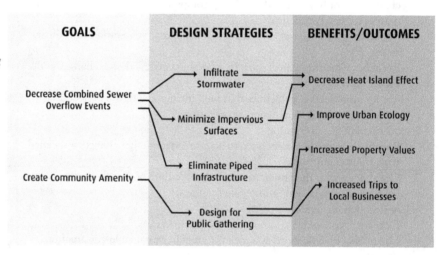

GOAL SETTING AT AQUATERA, FLORIDA

This large residential housing development on Florida's Gulf Coast was the area's first ecologically sensitive development of its size and nature. With the goal of meeting the county's requirements for improving the hydrological function of the site, the project's landscape architect came to Sherwood to explore landscape-based approaches to stormwater as part of its green streets initiative for the project.

On this type of development, the developer, home builder, and design team typically require buy-off over a multiple-year process that lends itself to value engineering and shortcuts in the field. Understanding the complexities of getting innovative ideas integrated into the project framework and actually built on this type of development, Sherwood proposed a unique method of applying a values inventory that had been developed with AECOM Design + Planning for a previous application in order to generate selection criteria and help prioritize design decisions. This process is detailed below and includes prioritizing project goals, scoring green strategies, and ranking these strategies based on the weighted goals. Because the proposed community center was slated to be a green building, the stakeholders rated the goals for it and for the overall development separately.

STAKEHOLDER RESPONSE: RATING AVERAGES

SHERWOOD Design Engineers

Strategy Division	Project Goal	Averages — Community Center (1=LOW) Total=100	Overall Development (10=HIGH) Total=130	S1 CC	S1 OD	S2 CC	S2 OD	S3 CC	S3 OD	S4 CC	S4 OD	S5 CC	S5 OD	S6 CC	S6 OD	S7 CC	S7 OD	S8 CC	S8 OD	S9 CC	S9 OD	S10 CC	S10 OD
				Director of Product Design		Manager, Land Acquisitions		Associate VP, Sales & Marketing		Vice President, Planning & Development		Vice President, Sales & Marketing		Director of Construction		Manager, Planning & Development				Director of Planning & Development		Director of Construction	
Adopt LEED NC																							
	1 Adopt LEED NC	9.0		10		8		9		10		8		9		10		8		9		10	
COMMUNITY																							
	2 Improve Home Site Aesthetics		7.7		2		5		8		10		7		9		10		10		8		9
	3 Heighten Home Site's Sense of Uniqueness		6.6		2		7		5		10		7		7		10		7		4		8
	4 Improve Development Amenities		7.3		10		4		7		10		6		7		10		8		4		10
	5 Improve Development Aesthetics		7.9		10		6		8		10		8		7		10		8		4		10
	6 Heighten Development's Sense of Uniqueness		8.4		10		7		9		10		8		9		10		7		6		10
	7 Improve Road and Driveway Aesthetics		6.4		5		7		7		10		3		8		10		5		3		10
	8 Increased Pedestrian Connectivity	6.8	5.8	7	7	7	3	6	8	5	1	8	9	8	8	5	1	7	7	8	8	10	10
	9 Expand Multi-Use Functionality	6.4	5.4	2	2	8	2	7	7	7	6	8	6	6	6	7	6	5	6	8	8	10	10
ENVIRONMENT																							
	10 Improve Energy Efficiency	7.2	8.0	10	10	3	8	7	10	8	8	9	9	8	7	8	8	7	7	5	5	10	10
	11 Reduce Carbon Emissions	3.1	3.3	2	2	2	5	2	5	1	1	7	3	6	6	1	1	3	3	4	4	10	10
	12 Minimize Embodied Energy	1.9	1.9	1	1	4	3	2	3	1	1	1	1	1	1	1	1	3	3	3	3	10	10
	13 Increase Water Efficiency	6.2	6.7	10	10	2	6	8	8	7	7	4	4	7	7	7	7	5	5	6	6	10	10
	14 Improve Water Recycling	3.6	3.0	2	2	7	1	7	6	1	1	6	8	4	4	1	1	3	3	1	1	10	10
	15 Reduce Stormwater Runoff	3.7	3.8	2	2	4	5	5	5	4	4	3	3	4	1	4	4	4	4	3	6	10	10
	16 Improve Stormwater Quality	2.7	3.1	1	1	3	2	7	4	1	4	2	2	4	3	1	4	4	4	1	4	10	10
	17 Expand Local Material Use	3.0	2.7	2	2	2	1	2	2	5	4	1	1	3	3	5	4	1	1	6	6	8	8
ECONOMICS																							
	18 Increase Marketability and Perceived Value to Potential Buyers	7.4	7.9	10	10	4	6	6	9	8	8	8	9	9	8	8	8	8	8	6	5	10	10
	19 Stay within Budget Limits	7.0	5.7	10	10	5	7	7	7	8	4	7	7	6	1	8	4	7	6	6	5	10	10
	20 Optimize Maintenance Requirements	6.7	5.1	10	10	7	8	7	5	6	3	4	4	7	1	6	3	5	4	8	8	10	10
	21 Increase Systems Durability	6.0	5.1	10	10	6	7	7	5	5	5	3	3	7	1	5	5	5	4	6	6	10	10
CONTEXT																							
	22 Maximize Practice of Locally Appropriate Construction	3.1	1.8	2	2	4	2	0	0	5	2	3	3	1	1	5	2	7	2	1	2	8	8
	23 Create Positive Influence on Future Development	2.7	3.4	4	4	5	4	0	0	1	1	6	6	1	9	1	1	2	2	4	4	9	9
	24 Reinforce Good Neighbor Policy		2.9		1		7		0		3		2		2		3		4		4		10
	25 Advance Codes to Support Project Goals	2.3	2.3	1	1	7	7	0	0	1	1	2	2	1	1	1	1	2	2	6	6	10	10
	26 Encourage Positive Influence on Lifestyle/Awareness	6.1	3.9	2	2	9	7	6	1	8	3	5	6	4	3	8	3	8	5	5	5	10	10
	27 Expand Positive Influence on Environmental Stewardship	4.9	2.9	2	2	3	3	5	1	8	3	3	3	4	1	8	3	6	5	5	5	10	10
		100	129	100	130	100	130	100	130	100	130	100	130	100	130	100	130	100	130	100	130	195	262

Prioritizing Project Goals

As per Figure 1-8, the stakeholders listed across the top were asked to rate each of the project goals listed down the left side for both the community center and the overall development. Each goal could be scored from 1 to 10, but the total points had to add up to a specific number, thereby requiring the stakeholders to prioritize goals. (One individual, at the far right, didn't follow these instructions and ranked virtually every goal a 10, for a total score of 262; his numbers had to be recalibrated.)

After everybody ranked the project goals, they were given a combined weighting factor, which indicated their overall importance to the team. In this

Figure 1-8 Stakeholder response: rating averages. A stakeholder survey for a project allows the design team to prioritize and weight the client's goals. © Sherwood Design Engineers.

case, the highest priority for the community center was to adopt the LEED for New Construction Rating System (LEED-NC), while the winning priority for the overall development was "heighten development's sense of uniqueness."

Scoring Green Strategies

In the next phase of the exercise, the design team scored a list of green strategies in terms of their impact—positive, negative, or neutral—on each of the project goals from the survey results. For instance, a materials strategy like "reusing local aggregate for landscaping" has no impact on the project aesthetics, because it is buried and invisible. But reusing that heavy material on-site does reduce the embodied energy of the project.

Ranking the Winners

The green strategies' scores were then multiplied by the weighted ranking given to each goal by the stakeholders. In this way, each of the green strategies was given a final ranking based on its overall impact on the project goals that were of high priority to the stakeholders.

For the Aquatera Project, the top five goals were as follows:

Community Center Goals
Overall Development Goals

1. Cisterns for rainwater collection on rooftops
   Stormwater capture parks/Outdoor event parks
2. Landscape irrigation via harvested rainwater
   Sustainable living maintenance manual
3. Sustainable living maintenance manual
   Visible stormwater feature/Art installation

4. Stormwater capture parks/Outdoor event parks
   Community nursery/Greenhouse
5. Locally appropriate plantings
   Locally appropriate plantings

This process yields a wealth of data about the project and clarifies why some strategies are getting prioritized. For instance, the second-ranked goal for the community center was "landscape irrigation via harvested rainwater." This strategy scored high for its positive impact on important goals like "increase water efficiency" (weighted 6.3) and "increase marketability to potential buyers" (weighted 7.4), while having no negative scores, even on economic goals (including "stay within budget limits"). The second-ranked goal for the overall development was "sustainable living maintenance manual," which scored high on two important goals—"heighten development's sense of uniqueness" (7.8) and "improve energy efficiency" (7.6)—while having only one negative: "stay within budget limits." The number one goal for the overall development, "stormwater capture parks," was a mixed bag. Despite slight negatives on energy and economic goals, it ranked positively for a large number of community, environmental, and contextual goals, and received the highest ranking.

This type of sophisticated analysis integrates values, goals, and strategies in a transparent, participatory way that allows a group of stakeholders to gain clear consensus on their programming priorities. As the landscape design moved forward, it focused on xeriscaping strategies wherever possible to minimize water use and lend a unique flavor not found within other projects of this scale in the area.

CHAPTER 2
Sustainable Infrastructure Frameworks

Several years ago, a team from Sherwood walked into a meeting for a large new development project in Colorado. The developer was accustomed to creating a certain product over and over. At the first meeting, however, it became clear that the client was interested in an innovative and sustainable project, but had never tackled anything like that before. For about an hour, people pitched ideas—some good, some not so good—but with no clear direction or organizing principle. So Sherwood suggested the adoption of a framework, a system that allows teams to rank priorities by category, to define success within those categories, and to select strategies that meet as many of the criteria as possible. By the next meeting, consensus had coalesced around a version of Sherwood's pillars of sustainability framework, with its goal of striving for Leadership in Energy and Environmental Design for New Development (LEED-ND), level gold. As a result of identifying goals within the framework, the design team and client were able to conduct focused and directed meetings, swiftly and productively moving toward a shared vision.

The five pillars model for using sustainable infrastructure frameworks grew out of the challenge of designing for complex projects characterized by a myriad of interrelationships—projects requiring clear systems to focus and direct the design process. More specifically, designing sustainable infrastructure requires integrated strategies for managing water, wastewater, energy, and solid materials systems. It also requires integrating these systems into the local ecological context in a positive way, while creating designs that meet the needs of a variety of human stakeholders. Factors that play a role in determining appropriate strategies for a project may include the following:

- Scale of the project
- Density of development
- Local climate
- Ecological opportunities
- Available technology
- Cultural context
- Regulatory environment
- Development and construction costs
- Operations and maintenance considerations

Finding a common framework that addresses all these project drivers allows the designer to look beyond a checklist or single point of view and embrace multiple aspects of sustainability for each design decision. A framework may also be used to assess the ecological context of a project, identify opportunities for sustainable design, and evaluate the impacts of design choices.

Building new developments on an already overburdened planet requires sensitivity to the impact of additional infrastructure on local ecosystems. Every development has the potential—and the responsibility—to respect and restore healthy cultural traditions and ecological conditions. Choosing an appropriate infrastructure framework can help any project live up to that responsibility.

This chapter discusses four sustainable infrastructure frameworks that Sherwood makes effective use of:

1. The pillars of sustainability
2. The scale-density framework
3. The transect
4. The built form–ecology framework

The frameworks presented here are in no way an exhaustive list or a complete formula for solving sustainable infrastructure design problems. They represent a good starting point. Typically used as a frame of reference to organize the early thinking in a project, they are also something the design team can come to back regularly to make sure they are on track. In the midst of design, it is easy to get focused on one or two driving ideas and lose sight of the overarching objectives. By implementing a framework, a common set of project-unifying values can be established.

A project may use one or more frameworks, and there are usually some that fit more naturally with a project or resonate better with a client than others. From that starting point, the frameworks are usually customized slightly for each project. They are presented here in the order of frequency in which they are used at Sherwood:

1. *The pillars of sustainability:* This framework organizes the design systems into five categories: water, energy, materials, community, and ecology. Each "pillar" is carefully examined in terms of both the possible degrees of sustainable achievement for a given project and the potential interrelationships and synergies they may share. The pillars of sustainability model emphasizes that each of these areas is important and allows a clear demonstration of the balance necessary between them.

   The pillars of sustainability is a useful framework to apply to most projects, regardless of scale, density, or design priority, but it is frequently adopted on projects that require a deep level of sustainable design exploration. This framework is particularly suited for optimizing system synergies and advancing regenerative designs. By incorporating sustainability metrics that bind the pillars together—strategies that yield both water and energy savings, for instance, or measures that improve both the ecology and the community—the framework can be used to make design decisions that promote improved performance within each of the five pillars while optimizing synergies with the others.

2. *The scale-density framework:* Many designers are accustomed to thinking in terms of scale. It is obvious that single structures or community neighborhoods require different strategies than whole cities or entire regions. Yet the density of development is also an important consideration. For example, the considerations that came into play in the 50-square-mile conservation development in rural China near the Great Wall were entirely different than those encountered in a high-density brownfield redevelopment planning effort for a district of the same size in the Chinese city of Guangzhou. The scale-density framework combines these two key elements and can be used to illustrate a variety of potential responses.

The scale-density framework is practical for presenting specific ideas and demonstrating the relationship of selected strategies, from the single-building scale to the regional scale. It can also be used to show the reasons behind the solution for a given project by illustrating where certain designs are appropriate and where they are not. For example, at the Ahwahnee project discussed in chapter 3 (see page 72), the overall strategy for stormwater management involved creating a series of large restoration and retention wetlands for low-density areas of the plan, whereas rain gardens were incorporated into streets within the limited space available at the core of the development. The scale-density framework allowed the team to organize the design response and to show the relationship between the selected strategies within different densities of the project.

3. *The transect:* This model of urban planning was created by Andres Duany, one of the leaders of the New Urbanist movement. The transect is used to create an urban cross-section that offers a range of organized design and planning responses. The feasibility of common infrastructure systems from wastewater treatment to energy generation are driven by factors including density of development, intensity of use, environmental constraints, and other land-use restrictions. Because the transect clearly labels these drivers and constraints, it is a valuable tool to use when looking for sustainable infrastructure opportunities. Working within the transect framework also demonstrates how to incorporate mixed uses and mixed densities within a project in order to achieve a healthy urban ecology.

   The transect is applied in many projects, both in a redevelopment condition and in greenfield development. Often used for establishing land-use parameters, this tool has been adopted by many U.S. cities as an alternative to conventional zoning tools. Highly effective as a mechanism for transforming cities into more walkable and sustainable environments, the transect is also effective on private development projects. It allows designers to guide development patterns and infrastructure responses according to specific land uses in a density-appropriate manner.

4. *The built form–ecology framework:* Analyzing the interrelationship between natural ecosystems and human environments is another way to establish a framework for designing sustainable infrastructure systems. Examining a site's current or past natural conditions—its ecological baseline—allows a project's regenerative progress to be measured and can help ensure or promote a balanced relationship with ongoing human development patterns. An understanding of the ecosystem services provided by open space, wildlife corridors, and biodiversity can help designers justify incorporating these natural components into their projects. Understanding local ecology is also essential for mitigating the impacts of development.

   The built form–ecology framework is effective for projects in or adjacent to natural areas, or with large planned or existing components of natural systems within the project boundaries. This tool is also pertinent to the application of regenerative designs in areas where the reintroduction of natural systems and ecologies is a top priority. Finally, this system can be helpful in establishing regional growth and conservation plans. Because of its focus on the relationships between human-made and natural environments, this framework is useful for balancing elements at critical boundary zones.

ESTABLISHING A FRAMEWORK

As discussed in chapter 1, many factors drive a project, and frameworks can be developed to incorporate a variety of sustainability metrics. Frameworks can be established by the type of development the client is looking for (brownfield redevelopment, walkable communities, low-impact development), the goals the team is after (community engagement, environmental restoration, increased public transit), or by the systems that are being dealt with (water, energy, transportation).

A design team will often select a single framework for a project, but there are many ways the frameworks can complement each other as well. The scale-density framework can be used to generate a range of technologies and design solutions that can then be tracked into the transect, for example. Either the pillars of sustainability or the built form–ecology framework can be used as a big-picture, goal-setting tool in the early conceptual design phase of a project. The structures, goals, and metrics identified can then feed into either the scale-density framework or the transect framework as implementation tools.

These frameworks can also be complemented by other systems or approaches for organizing a sustainable development strategy. For example, many projects adopt LEED and use the LEED matrix as the design strategy organizing tool. The following systems and design philosophies are often used in conjunction with the frameworks identified above:

- LEED rating systems
- The Building Research Establishment Environmental Assessment Method (BREEAM)
- Net-zero energy development
- Regenerative development
- Permaculture
- Light imprint
- SmartCode
- Living Building Challenge
- Rocky Mountain Institute's urban framework
- Melbourne Principles for Sustainable Cities
- One Planet Living's ten principles
- American Institute of Architects (AIA) Committee on the Environment's (COTE) Ten Measures of Sustainable Design
- American Society of Landscape Architects (ASLA) Sustainable Sites Initiative Benchmarks and Performance Guidelines

For more information on related topics please see www.sherwoodinstitute.org/ideas.

There has been a lot of discussion about the role that rating systems play in promoting sustainable development. Some argue that they offer much needed standards for the industry, others that they reduce sustainability to a checklist. For an architect's perspective, see the feature below. Using the rating systems as a guidepost or an incentive toward better design is generally a good thing. But they shouldn't be the sole goal or measure of a project's sustainability. Each site is unique, and efforts to make it more efficient, more integrated with the environment, and more responsive to the community must be unique as well. The frameworks offered in this chapter serve to get the design conversation started and to point it in the right direction; the next section covers how to use them effectively.

GREEN BUILDING RATING SYSTEMS: HELPING OR HURTING? AN ARCHITECT'S PERSPECTIVE

Erin Cubbison/Gensler

The last ten to fifteen years has seen the creation of a number of green building organizations: the U.S. Green Building Council, the Building Research Establishment, Energy Star, the Green Building Initiative, and many others. During the last five years, there has been widespread adoption of the rating systems created by these organizations—LEED, BREEAM, Energy Star, and Green Globes, respectively—as well as many others. All of these systems quantitatively evaluate the benefits of sustainable strategies and give projects an overall rating.

The discipline of architecture is fundamentally about the experience of built form, an intangible and arguably unquantifiable pursuit. Many view this kind of rating as an overly simplistic representation of a building that does not honor its full value. This critique can take several directions. Some simply maintain that a sustainability rating serves no benefit—that good design *is* sustainable design. Some argue that the rating systems actually do more harm than good because they encourage simplistic solutions.

The basis of this argument comes from the very nature of the rating systems: because so many projects must be evaluated, because the process must be objective, and because the market favors systems in which requirements are known up front, the rating systems reward strategies that are easily evaluated, not necessarily strategies that produce the most sustainable outcome. The rating systems are not able to fully evaluate and reward a project that achieves a high level of sustainability but does so through strategies that are outside the system's framework. Additionally, some believe the rating systems do more harm than good because they feel they have set the bar too low. Each system has various levels of achievement, but the base level typically requires little improvement over conventional design. Critics argue that these easily achievable base levels encourage projects with minimal sustainability goals.

The positive effects of the rating systems are, however, undeniable. They have brought the concept of green building into the mainstream and have created a market-based movement. While their evaluation systems may be overly simplistic from the perspective of some, they seem to be well matched to the level of risk that most clients are willing to take. Finally, by setting the bar within reach of most conventional projects, the rating systems have engaged a significant proportion of the industry. Most recently, they have become part of municipal building requirements and corporate building standards.

USING SUSTAINABLE INFRASTRUCTURE FRAMEWORKS

Sustainable infrastructure frameworks help the design process in several key ways:

Understanding opportunities: Because sustainable design is a systemic, holistic process, it is useful to have a framework that integrates multiple components of a project. This can provide a more complete assessment of existing conditions and assist in identifying potential solutions and measuring the costs, impacts, and benefits of various strategies. A framework can also show how changes in one part of a project will affect other areas. This is important for getting beyond a bottom-line approach or an unbending focus on a single area of interest, pet project, or stakeholder agenda.

Communicating options: Frameworks are useful for communicating with stakeholders. Planners, engineers, architects, regulators, and community members often come from different backgrounds. They have different concerns, different needs, and different areas of expertise. By identifying project elements and clearly establishing their relationships, frameworks help take the mystery out of the sustainable design process. Providing a common framework that everybody understands can increase clarity and foster the development of shared solutions. As a simple means of presenting a project's critical issues, a good framework allows a wide range of stakeholders to participate effectively in the decision-making process. By getting all team members to share common objectives from the start, frameworks can be effective at streamlining design.

Establishing priorities: Once the available options have been clearly communicated, the team or stakeholder group has the ability to weigh relative priorities. For example, in a project's early stages, achieving carbon neutrality might be identified as the primary goal, while stewardship of water resources might be recognized as important but secondary. Without an overarching framework, design priorities can be focused too narrowly or solve one set of problems at the expense of another.

Setting goals: It is easier to set goals after priorities have been established. These goals can then be used to establish performance metrics for the design of all of the project's infrastructure components. Synergistic solutions that achieve environmental, energy, and economic goals simultaneously would be given top priority. A framework unites good ideas and improves the project's overall sustainability by optimizing synergies, increasing buy-in, and reducing costs.

Using Frameworks for Different Types of Development

The type of development taking place on a project will help determine the appropriate framework to use. The work of design engineers can be divided into three types of development:

Restorative development seeks to enhance or revive traditions, cultures, and natural conditions. At the Jiankou project north of Beijing, Sherwood used the pillars of sustainability framework to help preserve community steward-ship of local land. Faced with the kind of urban expansion that threatens tra-ditional ways of life around the world, the client was seeking to develop the site in a way that would preserve the livelihoods of local farmers while pro-viding the community's younger generation with income and opportunities for improving its outlook.

Regenerative development helps a community transition toward a more sustain-able society by reducing dependence on polluting energy systems, designing more efficient buildings and transportation systems, and reintroducing lost ecosystem services to the community. These projects often include brown-field development for its emphasis on regenerating degraded urban or indus-trial areas. In developing general master plans for several towns in rural California, Sherwood used the transect as a framework for identifying appro-priate densities within the plan, establishing form-based codes to guide responsible redevelopment and aligning green infrastructure with historic creeks, contours, and watersheds.

New development means breaking fresh ground. Sometimes referred to as greenfield development, it bears the responsibility of infringing upon natural systems but is often free to implement sustainable strategies without cultural or historic limitations on infrastructure design. In developing a new commu-nity in the Arizona desert, Sherwood was able to align the street grid with the sun paths and prevailing wind patterns to create favorable shades and breezes that significantly reduce energy loads for air-conditioning. The scale-density framework was used to establish a transportation system organizing strategy that would foster mixed-density communities and encourage respon-sible development while avoiding urban sprawl.

The frameworks are presented on the following pages in order to demonstrate the kind of holistic planning and design that makes all three of these types of develop-ments—as well as the full spectrum of their combinations often encountered in real-world scenarios—more sustainable.

Framework #1: Pillars of Sustainability

Five Elements of Sustainability

The pillars of sustainability is a model that looks at the five key elements of a proj-ect that form the foundation for sustainable development. The pillars create a frame-work for establishing performance metrics and maximizing opportunities for synergies among the five elements:

Water embraces all aspects of hydrology, including oceans, rainfall, snowpack, rivers, permanent freshwater bodies, and aquifers. It encompasses the water resources piped onto a project, water treatment and reuse methods, as well as stormwater, graywater, and blackwater flows. A full consideration of water also includes water vapor and the effects of evaporation and transpiration on the atmosphere and environment.

Energy is the flow of energy to, from, and within a site. It includes transportation and other activities that use energy; it also encompasses the impacts that power production and energy flows have on humanity, the atmosphere, and other elements of the environment.

Materials include all the physical components involved in the functioning of the built environment and range from soil nutrients to building materials to solid waste management.

Ecology embodies all natural and geophysical systems related to a site and the ecosystem services they provide.

Community represents the social networks within the built environment and the physical places that foster the cultural interactions that sustain our social systems. Community includes all people in and related to the site, with a special emphasis on adjacent populations and place-making within the project.

There are three steps involved in applying the pillars:

1. Present the pillars to the team, pointing out that there are several levels of potential achievement within each, from reducing harm to regenerative designs.
2. Demonstrate a variety of strategies for reaching the various levels of achievement for each pillar. Having a clear understanding of the steps necessary to reach a desired level of achievement for each pillar can help the design team

Figure 2-1 Step 1: The five pillars framework at the early stage of a project is shown with basic levels of achievement, from reducing harm to increasing positive impact. Within each pillar, the four levels of achievement offer the design team a tool for prioritizing its decisions across all five pillars. © Sherwood Design Engineers.

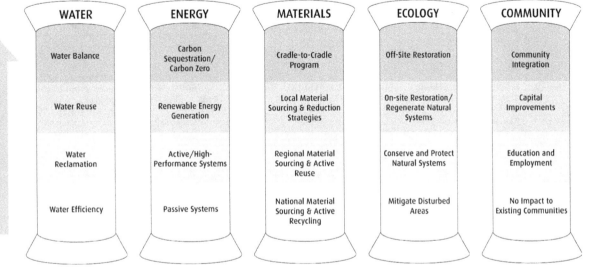

assign priorities. It will not usually be possible to reach the highest levels on every pillar right away; viewing the strategies required for each of them in tandem with the others, however, can often help designers find synergies between the different pillars. This can lead to reduced costs and higher-performing designs.

3. Update the pillars with the desired strategies and approaches selected. This then becomes a clearly identifiable framework that everyone on the design team can use throughout the life of the project.

	LEVEL ONE: REDUCE HARM	LEVEL TWO: SUSTAINABILITY SOURCING	LEVEL THREE: SYSTEMS INTEGRATION	LEVEL FOUR: REGENERATIVE DESIGN
COMMUNITY	Integrate project into local context Minimize infrastructure impacts Minimize circulation impacts Reduce air pollution	**EDUCATION AND EMPLOYMENT** Improve local training and workforce development Access to health care and family planning	**CAPITAL IMPROVEMENTS** Improve/expand infrastructure in surrounding communities Generate additional tax-based revenue for local communities	Achieve lasting economic and social benefits Optimize systems of learning and education Expand and enable cooperative networks
ECOLOGY	**MITIGATE DISTURBED AREAS** Mitigate wetland impacts Incorporate open space Minimize negative impact on habitat	**CONSERVE & PROTECT NATURAL SYSTEMS** Monitor sensitive species Preserve wildlife corridors Improve natural hydrology Landscape with native plants	**ON-SITE RESTORATION** Regenerate native systems Restore native species in wildlife corridors Coral reef propagation On-site & off-site reforestation	Maximize biodiversity and restore when necessary Model on ecosystems, biomimicry at macro and micro scale Appropriate use of environmentally sound technologies
ENERGY	**EFFICIENCY** Reduce carbon emissions Energy-efficient appliances Building-scale energy demand reduction strategies Promote public transportation	**ACTIVE HIGH-PERFORMANCE SYSTEMS** Solar-powered air-conditioning Transit-oriented development Energy monitoring systems Promote passive energy design	**RENEWABLE ENERGY GENERATION** Photovoltaic (PV) cells Wind power Zero-emissions transportation Carbon sequestration	**CARBON ZERO** Facilitate a net uptake of atmospheric carbon dioxide Continually minimize energy use through aggressive auditing
WATER	**WATER EFFICIENCY** Water conservation Xeriscaping Low-impact development	**WATER RECLAMATION** Graywater recycling On-Site wastewater treatment Retaining water on-site	**WATER REUSE** On-site rainwater harvesting Use of water-recovery systems Water withdrawal offset by groundwater recharge	**WATER BALANCE** Effective demand management Strive for Net Zero use Match predevelopment hydrologic conditions
MATERIALS	**NATIONAL MATERIAL SOURCING** Active recycling Reduce toxic materials	**REGIONAL MATERIAL SOURCING** Active reuse of materials On-site composting	**LOCAL MATERIAL SOURCING** Design for deconstruction On-site agricultural production	Minimize ecological footprints through construction and operations Minimize waste production and promote responsible recycling and reuse

Figure 2-2 Step 2: This framework is usually complemented by the development of a matrix with specific strategies, ranging from modest goals at level one to more comprehensive, sustainable development objectives at level four. Since developing this framework, Sherwood has found examples of related frameworks used by the Environmental Protection Agency (EPA) and others. © Sherwood Design Engineers.

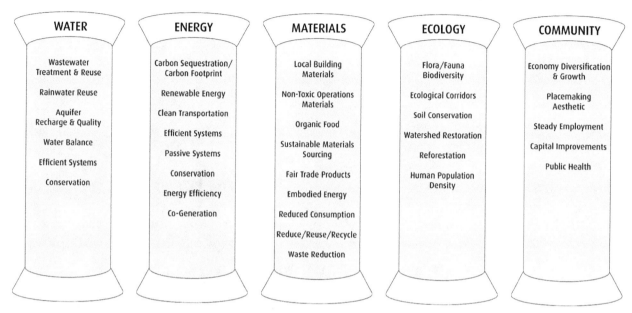

Figure 2-3 Step 3: Once the strategies are selected, they are applied as a project roadmap for achieving goals related to the various components within each of the five pillars. © Sherwood Design Engineers.

PILLARS OF SUSTAINABILITY AT THE GREAT WALL ECO VILLAGES

Collaborator Perspective: Robert Devine, Managing Director, Great Wall Resort

In 2007, Sherwood began working on concepts for a luxury resort project located amid 15 square kilometers of land 60 kilometers north of central Beijing. The project site is surrounded by 20 kilometers of original-state Great Wall, in the jagged, rocky terrain adjacent to the famous Beijing Knot, a key stronghold where three strands of the wall converge.

China's incredibly rapid development over the last twenty years has led to low-quality, poorly planned sprawl in the formerly rural areas around the major cities, leaving few openings for more sustainable development. However, in this case, the client leased the property in 1999 and had the foresight to leave it untouched while a market for a low-impact eco-resort crystallized. In the interim, the client had also rejected other master plans

because of their insensitivity to the valley's environment and cultural assets, the local village, and the Great Wall.

North China's ecosystems are extremely fragile, with limited water supplies, thin soil, and relatively harsh winters. Historically very lightly inhabited, the area's prewar and postwar population booms led to an overburdened environment. Scarce water resources were overused, deforestation—particularly during the 1960s and 1970s—was severe, and the regular use of pesticides and poisons drove native wildlife out of the valley.

Ten years ago, the project site was a roughly two-and-a-half-hour drive from Beijing. Significant government investment in road infrastructure reduced that time by half, pulling the land and its inhabitants more directly into Beijing's economic orbit. The question facing the client

Figure 2-4 The Great Wall along the Great Wall Villages' southern project boundary. © Sherwood Design Engineers.

and the planners was how to leverage that increased value potential in a way that had positive benefits for the local community and restorative impact on the natural and historical environment, all while ameliorating or eliminating any negative effects from increased usage.

With the developer, the team of Hart Howerton and Sherwood Design Engineers jointly viewed a multifaceted approach to sustainability as the organizing principle. Using the five pillars framework, Sherwood performed an initial analysis of the project. The core challenge was identifying and abiding by the environment's natural and historical sustainable carrying capacity while also generating the required economic surplus necessary for investing in improving the villagers' lives, as well as for desperately needed restoration and preservation work on the Great Wall.

We recognized that, in order to achieve sustainability in such a complicated case, we had to think holistically—to consider the interplay between economics, environment, and community.

To provide a strongly integrated framework, metrics were identified and obtained for each pillar, and a baseline picture of the project site as it existed emerged. Using this data, the project was conceptualized using the pillars of sustainability framework as follows:

Ecology

The initial state of the ecology at Jiankou was poor. Years of relative overpopulation in a sensitive biosphere combined with a lack of government policy focused on sustainable natural resource use had left the hillsides denuded and the biosphere sparse.

When the client first leased the land from the village (years before any project was outlined), an initial commitment was made to reforestation; it included direct cash payments to the villagers in return for their ceasing the harvest of healthy trees.

Once the project was underway, the goal was clear: provide a net increase in biodiversity, habitat, and environmental quality. This was accomplished first by understanding the ecology and identifying critical and sensitive habitats on-site. Next, an extensive conservation and restoration strategy was envisioned, with a total construction density of less than 1 percent of the whole valley and tilled agriculture accounting for only another 5 percent. The remainder is zoned as green space, including a 500-meter development exclusion zone around the Great Wall.

Extensive reforestation efforts are underway, with the aim of making the project a carbon sink, while the elimination of pesticides and poisons is allowing a slow recovery of birds and fauna. The intention is to increase the value of per-unit biosphere use while reducing its intensity.

Water

In the traditional Chinese conception of a harmonious living environment, the interplay between water and mountains is fundamental. Additionally, hot springs and water therapies are planned as a central feature of the spa resort. But more importantly, in North China, water is always the scarcest resource. Beijing is the most water-starved large city in the world. Its water resource per capita is already less than 300 cubic meters—one-thirtieth of the world average—and groundwater tables have been dangerously depleted over the last several decades.

To ensure a sustainable water resources system, a water-balance analysis was performed, and the goal of limiting groundwater use to 600 millimeters per year was established. This level will not only prevent further groundwater depletion, it means that the project site will be net additive to the water system—at an average increase of 200 millimeters per year in aquifer level.

At the macro level, planning was focused on land use. The total amount of cultivated acreage has been decreased, a winter fallow season reintroduced, and the use of greenhouses considerably increased. All these measures have reduced system water loss due to evapotranspiration.

Additionally, to increase water efficiency

- rain harvesting infrastructure is being introduced at each individual resort unit and throughout the project site;
- maximum-efficiency water technologies are being built into the architecture;
- the whole constructed infrastructure is being located on the upstream side of the project site so that graywater and even blackwater can be treated and reused for irrigation and aquifer recharging;
- efficiency technologies are being built on the land surfaces so that stormwater can be routed through the site and have its energy dissipated in water features, and so precipitation can be prevented from leaving the system as runoff;
- extensive mulching is being used at the agricultural level, reducing evapotranspiration up to 100 millimeters per year.

In this way, we developed an expanded water system that continued to provide for agricultural and groundwater recharge but also met the needs of the expanded community under development.

Energy

The project was designed to be fully off-grid as well as a net carbon sink, absorbing more carbon dioxide than it releases. Energy demand reduction technologies are integrated into the building design where possible, but the requirements of a luxury, branded resort affected what could be imposed. Instead, considerable thought went into the energy supply concept:

- First, a baseline of geothermal heat exchange pumps was specified to level interior temperatures year-round at about 14°C. This is particularly crucial to the idea of basing design on North China rural vernacular but opening up the traditionally "hunkered-down" courtyard to better absorb the views of the wall and valley. Without heat pumps, heating costs in this mountainous climate would be prohibitive.
- Second, dispersed biomass is key to power generation. An aggressive hillside reforestation program has been undertaken using a hybrid willow suitable to the local environment, and biomass material collection takes place throughout the valley. Additionally, farm and kitchen waste are collected and utilized for biomass energy generation.
- Third, additional on-site power is generated through low-visual-impact solar thermal heat and photovoltaic production.

Transportation was also a key concern. Rather than overpaving the site for low volumes of automobile traffic, smaller, low-impact trails have been designed for use with electric carts, bikes, and horses.

Materials

The materials pillar is challenging and often overlooked. At Jiankou, our approach was to maximize the use of local, renewable, and reusable materials to reduce the project's overall energy intensity and waste production. Sherwood started this process by completing a baseline nutrient balance to understand how nutrients flowed to and from the site in the form of food, fertilizer, and waste.

The dominant aesthetic of the village is stone buildings, gray brick and tiles, and wood. The many handmade stone walls, roads, and structures on the site were obviously a crucial piece of cultural heritage, as well as being the dominant form of local infrastructure. While most of the structures were not of historic value, one of the smaller villages is being preserved and renovated in order to provide a historical touchstone for the project. Elsewhere, as structures are dismantled, the materials are retained for reuse. The majority of the new stone material needed for the project is being sourced on-site from back-valley quarries, reducing transport emissions and ensuring the quarrying will be undertaken cleanly. Much of the gray brick and tile will be kilned on-site—just as Great Wall bricks were nearly six hundred years ago. (The site still has the remnants of brick kilns used for that very purpose.)

The materials pillar also encompasses food provision and the nutrient cycle. The project is planned as a fully functioning biodynamic farm. The restaurants will feature locavore menus, and the controlled food supply and organic nature of the valley are key marketing points for the project. Special focus has been placed on grapes, fruits, vegetables, spices, mushrooms, honey, and nuts.

Pasture-fed livestock and poultry will be raised on-site, as will limited amounts of corn, barley, soybean, and wheat.

Approximately 400 acres of hillside land (about 10 percent of the site) will be planted with a fast-growing hybrid willow that will be used for dispersed biomass power generation. Additionally, all biowaste will be recycled for fertilizer or, where possible, power generation.

Community

The Jiankou site is important not only for its cultural resources but also as a home to 140 peasant households scattered in seven villages throughout the valley. Upholding the pillar of community meant incorporating and enhancing these existing inhabitants' quality of life. The crux of sustainability revolves around inhabitants, economics, and preservation—in this case, both natural and cultural.

For the peasants in the valley, agriculture alone provides only a subsistence existence, one that depletes the natural resources of water, wood, and soil. But a development program that opened this area to unfettered tourism would quickly erode the area's traditional culture and damage the Great Wall and its surrounding ecosystem. This project sought to find a middle ground, one that

Figure 2-5 For this project, building a strong community pillar meant preserving traditional ways of life while providing modern opportunities for village inhabitants. © Sherwood Design Engineers.

opened the wall to outsiders in a way that preserved the place's unique local character.

The project offers all inhabitants upgraded living facilities (including basic utility upgrades, better water pressure, more consistent electricity, and simpler sanitation disposal) and cash compensation, as well as stable employment at the resort and incorporation into the urban social security net. The project also allows for straight cash payments to households wishing to relocate to the city. (To the client's surprise, this has proven to be the somewhat more popular option.)

For the community pillar to be strong, the local economy had to be developed as well. To increase and diversify economic opportunities, we sought ways to provide a healthy market for local products and incorporate local labor into the expanded service opportunities presented by the development of a spa resort and boutique international conference center.

By bringing together investment, planning, and design capability, the project seeks to break the depletion cycle by generating a revenue stream large enough to restore and preserve the site's cultural and natural environment while also providing an improved life for the local inhabitants—a sustainable community and economy that enhances the lives of all those who interact with the project.

By considering the needs of the existing community in tandem with the opportunities of the developing community, we were able to create a synthesis of the modern and the traditional. Visitors to the Great Wall can now see more than just the ancient stones.

PlaNYC: Pillars of Sustainability in Action

Over the next twenty-five years, New York City will get bigger, its infrastructure will get older, and its environment will be increasingly threatened by poor air quality, heightened storm intensity, and rising sea levels. To tackle these challenges, city planners developed a framework of six critical areas to target: land, air, water, transportation, energy, and climate change.

Working closely with the community, New York developed goals for the year 2030 in each of these target areas:

Land: Create more homes and more affordable homes, promote open space and ensure all residents live within a ten-minute walk of a park, and clean up the more than 1,700 acres of contaminated brownfield in the city environs.

Water: Improve the water network to ensure a reliable clean water supply. New York's aging pipes lose millions of gallons of water a day. Conservation efforts, new facilities, watershed protection, and increasing the rate at which aging infrastructure is repaired will all work toward clean water. The second goal, improving the health of New York's waterways and watersheds, includes traditional solutions like expanding stormwater capacity in sewers and at treatment plants; green technologies like green roofs and pervious parking lots; natural solutions like wetland restoration; and

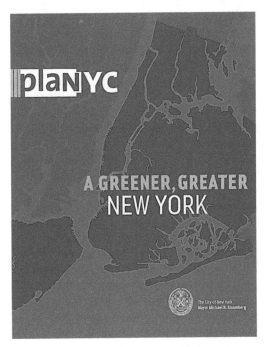

Figure 2-6 PlaNYC identifies sustainability goals for New York City for the six "pillars" of land, air, water, transportation, energy, and climate change. PlaNYC, the City of New York.

promising best practices like vegetated swales, tree planting, and mussel beds, which naturally cleanse water.

Transportation: New York is developing a sweeping regional transportation plan to reduce gridlock and improve public transit. Over seventeen initiatives will expand bus, ferry, and train routes; manage roads more efficiently; stay current with repair needs; and promote cycling on the city's 1,800-mile bike master plan. They will also introduce a congestion pricing program to control traffic into the city center and experiment with street closures to reclaim space for pedestrians.

Air: Over 50 percent of air pollution in New York comes from transportation, making it an essential element in the success of any clean air program. Cleaner cars, trucks, and buses; better fuels; and more efficient vehicles are all necessary from an air-quality standpoint. Reforesting parkland, planting street trees, cleaner waterways, and renewable energy will also improve air quality.

Energy: To curb ever-expanding energy demand while increasing supplies of clean energy, the city's plans include awareness campaigns, training, and incentives for conserving energy; improving the city's power grid; and fostering renewable energy. Because energy is a regional issue, the city is forming an energy power board to coordinate energy objectives with New York State.

Climate change: To deal with increased storm intensity and rising sea levels, New York needs to protect vital infrastructure systems, including water supply, sewer, and wastewater, as well as major airports and subterranean subways and tunnels. The city is creating an interagency task force to deal with the enormous challenge of developing coordinated responses among these different agencies. To help communities prepare and adapt to climate change, the city is reaching out to its communities with site-specific planning measures and climate-adaptation strategies. As part of its citywide planning efforts, it is updating the one-hundred-year floodplain map of New York.

New York's PlaNYC was developed around a framework similar to the pillars of sustainability that focused on three natural systems (land, water, air), two man-made systems (transportation and energy), and the great global challenge of our time, climate change. By targeting sustainability efforts toward strengthening each of these pillars, the city is finding many mutually reinforcing strategies.

PlaNYC demonstrates that diverse challenges require an integrated, comprehensive approach to overcome jurisdictional obstacles and create solutions that work synergistically. The plan encompasses many city departments and agencies, and its agenda stretches over many years. To date, the plan has made progress in a number of areas. The following are examples of the diverse objectives and programs achieved as part of PlaNYC*:

Energy: Established the New York City Energy Planning Board to coordinate energy efficiency, renewable energy, and energy infrastructure programs.

Expanded peak load management: Deployed advanced meters to monitor power usage.

Solar incentives: Created property tax abatement for solar installations.

Producing energy from solid waste: Initiated feasibility studies for anaerobic digestion in Hunts Point Water Pollution Control Plant and began the process of siting alternative waste conversion technologies in all five boroughs.

Green roof/blue roof pilot study: Compared various methods on adjoining roofs to determine the most effective methodology.

Sustainable stormwater management plan: Launched an interagency best management practices (BMP) task force to complete a comprehensive BMP plan for the city.

For more information on this subject please see www.sherwoodinstitute.org/resources.

*Source: PlaNYC Progress Report 2009. www.nyc.gov/html/planyc2030/. Accessed 3/27/2010.

Framework #2: The Scale-Density Framework

This framework offers the ability to quickly define the various strategies that operate over a range of different scales and densities. It makes evident how these strategies interrelate or overlap. It also allows for a deeper examination of relative value to ensure that systems are integrated. The application of scale is clear: as you go from building scale to city scale, the strategies change. This is complemented by strategy options within a block or district based on the density. For example, stormwater management in a dense neighborhood may be accomplished with green streets and green roofs, whereas in a less dense neighborhood, bioretention wetlands incorporated into open space might be the selected strategy.

Figure 2-7 Scale-density matrix. Sustainable opportunities at various scales and densities are shown in matrix format as part of the application of the scale-density framework. © Sherwood Design Engineers.

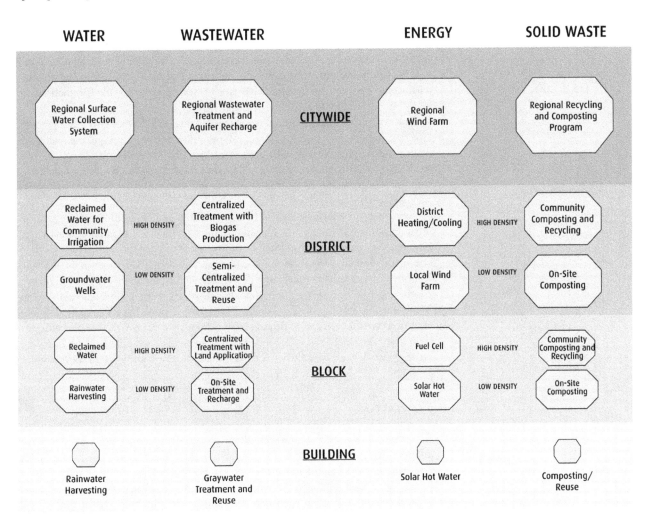

Scale

So-called economies of scale have become a dominant part of modern design strategy. This thinking has led to the development of single solutions at larger and larger scales, from centralized water projects to sprawling suburbs and interstate freeways. But these systems often become energy intensive, degrade the environment, have high up-front costs, or lack efficiency. Sustainable design focuses on what might be termed synergies of scale—finding the most appropriate scale for the infrastructure of an individual project and integrating it with other local systems.

This book deals primarily with three scales common to Sherwood's projects: site, community, and city scale. At the smaller end of the spectrum are single buildings or single sites, such as a plaza. The community scale involves a number of buildings, the circulation networks that connect them, and the infrastructure systems they share. At the city scale, a collection of communities and their shared infrastructure networks and open spaces are considered. Technologies and systems that are not viable at the building or community scale may become viable with the aggregated investment of an entire city. Likewise, some strategies, like reclaiming water, can be found at all scales, from harvesting rainwater on a single residence to recharging aquifers with a city's treated wastewater. This is why having a framework is important: it allows similar strategies across varying scales to be accounted for.

In a city such as San Francisco, resources are available to establish a comprehensive municipal water recycling system. The resource constraints, combined with the scale of the support district—a large city—make such a system viable. Across the bay, smaller towns with similar climatic and environmental conditions do not have recycled water systems, due to their smaller scale and the scarcity of resources to support such a system.

Infrastructure responses depend in part on the height of buildings, the number of units on a single site, and the range of uses on a single block. Neighborhoods where businesses are separated from residences, for instance, need different strategies than ones with commercial uses on the first floor and residential apartments above them. Running a quick errand (like going to the cleaners) in a Phoenix suburb involves a trip in a car, often of several miles, while the same errand can be accomplished in Manhattan by walking to the corner. These two options have markedly different environmental footprints. Multiuse neighborhoods are more walkable and efficient than zoned developments where residential, commercial, and industrial development are segregated. Scale alone, therefore, is not a sufficient consideration for determining appropriate development strategies.

Density

Regardless of the scale of a project, all cities, and even many neighborhoods, have different densities within them. Properly assessing scale and density is thus critical for designing appropriate infrastructure systems. Strategies that work for single-family homes—like leachfield septic systems or drinking from well water—may be inappropriate for multiunit urban apartment buildings. Large buildings and high-rises may require fuel cells, advanced HVAC systems, or stormwater retention cisterns. Lower densities permit the use of less technology, allowing open spaces and native systems to naturally clean the air and absorb water. Moderate- or mixed-density projects can more easily use passive techniques and naturally engineered technologies like landscape-based stormwater management features and passive solar heating designs.

Usually, as density increases, more intensive technology is required. As the volume of water, energy, and material flows on a given site grows, engineers must shift the burden from natural systems to man-made systems. Modern technologies can handle enormous flows of water and waste, treating more material with less time on less space than natural methods. The tradeoff is that they usually require imports of energy or generate carbon dioxide and other waste products. Sustainable design, then, becomes the art of satisfying the same human needs with less energy and materials by increasing efficiency, and also reducing the environmental impact of the energy and materials we do use.

Impact reduction may be achieved by shifting back to natural systems for absorbing waste, cleansing water, and purifying air, or by developing technologies that replicate these systems for use in denser developments. Many sustainable or green technologies are engineered methods for increasing the performance of natural systems and integrating them with human development. This aim underlies green roofs, rain gardens, and living machines. The more we integrate natural systems into our developments, the more we gain the benefits those systems provide. This is why parks, waterways, and urban forests are so important.

APPLYING THE SCALE-DENSITY FRAMEWORK TO NEW DEVELOPMENT
New City Planning in the Southwestern United States

Sherwood has been working as part of a multidisciplinary team on the planning and design of a new city-scale project in the Southwestern United States. This project has included a variety of uses, including institutional, commercial, hospitality, recreation, and residential, as well as varying degrees of density. As the Southwest continues to grow, this project has, at its core, a more than twenty-year vision for how it can become a model for new large-scale development set adjacent to the existing fabric of suburban sprawl and its corresponding infrastructure.

As we began to look holistically at this project, weighing the developer's objectives and the constraints of the site, we realized that it would not be able to maximize its sustainability potential with multiple city-scale solutions to its infrastructure design. Instead, we explored solutions at a variety of scales to maximize the give-and-take of resource flows between the various land uses within the project.

At the project scale, we were looking at a development with infrastructure requirements—including substantial water demands—that would need to be fed by a combination of sources, including from the state water project; power demands that would require the construction of new substations and distribution infrastructure; wastewater generation that would require new treatment plants or, at a minimum, extensive upgrades of some of the regional plants; transportation infrastructure that would need to connect into regional highways and rapid transit systems; stormwater management infrastructure to detain and convey the potential flash floods that move out of the surrounding foothills and through the site; and ecological infrastructure to support the site and region's existing flora and fauna. Each of these infrastructure systems had its unique conditions and requirements with respect to how it connected to the greater regional systems, as well as how it was designed internally.

As we worked to understand these overall resource flows (potable water, blackwater, irrigation water, electricity, natural gas, etc.), it became imperative to work at a range of scales simultaneously in order to advance our overall infrastructure design in a meaningful way. This included working both at the intermediate scale of districts and neighborhoods, looking for efficiencies and feedback loops, and identifying integrated strategies at the scale of the individual buildings and site.

Simultaneously, we looked at densities within the project's districts, as high, medium, and low densities have significantly different infrastructure requirements across the various proposed land uses. The highest densities tended to occur in the proposed central business district and neighboring multistory residential condo buildings, while the lowest densities occurred in the most outlying residential neighborhoods and along the network of open space. Medium densities occurred within the tighter fabric of two- and three-story neighborhoods, some of the areas dedicated for institutional uses, and a portion of the site dedicated to hospitality. At each of these densities, we were again able to explore various opportunities for efficiencies and synergies between the various resource flows.

Critical to analyzing the pros, cons, and cumulative effects of various design strategies proposed at the various scales and densities across the project was the use of the scale-density framework as an organizing principle. Our first step included developing a matrix of potential infrastructure solutions at the various project scales and densities, similar to Figure 2-7. Working with the client, design team, and local municipalities, we were then able to eliminate strategies that did not meet budgetary, permitting, or aesthetic requirements. At that point, we were left with a toolkit of strategies. These could be implemented at various scales and densities that, in aggregate, formed the backbone of our infrastructure design. Using resource (irrigation, electricity, potable water, etc.) design calculators, we were then able to model the smaller individual strategies, as well as their cumulative makeup, in real time, to explore the impacts of land-plan changes on infrastructure thresholds when it came to supply, cost, environmental impact, and so on.

Some of the most interesting resource flow manipulations for this project occurred around the region's most precious resource—water. Set in an area with limited water supplies, there were both legal and practical (cost, maintenance, operations, etc.) constraints to work through. Central to this debate was how much stormwater and blackwater the project would recycle and reuse on-site and how much it would supply to the regional infrastructure systems. One of our overarching design concepts was to keep as much water within local water reuse networks as possible in order to minimize the energy required to transport the water to and from the site, and to implement landscape-based treatment systems wherever possible throughout the project.

Starting at the building scale, we identified strategies that would complement those working at each of the successively larger scales. In a region with an average annual rainfall of under 8 inches, conservation was at the cornerstone of home design and the assumptions that went into demand calculations. Within the low-density areas, separate plumbing for graywater systems and on-site reuse as an irrigation source was proposed. Additionally, on-lot stormwater management was designed to support the native landscaping palette, maximize infiltration, and minimize downstream stormwater infrastructure capacity upgrades. Although not required for all lots, rainwater harvesting was supported and made attractive through incentives offered to neighborhood developers by way of decreased stormwater infrastructure requirements. Minimum coverage thresholds for living roofs within higher-density areas were implemented in an effort to decrease stormwater flows as well as for the synergistic effects of reduced heat island effect and improving urban ecology.

At the district scale, land use and density—both high density in the urban core and lower density in the residential neighborhoods—came under consideration. To make the most of the region's limited water supply, low-density areas included neighborhood-scale low-energy wastewater treatment technologies—including primary treatment at individual lots followed by secondary treatment through centralized media filters—that fed constructed wetlands for tertiary treatment prior to discharge to the open-space network. Wastewater management from the higher-density zones, on the other hand, was integrated into the city-scale strategies in an effort to capitalize on the efficiencies inherent in high-density shared infrastructure systems. Stormwater from these higher-density zones was routed through a network of green streets and parks to the larger reaches of the open-space greenbelt, where it supported the function and health of the natural system.

At a citywide scale, the introduction of a number of centralized systems became practical, from centralized wastewater treatment that, through a recycled water system, fed a community golf course, athletic fields, and municipal parks, to a city-scale greenbelt that retained and managed off-site stormwater flows in a capacity that mimicked the preexisting conditions. Finally, water from the state water project complemented the other water reuse, capture, and retention systems to make up the balance of the city's demand.

In aggregate, typical water demands were substantially decreased through the implementation of a variety of sustainable alternatives across the project's scales and densities. Figure 2-8 illustrates these interrelationships and the overall impact the individual solutions had on the project as a whole.

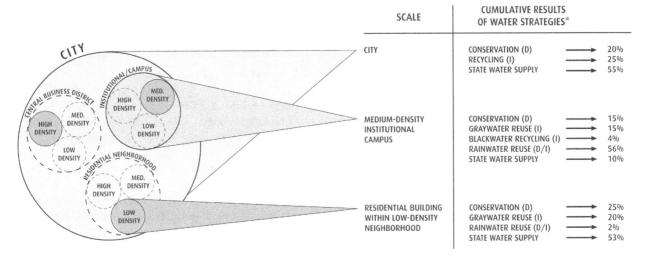

SCALE	CUMULATIVE RESULTS OF WATER STRATEGIES*		
CITY	CONSERVATION (D)	→	20%
	RECYCLING (I)	→	25%
	STATE WATER SUPPLY	→	55%
MEDIUM-DENSITY INSTITUTIONAL CAMPUS	CONSERVATION (D)	→	15%
	GRAYWATER REUSE (I)	→	15%
	BLACKWATER RECYCLING (I)	→	4%
	RAINWATER REUSE (D/I)	→	56%
	STATE WATER SUPPLY	→	10%
RESIDENTIAL BUILDING WITHIN LOW-DENSITY NEIGHBORHOOD	CONSERVATION (D)	→	25%
	GRAYWATER REUSE (I)	→	20%
	RAINWATER REUSE (D/I)	→	2%
	STATE WATER SUPPLY	→	53%

* As compared to a 'business as usual' scenario (baseline)

(D) denotes strategy that impacts domestic demand
(I) denotes strategy that impacts irrigation demand
(D/I) denotes strategy that impacts domestic and/or irrigation demand

Figure 2-8 The project's three scales are illustrated as circles of varying sizes, labeled "city" for the projectwide scale and "central business district," "institutional/campus," and "residential neighborhood" for three of the many intermediate scales; within those, "high density," "medium density," and "low density" were designated. Solid-lined circles indicate the scale/density relationship representative of the included project components; dashed-lined circles indicate other potential scenarios. This figure depicts just three of this project's many interrelationships and the corresponding makeup of water demands compared with a business-as-usual case. The cumulative result at the project scale was a new city that required 55 percent of the state-supplied water, compared with the baseline case. © Sherwood Design Engineers.

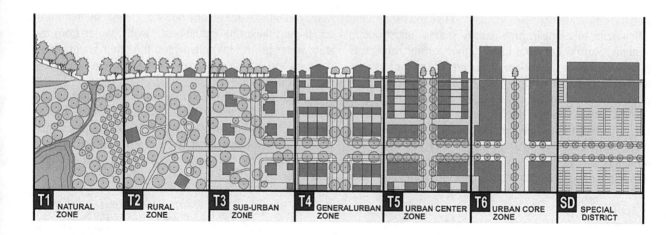

| T1 NATURAL ZONE | T2 RURAL ZONE | T3 SUB-URBAN ZONE | T4 GENERALURBAN ZONE | T5 URBAN CENTER ZONE | T6 URBAN CORE ZONE | SD SPECIAL DISTRICT |

Figure 2-9 The transect. Duany Plater-Zyberk & Company (DPZ).

Framework #3: The Transect

The urban transect divides land use into seven zones. The first is T1, the natural zone, which is undeveloped land or landscaping. This need not be wilderness—there are patches of T1 even in the heart of a city: parks, gardens, or empty lots can all be considered T1.

Moving along the transect toward greater density, from the T2 rural zone to the T3 suburban zone, the space between buildings diminishes, limiting the ability of open and landscaped spaces to perform natural functions like stormwater retention. In T4 and T5 are denser zones of development where building-integrated infrastructure takes over from site-integrated infrastructure. These denser zones also support centralized infrastructure systems, including wastewater treatment and public transportation, to a greater degree than rural and suburban zones.

Finally, T6 is a dense urban core or business district featuring high-rises and a multistory skyline. It is important for cities to contain a balance between these zones. On a map of New York City, Central Park represents a T1 zone, while Times Square is a T6. The major park right in the city center literally provides a breath of fresh air for city residents. An additional category is labeled special district (SD); it includes places like industrial facilities, campuses, or other unique uses.

As a planning method, the transect promotes community by offering people a variety of housing and commercial opportunities within each neighborhood. While conventional zoning calls for business, commercial, and residential areas in separate zones, the transect accommodates mixed-use environments by organizing around specific densities instead of specific land uses. By allowing density-appropriate mixes of commercial, residential, and open spaces, the transect aims to create complete neighborhoods, whether in a small town or a dense city block. This avoids some of the downsides of conventional planning that have led to sprawling houses miles from any store, or big-box stores that put a nearby historic Main Street out of business. The transect framework helps planners control growth by determining the right mix of building types and public spaces for a certain district, as well as where those districts should be in relation to one another.

As engineers, we examine water, wastewater, energy, and material flows across the spectrum of the transect to reveal different opportunities for implementing sustainable development strategies.

The transect is useful for identifying

- scale-appropriate infrastructure
- density-appropriate technology
- climate-appropriate and regionally specific designs
- opportunities for the preservation and augmentation of public spaces
- linkages and overlaps between building and streetscape solutions
- connectivity between on-site and off-site infrastructure
- the integration of regional hinterland resources

Achieving a Balanced Transect

Many studies have shown the efficiencies of dense urban living. Apartment residents use less water and energy than their suburban counterparts. Walking to the store and taking the train to work are less energy intensive than driving everywhere. As density increases, a variety of infrastructure efficiencies develop naturally. But that does not mean the greatest possible density is always best. There are sometimes reasons for development in new or outlying areas that lack infrastructure. The purpose of having a transect is not to identify the "best" level of density, but rather the optimum balance among the different levels of density that occur in every community.

If a community goes from an area at T6 to a few miles of T1 to another clump at T6 and then a neighborhood of T3, efficiency of infrastructure is lost from every perspective: traffic, water, and energy. The transect allows planners and engineers to achieve a balance among density, efficiency, and the cultural needs and character of a community.

For more information on related topics please see
   www.sherwoodinstitute.org/resources.

T1: Natural Zone

This zone is characterized by natural areas, the area surrounding a development, or preexisting conditions of the area before development began. In designing sustainable infrastructure, the first step is to look at regional ecosystems, including local watersheds and the groundwater basins they overlie. Where does water come from, what is available locally, and what are the major uses of that water? Mapping natural boundaries over jurisdictional boundaries is also important. A community may straddle several watersheds, or share its water with other jurisdictions. Virtually all communities are importers of food, energy, water, and materials as well, which means transmission lines and other delivery networks are required to pass through the T1 zones of the hinterland surrounding the community. Understanding the natural environment and climate of T1 has a critical influence on many other planning decisions.

Figure 2-10 Stormwater design using the transect. For a project in Garfield County, Colorado, Sherwood developed water-quality sizing criteria for the varying streetscape sections as defined by the transect. For the different road types, this included the selection of methods (function) and features (form) for removing contaminants and facilitating infiltration. Sherwood Design Engineers with Hart Howerton.

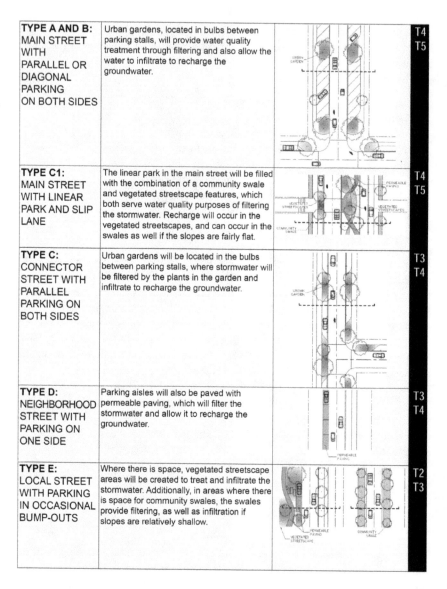

TYPE A AND B: MAIN STREET WITH PARALLEL OR DIAGONAL PARKING ON BOTH SIDES	Urban gardens, located in bulbs between parking stalls, will provide water quality treatment through filtering and also allow the water to infiltrate to recharge the groundwater.	T4 T5
TYPE C1: MAIN STREET WITH LINEAR PARK AND SLIP LANE	The linear park in the main street will be filled with the combination of a community swale and vegetated streetscape features, which both serve water quality purposes of filtering the stormwater. Recharge will occur in the vegetated streetscapes, and can occur in the swales as well if the slopes are fairly flat.	T4 T5
TYPE C: CONNECTOR STREET WITH PARALLEL PARKING ON BOTH SIDES	Urban gardens will be located in the bulbs between parking stalls, where stormwater will be filtered by the plants in the garden and infiltrate to recharge the groundwater.	T3 T4
TYPE D: NEIGHBORHOOD STREET WITH PARKING ON ONE SIDE	Parking aisles will also be paved with permeable paving, which will filter the stormwater and allow it to recharge the groundwater.	T3 T4
TYPE E: LOCAL STREET WITH PARKING IN OCCASIONAL BUMP-OUTS	Where there is space, vegetated streetscape areas will be created to treat and infiltrate the stormwater. Additionally, in areas where there is space for community swales, the swales provide filtering, as well as infiltration if slopes are relatively shallow.	T2 T3

T2 and T3: Rural and Suburban Zones

In the T2 and T3 zones, there is space to use passive techniques such as building orientation and shade trees for heating and cooling and bioswales for water management. Knowing where stream courses would naturally have run allows engineers to daylight creeks and reintegrate natural water systems. These can serve as flood zones and natural drainage ways, allowing water to get back into underlying groundwater basins instead of leaving the basin rapidly as it would in a pipe. It also becomes an opportunity to develop waterways as open public spaces, with recreational and other uses well suited to the low densities found in these transect zones.

Like natural corridors, existing infrastructure corridors are also important. Planning development around existing infrastructure systems allows for increased density without requiring additional sewer, water, and power lines. Engineers and planners can use the transect as a tool to reveal where the natural and existing infrastructure systems are in their communities and aid lower-impact development.

T4–T6: Urban Zones

In the T5 and T6 zones of the transect, there is an increasing need to introduce active technologies to heat and cool buildings, provide light, manage stormwater, and treat wastewater. But there is also the opportunity for natural systems that are well engineered. Green roofs are an example of systems that are engineered at an advanced level, yet natural. They reduce demand on mechanical systems and capture and treat stormwater that would otherwise run off to stormwater systems. The process of integrating natural and engineered systems into effective hybrids requires careful thought, good design, and sometimes, the reshaping of local policy.

USING THE TRANSECT TO REDEVELOP TEHACHAPI

Tehachapi is a small agricultural town in the windswept foothills of eastern California. The town recently undertook a planning process with the objectives of growing economically, keeping its character as a small mountain town, and building sustainability into its general plan. Working with the planning and architecture firm Moule & Polyzoides, we used the transect framework to understand the existing conditions and infrastructure in the area, and then to map out sustainable strategies for further development.

Like many towns, Tehachapi had suffered from unplanned, discontinuous development. The town had originally sprung up alongside the railroad tracks. It was a quaint little town, charming but limited in size and economic potential. When some modern big-box stores were built a few miles away, the population expanded. Inexpensive farmland was soon covered with sprawling, single-family dwellings; suburban cul-de-sacs paved over the fields outside of town. With houses, shops, and work all separated from each other, people were forced to drive everywhere.

From a transect perspective, the developed edges of town (T4) went suddenly to T1, with undeveloped fields directly abutting the expanded town core. Because several miles of open farmland (T1) separated the recently developed suburban homes (T3) from the town, residents were required to drive for daily errands. Likewise, another stretch of open land (T1) separated a patch of older, rural homes (T2) from both the suburbs and the town itself.

Without a framework to integrate development and match mixed uses at common densities, the town had pockets of development separated by miles of undeveloped land. This type of haphazard development based on conventional zoning regulations is not uncommon. Unfortunately, it is inefficient, resulting in traffic congestion and a decreased quality of life, while threatening the culture of the small town it serves.

Tehachapi is not unlike many small towns in California and around the world that experience unexpected transformation when new economic drivers sweep in a wave of growth. Integrating infrastructure and city planning using a tool like the transect (see pages 44–45) allows these towns to be prepared and to direct appropriate development. With the right tools in place, cities can share the burden and expense for infrastructure extensions and upgrades accordingly.

Figure 2-11 Watershed analysis. To help inform new strategies related to urban form and future development patterns, our first step was to look at the regional climate and watersheds that support Tehachapi. The area is barren, windy, green for only a few months a year, and snowy in the winter. This is a diagram of the watersheds surrounding Tehachapi. Notice that the town is straddling the line between two major watersheds. Understanding this physical and environmental context is the first step in designing a response that will improve the relationship of the town with its surroundings and natural resources. © Sherwood Design Engineers.

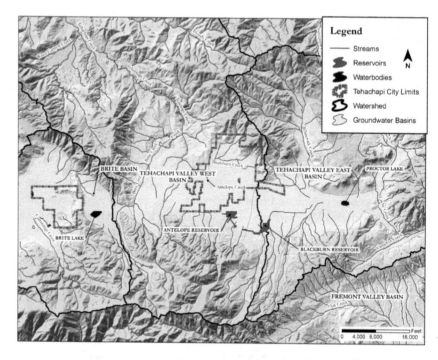

Figure 2-12 Wind-power mapping. The area of darkest shading on this map shows the windy ridges east of town that are best suited for generating wind power. Just as we try to draw water from local sources and use it in a way that replenishes as much groundwater as possible, we also incorporate local sources of energy into our understanding of the T1 zone of the transect. Tehachapi already has significant wind power development in place, and it was important to coordinate proposed wind development plans with the town's general plan. © Sherwood Design Engineers.

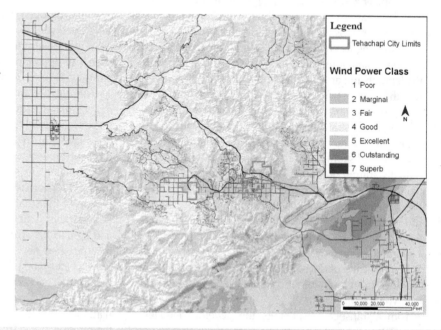

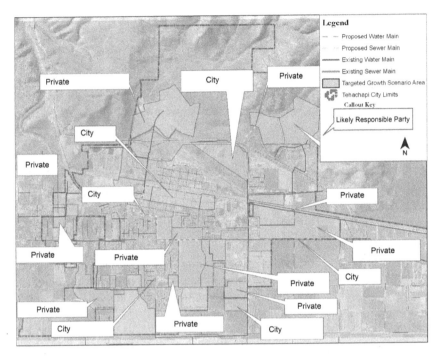

Figure 2-13 Infrastructure mapping. Honing in on the town itself, this diagram maps existing sewer infrastructure over proposed development areas. Building new development around the existing infrastructure is more efficient than building from scratch in unserviced areas. But care must be taken not to overburden existing systems or load them unevenly. Using a transect helps identify the appropriate densities for a given area and keeps planning efforts in line with infrastructure capacities. Guiding development based on existing infrastructure is a more organic and sustainable form of planning than simply developing on the lowest-cost land. Because land is cheaper the farther it is outside of existing established areas, development based on land cost alone tends to increase sprawl and lead to the discontinuous pockets of development that had plagued Tehachapi. © Sherwood Design Engineers.

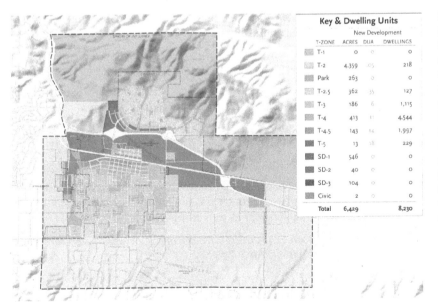

Key & Dwelling Units

| | New Development | | |
T-ZONE	ACRES	DUA	DWELLINGS
T-1	0	0	0
T-2	4,359	.05	218
Park	263	0	0
T-2.5	362	.35	127
T-3	186	6	1,115
T-4	413	11	4,544
T-4.5	143	14	1,997
T-5	13	18	229
SD-1	546	0	0
SD-2	40	0	0
SD-3	104	0	0
Civic	2	0	0
Total	6,429		8,230

Figure 2-14 Transect planning. This diagram shows the general plan of the town and how the transect was applied. The infrastructure systems delineated in Figure 2-13 provided a road map for the plan, and a series of community workshops allowed the townspeople to contribute significantly to the plan's development. The densest development is situated adjacent to the rail line and the historic town center, while neighborhood commercial centers are established where appropriate to enhance walkability. Moule & Polyzoides.

AIA/COTE TEN MEASURES OF SUSTAINABLE DESIGN

The sustainability frameworks presented in this chapter are by no means mutually exclusive; there are a variety of frameworks for defining sustainability. They have been developed by different organizations with a variety of different emphases. The Ten Measures of Sustainable Design were developed by the American Institute of Architects' Committee on the Environment (AIA/COTE).

Measures of Sustainable Design

COTE definition of sustainability and sustainable design:
   Sustainability envisions the enduring prosperity of all living things.
   Sustainable design seeks to create communities, buildings, and products that contribute to this vision.

Measure 1: Design & Innovation

Sustainable design is an inherent aspect of design excellence. Projects should express sustainable design concepts and intentions and take advantage of innovative programming opportunities.

Measure 2: Regional/Community Design

Sustainable design values the unique cultural and natural character of a given region.

Measure 3: Land Use & Site Ecology

Sustainable design protects and benefits ecosystems, watersheds, and wildlife habitat in the presence of human development.

Measure 4: Bioclimatic Design

Sustainable design conserves resources and maximizes comfort through design adaptations to site-specific and regional climate conditions.

Measure 5: Light & Air

Sustainable design creates comfortable interior environments that provide daylight, views, and fresh air.

Measure 6: Water Cycle

Sustainable design conserves water and protects and improves water quality.

Measure 7: Energy Flows & Energy Future

Sustainable design conserves energy and resources and reduces the carbon footprint while improving building performance and comfort. Sustainable design anticipates future energy sources and needs.

Measure 8: Materials & Construction

Sustainable design includes the informed selection of materials and products to reduce product-cycle environmental impacts, improve performance, and optimize occupant health and comfort.

Measure 9: Long Life, Loose Fit

Sustainable design seeks to enhance and increase ecological, social, and economic values over time.

Measure 10: Collective Wisdom and Feedback Loops

Sustainable design strategies and best practices evolve over time through documented performance and shared knowledge of lessons learned.

Source: AIA COTE Mission. http://www.aia.org/practicing/ groups/kc/AIAS074684

Framework #4: The Built Form–Ecology Framework

All human development occurs within the context of natural systems. We depend for our survival on ecosystem services (see Figure 2-15), including the production and recycling of our most vital resources: air, water, and food; the energy we derive from natural forces (such as fossil fuels, water, wind, and the sun); and the stunning range of biological diversity found in the world's ecosystems, which provide many cultural and recreational opportunities. Mapping the interactions between human-made and natural systems can provide a useful framework for evaluating sustainable development. This framework also allows us to consider the regenerative possibilities of development.

Designer Bill Reed, author of *The Integrative Design Guide to Green Building*, is one of the numerous designers who have observed that many Native Americans do not conceive of the environment as being somehow separate from themselves. In designing infrastructure systems, we often think of the hinterland as the natural resource banks and support systems outside developed areas. But our ecological footprint does not stop at a project's property line or at a city boundary. In an overcrowded world in which we are changing the chemistry of the atmosphere and the oceans, there is no separation between us, our communities, and the environment. It is no longer enough to simply "leave nature alone." The regeneration of natural systems must be successfully integrated into the development process.

By approaching a project site with an eye for the interaction between natural systems and human activity, we can measure the flows between them and the impacts they have on each other. In this way, we can shift the relationship between the natural and built environments from an intersection to an integration.

In greenfield development, this means ensuring that intact ecosystems are not harmed. In brownfield development, it means restoring natural ecosystems—not merely building healthy human systems on top of degraded natural systems. And in urban infill development, regeneration means bringing nature to the city. Incorporating ecological systems into the urban environment can help clean the air, treat water, provide shade, and add recreational opportunities.

Ultimately, the goal of sustainable design is to develop human systems that make positive contributions to the natural systems with which they interact. Much of humanity's impact on these natural systems can be considered in the context of three major drivers of expansion: how we live, how we work, and how we play. It is worth considering these drivers because they are important to many design decisions, and the way these systems are designed can greatly affect the impact they have.

Drivers of Human Environmental Expansion

Sustainable development requires understanding a wide range of human impacts on natural systems and implementing effective strategies to counteract them. Successful eco-tourism practices can protect biodiversity and use less energy while encouraging an appreciation of and respect for nature. Sporting and tourist facilities can strive for net-zero water use and carbon-neutral structures and transportation options. Cleaner forms of electricity and self-sufficient renewable energy can greatly reduce the impact of major cities as well as support developing and remote communities. There are many ways to restore a balance between ecological services and urban impacts: better stewardship of parks and open spaces, policies to control groundwater depletion and erosion, wetland restoration and wildlife habitat protection—all of these can work to better integrate the natural and built environments.

Habitation and Settlement

Human habitation and settlement has long been our primary impact on nature. It is only recently that industry has overtaken housing in terms of cumulative impact. We have doubled our population in the last forty years, moving off rural farms and towns and crowding into cities. Urban areas are now responsible for nearly 75 percent of global energy use and greenhouse gas emissions, over 50 percent of which comes from the buildings.2 In the United States, sprawling suburban development has consumed vast tracts of open land. Native forests across Europe and North America have been razed and covered with impermeable surfaces. Increased population has led to expanded agricultural production and factory farming practices. These, in turn, have damaged our lands through habitat destruction and topsoil erosion and contaminated our rivers and water tables with billions of gallons of severely polluted runoff, creating enormous dead zones in our oceans. Population growth has impacted many natural system processes. The urban heat island effect, for example, has changed urban climatic systems as a result of paving over the landscape. (The impact on hydrological cycles is discussed in chapters 3 and 4.)

Industry

Human industry affects natural systems primarily in two ways: through what we extract from nature, and through what we give back. Historically, we have extracted resources like timber, fish, metals, minerals, freshwater, and fossil fuels. What we give back is predominantly the extraordinary amounts of waste our industrial processes generate. Carbon dioxide, nitrogen oxides, methane, and other gases are emitted into the atmosphere through industrial processes and by burning solid materials; chemical effluents from factories, agricultural pesticides, fertilizers, and animal waste are discharged into rivers and seas; and plastics, electronics, construction materials, paper, food waste, and household goods are piled up in landfills.

Central to the promise of sustainable development is the ability to break the connection between industrial processes and environmental devastation. Developing products that can be reused or safely broken down under natural conditions; closing the loop in industrial processes to prevent waste production; and transforming waste into fuels, energy, and useful products are all strategies for reducing industrial impacts on natural systems.

In his groundbreaking work *Cradle to Cradle: Remaking the Way We Make Things,* William McDonough writes that we must learn to think of our materials as "technical nutrients" operating in an industrial ecosystem. Just as nature has no waste, using and reusing everything, we must prioritize development strategies that reduce or eliminate waste production as well. But because industrial processes invariably have inputs and outputs, the ultimate goal is not to eliminate output, but to make our industrial outputs positive contributions to the biosphere. Buildings and factories that clean the air and water they use are now being built. The ultimate goal of sustainable development is to create an environment in which natural and human-made systems work in a symbiotic relationship, integrating and supporting each other.

Recreation

According to the International Ecotourism Society, global travel and tourism represent the largest business sector in the world economy; they are responsible for over 10 percent of gross domestic product worldwide. They are also the primary source of foreign currency for over sixty countries, including 83 percent of developing countries. Despite these economic benefits, recreational activities exact an environmental cost. Coral reefs are being damaged all over the world by cruise ship anchors and sewage, while an average eighteen-hole golf course uses over 500,000 gallons of water per day.[2]

Figure 2-15 Man-made environment/natural systems integration. This chart shows strategies for sustainable transformation at the intersections between natural systems and the major human activities that impact them. © Sherwood Design Engineers.

		NATURAL SYSTEMS			
		Biological Diversity	Water	Air	Land	Energy
MAN-MADE ENVIRONMENT EXPANSION	Habitation/ Settlement	Expand open space, urban forests, wildlife corridors, promote Low-Impact Development and climate-appropriate landscaping, limit building in environmentally sensitive areas, protect endangered species and habitats	Promote net-zero water use, rainwater harvesting, graywater recycling, reduce groundwater depletion and degradation	Reduce transportation-related emissions, improve urban air quality and indoor air quality	Promote Low-Impact Development, Transit-Oriented Development, protect productive land from development, eliminate construction-related erosion, eliminate landfill, recycle building materials	Improve energy efficiency and green building, develop energy-neutral cities
	Industry/ Resource Extraction	Reduce monoculture, expand permaculture, preserve biodiverse areas, promote sustainable forestry and fisheries, reduce polluting industries, reduce agricultural runoff, eliminate mountain top removal mining	Prevent industry from degrading surface waters, aquifers and oceans, eliminate ghost-fishing, blast-fishing, and other harmful practices, reduce agricultural runoff	Eliminate polluting emissions from power production, reduce GHG-producing transport	Reduce deforestation, reduce monocrop agriculture and factory farming, promote permaculture, reduce agricultural-related erosion and soil depletion, protect top soil and promote net-zero soil nutrient loss, close material loops in manufacturing	Transition to clean, renewable energy, limit fossil fuel extraction, develop waste-to-energy technologies
	Recreation	Promote 'eco-tourism' practices, protect national parks and wilderness areas, expand urban 'green belts'	Promote net-zero water use for recreation fields and tourist facilities, eliminate trash dumping by cruise ships, restore riverfronts and beaches, eliminate pollution of bays, lakes and rivers	Shift to cleaner vehicles for recreation, reduce airline emissions	Protect national parks & wilderness areas, restore wildlife corridors and 'green belts'	Promote energy-neutral tourist facilities and transportation

Values in table represent regenerative possibilities.

Experts at Oxford University's Centre for the Environment (OUCE) estimate that tourism's overall greenhouse gas emissions from travel-associated transport, accommodation, and activities could, in real terms, be responsible for up to 14 percent of the global warming effect.[3] Hotels, ski resorts, sporting events, off-road vehicles, and vacation driving habits all add to the total impact that recreational activities have on the environment. These impacts are felt directly in terms of human encroachment on natural ecosystems, and indirectly in terms of the habitation and industrial activities associated with recreation.

Regenerative Possibilities: Having a Positive Impact on Natural Systems

The chart on page 49 demonstrates regenerative possibilities for the three major areas of human impact on natural systems, and its application is elucidated through the case study of the Santa Lucia Preserve that follows.

BALANCING HUMAN AND ECOLOGICAL DEVELOPMENT ON THE SANTA LUCIA PRESERVE

The Santa Lucia Preserve is situated on 20,000 acres of rolling hills between Monterey and Big Sur in the central coast region of California. This large piece of property contains five distinct watersheds and multiple habitat zones. The land had been a cattle ranch for many years before it was designated for development. The original design for the project called for 11,000 homes, but consistent environmental pressure in the community reduced that number to under 300 in a master plan led by Hart Howerton of San Francisco.

In recognition of the sensitive nature of the land, the owners committed to setting aside 90 percent of the property as permanent open space and formed the Santa Lucia Conservancy to oversee the protection of the land as a permanent preserve. Proceeds from real estate sales helped create a $25 million seed endowment to fund the maintenance and preservation of the land in perpetuity. The Santa Lucia Preserve is a good example of how habitation and settlement affect the landscape in terms of roads, driveways, and home sites. The site's eighteen-hole golf course is an example of how recreation impacts the landscape. Designing these systems and their necessary support structures in a way that minimized impact to the landscape was a formidable challenge.

Habitation and Water

As previously noted, the Santa Lucia Preserve encompasses five different watersheds, and the conservancy undertook several years of groundwater monitoring and model development in order to establish a sustainable water balance. Long-term stewardship of the watershed requires ensuring the perpetuation of critical base flows in the various streams running through the site and sustaining the water flow necessary to support critical wetland habitat on the property, as well as groundwater levels.

The water system that was developed works as a combination of an integrated network of wells, rainwater harvesting, and water recycling. All the water that comes off of the golf course and all the water that comes out of the treatment plant, as well as stormwater from all the home sites and the community center, is blended, treated, and then reused for irrigation. By minimizing water demand through this integrated strategy, the project is able to satisfy all its nonpotable water needs through on-site water reuse, thus saving hundreds of thousands of gallons of water annually.

Source: www.santaluciapreserve.com, www.slconservancy.org

Figure 2-16 The hacienda at the Santa Lucia Preserve. Hart Howerton.

Habitation and Biological Diversity

The nonprofit Trust for Public Land served as an advisory body to the Santa Lucia Conservancy, and a public-private model was developed that, in effect, created a series of wildlands. Each of the lots purchased by individuals contains open land that is privately owned but that must be preserved as natural, wild, open space. These wildlands are actively managed by the conservancy and help to create a contiguous greenbelt throughout the developed area of the property that preserves the rural character of the land and maintains wildlife migration corridors.

Originally, the entire 20,000 acres was a cattle ranch. The conservancy began the reduction of cattle grazing and the expansion of ecosystem restoration activities nearly a decade before the first new homeowners occupied the property. It introduced fencing to keep the cattle from grazing in riparian and wetland zones. Over time, the size of the herd has been decreased and consolidated in the least environmentally sensitive areas. The conservancy began a large nursery to propagate native plants, and the site's ecologists began removing invasive species such as Scotch broom while reintroducing native plantings around the property. Extensive mapping identified endangered species and rare habitats, including patches of coastal buckwheat, which supports the endangered Smith's blue butterfly. Other critical protected areas include habitats for endangered amphibians like the California red-legged frog and the California tiger salamander. All of the development was done in a way that preserved significant buffers and avoided disturbing these sensitive areas, whether by utilities access, driveways, roads, or buildings.

Habitation and Land Use

Roads, buildings, and utilities have one of the largest impacts on the landscape in this kind of development. Working around sensitive groves of trees, heritage oaks, butterfly habitats, and wetland areas required finding ways to minimize that impact. We redefined minimum centerline radii to allow these roads to fit into the land and min-imize earthwork. We worked with the fire department to get narrow road standards with widened shoulders and turnouts accepted. We established geometries for getting over the steep hills while minimizing disturbance of the landscape. Finally, fitting the homesites into the least sensitive landscapes and finding opportunities to observe and engage nature through the building placement without invading it became the overarching driver.

ECOSYSTEM SERVICES

The World Resources Institute has calculated that nature's ecosystem services are worth over $33 trillion dollars a year[Footnote]—nearly double the size of the global economy. And while that figure is important for putting a value on nature's contributions to the economy, it underscores the fact that without nature, we could not survive at all. Understanding the character and interdependence of these systems is necessary to ensure that development practices do not impair these vital services.

In their seminal work *Sustaining Life: How Human Health Depends on BioDiversity*, two Harvard physicians teamed up with Oxford University Press, the United Nations Environment Programme (UNEP), and famed biologist E. O. Wilson to compile a comprehensive picture of how diverse species and ecosystems provide "materials, conditions, and processes that sustain all life on this planet, including human life."*

1. *Net primary production (NPP):* The total amount of plant material produced during a year through photosynthesis. This organic matter is not only the base of the entire food chain but also the foundation for all other ecosystem services.
2. *Plant and animal products:* Nature provides our food, fuel, and medicine. The world's grasslands support the animals that give us meat, milk, wool, and leather, while forests give us timber for shelter, furniture, and paper. Fisheries are the primary source of protein for millions of people around the world. Organic material from plants and trees also supplies 15 percent of the world's fuel—40 percent in the developing world—as well as hundreds of other industrial products, including resins, dyes, and insecticides. Plants and animals also produced the fossil fuels that we depend on so heavily.
3. *Pollination:* Bees alone pollinate one-third of the nation's food supply and are vital to major economic drivers like California's billion-dollar agriculture business. Preserving natural areas bordering fields has been proven to increase pollination rates and reduce pests by supporting natural predators.
4. *Cleaning the air:* Plants—especially forest canopies—clean the air we breathe. By filtering out the particulate matter from our fossil fuel combustion, cement production, waste incineration, and crop burning, plants can greatly reduce the toxins we spew into the air. Trees along roadsides and freeways, and in congested urban areas absorb nitrous oxide with their leaves; they also soak up carbon dioxide, giving off fresh oxygen in return.
5. *Purifying the water:* Nature's forests, soils, and wetlands are so effective at removing toxins, heavy metals, and organic matter from water that engineers are now building "living machines"—constructed wetlands—to treat wastewater. Sand and gravel filter particulates from water, while microbes and bacteria feed on organic matter. Freshwater is our most precious resource, and it is nature's clouds, snowbanks, and watersheds that cleanse, store, and transport that water for us.
6. *Mitigating floods:* Floodplains are nature's safety valves, allowing a river to overflow its banks and deposit fresh soil on the land as part of its natural cycle. But as urban development and farmland

have encroached on the rivers, we have drained these wetlands and put ourselves in harm's way. As a result, floods cause billions of dollars in damage annually.

7. *Controlling erosion:* Plant canopies intercept and soften rainfall. Their roots bind the soil in place, while root channels and animal burrows act like natural drainage networks, helping water soak deep into the ground. By clearing plants, we expose dry, unbinded soils to pounding rains which simply wash it away. The Food and Agriculture Organization of the United Nations estimates that erosion ruins over 10 million acres of cropland per year. Lands cleared for agriculture suffer increased damage during storms and hurricanes, while places with intact coral reefs, vegetated dunes, and healthy forests are more protected.

8. *Detoxifying pollutants:* Many common plants can absorb the toxins, heavy metals, pesticides, and radioactive materials we release into the earth and atmosphere. Bioremediation by mustard plants has been used to remove lead, nickel, copper, and a host of other metals from contaminated soils; aquatic hyacinth has been used to remove arsenic from drinking water; and the common sunflower was used to soak up radioactive substances in ponds after the nuclear disaster in Chernobyl.

9. *Controlling pests and disease:* We have learned the hard way that targeting one particular pest often creates unintended consequences. But in many cases, we still do not know what species are necessary for ecosystems to function properly, or in what proportions they must be present. Maintaining natural places, with their complex webs intact, is often a safer, more reliable way to deal with pests than simply killing them off.

10. *Regulating climate:* Nature is what makes our planet habitable and enjoyable. It was microorganisms that created our oxygen atmosphere, and it is plants that sustain it. Forests and soils are also the world's largest storehouses of carbon. Nature cycles the hydrogen, nitrogen, phosphorus, and sulfur—which together with carbon and oxygen comprise 95 percent of the biosphere. Nature provides refuge, recreation, and relaxation.

* Eco-Solutions All About: Cities and Energy Consumption, http://edition.cnn.com/2007/TECH/12/31/eco.cities (accessed 3.13.10).

Adapted from Andrew Mannle, "Top 10 Reasons Mother Nature Is 'Too Big to Fail,'" SolveClimate, April 22, 2009, http://solveclimate.com/blog/20090422/top-10-reasons-mother-nature-too-big-fail.

SYNERGY AND SUSTAINABLE COMMUNITY DESIGN

Jim Heid, Founder, UrbanGreen

Thought leaders in design and community planning have advanced a number of core ideas for making communities sustainable. These include urbanism, increased social interaction, resource conservation and regeneration, mixed use, and increased walkability. But no single strategy will make communities sustainable. Instead, the focus should be on achieving synergy among infrastructure elements, the design program, ecosystem services, and community users.

While building science has advanced significantly through the development of numerous rating methods, the art of designing sustainable communities is still in its infancy. Sustainable communities cannot be created with a checklist; they emerge from an integrative process that is both art and science. Buildings focus on material, structure, and systems. Communities focus on site, infrastructure, and program. The complex ideas and synergies that come with sustainable community design must reduce resource consumption while creating places that are both livable and memorable.

Imagine designing a community where a conscious decision has been made to emphasize mobility and introduce transportation methods beyond private automobiles. This would reduce the number of cars driving through the development on a daily basis, allowing for reduced road widths. Reduced road widths would, in turn, slow (or calm) traffic, increasing the likelihood that people will walk. If community facilities and some daily goods—a bakery, a small grocer, and cafés, for example—were introduced into the community, it would give people a reason to walk. And if these uses were clustered, it would provide a gathering place or focal point for the community.

As roads became narrower, low-impact storm drainage techniques could be used, increasing the amount of "tree lawns" adjoining the road, helping the developer redirect the significant dollars normally invested underground in invisible gray infrastructure into surface improvements such as trees and landscape—very visible green infrastructure. This would lead to increased shade, further reduce heat island impacts, and improve the image of the community. All of this would increase the value of the land, lots, and homes while fostering greater pride in the community. The result would be a more vital, memorable, and desirable place to live: a community with deepened social, economic, and environmental sustainability.

None of these outcomes could be created by a single consultant or advanced by a single design action, and none of these ideas, on its own, would constitute sustainability. However, each action in combination with the others creates a sum greater than its parts. This is the result of synergy, which should be the primary goal of sustainable design.

Synergy requires a different approach to design and planning. The conventional patterns of linear, sequential design processes or ego-driven dogmatic designers will not lead to sustainable outcomes. A more effective approach is the integrative design process, which moves the practice of community design to more sustainable outcomes by changing the way teams work. The integrative design process takes recent learnings about what makes a community sustainable and helps teams understand how they should be interacting and working to accomplish the end goal.

Here are some guideposts for successfully using the integrative design process as part of the master planning:

- Include all team members in core meetings and consider them co-learners.
- Create a clear and powerful core purpose for the project and make sure all team members have bought into that purpose.
- Create clear metrics for measuring progress toward the purpose and project principles.
- Take the time to create a roadmap for the planning process, including time for design iterations and testing against established metrics.
- Set up a feedback process and use it often to ensure you are learning and improving as you move forward.

ONE PLANET LIVING FRAMEWORK: SONOMA MOUNTAIN VILLAGE

One Planet Living is a framework for sustainability developed by the World Wildlife Federation (WWF) and BioRegional, the British sustainability experts, to showcase how we can live sustainably on one planet. The initiative is based on the idea that if everybody lived like an average European, we would need three planets to support us all; if everybody consumed resources and emitted carbon like an average North American, we would need five planets. The One Planet Living framework is composed of ten sustainability principles:

1. Zero carbon
2. Zero waste
3. Sustainable transport

4. Local and sustainable materials
5. Local and sustainable food
6. Sustainable water
7. Natural habitats and wildlife
8. Cultural heritage
9. Equity and fair trade
10. Health and happiness

There are several One Planet communities around the world that are putting these principles into practice, beginning with the famous BedZED (an acronym for Beddington Zero-Energy Development), the United Kingdom's largest mixed-use, sustainable community, and including Masdar in Abu Dhabi, an ambitious project to build the greenest city in the world. By 2016 Masdar hopes to house fifty thousand people in the world's first zero-car, zero-carbon, zero-waste city.*

Sonoma Mountain Village is the first official One Planet community in North America. The 200-acre project in Rohnert Park, California, is built on the site of a high-tech office park that closed in 2003. Now the site is being restored as a walkable mixed-use community of shops, houses, and green-tech businesses. The project features a 1.14-megawatt solar array that will power one thousand homes; a high percentage of green space that includes gardens, street trees, and stormwater features; and a water plan that emphasizes communitywide conservation measures, graywater reuse, and rainwater harvesting.** The following is a list of the ten measures of sustainability outlined in the One Planet Living framework. After each one are listed the goals of the One Planet community and the steps Sonoma Mountain Village is taking to meet them:

1. *Zero carbon:* Achieve net-zero carbon dioxide (CO_2) emissions from building operations in One Planet community developments through energy efficiency and renewable energy.
   Sonoma Mountain Village aims to achieve carbon neutrality by 2020. New buildings will be 80 percent more efficient than California's Title 24 building code requires, and retrofits will reduce energy by 50 percent. Renewable energy supplies on-site include the 1.14-megawatt rooftop solar array that will power a zero-carbon data center as well as solar-electric and ground-source heat pumps, biomass, and biogas.
2. *Zero waste:* Eliminate waste going to landfill and incineration through resource efficiency, reuse, recycling, composting, and generating energy from waste.
   Sonoma Mountain Village plans to recycle and compost up to 70 percent of its waste, reducing the amount sent to landfill by 98 percent by 2020. The village has a solar-powered steel factory on-site that creates deconstructible steel-frame building assemblies that are 100 percent recyclable.
3. *Sustainable transport:* Provide transportation systems that reduce the use of private vehicles and offset transportation emissions.
   The Sonoma Mountain Village begins with walkable

neighborhoods, bike paths, and electric vehicles charged on solar power. Local businesses, live/work housing, grocery stores, farmers markets, and restaurants will all reduce the need for daily vehicle trips off-site. The project plans include a biofuel filling station; carpools and car-sharing programs; and a bike path and alternative fuel shuttle to nearby Sonoma State University.

4. *Local and sustainable materials:* Use local, renewable, and recycled materials.
   Sonoma Mountain Village plans to manufacture 20 percent of all materials on-site and get 60 percent from within 500 miles. The project has developed comprehensive standard specifications that call for low-impact materials and cradle-to-cradle accounting to calculate the embodied carbon of all products, activities, and material.
5. *Local and sustainable food:* Reduce impacts of industrial agriculture and long-distance food transportation by supporting local, healthy food production.
   Sonoma Mountain Village features community gardens, fruit trees, and a daily farmer's market. Local biodynamic food will be served in its restaurants and carried by its grocery stores. The 2020 goal is to source 65 percent of all food from within 300 miles and 25 percent from within 50 miles.
6. *Sustainable water:* Promote water efficiency and reuse, restore natural water cycles, and implement landscape-based water treatment.
   The water plan for Sonoma Mountain Village includes conservation efforts, rainwater harvesting, and graywater reuse. The plan allows the development to add 1,900 homes without increasing its use of municipal water supplies. Stormwater will be managed using porous pavements, structured soil, swales, and mycoremediation. All irrigation (including the watering of backyards) will be done with nonpotable water, all water fixtures will have strict efficiency standards, and toilets will use rainwater or graywater for flushing. The project is also developing a reed-bed filter for treating graywater from showers, installing large-scale on-site cisterns for rainwater storage, and researching on-site blackwater treatment as well.

7. *Natural habitats and wildlife:* Restore biodiversity and degraded environments.

   The development is reserving 10 percent of the site as a high-biodiversity zone of native plantings and undisturbed areas protected by conservation easements. Another 40 percent of the site will consist of various forms of green space, including restored seasonal wetlands and riparian corridors, community gardens, a wide variety of street trees, recreation fields, trails, backyards, and nesting habitats on green roofs. To offset the developed areas of the project, Sonoma Mountain Village has agreed to conserve an additional 70 acres off-site, but within 200 miles of the project, to be protected in perpetuity.

8. *Culture and heritage:* Protect and enhance local cultural heritage and regional identity.

   Anchored by a town square, the central focus for the community, Sonoma Mountain Village will maintain local culture through a farmers' market, public art exhibits, festivals, and murals. The construction of the Sonoma Mountain Business Cluster, an incubator for businesses developing sustainable resource technologies; the Codding steel-frame technology factory; and the zero-carbon data center will all help generate local jobs on the site. Creating a culture of community involvement in planning, design, and local governance will also help strengthen the sense of local culture.

9. *Equity and fair trade:* Promote equity and fair trading relationships to ensure One Planet communities have a positive impact on other communities both locally and globally.

Sonoma Mountain Village has committed to re-creating the jobs that were lost when the office park that originally occupied its site was closed. To allow people to live close to those jobs, the village features a range of affordable housing units for rental or purchase. Businesses are required to promote local business and fair-trade products.

10. *Health and happiness:* Promote healthy lifestyles and quality of life through well-designed and socially engaged communities.

   Sonoma Mountain Village will promote healthier, happier lifestyles through safer streets, fresher foods, cleaner materials, and an environment conducive to outdoor activity and community involvement. Community meetings will conduct surveys and gather input about what is or isn't working within the community and attempt to involve people in the larger community vision. By emphasizing local job creation and local business spending, more wealth will be kept in the community, and long commuting hours will be reduced. Volunteer and community activities, as well as walkable access to daily needs, will encourage community members to interact in positive ways, which strongly correlates to overall health and well-being.

* BioRegional, "BedZED," *http://www.bioregional.com/ what-we-do/our-work/bedzed/*; One Planet Communities, "Masdar City," *http://www.oneplanetcommunities.org/ Masdar/index.html.*
** One Planet Communities, "Sonoma Mountain Village," *http://www.oneplanetcommunities.org/Sonoma/.*

For more information on related topics please see www.sherwoodinstitute.org/resources.

Notes

1 Eco-Solutions All About: Cities and Energy Consumption, http://edition.cnn.com/2007/TECH/12/31/eco.cities (Accessed March 13, 2010).

2 The International Ecotourism Society, Global EcoTourism Fact Sheet, 2006, www.ecotourism.org.

3 Arcwire.org, "A Path to Sustainable Tourism?"

PART II
SUSTAINABLE RESOURCE SYSTEMS

When we look at the trajectory of recent human development patterns, we recognize that we are rapidly heading down an irreversible path of environmental destruction and risk the disintegration of traditional and contemporary cultures. Sustainable infrastructure design is the art of taking a systems approach to ecology, engineering, and culture; realizing these are interconnected realms; and seeking solutions that address them with coordinated, rather than separate, strategies.

Too often, project design has been approached as a simple problem-solving exercise. Although often effective in addressing isolated aspects of a project, this approach can obscure a view toward the larger-scale opportunities presented by considering the externalities and interrelated elements of any design.

Nevertheless, to understand how these systems interrelate, it is instructive to first examine them individually in detail. Each of the primary systems we design is covered individually in Part II of this book. Together, they comprise the primary building blocks of engineering sustainable infrastructure.

Chapter 3 covers water conservation and supply. We discuss water management plans; achieving water balance on a site; and analyzing different water sources. We also cover strategies for designing sustainable water supplies, beginning with reducing water demand and improving water infrastructure. Finally, we look at methods and challenges of expanding water supply, including rainwater harvesting and desalination.

In chapter 4 we look at strategies for integrated water management, including harvesting stormwater and developing greenstreets programs; treating and reusing graywater; and improving blackwater treatment systems.

Chapter 5 covers energy and greenhouse gases, including methods for reducing energy demand through design; how to design for energy efficiency; a variety of sustainable power systems that engineers are encountering with increasing frequency; and addressing carbon footprint and climate change from a design and policy perspective.

Chapter 6 discusses sustainable site planning, including baseline analysis of existing land patterns and ecological systems; as well as sustainable methods for integrating site infrastructure. We also discuss green streets and sustainable transportation networks; as well as methods for improving material selection and use; and solid waste management.

CHAPTER 3
Water Conservation and Supply

Figure 3-1 Urban water use. The complexity of water movement and use through urbanized systems presents the designer with particular challenges when contamination or resource shortages come into question. © South East Queensland Healthy Waterways Partnership.

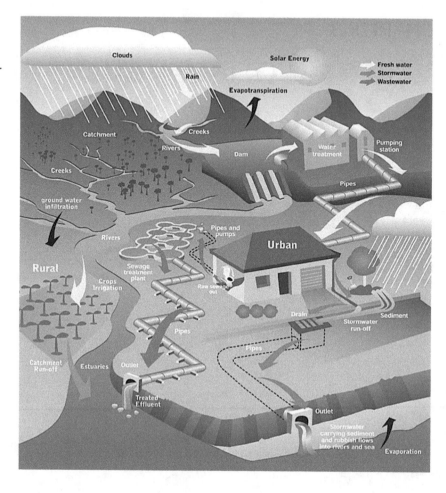

In the natural world, water moves in continual cycles, constantly changing form and mixing with its surroundings. Yet in much of our urban environment we have a system that uses water once and then treats it as a waste product. The perspective of millions of homeowners and businesses—and that of most cities—is that fresh water comes out the tap, and dirty water goes down the drain: most people are only seeing one tiny piece of the water cycle. As designers, we need to consider the whole water cycle in order to build sustainable systems that restore the natural balance of water by reducing the negative impact of our current use.

There are two main ways that humans impact the water cycle through development. First, by building impervious surfaces that cover the earth with asphalt, we have disrupted the natural cycle that allows water to soak into the ground and nourish plants. Instead, water falls on our sidewalks and freeways, and picks up pollutants. Second, our pervasive use of pesticides, hormones, antibiotics, and chemical fertilizers means that the water running off our farms and fields is also polluted. Likewise,

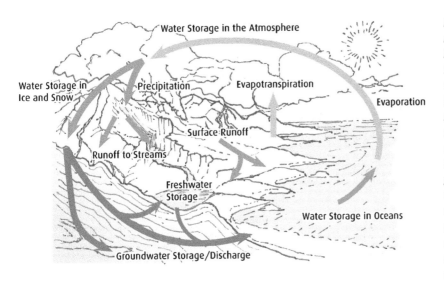

Figure 3-2 The water cycle. The natural movement of water on earth is known as the water cycle or hydrological cycle. Water migrates through the water cycle in various states, including liquid, vapor, and solid (ice and snow). As engineers, we typically make distinctions between types of water based on source and quality. Freshwater resources include ice caps, glaciers, surface water, and groundwater. These freshwater resources are diminished by evaporation, flowing to the ocean and mixing with saltwater, and pollution by natural or human means. Our freshwater sources are replenished by precipitation, runoff from mountain snowmelt, and springs welling up from the groundwater.
© Sherwood Design Engineers.

water coming out of our showers and toilets is laden with pharmaceuticals, preservatives, petroleum-based cosmetics, and other chemicals. The net result is that we are overloading our rivers and oceans with polluted water.

In conventional water management practice, water is treated as three distinct systems. In the first, water is treated to potable levels and distributed through pipes to users. A second network collects the water from toilets and drains, pumps it to wastewater treatment facilities, and then discharges the treated water back into the environment. A third network collects stormwater and discharges it back into local fresh water bodies or the ocean.

For the past century, engineers have tried to control and improve on nature with these pipes, pumps, culverts, and storm drains. Now we are finding better ways to let nature do her work. We have an increased understanding and appreciation for natural technologies, an increased ability to adapt natural systems so they can be more effectively integrated into urban environments, and a pressing need for more cost-effective ways to both treat and supply water. All of these drivers cause engineers, land planners, and architects to take a fresh look at the water cycle in order to find ways to improve viable water systems. This chapter demonstrates how the engineers at Sherwood approach these challenges and also introduces the prioritized strategies for planning, upgrading, or retrofitting a water supply system.

This chapter introduces the natural and urban water cycles, the common sources of water that engineers deal with, and the concept of establishing a water balance for a project. It then discusses, in order of priority, strategies for sustainably improving and expanding water supply on a project. It provides details on rainwater harvesting and examines the challenge of desalination.

Despite the vast oceans covering the planet, less than 1 percent of the world's water is both fresh and accessible for human use (see figure 3-3). Today, even with conventional water supply strategies and technologies, water shortages commonly plague communities around the globe. The World Health Organization (WHO)

Figure 3-3 All the water in the world. If all the water on earth were gathered in a ball, this is how large it would appear in relation to the earth (superimposed over the North Atlantic Ocean). Although it may seem that water is everywhere, it is in fact a very limited resource. Approximately 97.5 percent of the water on earth is saltwater. Of the remaining 2.5 percent, most is freshwater frozen in polar ice caps and glaciers. 99 percent of the freshwater that is not frozen is inaccessible groundwater, with the remainder contained in shallow aquifers, surface water, swamps, and the atmosphere. It is this tiny fraction of water—less than 0.1 percent of the total—that is available for human use without significant treatment or energy expenditures. From this minute volume comes virtually all the water we use for our agricultural, industry, electricity generation, and homes. © Sherwood Design Engineers. Data source: CircleofBlue.org.

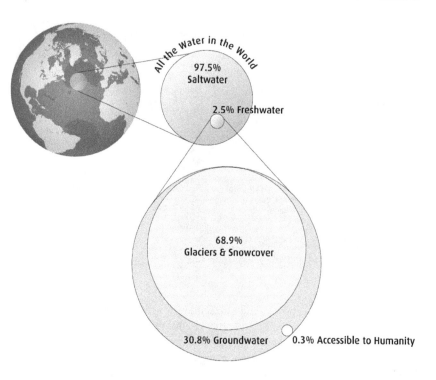

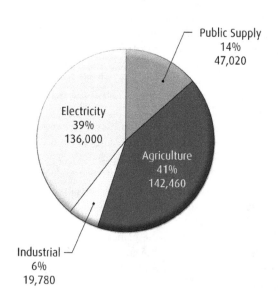

Freshwater Withdrawals in U.S. in 2000 (Mgal/day)

Figure 3-4 Freshwater withdrawals. Overall, the two largest uses of water are agriculture and electricity generation, which together amount to over 80 percent of the water we use each year. Data source: U.S. Geological Survey. Re-created by Sherwood Design Engineers.

SEASON	3-MONTH RAINWATER COLLECTED VS. UNUSED		END OF SEASON RAINWATER STORAGE	3-MONTH DEMAND			

WINTER — WINTER RAINWATER COLLECTED — WINTER RAINWATER UNUSED — GRAYWATER AND BLACKWATER SUPPLY AND USE — RAINWATER USE — MUNICIPAL SUPPLY (IRRIGATION USE) — MUNICIPAL SUPPLY (DOMESTIC USE)

SPRING — SPRING RAINWATER COLLECTED — SPRING RAINWATER UNUSED — GRAYWATER AND BLACKWATER SUPPLY AND USE — RAINWATER USE — MUNICIPAL SUPPLY (IRRIGATION USE) — MUNICIPAL SUPPLY (DOMESTIC USE)

SUMMER — SUMMER RAINWATER COLLECTED — (NONE UNUSED) — GRAYWATER AND BLACKWATER SUPPLY AND USE — RAINWATER USE — MUNICIPAL SUPPLY (IRRIGATION USE) — MUNICIPAL SUPPLY (DOMESTIC USE)

FALL — FALL RAINWATER COLLECTED — (NONE UNUSED) — GRAYWATER AND BLACKWATER SUPPLY AND USE — RAINWATER USE — MUNICIPAL SUPPLY (IRRIGATION USE) — MUNICIPAL SUPPLY (DOMESTIC USE)

reports that over two billion people—roughly one out every three people on the planet—live in a water-stressed area.[1]

For more information on this subject please see www.sherwoodinstitute.org/research.

Managing the quality of surface water resources both upstream and downstream from human settlement has become one of the greatest challenges of our time. History demonstrates that properly managed water resources can be the deciding factor in determining the habitability of an individual site, the sustainability of a community, or the survival of an entire civilization.

Both human and natural water cycles vary widely by region and depending on climate, geological conditions, vegetation, development density, and seasonal weather patterns. It is important for designers to thoroughly identify and understand all aspects of local water cycles when embarking on a project in order to develop appropriate supply, use, and management strategies. The first step involves modeling and measuring water flows to determine water balance (see figures 3-4 and 3-5).

Figure 3-5 Water supply analysis. The seasonal availability of water resources for a residential project on the California coast. Average demand and storage volumes are graphically illustrated to aid in the communication of water conservation and reuse strategies. Diagrams such as these help designers establish priorities and strategies with clients. © Sherwood Design Engineers.

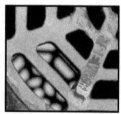

THE ASPEN INSTITUTE
ENERGY AND ENVIRONMENT PROGRAM

THE ASPEN INSTITUTE: ENERGY AND ENVIRONMENT PROGRAM

In the fall of 2008, the Aspen Institute's Energy and Environment Program held a series of dialogues with top water experts from a variety of fields. In 2009, it issued a report based on those dialogues entitled *Sustainable Water Systems: Step One—Redefining the Nation's Infrastructure Challenge.* In the report's executive summary, it outlined a "sustainable path" to addressing our water issues based on three key principles:

"The first principle is that the traditional definition of water infrastructure must evolve to embrace a broader, more holistic definition of sustainable water infrastructure that includes both traditional man-made water and wastewater infrastructure *and* natural watershed systems.

"The second key principle is that this definition of sustainable water infrastructure should be embraced by all public and private entities involved in water management, and that these same entities have a shared role in ensuring their decisions consider and integrate a set of criteria that include environmental, economic and social considerations (the Sustainable Path)....

"The third principle developed by the dialogue participants is that a watershed-based management approach is required for drinking water, wastewater and stormwater services to ensure integrated, sustainable management of water resources."

Source: http://www.aspeninstitute.org/publications/ sustainable-water-systems-step-one-redefining-nations- infrastructure-challenge

THE ASPEN INSTITUTE

WATER MANAGEMENT PLANS

A water management plan is a vital tool for the sustainable management of water resources. A water management plan should, at a minimum, include an assessment of supply and demand, energy, environmental impacts, and the financial implications of systems. The evaluation should also include projections for future conditions and address how the project fits into the watershed of the surrounding city and/or region. Generally, a key goal of a water management plan should be to have a self-sufficient, economically viable, and reliable water portfolio that maximizes and diversifies the use of water resources.

The primary strategies of a water management plan should include

- water conservation and use reduction
- conjunctive use
- water recycling
- improvements to infrastructure

A water management plan for a city or region is an important part of achieving a sustainable and life-sustaining hydrologic cycle. This involves assessing and comparing predevelopment and postdevelopment hydrologic conditions. Predevelopment conditions that should be assessed include precipitation, evaporation, evapotranspiration, infiltration, and runoff. In existing cities, some research or modeling of local conditions may be required in order to gain a good understanding of the region's historical conditions. Postdevelopment scenarios that should be assessed include city water demands and sources used to meet those demands, increases in impervious areas (which decrease infiltration and increase runoff), and stormwater management systems that alter the hydrologic cycle. In addition, communities within the city may have private water supplies (such as groundwater or lakes) that can be utilized with backup from a municipal water system.

After the assessment, predevelopment and postdevelopment conditions can be compared to see how the city's operations affect the hydrologic cycle. Many cities import drinking water from far away, thereby affecting not only the city's hydrologic cycle but also that of the region the water came from. Likewise, many cities depend on groundwater resources for their drinking water but do not adequately replenish their aquifers. Both of these situations have a significant impact on a region's hydrologic cycle in the long run, so it is essential to look at how the water withdrawals can be more balanced for maximum sustainability.

Other important aspects of water management plans to consider are

- projections for population changes over the long term and provisions in water supply;
- the impact of climate change on water resources and infrastructure;
- the financial, environmental, and social aspects of planning, designing, constructing, operating, and maintaining water supply and delivery systems.

Energy has important financial and environmental implications on the daily operation of a city's water system, so mapping the system's energy needs, costs, and carbon footprints is a necessary step in shaping a sustainable water management plan. Large pump stations, water treatment works, and desalination plants are likely to be the largest energy users. Recycling water to reduce the amount of water that needs treatment and maximizing pump efficiencies can provide significant energy savings and help achieve a carbon-neutral water system. Decentralization can reduce the energy costs of pumping water throughout a city, helping to make the water system more sustainable.

(When robust water management plans are not feasible due to project constraints, the strategies listed above and described further in subsequent sections can still be referenced to guide project implementation.)

ACHIEVING WATER BALANCE

Modeling the water balance for a project is a complementary step to creating a water management plan. Water balancing is appropriate for building-scale projects for which a water management plan may not be introduced. Additionally, water balancing is an invaluable tool when looking at strategies to revitalize larger systems and reestablish hydrological processes all the way up to the watershed-scale study area. A water balance begins by establishing a boundary around the site under consideration and analyzing how water flows onto the site, how it is used on the site, and how the remaining water flows off of the site. The boundary could define a single building or a large regional watershed, depending on the scale of the project.

The balance is obtained by retaining the same flows after development as existed when the site was in a natural condition. Full water balance is not always achievable on every project, but the impact of a site's development can be significantly lessened if the goal of achieving basic water balance is used consistently as a guiding principle in the design process.

Figure 3-6 Water balance. A water balance must look at off-site and on-site sources and balance them with on-site and off-site sinks (or demands). © Sherwood Design Engineers.

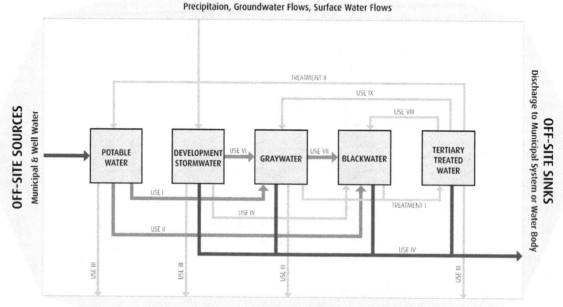

Planning, designing, operating, and maintaining sustainable water supply systems requires a holistic approach to water resource management. This can be accomplished through regulations, the development of alternative water sources, or the use of innovative technologies and infrastructure. Water supply systems should be evaluated with respect to the supply source, climate, water quality, proposed layout, and cost. For a water balance to be achieved, supply will be allocated to demands based on availability and water quality. A description of the steps and considerations for evaluating supply and demand and achieving a water balance follows:

When considering a water network, the first step is to understand the water demand for the proposed project.

The second step is to determine which of the water demands for the project can be served by nonpotable water. If nonpotable demands are significant—especially if the demands are centralized or a public demand, such as for a golf course or streetscape irrigation—then examination of the local regulations is necessary to determine nonpotable water use requirements and guidelines.

The third step is to determine the volumes of nonpotable water that the project generates, either through graywater or treated wastewater, as well as the rainwater harvesting potential of the project area. If the rainwater harvesting potential is high, look at the collection potential on a monthly basis to compare it to monthly

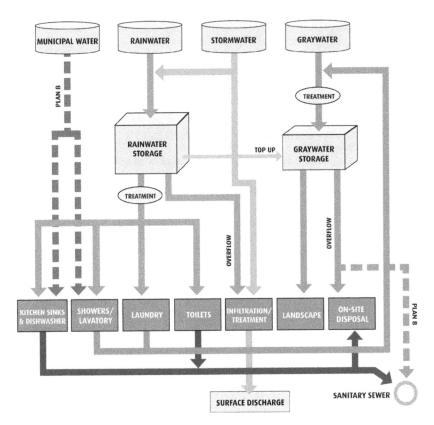

Figure 3-7 Water flow diagram. Part of a water management plan and achieving water balance is establishing the flow volumes, identifying sources of water, and quantifying the various reuse opportunities.
© Sherwood Design Engineers.

water demands. Monthly analysis is also useful for areas that have significant variations in occupancy during the year or a variation in irrigation demands.

After these components are calculated, a water balance can be created to determine whether nonpotable demands can be met through reclaimed water and/or rainwater harvesting. If rainwater is abundant and local regulations allow for it, the water balance can clarify whether rainwater harvesting can supply some or all of the potable water needs as well.

Managing stormwater is another important component of the water balance, and the project should strive to ensure that groundwater recharge, evapotranspiration, and runoff are the same as in predevelopment conditions. This will allow the local aquifer to remain healthy, maintain local weather patterns by not affecting the water returned to the atmosphere locally, and prevent increased erosion or altered animal habitats downstream.

Once the water demand is understood, the water supply must be determined. In some cases, the water supply may be from municipal water mains from either a nearby or faraway surface-water source (such as a river, lake, or reservoir), a network of public and private wells, a desalination plant (especially in many island locations), or a combination of these. In any case, the proposed water demand must be verified against the available supply to better understand if the development needs can be met and if considerations for reuse and reduction can be evaluated.

For more information on related topics please see www.sherwoodinstitute.org/ideas.

Looking at a Water Balance for a Retreat Center

Sherwood was recently invited to an expansive retreat center on over 100 acres of rolling hills and woodlands on the United States' West Coast. The client wanted to build to the LEED Platinum standard for the new buildings. In order to support more people on the property, the on-site water supplies needed to be increased in a sustainable way. In collaboration with the architects and mechanical engineers, our team developed an integrated water master plan for harvesting, storing, treating, and distributing natural water resources throughout the property.

The first step in this process involved establishing a water balance for the site. We started by analyzing the property's existing water system and demands and then developed strategies to achieve future sustainable water balance.

Existing Conditions

The center is located in an area of steep coastal hills that does not support an aquifer big enough to supply its year-round needs, despite a pattern of above-average rainfall when compared with baseline values for the county. When we started the project, water was pumped from six shallow wells spread across the property, then treated and stored in a 212,000-gallon storage tank. The center was only able to collect enough well water to meet its existing domestic demands—estimated to be 75 gallons per person per day for guests and staff—as well as the irrigation demands for the property. But laundry had to be hauled off-site, and during dry months water was purchased and trucked in. The facility had an average occupancy of fifteen to thirty people, with peak attendance in the summer and low attendance in the winter.

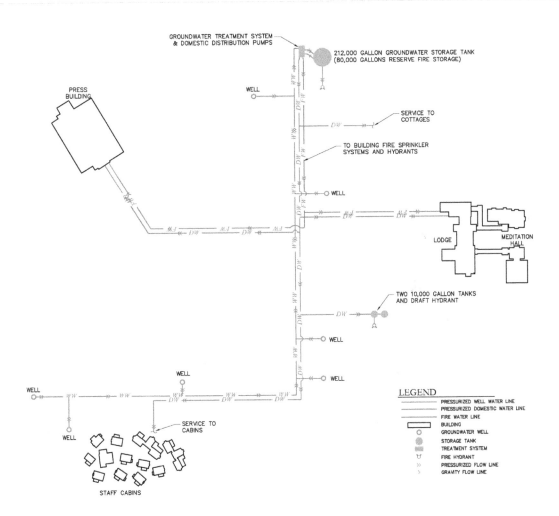

GROUNDWATER TREATMENT SYSTEM
& DOMESTIC DISTRIBUTION PUMPS

212,000 GALLON GROUNDWATER STORAGE TANK
(80,000 GALLONS RESERVE FIRE STORAGE)

PRESS
BUILDING

WELL

SERVICE TO
COTTAGES

TO BUILDING FIRE SPRINKLER
SYSTEMS AND HYDRANTS

WELL

WELL

LODGE

MEDITATION
HALL

TWO 10,000 GALLON TANKS
AND DRAFT HYDRANT

WELL

WELL

WELL

WELL

WELL

WELL

SERVICE TO
CABINS

STAFF CABINS

LEGEND
——————   PRESSURIZED WELL WATER LINE
——————   PRESSURIZED DOMESTIC WATER LINE
——————   FIRE WATER LINE
☐   BUILDING
○   GROUNDWATER WELL
   STORAGE TANK
   TREATMENT SYSTEM
   FIRE HYDRANT
»   PRESSURIZED FLOW LINE
›   GRAVITY FLOW LINE

Proposed Build-Out Conditions

In keeping with the client's tradition of living gently on the land, we sought ways to utilize the area's abundant rainfall by collecting and conveying it to a new reservoir. We also designed a graywater treatment system to allow water from laundry and showers to be reused for irrigation.

To capture rainwater, we created an integrated rooftop collection system for the primary buildings to transfer the water to a storage reservoir. In order to gather even more rainwater, a series of shallow, rock-lined trenches spread over a 4-acre area above the reservoir were designed to collect surface runoff. This upland collection system gathers surface water and routes it to the reservoir to maximize water availability throughout the year.

Figure 3-8 Existing system: process/flow diagram. The existing condition at project start-up was reliant upon a network of energy-intensive, low-volume-producing wells. © Sherwood Design Engineers.

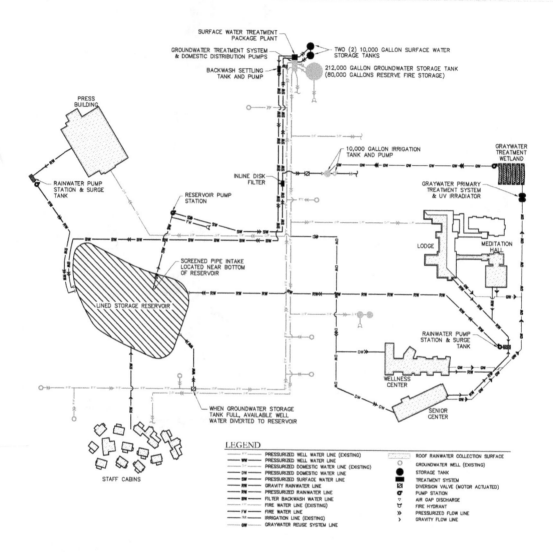

Figure 3-9 Proposed water process/flow diagram. In order to create a fully integrated water system, the water supply and wastewater flows were optimized though a variety of strategies. Existing systems were augmented by an extensive roof rainwater harvesting program and a graywater treatment and reuse system.

To better harvest graywater for irrigation, we designed a gravity-fed primary treatment system, a constructed wetlands for secondary treatment, and an ultraviolet (UV) system for additional disinfection purposes.

For additional discussion of the water system on this project, including a list of system components, see chapter 4, page 144.

By using a comprehensive water balance approach, we were able to see how much water was needed in order to then design strategies that best met those needs. We also incorporated heavy rainfall conditions—as well as twenty-five-year drought conditions—into our water balance to ensure that the system would have neither too much water in wet years nor too little water in dry years.

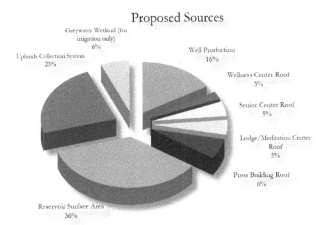

Proposed Sources

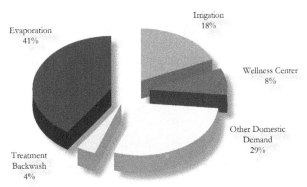

Proposed Sinks

Achieving a complete water balance produces the desired goal of net-zero water development. By harvesting and storing water on-site, treating it minimally, and using it to meet on-site water demands, it is possible to close the loop of the water cycle and restore a natural balance. This generally requires managing stormwater on-site and reusing water for nonpotable needs like toilets and irrigation. If done properly, the amount of water exiting the development does not increase from the pre-development condition, nor does it decrease in quality.

While it may not be possible to achieve 100 percent water balance on every project, using this goal requires designers to quantify water sources and sinks on-site, identify potential reuse opportunities, and then determine appropriate tools for the project. Once these values have been quantified, the performance of the mitigating technologies or approach can be measured throughout the design process.

Sources and Sinks

Proposed Sources		Proposed Sinks	
Well Production	1.81 (ac-ft)	Irrigation	2.31 (ac-ft)
Wellness Center Roof	0.28	Wellness Center	1.03
Senior Center Roof	0.52	Treatment Back-wash	0.49
Lodge/Meditation Center Roof	0.52	Evaporation	5.09
Press Building Roof	0.71	Other	3.64
Reservoir Surface Area	3.98		
Uplands Collection System (includes cabin roof catchment)	2.59		
Graywater Wetland	0.69		

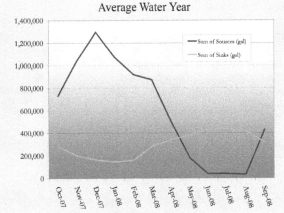

Figure 3-10, a–c Water system sources and sinks. These diagrams provide an overall snapshot of the water supply sources and sinks, as well as an annual flow chart used to optimize the campus water balance (Figure 3-10c). © Sherwood Design Engineers.

Water Balance on the "Ahwahnee" Project

In California's Central Valley, Sherwood Design Engineers teamed with Gensler's urban planning group and SWA Group's landscape architects to find a creative way to get a stalled large-scale greenfield development back on track. The combination of the state's pressure and a Sierra Club lawsuit required the project to adopt the Ahwahnee Principles and to look comprehensively at this development's implications on the city's growth plans. As a result, the design team developed a master plan that integrates transit and maximizes open space, closes the water loop, and finds ways to move toward net-zero carbon at a scale that's replicable for other developers.

The Ahwahnee Principles for Resource-Efficient Communities were authored in 1991 by New Urbanists Andres Duany, Elizabeth Plater-Zyberk, Stefanos Polyzoides, Elizabeth Moule, Peter Calthorpe, and Michael Corbett as part of the Local Government Commission, a California-based nonprofit membership organization composed of planners, architects, local government officials, and community leaders dedicated to promoting resource-efficient and livable communities.*

The Ahwahnee Principles were based on new and emerging ideas in community design and planning that include the provision to encourage "[c]ommunities [to] provide for the efficient use of water through the use of natural drainage, drought-tolerant landscaping, and recycling."** Figures 3-11 and 3-12 demonstrate the water inputs and outputs for a conventionally developed 1,400-acre site and the more balanced approach we pursued, which adheres to the tenets of the Ahwahnee Principles.

* Judith Corbett and Joe Velasquez, "The Ahwahnee Principles: Toward More Livable Communities," Local Government Commission, http://www.lgc.org/freepub/community_design/articles/ahwahnee_article/index.html.
** Local Government Commission, "Original Ahwahnee Principles," http://www.lgc.org/ahwahnee/principles.html.

For more information on this subject please see www.sherwoodinstitute.org/casestudy.

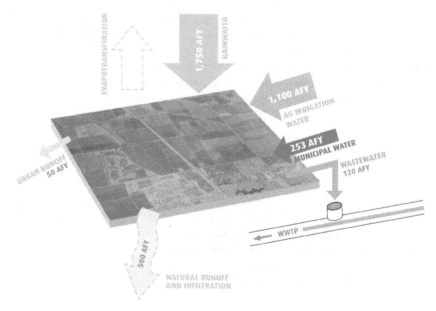

Figure 3-11 Conventional development water cycle. This diagram illustrates the water inputs and outputs for a conventional development approach. In addition to the natural inputs and outputs, the site will receive water from an off-site municipal source, discharge to an off-site wastewater treatment plant, and produce a large amount of stormwater runoff after development occurs. © Sherwood Design Engineers.

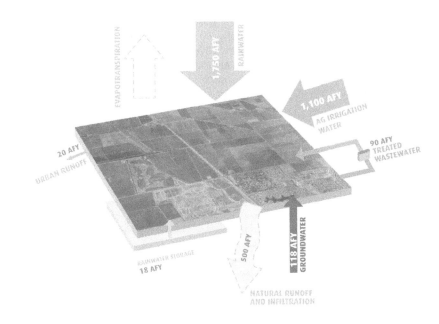

*Figure 3-12 Water-balanced develop-
ment water cycle. In this alternative
scenario for the same site, a stormwater infiltration strategy recharges
the aquifer, which then provides an
adequate domestic water supply
resource. Since stormwater is being
intercepted to recharge the aquifer,
there is less urban runoff.
Additionally, an on-site wastewater
treatment system is used to provide
water for irrigation, thus closing the
water-use loop for the property.
© Sherwood Design Engineers.*

THE LIVING BUILDING CHALLENGE: WATER

"The Living Building Challenge envisions a future [in which] all buildings are designed to harvest sufficient water to meet the needs of occupants while respecting the natural hydrology of the site, the water needs of the neighbors, and the ecosystem it inhabits. Indeed, water can be used and purified and then used again. Currently, such practices are often illegal due to health-code regulations in North America. Therefore, reaching the ideal for water use presently is dependent on what is allowable by code."

The Living Building Challenge requires net-zero water usage at the building such that no water comes from off-site, other than rainwater harvesting. If local regulations prohibit the use of rainwater for potable water use, then municipal water use is only allowed for potable needs.

Prerequisites include:

- "Net-zero water: 100 percent of occupants' water use must come from captured precipitation or

closed-loop water systems that account for downstream ecosystem impacts and that are appropriately purified without the use of chemicals.
- "Sustainable water discharge: 100 percent of stormwater and building-water discharge must be managed on-site and integrated into a comprehensive system to feed the project's demands."

Exceptions: The Living Building Challenge does allow an exception for "water that must be from municipal potable sources due to local health regulations, including sinks, faucets, and showers, but excluding irrigation, toilet flushing, janitorial uses, and equipment uses."

Source: The Living Building Challenge

🖱 For more information on this subject please see www.sherwoodinstitute.org/resources.

LEGEND

- - - - - - - - - **TREATED RAINWATER**
- - - - - - - **UNTREATED RAINWATER**
—————— **WASTEWATER**
- - - - - - - **GRAYWATER**
▨▨▨▨▨ **TREATED GRAYWATER**
▨▨▨▨▨ **STORMWATER**

Figure 3-13 Designing for net-zero water. This section diagrams the water systems for the net-zero condition that Sherwood Design Engineers applied for a project in Northern California to meet the Living Building Challenge. All water demands are met with harvested rainwater and reused water. Wastewater and stormwater are managed on-site. © Sherwood Design Engineers / W. David Winitzky, AIA / Carrie M. Burke, AIA/VA.

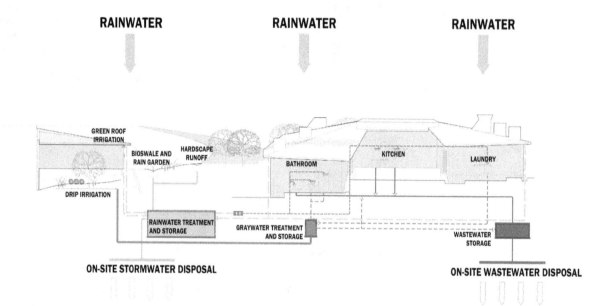

ANALYZING WATER SOURCES

Understanding the various types of water that we work with as engineers, hydrologists, and landscape architects, as well as the sources of that water and the relative water quality of those sources, helps us determine the best ways to treat and use the water we find on any given project. Below are introduced the most common sources of water, including stormwater and reclaimed water, which are essential factors in water resource management. Specific strategies for stormwater, graywater, and blackwater are discussed more fully in chapter 4.

Groundwater

Groundwater resources include both seasonal flows that are renewed annually and ancient aquifers, which can be millions of years old and are essentially nonrenewable. Much of the earth's groundwater is not accessible for human use. Relatively shallow groundwater that exists just beneath the earth's surface fluctuates with rainfall and seasonal changes, and can be accessed through wells and springs. This is a fragile resource and must be regarded as precious. Development of buildings, roads and the compacting of soils hinders the natural process of aquifer recharge by sending urban runoff to the oceans.

Pristine groundwater quality is often very good, requiring little treatment to meet drinking water standards. Because it is filtered through soil and rocks, it is less susceptible to bacterial contamination than surface water. However, groundwater may contain high levels of dissolved substances and minerals from the rocks it comes in contact with. Water table aquifers are most vulnerable to contamination because they are usually closer to the surface. The most common contaminants are road salt in colder climates, bacteria from septic systems in rural areas, and pesticides and fertilizers from lawns and crops.

As communities mine deep underground aquifers, they are also consuming these nearly nonrenewable water resources. In coastal communities, this can cause saltwater to intrude into the aquifers, contaminating water supplies. In countries around the world, excessive groundwater pumping causes water tables to drop, requiring deeper and deeper wells to access water or creating shortages when the aquifers run dry.

Surface Water

Surface water includes water that falls from the air, flows through streams and rivers, or exists in oceans, bays, lakes, ponds, and reservoirs—all common sources for municipal water supplies. These surface waters tend to be farther away from developed areas than other water sources, and their treatment and conveyance often requires large infrastructure networks. Surface water sources are prone to contamination from human and animal waste and other pollution, making their quality lower than that of groundwater or rainwater. Surface water sources are well suited for irrigation needs (because little to no treatment is required); they must be subjected to proper treatment, including filtration and disinfection, before being considered safe to drink. New York City, for example, has invested considerably in protecting the watersheds that are the source of much of its water.

Rainwater

Rainwater is typically high in quality and when captured from rooftops, contains relatively few contaminants. When contamination does occur, it is most often due to biological pathogens or chemicals on roofs, animal or insect infiltration into tanks, or algae growth in tanks. The most common treatment technologies include sand filters, gutter screens, and chemical additions that are passive and require no energy to function. Rainwater tends to be slightly acidic but can be treated easily with the addition of lime or limestone. Harvested rainwater can be used for irrigation with just a prescreening or first-flush diversion. Because the first several inches of rain clean the dust and particulate matter off of roofs, first-flush devices allow for diversion of that initial contaminated water in order to harvest cleaner water for the remainder of the rainy season.

Brackish Water

Brackish water has a salinity level between that of freshwater and seawater. It occurs naturally and is common in estuaries where freshwater and seawater mix and may also occur in brackish fossil aquifers. Many species of fish and plants thrive in brackish water; however, it is not suitable for drinking or for the irrigation of most plant species without desalination.

Treating brackish water involves removing dissolved solids or salts, generally through reverse osmosis. Originally used to produce ultra-pure water for industrial processes, reverse osmosis is now being used in many coastal areas as a way to supplement domestic water supplies. However, the desalination process is both energy intensive and produces a saline byproduct that is environmentally damaging if not passed through a costly treatment process.

Seawater

Figure 3-14 Four types of stormwater. © Sherwood Design Engineers.

Seawater makes up the vast majority of the water sources on earth. It possesses salinity levels higher than brackish water and significantly higher than that of freshwater. These levels vary from place to place; they are higher in areas with high rates of evaporation and low precipitation. Seawater, like brackish water, must be desalinated before it can be considered a source of either domestic or irrigation water.

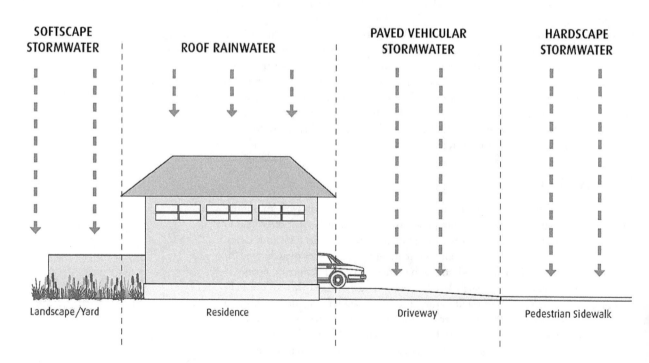

Stormwater

Once rainwater hits the ground, it is considered stormwater. The quality of stormwater varies greatly, depending on where it falls. Water that falls on paved pedestrian-only areas is the second-most pristine water for harvesting—after roof rainwater—because the contaminants introduced by wind or foot traffic are relatively mild. This water is easily appropriated for groundwater recharge and irrigation. Stormwater collected from vehicular paved areas, however, tends to carry hydrocarbons, including gasoline, oil, asphalt, and tire particles, as well as metals and paints that flake off vehicles. These contaminants are not easily removed, so this water is should be filtered through the stormwater treatment techniques (discussed in chapter 4). After initial treatment, vehicular stormwater can be used for irrigation or landscaping.

Water that runs off of planted areas often contains silt sediments, fertilizers, pesticides, and other contaminants. Because of the filtering nature of soil and rocks, this water is appropriate for groundwater recharge but is typically of inadequate quality to be captured and reused for applications other than irrigation.

WATER SUPPLY STRATEGIES

The next section discusses strategies for conserving water, improving existing resources, and providing alternative methods for supplying water. Two methods for provision of alternate supply covered in detail are rainwater harvesting and desalination, both of which come with unique challenges and constraints. The former is a relatively simple method for increasing water supplies; the latter is both more complicated and potentially more damaging to the environment, but can ultimately provide a large-scale source of water in arid, coastal environments.

The first water supply strategy should always be to reduce demand. Water conservation measures include water-efficient fixtures at the building scale, water conservation and green streets programs at the community scale, and education about green building programs at the state or national level. Water-efficient irrigation, landscaping, and agriculture remain important at every level.

The second step is to improve the performance of existing water systems by monitoring water use, reducing leaks, providing appropriate backup and safety measures, and using water more efficiently.

Thirdly, new sources of water can be identified and developed. Rainwater harvesting makes use of a readily available supply of nearly potable water, while desalination makes use of the world's most widely available form of water—saltwater.

Reduce Demand/Conserve Water

Research shows that usage efficiency and conservation are the most environmentally and financially sound water provision strategies. Transitioning to low-flow plumbing fixtures, increasing water or sewage rates to incentivize households and businesses to use less water, and providing education about simple household water-saving

Figure 3-15 Average annual water rates. Water costs vary widely across the nation, but they are rising every-where. The San Francisco Public Utilities Commission is spending billions of dollars to upgrade and expand its water system, costs that are invariably felt by the consumer. PlaNYC Sustainable Stormwater Management Plan.

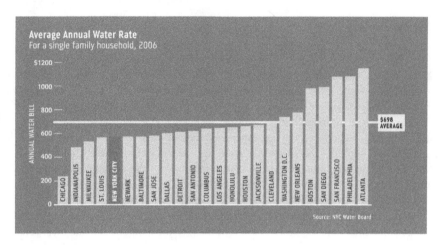

techniques have enormous leverage on upstream resources. Effective water conservation programs can lower costs considerably by reducing municipal demand and the associated infrastructure development and maintenance necessary to support that demand. Additionally, with reduced water use, associated wastewater costs also go down. In turn, the energy demands and consequent greenhouse gas emissions of supply systems and wastewater treatment facilities are also reduced through water conservation.

While conservation is an important water management strategy, conservation alone is often not sufficient to keep up with rising demand. In California, for example, projections demonstrate an absolute maximum feasible savings of about 3.2 million acre-feet per year by 2030 through conservation and efficiency measures.[2] These potential savings from conservation would still fail to bridge the gap between future demand and supply. The state's population is projected to increase by another 14 million between 2010 and 2030, translating to an additional water demand of 3.6 million acre-feet.[3] California is not alone in this challenge: across the United States, thirty-six states are facing water scarcity issues, while water costs nationwide have risen nearly 30 percent in the last five years.[4]

Furthermore, studies have shown that hastily applied stopgap water restrictions are not effective at transforming long-term public consciousness because people tend to overcompensate once restrictions are lifted. Creating an enduring perception of water as a limited and valuable resource will require a fundamental shift in the way we build water systems, purchase water rights, and evaluate water safety. Meanwhile, alternative water sources, such as graywater reuse and rainwater harvesting, are increasing available water while also encouraging conservation by improving individual and public awareness of water systems and their purpose.[5]

In regions where water resources are stretched by increased development, the most practical conservation method is to adjust current water-use patterns to maximize the existing water supply. Water conservation measures represent the first best practice related to adapting an existing water supply to a growing population. However, the actual water savings must first be compared to the relative cost of implementing a specific conservation measure. Comparing the volume of water savings associated with each measure to the cost of implementing it will determine whether the measure is both feasible and cost-effective. By calculating water savings first, designers can more accurately gauge the need to import off-site water supplies or develop additional water resources to support a project.

Conservation measures can also be implemented on a community scale through regulation, community design guidelines, homeowners associations, economic incentives, and education programs.

The following are examples of community conservation and use-reduction programs:

- Institute financial incentives that use a tiered billing system: customers using less water are rewarded with lower prices.
- Require water purveyors to audit residential customers and make them aware of both their water usage and the potential to receive incentives or reduce water costs.
- Require that public and large-scale private landscaping consist of drought-resistant plants native to the region so that supplemental irrigation is not necessary.
- Offer incentives for retrofitting household appliances with reduced water demands, such as high-efficiency washing machines, low-flow showerheads, and ultra-low-flow toilets.
- Use the public schools to educate the next generation of decision makers about the value of water conservation.
- Offer financial incentives to the public for identifying and repairing leaks on private property.
- Limit (and levy fees on) wasteful activities such as washing driveways and sidewalks instead of sweeping them, watering lawns during the day, and so on.
- Require water purveyors to dedicate a member of their staff to water conservation coordination in order to centralize conservation efforts and make such programs more efficient and more accessible to the public.
- Forbid potable water from being used for irrigation.

The success rates of such programs can be increased by encouraging a competitive environment and making water-use and conservation metrics visible to all participating in the competition. For example, one block or neighborhood could compete against another for the lowest water-use metric in the same community. Incentives such as lower water rates and discounts donated by local merchants could be provided to the winners. Bringing a community together in the spirit of friendly competition can be an effective educational opportunity.

For similar programs at Stanford University refer to the following link: http://sustainability.stanford.edu/conservationcup.

Conserving Water through Improved Irrigation

Significant opportunities to conserve water through better planning, better monitoring, and better irrigation technologies exist in landscape and agricultural irrigation applications. More than half of urban water is used for landscaping, and a considerable amount of that is lost to overwatering or inadvertently watering hardscape—which not only wastes water but contributes to stormwater runoff. The Environmental Protection Agency (EPA) estimates that over two-thirds of that wasted water could be conserved through better irrigation practices. A variety of technologies offer improvements over standard sprinkler systems for both landscaping and agricultural settings.

Microirrigation systems such as drips, bubblers, and microsprinklers are ideal for arid climates and plants susceptible to dampness-related problems like mold and rot. The advantages of these systems are that they apply water directly to plants, can irrigate irregularly shaped land, operate with smaller power units than conventional sprinkler systems, and can also distribute water-soluble fertilizer. The disadvantages of microirrigation systems include higher installation costs and greater maintenance requirements, as they are prone to clogging.

With *subsurface capillary irrigation*, the water supply is buried below the surface of the ground, and plants draw the water up to their roots. One type of system uses flow chambers to distribute water throughout the ground; accompanying pans retain excess water that would otherwise seep deeper into the ground and become inaccessible to shallow-rooted ground cover. Other types of subsurface capillary irrigation systems incorporate strips of different geotextile fibers and tapes to create a subsurface water distribution system. If installed and operated properly, these systems can use up to 85 percent less water than traditional irrigation systems. There is, however, a learning curve associated with their use, and improper subsurface irrigation can lead to overwatering and soil saturation.

Flood irrigation is one of the most common irrigation methods because it is inexpensive and simple. It can, however, be very inefficient, as a lot of water is wasted through evaporation and transpiration. Methods to make flooding more efficient include leveling fields so that the water reaches all places equally, incorporating surge flooding that reduces runoff, and capturing runoff in ponds and pumping it back to the top of the field for reuse as irrigation water.

Spray irrigation systems are used on large farms. The most common spray system is the center-pivot sprinkler, which uses high pressure to spray water on crops in a circular manner. This method covers a large area of land, but 40 percent of the water pumped is lost to water evaporation and wind affecting the spray. Low-energy precision application (LEPA) center-pivot systems are an alternative technology capable of achieving 80 to 95 percent efficiency by hanging bubblers and sprayers 8 to 18 inches from the ground, thus reducing the amount of water lost to evaporation and wind.

Smart irrigation controllers are used for landscape and agricultural irrigation in both the commercial and residential sectors. The technology monitors environmental changes via sensors and weather information in order to best manage watering frequency. Using these "smart" devices can eliminate overwatering and reduce water use by 15 to 30 percent.

Improvements to Infrastructure

Strategies to optimize the performance of existing water systems can also be applied to centralized water management facilities. The extensive network of pipes, valves, and other appurtenances in a built system will often have significant leaks that can be difficult and expensive to repair. If leaks go undetected, they eventually manifest as burst pipes, broken pumps, and other system failures that can disrupt supply or endanger public health and safety through flooding or by undermining buildings and roads. Conventional identification methods used to estimate the lost water volume and inherent repair costs include installing and periodically calibrating meters, pressure testing, and computer modeling the existing distribution system.

More advanced leak-detection techniques include the use of acoustic devices, tracer gas, infrared imaging, and ground-penetrating radar. These methods can provide varying results based on the pipe material, soil conditions, and the ambient temperature of the ground.

Acoustic devices: These methods include listening devices and leak noise correlators that detect the sounds or vibrations caused by water leakage in pressurized pipes. This method is less effective in plastic pipes than in metallic pipes.

Tracer gas: Nontoxic gas is inserted into an isolated section of pipe. If there is a leak, the gas will escape at the damaged section of pipe or joint and filter through the above soils. Gas detectors scan the area above the pipe and locate the leak's location.

Tracer chemical: Nontoxic compounds blended into an isolated section of pipe can measure the variation in chemical concentration between the input and output (given specific flow rates) and determine the volume of water lost and the severity of the leak.

Infrared imaging: This technique uses heat detection to locate leaks. The leaking water changes the temperature of the soil around the pipe. Imaging detects differences in temperature between the leak site and surrounding area.

Ground-penetrating radar: The radar detects voids in the soil caused by leaking water.

In addition to these methods of physical leak detection, water purveyors have the option of using advanced electronic metering and communication systems to identify and mitigate leaks. In such systems, remote metering throughout the distribution network communicates to a central control facility. This facility can then identify pressure and flow rates at various locations, which can be compared to "standard" conditions. For example, flow at night—during off-peak hours—should be lower than that during the peak morning and evening hours. By observing pressure and flow anomalies during these hours, leaks can be identified. Implementing a computerized monitoring system for an entire neighborhood can allow for early detection and focused repair.

At a smaller scale, the individual homeowner or business can install a "building dashboard" that compiles electricity, water, and natural gas data from an energy management system and displays it in a real-time interface accessed via the Internet. The dashboard monitors a building's water use to help occupants identify leaks, saving water and preventing water damage. These systems have the added benefit of highlighting water uses and patterns so the occupant can better understand consumption trends and respond by making adjustments.

Expansion of Existing Water Resources

Other strategies can further extend the effectiveness or enhance the productivity of existing water infrastructure. The approaches defined below provide complementary tools to those already presented in this chapter.

Conjunctive Use

Conjunctive use strategies involve an integrated management of water supplies—typically at a watershed or regional scale, and over a long time period—in an effort to optimize the coordination of multiple supply sources, such as rainwater, stormwater, surface water, recycled water, and groundwater. When the capture, treatment, storage, and delivery of multiple sources are well planned and coordinated, demands can be met efficiently and reliably on a long-term basis. Such management programs result in increased reliability of supply, reduced need for system infrastructure, optimized efficiency, reduced risks (such as seawater intrusion), and reduced water losses in the system.

Water purveyors, districts, and cities are often constrained to established boundaries based on local and regional development rather than natural hydrologic drainage boundaries. This has resulted in complex water rights and management systems for groundwater basins, streams, rivers, and lakes. Additionally, a city's water demand often peaks at the opposite time of peak supply. These factors result in inefficient conventional solutions, such as importing water over large distances or the construction of large dams and reservoirs to meet demand.

The ideal conjunctive-use strategy assesses water resources across political boundaries as well as

- meeting demands more efficiently
- reducing infrastructure
- reducing the energy needed for conveyance
- optimizing use of gravity-fed systems
- providing system redundancy

Creative Water Solutions

Because water is a complex, vital issue, designers will need technical solutions as well as creative thinking to solve the world's water problems. The following are creative and alternative ways to generate drinkable water: innovative, artistic strategies born of necessity that demonstrate out-of-the-box thinking for solving water problems.

Evapotranspiration in Urban Greenhouses

The increasing practice of indoor urban agriculture, or building-integrated sustainable agriculture (BISA), provides a unique opportunity for harvesting water. Gas-cooled tubes running across the roofs of warm, humid greenhouses will facilitate the condensation of water. As a technical application of the natural process of evapo-

Figure 3-16 Desert dew harvester. Visiondivision.

transpiration, this is an easily harvested source of highly purified water condensed right out of the air. This technique allows crops that are watered with treated gray-water to become a potential source of potable water for the community or facility, or an additional revenue source to offset the costs of urban farming facilities.

Desert Dew Harvesting

Under favorable climatic conditions, dew forms overnight when ambient air temperature drops, causing atmospheric water vapor to condense on surfaces it comes into contact with. Dew can be harvested with simple or complex nets or other objects where it collects, coalesced into larger droplets of water, and dripped by gravity to a collection system without the use of electricity.

An innovative idea for dew harvesting (Figure 3-16) was put forth by the Swedish design firm Visiondivision as an entry in the 2009 Design for the Children Competition. This could be a hospital tent shaped like an upside-down sun hat, with a broad surface area overhead that slopes down toward the center. The roof provides shade during the day and harvests dew at night. The dew is funneled to a barrel in the center of the structure, which acts as a passive cooling device as well.

Fog Harvesting

Fog can also become a source of freshwater, harvested without using electricity. Simple or complex nets or other objects can be used to intercept tiny water droplets from wind-driven fog. As the droplets collect and join, they are conveyed by gravity to a collection system at the bottom of the fog catcher. The frequency, variability, and water content of the fog must be considered for each specific site. There is a model fog catcher at the Chartwell School that Sherwood worked on in Monterey, California, and the technique is being explored on a larger scale by rural communities in the deserts of Chile.

Figure 3-17 Roundabout pump at a school in Uganda. The organization Drop in the Bucket was formed in 2006 with the goal of providing wells to large rural schools in sub-Saharan Africa. During the next three years it installed over sixty wells and sanitation systems in six different countries. This roundabout will pump water 80 meters up and is perfect for moving water from the well to places where it is needed. John Travis, Drop in the Bucket.

Creative Ways to Pump and Carry Water

Rotary water pumps designed as merry-go-rounds operated simply by children playing on them are a creative solution with multiple synergies—recreation, education, community involvement, and energy. They can be fitted to pull water from wells or underground storage tanks, which can then be used as needed. Another creative technology is the Hippo water roller, which consists of a barrel that can be filled with water, turned on its side, and rolled from source to destination as an alternative to carrying water by hand.

Rainwater Harvesting

Beginning in the late twentieth century, rainwater harvesting reemerged worldwide as a significant water supply strategy. Modern installations bear some resemblance to the simple technology of ancient practices; much of modern rainwater harvesting occurs via roof catchment systems that feed storage tanks or cisterns. A roof design that is explicitly intended to detain water on the roof surface itself is known as a blue roof. Other variations, such as earthwork catchment systems and in-ground storage facilities, are also in use around the world.

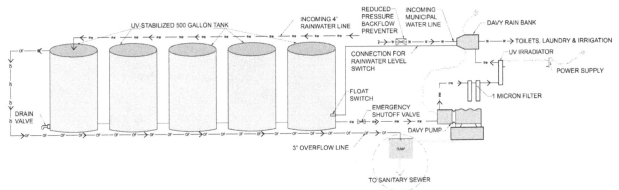

Figure 3-18 Rainwater harvesting schematic diagram.
© Sherwood Design Engineers.

RESIDENTIAL RAINWATER HARVESTING IN SAUSALITO

In 2004, Sherwood was approached by 450 Architects Inc., a San Francisco–based green architecture firm with a client who had a residential property in Sausalito, California, a hilly town overlooking San Francisco Bay. The client wanted to collect the rainwater falling on his property to water his garden and do his laundry, thereby minimizing his dependence on municipal water supplies and reducing stormwater runoff to the bay. He had grown up in Germany, where rainwater harvesting is more common. But when he began to pursue the idea of building a rainwater harvesting system into his home, he was surprised to discover that while many permitted rainwater harvesting systems exist around the country for other uses, no one in California had ever gotten approval to use harvested rainwater inside a home.

Based on Marin County rainfall data and the plan area of the proposed residence, our research showed that the amount of water used for laundering would be comparable to the estimated annual rainfall expected on the residence's primary 600-square-foot roof. In collaboration with the client and the architect, we set about designing a system that would be safe, efficient, and reliable. Then we had to convince city and county officials to approve the use of rainwater for doing laundry. We presented a list of similar rainwater harvesting precedents and answered concerns about the safety, design, and maintenance of the system.

After an extensive design and approval process, we eventually succeeded in setting a new precedent by building California's first residential rainwater harvesting system that is actually permitted to use rainwater indoors. System designer Carl Nelson noted, "I am hopeful that the collaborative approach adopted for this project can be built upon to advance progressive engineering. Considering the increasing pressure on water supplies, people will need to take advantage of the precious resource that falls from the sky."[*]

Rooftop catchment systems like these provide a scalable method of water harvesting that can be designed for a variety of sizes and budgets. They also provide flexibility in treating water to the appropriate quality for its intended use by incorporating various site-specific treatment methods. This rooftop rainwater, which would otherwise run into the gutter, then becomes available for landscape irrigation, washing clothes, emergency water supplies, or use in fire prevention.

Beyond scalability and flexibility, most common treatment technologies, such as sand filters, gutter screens, and chemical additions, are also passive. They require little electricity or chemicals and can be easily maintained or upgraded. As more projects get approved and the attitude toward water harvesting changes, these systems are becoming increasingly common.

Figure 3-19 Residential rainwater cistern. © Sherwood Design Engineers.

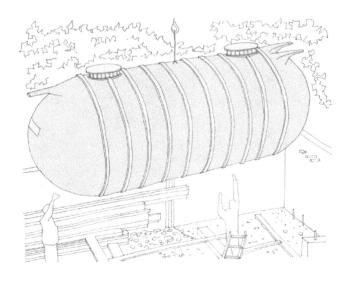

Figure 3-20 Diagram of cistern component parts. © Sherwood Design Engineers.

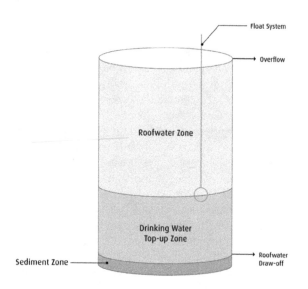

Rainwater Harvesting Systems Overview

In preliminary meetings with local city and county agencies, various questions and concerns were raised about the rainwater harvesting system. Officials wanted assurances that rainwater would not be allowed to enter domestic or municipal potable water supplies, that the water entering the house's laundry facilities would be properly treated, and that the copper roof was safe for harvesting water.

For the Sausalito home, we decided on a copper roof because it provides a clean harvesting surface that is relatively inert once it achieves its patination and is almost perfectly recyclable, thereby reducing its long-term environmental impacts. While copper poses a potential risk to waterways, the leaching of copper is caused principally by corrosion and enhanced by factors such as high-velocity flows, high temperatures, stagnant water, and mechanical abrasions. Our relatively flat roof design provides low-velocity, nonstagnant flows, and the water temperature is much lower than that associated with temperature-based corrosion.

When it rains, water runs off the copper roof and passes through gutter screens that prevent debris from entering the downspouts. The rainwater downspouts connect to a 6,000-gallon storage tank built under the back patio. A drain valve at the bottom of the tank connects to the municipal stormwater system, allowing the tank to be emptied for cleaning or maintenance. Bolted manholes at each end of the tank provide access from the top.

When the water in the tank drops below a specified level, a fill valve opens from the domestic water supply, allowing water into the tank until it reaches the fill-off level (see figure 3-20). The water level is specified so that the tank maintains a minimum water level but does not remain full during the rainwater season, providing sufficient room for incoming flows. The system was designed with air-gap assemblies that conform to the Uniform Plumbing Code (UPC) to ensure that no water enters the domestic supply. An additional level of protection for municipal water supplies is ensured by a backflow prevention valve with reduced pressure principle (BPV-RPP) according to California code for well water or other alternative water supplies.

To ensure the rainwater is safe to use, water is first screened and filtered to remove debris, sand, silt, and other particulates; it is then disinfected using an ultraviolet system that destroys bacteria and microorganisms.

Following treatment, the plumbing lines serve the laundry and exterior irrigation needs. All faucets and valves are labeled "Rainwater: Do Not Drink." This rainwater supply system is independent of the household water supply, and the features that make use of the rainwater are not connected to the domestic water supply system.

* Sherwood Design Engineers, "The First Permitted Rainwater Harvesting System for Residential Interior Use in California Approved by the City of Sausalito" (press release), November 21, 2005.

Benefits of Rainwater Harvesting

As they evaluate the opportunities for the integration of rainwater harvesting systems into project design, designers should be aware of the following benefits of rainwater harvesting:

Supports municipal water supplies: Rainwater harvesting systems can alleviate municipal water shortages by increasing the volume of water entering public systems. As a rough estimate, a 1,000-square-foot roof area harvests about 600 gallons per inch of rainfall. The amount of rainfall varies by region, and the seasonal distribution can be a significant factor in further determining rainwater harvesting's benefits.

Reduces infrastructure costs: By reducing loads on municipal supplies, rainwater systems can reduce the frequency and expense of maintaining and upgrading municipal water systems. In areas heavily dependent on long-range water infrastructure systems, increased rainwater systems translate into considerable financial savings.

Reduces energy and greenhouse gas emissions: Harvesting rainwater reduces the energy and associated emissions needed for pumping, treating, and distributing water. Because rain falls everywhere, it is a naturally decentralized water source. When collected on-site, it is gravity-driven from roofs through treatment processes and storage units.

Increases water security: Rainwater harvesting adds resilience to large centralized water systems by lowering demand in the communities they serve. By harvesting and maintaining independent water supplies, cities can minimize or prevent water loss in the event of an earthquake, energy blackout, or other disruptive occurrence.

Provides savings to residents: Augmenting centralized water systems with rainwater can save people money in a variety of ways. Several studies have shown that local harvesting can be more cost-effective than long-distance supply systems.[6] In addition to saving on their water bills, people may save

Figure 3-21 Average annual rainfall distribution in the United States.

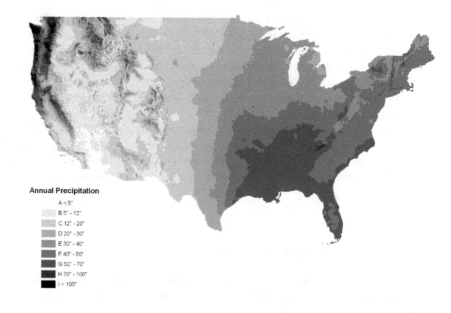

Annual Precipitation

    A < 5"
    B 5" - 12"
    C 12" - 20"
    D 20" - 30"
    E 30" - 40"
    F 40" - 50"
    G 50" - 70"
    H 70" - 100"
    I > 100"

Figure 3-22 Marin Country Day School rainwater cistern installation. The cistern being installed in a school in Marin, California, is positioned below grade. Water harvested is used for the mechanical system makeup water and for irrigation. © Sherwood Design Engineers.

on their sewage bills as well, because many agencies calculate sewage rates as a percentage of municipal water-supply use. Indirect, communitywide savings also include lowered maintenance costs for storm and sewage systems due to decreased water volumes and savings on repair costs because harvesting allows storm surges to be more evenly and slowly released into municipal system, causing less damage.

Improves flood control: Impervious urban surfaces shunt water to storm drains instead of allowing it to soak into the ground. When these pipes back up or clog, it causes flooding. Upgrading these pipes to larger volumes is both cost-

Figure 3-23 Chartwell School cistern installation. The cistern installed at the Chartwell School offers students an interpretive element designed to complement the school's science curriculum. Michael David Rose Photography.

ly and time-consuming. Rainwater cisterns serve as effective stormwater detention tanks by slowly releasing captured water. With less piping, smaller, dispersed on-site tanks provide better surge control than large, centralized detention tanks by reducing stormwater volume during high-impact natural events.

Increases surface water quality: Stormwater that runs over city surfaces picks up heavy metals, motor oil, trash, and other contaminants. In most cities, storm drains release captured flows directly to local surface waters without treatment, contributing to the pollution of streams, bays, and oceans. Because rooftop rainwater is typically the cleanest form of stormwater, harvesting it before it picks up extra pollutants both reduces the flow of stormwater and lowers the amount of pollutants being "scrubbed off" into local waters.

Reduces sewer overflow: Cities that do not discharge storm drains directly into local surface waters typically combine rainfall with sewage for treatment before it is discharged. Ideally, this reduces the amount of pollution from stormwater in local surface waters. In practice, however, sewage systems are periodically inundated with millions of gallons of relatively clean rainwater during a storm. Treated as blackwater, this huge combined volume creates significant energy and financial costs. In San Francisco, the combined system actually overflows an average of ten times per year, releasing raw sewage into San Francisco Bay and the Pacific Ocean.[7] Capturing rainwater could reduce surges on the sewer system, prevent overflows, improve local water quality, and save significant amounts of energy required for sewage treatment.

Offers community benefits: In addition to the financial and environmental benefits of rainwater harvesting, there are community and educational benefits. Well-designed rainwater systems can decrease pollution and increase public green space, adding benefits including shade, noise reduction, and improved air quality. Additionally, these systems can increase awareness of water resources, improve water management, increase public knowledge of water-saving strategies, and contribute to community self-sufficiency and security by maintaining independent water supplies. All of these contribute to healthy, beautiful communities that improve quality of life for everyone and increase property values.

Water Quality Concerns for Rainwater

For all rainwater harvesting systems, it is important to match the level of treatment with the intended uses in order to maximize system efficiency, safety, and user satisfaction. A system that treats rainwater to potable standards should be used for drinking and cooking to justify the cost and energy required. Conversely, irrigation-quality water should never be used for drinking due to health concerns.

Builders and homeowners must take local regulations into account. Each local agency has specific considerations and standards that should be met for safety and legal reasons. For example, Ohio's rainwater harvesting laws are some of the most detailed in the country,[9] while the wide variety of rainwater harvesting systems in Texas are only subject to regulation if the household also has a municipal connection.

Rainwater is a high-quality water source that can be a superior alternative to ground or surface waters in developing countries. Many people are able to drink rainwater untreated without ill effect despite its periodic failure to meet World Health Organization standards.[9] But rainwater should only be used for drinking when other high-quality sources are unavailable.[10] Drinking and cooking account for only 5 to 10 percent of total residential water use, so there are still great water savings to be had without increasing risk if used for other purposes.

Unregulated conditions: It is estimated that there are over five hundred thousand residential rainwater systems in the United States alone, and many thousands more all over the world.[11] In areas without a streamlined permitting process, individuals have created do-it-yourself catchment systems without regulation or guidance regarding proper system design. Instead of ignoring or marginalizing the initiative of such individuals, municipalities should cultivate the collective energy of its citizenry and create safe practices through education and support.

Health concerns: Scientists estimate that up to seven million Americans fall ill from municipal-supplied tap water per year.[12] From collection onward, rooftop rainwater is exposed to fewer potential pathogens than centralized water supplies.[13] While there have been cases of human illnesses attributed to drinking rainwater, these reports are infrequent when compared to the numbers of municipal outbreaks.

Contamination pathways: Despite the high initial quality of rainwater, studies have revealed that contamination pathways do exist during collection, storage, and distribution.[14] For example, a 1997 outbreak of campylobacter in Queensland, Australia, was attributed to animals that had infiltrated a tank.[15] Two separate cases of salmonella in Trinidad and New Zealand occurred due to bird and animal fecal contamination.[16] An outbreak of giardiasis and cryptosporidiosis was reported when rainwater tanks were found to have been structurally compromised and infiltrated by a nearby septic tank.[17] Cases of Legionnaires' disease[18] and gastroenteritis[19] have also been documented. In most of these instances, rainwater was consumed from a compromised system without any prior treatment or filtration.

Biological pathogens: Of all contaminants, microbial pathogens present the most serious health risks. These species, such as *Giardia, Cryptosporidium, Campylobacter enteritis,* and *Salmonella,* can originate from human or animal feces.[20] Human contamination can be avoided by securing access hatches and storing water away from septic tanks. Pruning branches to prohibit avian nesting can limit bird droppings on the catchment surface. Filters and gutter guards can prevent organic decay that can lead to elevated levels of fecal streptococci.[21] Performing visual checks of the system about twice a year is highly recommended to ensure animals do not infiltrate the tank. To remedy any biological contamination, remove the sources and disinfect the water and system with chlorine.

Chemical contamination: Unlike biological pathogens, chemicals may not cause immediate illness, but heavy metals, nitrates, and pesticides can present other serious health hazards. Metals such as lead, copper, and zinc can enter the system when water comes into contact with roofing materials, piping, or paints made of those elements. Usually, these materials are incompatible with rainwater harvesting. In some cases, lead flashings may be painted with an approved coating to eliminate exposure.[22] Lead levels have also been known to be high near automobile traffic. Similarly, nitrates from particulate fertilizer can settle on rooftops or uncovered tanks in agricultural areas, though such deposited particulates can usually be diverted with a first-flush device.[23] Pesticides may present problems when rain is exposed to treated wood, but these elements should be avoided altogether or counteracted with sealants or liners.

pH balance: The pH level of water is a measure of its acidity. Rainwater tends to be slightly acidic because it absorbs carbon dioxide on its flight through the atmosphere.[24] This causes leaching of metal ions from piping and other plumbing fixtures, leading to elevated heavy metal concentrations. Simple pH tests can demonstrate whether treatment is necessary. One such test option involves in-line calcium carbonate (limestone), calcium oxide (lime), or sodium carbonate (soda ash) pellets that dissolve only under acidic water. A less expensive option is to simply add baking soda to the tanks. If pH is between 7.0 and 7.4, add 1 pound of baking soda per 10,000 gallons of water to raise the pH by 0.1 units.[25] Below 7.0, double the amount and then retest after a few days. (Concrete storage tanks tend to impart some alkalinity to their contents.)[26]

Other concerns: Mosquitoes should be kept out of rainwater cisterns with mesh that is checked periodically, along with the rest of the working system. Algal growth can be avoided by using opaque cisterns and gutters to limit sun exposure. Most types of algae are not health hazards, but may create musty, vegetable, or fishy tastes and odors.[27] Other possible sources of odors include pollen on roofs or sediments in tanks or gutters. Thin biofilms or slimes, however, are universal to materials that continuously hold water and do not pose specific health threats. Lastly, water collected on newly painted roofs may have a soapy taste or frothy appearance; use such water for nonpotable needs for the first few rainfalls after painting.

⌒ For more information on this subject please see www.sherwoodinstitute.org/research.

Desalination

The process of desalinating seawater into potable water is not a new technology; it produces high-quality potable water and an extremely saline brine-waste effluent. A wide range of methods exist for acquiring saline water, removing salts, and disposing of the briny waste. Each process has a measurable impact on the environment. For example, suction pumps and intake valves can be intrusive to marine ecosystems, while saline effluents, usually discharged back into the ocean, can pose a significant environmental threat to marine life and habitat.

The most common desalination technology is reverse osmosis (RO), but newer desalination technologies that offer lower energy requirements, energy reuse potential, and other features are under development or in limited use. Yet for all of these technologies, disposing of the large quantities of saline waste generated still remains problematic.

Benefits of Desalination

Desalination technology has the ability to produce a year-round, reliable supply of high-quality water. Having a constant source of seawater makes desalination systems resistant to drought or other weather conditions. It can also be environmentally preferable to existing water practices in communities that are draining groundwater resources at an unsustainable rate. Adding desalinated water to a community's water supply can relieve the burden on aquifers and rivers, thus preserving the base flows required to support natural habitats.

Desalination can also be used to provide potable water for communities that may be located far from existing water infrastructure or for coastal communities not currently plumbed into municipal infrastructures. Purchasing a packaged treatment plant can offer an isolated community increased autonomy and flexibility for growth when other water resources are not available. The major drawback to this approach is that the water supply then becomes directly linked to available energy supplies that operate the desalination facility. Communities should not rely solely on desalination as a water source without having a reliable renewable energy source.

Desalination Best Practices

Best practices for desalination are specific to each location's natural and developmental constraints and should be based on site conditions, the quality of water needed, the availability of engineering and construction resources, and the potential impacts to existing water resources such as aquifers. Ideally, practices should include methods for the intake of brackish groundwater, alternative methods for pretreatment, specific desalinating processes, and brine disposal.

Given the state of the world's water resources and civilization's increasing encroachment into arid regions, desalination is becoming a more mainstream water resource. Because of its new high profile, innovations and efficiencies that use less energy and produce less waste are constantly being developed. In addition to technology modification, new process concepts are under consideration for possible water desalination in future decades. These include humidification/dehumidification processes, forward osmosis, membrane distillation, gas-hydrate affinity, capacitance deionization processes, carbon nanotubes, low-temperature desalination, and graphite electrodes. These innovations are currently all at early stages of process research, but they may one day provide long-term solutions to unleashing potable water from the world's oceans.[29]

Notes

1 World Health Organization, "10 Facts About Water Scarcity," March 2009, http://www.who.int/features/factfiles/water/en/index.html.

2 Public Policy Institute of California, "Water Supply and Quality," *Just the Facts*, (September 2008), http://www.ppic.org/main/allpubs.asp?

3 Public Policy Institute of California, "Does California Have the Water to Support Population Growth?" *Research Brief*, no. 102 (July 2005), www.ppic.org/main/publication.asp?i=624.

4 Michael Kanellos, "A Smart Grid for Water," Greentech Media, February 18, 2009, http://www.greentechmedia.com/articles/read/a-smart-grid-for-water-5743/.

5 Rain Bird, *Irrigation for a Growing World*, (2003), http://www.rainbird.com/iuow/whitepaper-growingworld.htm.

6 T. Herrmann and K. Hasse, "Ways to Get Water," *Water Science Technology* 26, nos. 8–9 (1997): 313–18.

7 http://sfsewer.org.

8 Ohio Administrative Code, Chapter 3701-28: Private Water Systems, http://www.odh.ohio.gov/rules/final/f3701-28.aspx.

9 V. Meera and M. Mansoor Ahammed, "Water Quality of Rooftop Rainwater Harvesting Systems: A Review." *Journal of Water Supply: Research and Technology-AQUA* 55, no. 4 (2006): 257.

10 C. A. Evans, P. J. Coombes, and R. H. Dunstan, "Wind, Rain and Bacteria: The Effect of Weather on the Microbial Composition of Roof-Harvested Rainwater," *Water Research* 40, no. 1 (2006): 37–44.

11 H. J. Krishna, "Development of Alternative Water Resources in the USA: Progress with Rainwater Harvesting" (paper presented at the 13th Annual International Rainwater Catchment Systems Conference, Sydney, Australia, August 2007).

12 National Resources Defense Council, "Issues: Water," http://www.nrdc.org/water/default.asp.

13 A. Spinks et al. "Urban Rainwater Harvesting: A Comparative Review of Source Water Quality," *Water Intelligence Online* 5 (February 2006).

14 Texas Commission on Environmental Quality, *Public Use Guidelines* (2007).

15 A. Merrit, R. Miles, and J. Bates, "An Outbreak of Campylobacter Entiritis on an Island Resort North Queensland," *Communicable Disease Intelligence* 23, no. 8 (1999): 215–19.

16 Hope Simmons, *Water Research* 35, no. 6 (2001): 1518–24; J. P. Koplan et al., "Contaminated Roof-Collected Rainwater as a Possible Cause of an Outbreak," *Journal of Hygiene* 81, no. 2 (1978): 303–9.

17 R. Lester, "A Mixed Outbreak of Cryptosporidiosis and Giardiasis," *Update* 1, no. 1 (1992): 14–15. Cited in enHealth Council (Australia), *Guidance on the Use of Rainwater Tanks*" (1998), enhealth.nphp.gov.au/council/pubs/pdf/rainwater_tanks.pdf.

18 German Schlech et al., "Legionnaires' Disease in the Caribbean: An Outbreak Associated with a Resort Hotel," *Archives of Internal Medicine* 145, no. 11 (1985): 2076–79.

19 J. Heyworth, "Consumption of Untreated Tank Rainwater and Gastroenteritis among Young Children in South Australia," *International Journal of Epidemiology* 35 (2006): 1051–58.

20 P. R. Thomas and G. R. Greene, "Rainwater Quality from Different Roof Catchments," *Water Science and Technology* 28, nos. 3–5 (1993): 291–99.

21 J. E. Gould and H. J. McPherson, "Bacteriological Quality of Rainwater in Roof and Ground Catchment Systems in Botswana," *Water International* 12 (1987): 135–38.

22 Australian Environmental Health Council, "Guidance on Water Tanks" (2004).

23 M. Yaziz et al., "Variation in Rainwater Quality from Roof Catchments," *Water. Resources* 23, no. 6 (1989): 761–76; World Commission on Dams, *Dams and Development: A New Framework for Decision-Making* (London: Earthscan, 2000).

24 P. R. Thomas and G. R. Greene, "Rainwater Quality from Different Roof Catchments," *Water Science and Technology* 28, nos. 3–5 (1993): 291–99.

25 Texas Commission on Environmental Quality, *Domestic Guide 2007*.

26 Lubinga Handia, "Operation Paper: Comparative Study of Rainwater Quality in Urban Zambia. *Journal of Water Supply: Research and Technology-AQUA* 54, no. 1 (2005): 55.

27 Australian Environmental Health Council, "Guidance on Water Tanks" (2004).

28 Michael Kanellos, "Forward Osmosis: Can a Startup Reverse Desalination?" GreentechMedia, February 17, 2009, http://www.greentechmedia.com/articles/read/forward-osmosis-can-a-startup-reverse-desalination-5735/.

CHAPTER 4

Integrated Water Management

WATER AS RESOURCE, NOT WASTE PRODUCT

When it comes to our relationship with water, redefining the concept of waste is especially important. A core principle of ecology is that nothing in nature is wasted; it is simply transformed into food for other parts of the ecosystem. In natural systems, dead or digested material is not transported, stored, or accumulated; it is absorbed on-site into the local food chain. Yet our current method of treating waste is to simply wash it away with drinkable water. The advent of modern sewage systems, for example, has given us the luxury of flushing away our waste with clean water, but it doesn't transform the waste into something useful: it simply transports it away from us. We then expend considerable financial and and energy resources to treat that water before discharging it back into the same rivers, oceans, and water tables that we gather our fresh water from.

In order to live sustainably, we need to find ways of transforming our "waste products" into useful nutrients or energy, without creating more pollution in the process than we started with, and without fouling the clean air and water we depend on for survival. In places where wastewater treatment systems are insufficient, we end up concentrating too much waste in one place, which disrupts ecological systems by overfeeding certain organisms. When these microbes absorb all the oxygen in the water, the ecosystem crashes, creating large dead zones in the receiving waters.

As a result of the increasing expense and negative impacts of our current systems of water and wastewater management, engineers and water planners are taking a fresh look at ways of recycling wastewater. The truth is that we have always been dependent on recycled water; we have simply relied on larger natural treatment cycles—via rivers, oceans, evaporation, and rainfall—to wash away our waste and return fresh water to us. As our waste production systems have expanded, increased in toxicity, and begun to include nonbiodegradable components, nature's ability to effectively treat our wastewater has been compromised. So we have begun treating it ourselves first before dumping it back into local water bodies to rejoin natural hydrological cycles.

Increasingly, however, engineers are realizing that these methods are inadequate. Sucking water from aquifers has lowered water tables and drawn saltwater into our wells. Pesticides and pharmaceuticals have infiltrated our groundwater. Our natural sources of water—watersheds, springs, rivers, and lakes—have become increasingly contaminated and polluted. While the earth is constantly flooded with abundant sources for renewable energy, we have only a finite supply of water. Holistic water management strategies adopt and enhance nature's original techniques to efficiently make the most of our water; to safely capture, treat and use our wastewater; and to make our communities more beautiful, resilient, and cost-effective in the process.

Impacts of Modern Wastewater Practice

Bringing water in via aqueducts or pipes and then flushing it away in a different set of drains and pipes has been the operating principle behind urban water management for over two millennia. These systems, however, are increasingly not meeting their goals. Aging, failing infrastructure and rapid population expansion are adding stress to water treatment systems in developed countries, even as developing countries are struggling to implement basic wastewater management systems. The United Nations Millennium Development Goals indicate that nearly one in four people in developing countries do not have access to any form of sanitation.[1] As a result, human health is still significantly impacted by the inadequate handling of sanitation around the world.

The conventional paradigm for treating wastewater regarded all nonpotable water as contaminated or polluted. This led to an external regulatory environment requiring all wastewater be treated to certain standards—typically concerning total suspended solids (TSS), biological oxygen demand (BOD), acceptable parts per million (ppm) of heavy metals and toxins, and the disinfection of biological pathogens—before being discharged into the "pristine" environment.

While these standards have been very effective in mitigating waterborne disease outbreaks and infections, this one-size-fits-all "treat-and-dump" approach has led to treatment methods and systems with much higher energy and chemical costs than is always necessary. Facilities have gotten cleaner and more efficient over the years, but the processes required for the highest levels of treatment still produce nitrous oxide (NOx), sulphur dioxide (SOx_2), carbon monoxide (CO), hydrochloric acid (HCl), chlorinated organics, and other contaminants in the process.[2]

Designers are increasingly recognizing that water efficiency and reuse strategies can provide numerous savings and benefits; that decentralized treatment systems perform better in many situations; that alternative sanitation technologies, like waterless urinals and efficient toilets, can greatly reduce water use; and that we can treat wastewater as an important nutrient stream. Despite these advancements, the majority of modern wastewater treatment is still a highly centralized and energy-intensive process.

Proper wastewater treatment systems are vital for maintaining human health and safety. Yet treating wastewater can be a toxic and dangerous process depending on the treatment method used. Because of global strains on water systems, designers are paying increased attention to ways that wastewater can be safely treated and reused: for irrigation and other nonpotable uses, to help achieve water balance by recharging groundwater, and even to reduce potable water demands.

If water pollution is not treated, it is just conveyed elsewhere; rather than solving the problem, it simply moves downstream to another community or ecosystem. Yet current systems for treating wastewater are undergoing the same strains as potable water systems. Aging infrastructure is expensive to maintain; it can leak or overflow, polluting groundwater and creating health hazards. Wastewater is routinely discharged into rivers, freshwater bodies, and groundwater from urban, agricultural, and industrial sources. A few examples of the many effects of these strains on the system are described below:

Figure 4-1 Nonpoint source pollution in Macon, North Carolina. Food production is one of our biggest users of water and has resultant runoff from rainfall and overwatering. On September 17, 2009, the New York Times *reported that "agricultural runoff is the single largest source of water pollution in the nation's rivers and streams, according to the EPA."[3] Paul Bolstad, University of Minnesota.*

Nonpoint source pollution: Rural wastewater treatment has only recently begun to get the attention it deserves. Rural wastewater from leaky septic systems and other distributed discharges is often called nonpoint source (NPS) pollution, to distinguish it from a point source such as a sewer effluent outfall. It can refer to blackwater from septic systems or animal waste on farms, or to stormwater that is contaminated with pesticides or nutrients from crops.[4] In the United States, the Clean Water Act was amended in 1987 to address nonpoint source pollution, which is regulated by either the Environmental Protection Agency (EPA) or individual states.[5] However, these regulations are not entirely effective in eliminating nonpoint source pollution. The full impacts of groundwater contamination are not yet fully understood, and both regulations and strategies for dealing with nonpoint source pollution are continually being developed.

Combined sewer water: In many parts of the world, blackwater and stormwater drainage systems in urban areas are combined in order to reduce the amount of piping required. This has had a lasting effect: older cities, such as New York and other cities in the eastern United States, still have a combined sewer system. The result is that while the sewer lines discharge to wastewater treatment plants during dry periods, the wastewater treatment plants can only accept a certain increase in flow during wet weather. To protect the treatment

Figure 4-2 Combined sewer outfall, Harlem River, New York City. Dahlia Thompson, Sherwood Design Engineers.

plant, the sewers are designed to overflow to the adjacent water bodies when those extreme wet-weather flows exceed the system's capacity, thereby sending raw, untreated sewage into the water bodies along with the stormwater. Engineers are working around the world to retrofit or transition from combined sewers where appropriate. Transformation is occurring at a very slow pace, due to the enormous costs associated with separating the systems. *Wastewater discharge:* Treated wastewater and untreated stormwater are typically discharged to open water bodies. Cities all across the Midwest get their drinking water from the Mississippi River, which also serves as the receptacle for wastewater from upstream cities. As populations have increased, so has the amount of water being discharged, as well as the level of agricultural, industrial, and automotive pollutants in that river water. This all-too-common situation creates health hazards for towns receiving polluted water or, at a minimum, increases the cost of treating water to potable standards. Despite public perception that well water is always clean, wastewater discharges often infiltrate groundwater tables, and well water is contaminated by heavy metals, toxins, pharmaceuticals, and other pollutants that many conventional wastewater treatment systems are neither designed for nor capable of removing.

New technologies allow wastewater to be effectively purified and treated to high-quality standards. Yet the groundwater replenishment system in Orange County,

California, for example, must inject its treated wastewater into an aquifer and withdraw the potable water elsewhere, even though the water quality is higher at the injection point than at the withdrawal point. Designers and engineers are working to shift water reuse policies toward an emphasis on water's quality, not the water's primary source, to reflect the current reality that sometimes treated blackwater or graywater is cleaner than degraded conventional water supply sources.

Redefining Wastewater

Because waste is an artificial concept, it has no taxonomic definition. Waste is not a scientific classification of materials or systems; it is a value judgment. We use the term *waste* to refer to things we think we don't need anymore and are ready to dispose of. Developing water systems around the concept of waste, therefore, is a historical legacy that needs rethinking. We can begin by redefining wastewater and dividing it into two sources: natural runoff and human runoff. Natural runoff is stormwater. Though it hasn't been used directly by us, it has fallen on our roofs and roads and been contaminated by artificial pollutants. What comprises human runoff is called graywater and blackwater—a combination of the grime of daily life, food scraps, and natural bodily excretions, as well as the water we use to wash it all away.

Figure 4-3 The transformation of water from source to sink. As water is transformed through various types of uses and treatment processes, the variation in the uses for which it is appropriate should be recognized as an opportunity. By maximizing reuse loops, projects can minimize the water required from off-site sources as well as the water discharged off-site. Balancing water resource flows with demands is an integral part of developing a sustainable water balance. © Sherwood Design Engineers.

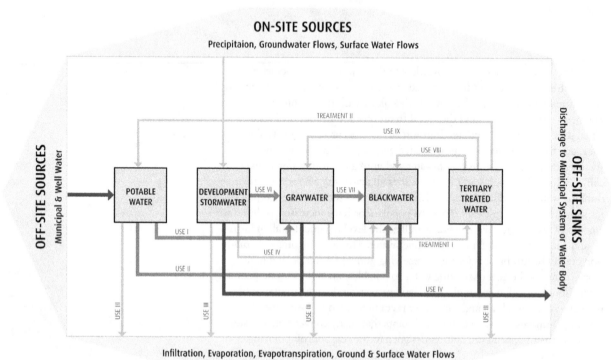

Stormwater: When rain falls on our fields, it is recognized as a life-sustaining resource. When it falls on our cities, it is generally considered a nuisance. During a storm, when more rain falls than the ground can absorb, it becomes runoff, which is what happens to most of the water in our highly paved cities. This natural runoff is called stormwater, and a significant portion of this chapter is devoted to appropriate ways to manage stormwater as a valuable resource, instead of as a waste product.

Graywater: Typically defined as wash water that comes out of sinks, showers, and laundry facilities, graywater comprises the majority of residential waste-water sources and can be reused directly for irrigation and cooling towers. After treatment, it can be used for domestic purposes such as toilet flushing. Because graywater contains few harmful pathogens, it can be recycled more easily than blackwater and treated to potable or near-potable condition using natural biological systems.

Blackwater: Blackwater consists of water that comes from toilets, kitchen sinks, and dishwashers. It can be reused only after tertiary-level wastewater treatment, and then usually only for nonpotable purposes. Blackwater contains significantly higher levels of contaminants, nutrients, and chemicals and therefore requires more significant treatment than graywater or stormwa-ter. Ironically, one of the simplest steps in treating blackwater is to remove the water from the equation. Composting food scraps instead of flushing them down the drain makes them much safer and easier to handle. Separating urine from feces with specialized toilets or using waterless com-posting toilets can also keep these resource streams separated. If we value water as a resource, then it makes sense to keep pathogens and chemicals out of our water systems. When overburdened or improperly designed, the prac-tice of combining waste with our water creates a downstream problem.

INTEGRATED STORMWATER MANAGEMENT

This section explores holistic methods for optimizing stormwater as a resource. Successfully implemented, these low-impact development strategies can decrease peak runoff rates and total runoff volume, dramatically reduce pollution and other negative effects of overdevelopment, restore habitat, and enhance the natural function and overall environment of the communities we live in.

Effects of Development on Stormwater Runoff

Over millennia, stormwater runoff has carved out a drainage network in the natural landscape. At the top of a watershed this network is defined by small rills, which combine into defined channels; water drains into creeks that flows into larger rivers,

Figure 4-4 The absorptive capacity of the natural landscape. Nevue Ngan Associates.

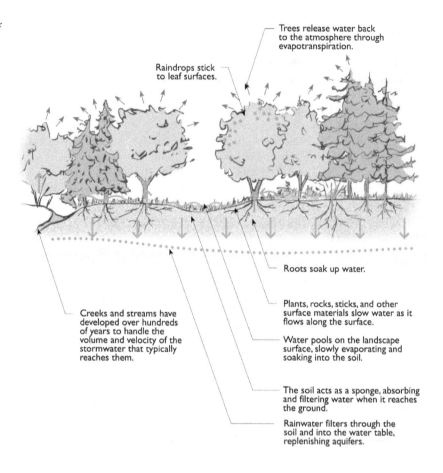

Trees release water back to the atmosphere through evapotranspiration.

Raindrops stick to leaf surfaces.

Roots soak up water.

Creeks and streams have developed over hundreds of years to handle the volume and velocity of the stormwater that typically reaches them.

Plants, rocks, sticks, and other surface materials slow water as it flows along the surface.

Water pools on the landscape surface, slowly evaporating and soaking into the soil.

The soil acts as a sponge, absorbing and filtering water when it reaches the ground.

Rainwater filters through the soil and into the water table, replenishing aquifers.

ultimately discharging to the ocean. At each step in this dendritic network, stormwater runoff gradually carves channels into the natural landscape. These channels have established a state of relative equilibrium changing gradually over time, accompanied by occasional periods of flood-influenced transformation. In natural watersheds, the vast majority of rainfall is intercepted by vegetation or infiltrates the soil, as illustrated in Figure 4-4.

Human development has ballooned since the Industrial Revolution, covering large sections of land with impervious surfaces such as rooftops, driveways, roadways, and parking lots. In the United States, over 100 million acres of land have been developed, and approximately 25 percent of that land is impervious. These surfaces absorb very little water, and the amount of surface runoff from them is many times higher than that from the natural landscape. Figure 4-5 shows the outcome of rainfall on landscapes with varying degrees of development. These changes accelerate the cycles of transformation and disrupt the dendritic network described earlier, creating unstable and disfunctional hydrologic systems.

When rain falls on paved urban surfaces, the water cannot be absorbed (as it would be naturally); this impacts the water cycle. Instead of soaking into the ground

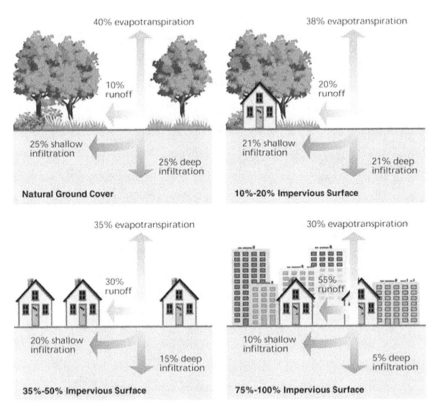

40% evapotranspiration

10% runoff

25% shallow infiltration

25% deep infiltration

Natural Ground Cover

38% evapotranspiration

20% runoff

21% shallow infiltration

21% deep infiltration

10%-20% Impervious Surface

35% evapotranspiration

30% runoff

20% shallow infiltration

15% deep infiltration

35%-50% Impervious Surface

30% evapotranspiration

55% runoff

10% shallow infiltration

5% deep infiltration

75%-100% Impervious Surface

Figure 4-5 The effects of development on stormwater runoff. (The relationship between impervious cover and surface runoff.) Impervious cover in a watershed results in increased surface runoff. As little as 10 percent impervious cover in a watershed can result in stream degradation. Federal Interagency Stream Restoration Working Group (FISRWG).

during a storm, all that water runs into storm drain pipes or directly into waterbodies. More water hits the system at once and the systems must therefore be built larger and stronger to handle these peak flows. While trees, reeds, and roots slow the movement of water, storm drain systems speed its flow. When these rushes of water impact stream channels and other natural systems, they cause erosion and sedimentation, leading to stream bank destabilization and habitat destruction. When they impact storm drain systems, they can cause overflows, localized flooding, and associated infrastructure and property damage. Figure 4-7 shows how the effects of urbanization can impact water flow with respect to timing, peak rate, and total quantity.

The net result of the large increase in surface runoff, which often contains elevated levels of contaminants, is a release of powerful erosive forces on the remaining natural landscape, especially the receiving streams. Studies have demonstrated that as little as 10 percent impervious surfaces in a watershed can have negative effects on water quality.[6]

The type and quantity of pollutants found in stormwater runoff vary by individual setting and location. In urban areas, the primary pollutants are related to machinery and industry, especially automobiles, which release hydrocarbons, heavy metals, and other chemicals, such as antifreeze, into the environment. In more suburban areas, pesticides, herbicides, and fertilizers are additional significant pollution sources. When a storm hits, these pollutants are rapidly flushed into local waterways.

Figure 4-6 Water treatment in a natural landscape. Natural landscapes absorb and filter water through rocks, roots, sand, and soil. Plants and trees also transpire moisture to the air, providing a cooling effect. © Sherwood Design Engineers.

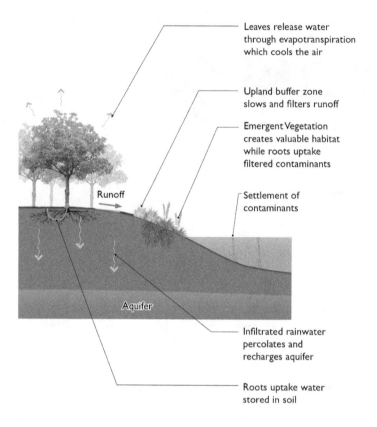

Leaves release water through evapotranspiration which cools the air

Upland buffer zone slows and filters runoff

Emergent Vegetation creates valuable habitat while roots uptake filtered contaminants

Settlement of contaminants

Runoff

Aquifer

Infiltrated rainwater percolates and recharges aquifer

Roots uptake water stored in soil

Low-Impact Development Design Principles

Low-impact development (LID) is a philosophy of stormwater management that seeks to repair hydrological and ecological function to urbanized watersheds. In a retreat from decades of large, centralized hard-pipe solutions that treat stormwater as a burden and ship it off-site as quickly as possible, LID is a paradigm shift that keeps stormwater on-site for longer periods and manages it as a valuable resource.

LID design aims to mimic natural hydrologic processes by making green space function to control stormwater at its source (see figure 4-6). These functional planted areas manifest as a distributed, interconnected system of vegetated nodes and pathways integrated into the built form. They incorporate natural processes to manage stormwater. Through efficient site design and the implementation of strategically placed landscape-based stormwater control features, stormwater runoff can be effectively utilized at its source instead of shipping it off-site in storm drains and culverts as a waste.

Optimal stormwater management systems focus on reduction of runoff and aim for simplicity of design. There are several central design principles that shape LID stormwater management designs. Each of them serves the underlying goal of employ-

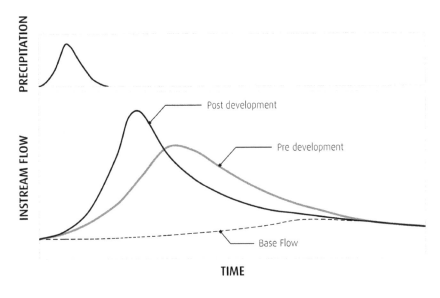

PRECIPITATION

INSTREAM FLOW

Post development

Pre development

Base Flow

TIME

Figure 4-7 The effects of development on in-stream flows. The curve on the top graph shows a rainstorm beginning, peaking, and stopping. Just after the rain starts, the in-stream flow begins. The predevelopment curve is gentler and slower, because water is being absorbed into the ground, and the overflow water that is moving into stream channels is taking longer to get there. The postdevelopment curve is much higher and sharper. It picks up just behind the rain and has a high peak because it has gathered all that water into the system very quickly. This causes increased runoff volume and alters the natural hydrologic cycle of the landscape. © Sherwood Design Engineers.

ing natural processes inherent in the landscape as a means of restoring hydrologic function to the built environment.

Treat stormwater as a resource: Conventional development favors drains and hidden pipes for removing stormwater from a site as efficiently as possible. LID favors natural solutions over constructed alternatives, using trees, swales, and ponds to deal with water at ground level in a multifunctional and aesthetically pleasing manner. Stormwater designs can support plants in urban environments in a way that does not use potable water for landscaping. The green spaces they create can improve air quality, provide shade, and reduce urban heat island effect.

Manage stormwater at its source: Instead of concentrating water treatment in large, centralized facilities, LID employs a decentralized system of structures that capture and treat precipitation where it falls, more closely mimicking natural systems. Impervious areas directly connected to storm drainage systems are the most critical to managing the quantity, rate, and pollutant loading of runoff. LID landscapes can channel overland flow through vegetated areas or allow water to form shallow ponds and slowly soak into the ground. This method of delaying stormwater in numerous small detention swales and holding ponds fulfills the primary function of keeping stormwater away from buildings and streets while reducing overflow and flooding during peak storm events. It also allows roots, soil, sand, and gravel to naturally filter, absorb, and treat water. Managing stormwater at its source provides a preliminary natural treatment that reduces the concentrations of pollutants carried. LID strategies thus reduce the amount and improve the quality of the stormwater entering municipal systems and receptive water bodies.

Retain and reuse water on-site: Centralized water facilities use pumps, chemicals, and other artificially constructed, energy-intensive processes and materials for treating and transporting water. LID uses vegetation, gravity, and living ecosystems to manage water on-site. In place of a one-use, linear system that uses drinkable water for irrigation and toilets and then pipes it away as wastewater, LID emphasizes circular, multiuse water systems that retain and reuse water. Stormwater best management practices (BMPs) such as constructed wetlands, vegetated flood plains, and cultivated ponds work with the natural ebb and flow of water across a site, remaining dry on most days and activating during rain events. By effectively reducing the quantity of water entering the system, stormwater BMPs save energy required to pump and treat water and, when incorporated into watershed-scale plans, can save on larger infrastructure expenses.

Benefits of LID Stormwater Management

Managing stormwater as a resource has numerous other benefits. LID features create engaging landscapes that celebrate natural water flows. As designed landscape elements, they nurture trees, plants, and flowers that provide shade; improve air quality; and increase the overall aesthetics of a site. Water features also perform evaporative cooling functions that can improve air quality and moderate temperatures in crowded urban environments.

The benefits of LID stormwater management are categorized here:

- Environmental
    - Improved air quality
    - Groundwater and aquifer recharge
    - Soil preservation and erosion control
    - Improved aesthetics
    - Wind and noise reduction
    - Energy-related pollution and emissions reduction
- Ecological
    - Habitat creation and increased biodiversity
    - Provision of critical links in hydrologic and nutrient cycles
    - Restoration of water balance
    - Reduction of discharge volumes to local waterways
- Economic
    - Lesser installation expense than conventional management systems
    - Energy savings in the elimination or size reduction of conventional systems
    - Energy savings through the stabilization of local climate and avoidance of urban heat islands
    - Increased property values
    - Increased patronage to businesses
- Social
    - Traffic calming
    - Passive recreation

- Increased urban green space, shade, and meeting and resting places
- Provision of evaporative cooling that hydrates and freshens air quality
- Mitigation or masking of urban noise via sound of trickling or running water and waterfalls
- Natural gathering points provided by fountains and ponds foster community interaction
- Educational opportunities in sanctuaries and other green spaces

Order of Design Operations

Designing an LID stormwater management system is a multistep process. Built facilities are ultimately the face of a finished project, but it is critical to first create the proper context and framework for their inclusion. The design process is broken out below into three steps in order to highlight the primary goals of each: site preservation, runoff reduction, and stormwater management facility integration.

Step 1: Site Preservation

To achieve site preservation, it is necessary to minimize site disruption during development. Soils house extremely complicated microecosystems, with delicately balanced levels of bacteria, fungi, nematodes, and protozoa. Mature soil strata are crucial for maintaining hydrologic, nutrient, and other biological cycles. When disrupted, it can take the soils years or even decades to reestablish their fully mature condition. The wisest approach is to disturb them to the least extent possible.

On previously undisturbed sites, scraping the dirt away to allow the site to be recontoured, then placing it all back and landscaping over the top, may create the appearance of a pristine condition. Such careful work, in fact, creates a deeply disturbed landscape. Wherever possible, designers and developers should avoid soil compaction, limit grading areas to the smallest possible footprint, and locate stormwater management facilities in the least sensitive areas of the site.

The final key element of site preservation is to preserve existing native vegetation, especially the mature tree canopy. A full canopy can actually intercept and absorb up to the first half inch of rainfall. All vegetation works to stabilize the soil, absorb and cleanse stormwater runoff, and provide a multitude of other environmental benefits.

Step 2: Runoff Reduction Strategies

Runoff reduction strategies must then be incorporated into the proposed site layout plan. Reducing the amount of hardscape and impervious surface is the easiest way to reduce runoff from a project; therefore, smaller buildings and minimized paving areas are the first step in this process. The footprint of built impervious structures should be reduced to the maximum extent practicable while allowing for full realization of site programming elements and their associated functions. The smaller the physical imprint of hard surface, the lower the long-term increase in stormwater runoff. Access points and circulation elements, including driveways, parking lots, and sidewalks, often provide significant opportunities for reducing hardscape through careful design. (See pp. 111–117 for a number of examples.)

After hardscaped areas are reduced, installing green roofs and pervious paving where possible will help with additional runoff reduction and detention. Pervious paving can act as a hidden detention pond, creating void space under the surface to store the stormwater until it either infiltrates slowly or is released from the storage area through an outlet pipe.

Step 3: Stormwater Management Facilities Integration

Finally, appropriate facilities for the site's typical stormwater flows should be designed. Before discussing the various types of treatment strategies, which are often used in combination with one another, here are some important design considerations common to them all.

Sizing the Facilities

One of the major questions that arises when designing a stormwater control plan is, how much room do we need to dedicate to facilities? A quick rule of thumb is that the required treatment area is approximately 5 to 10 percent of the tributary impervious area, depending on local climate and regulations. The primary determinants in sizing the facility are the level of storm to be captured, safety considerations with respect to the depth of ponding water, the intensity and duration of average local storms, and the native soil's infiltrative capacity. Thoughtful site design measures, described above in design steps 1 and 2, can reduce the amount of excess stormwater runoff produced and, correspondingly, the extent of the facilities needed to manage that runoff.

Siting the Facilities

Built stormwater management facilities must be matched with the proper setting within the built environment based on development density and land-use type. Since roadways and parking areas are the most significant contributors to nonpoint source pollution, it is particularly important to identify different typologies within that general category of land use with respect to the appropriateness of different facility types.

Natural Water Treatment Processes

Effectively gauging the various LID techniques—from rain gardens to bioswales—involves understanding how plants naturally filter and treat water. These natural treatment mechanisms include both physical and biochemical processes. Understanding the role these processes play helps designers make the most informed decisions.

Plantings reduce runoff velocity, which aids in the physical processes of sedimentation and provides some filtration and detention of larger solids. As water infiltrates the ground, many pollutants, including heavy metals and phosphorus, have a tendency to adsorb to soil particles and are therefore physically filtered out. On a larger scale, LID facilities can also function as effective trash collectors. While trash in the free environment is never ideal, it is better to collect and remove trash from LID facilities as part of their regular maintenance program than to allow debris to wash directly into streams, lakes, and oceans.

In order to remove coarse particles, prevent clogging, and reduce the overall maintenance burden, retention and filtration facilities should include some sort of pretreatment before runoff reaches the main facility. Pretreatment can be provided by a grass filter strip, a vegetated swale, or by a sediment forebay, which is a depressed ponding area about 10 percent of the size of the main facility. Through pretreatment, coarse sediments are trapped in smaller, more easily accessible areas, thereby simplifying maintenance practices.

In addition to physical filtration, healthy soils and plant life harbor rich ecosystems of microorganisms that can break down volatile organic compounds (VOCs). Some plants will uptake specific pollutants into their biomass: mustard can remove heavy metals from soil, while aquatic hyacinth has been used to absorb arsenic from drinking water. Also, simple exposure to sunlight and moisture can trigger photolytic reactions that also break down VOCs.

Mulch, plant litter, and clay remove pollutants through the adsorption of hydrocarbons, heavy metals, and nutrients, which are then broken down by bacteria or taken up by plant roots and assimilated. Microorganisms in the soil decompose organic content and degrade chemical- and petroleum-based compounds. Simply allowing water to flow through a planter box before entering the storm drain will provide some of these benefits; more sophisticated designs are capable of higher treatment levels.

However, infiltration strategies are not good solutions in areas with contaminated soils, incidences of high groundwater, or impermeable soils. Regulations governing minimum depth to groundwater vary regionally, and in situ percolation tests should be performed to determine the soil's infiltrative capacity.

Non-Landscape-Based Alternatives

In urban conditions where available space is hard to find and comes at a premium, underground and/or mechanical solutions are also options. While usually more expensive to construct and devoid of aesthetic and other auxiliary benefits, they can nonetheless perform the same detention, retention, and water quality functions as naturalized facilities. Many proprietary stormwater devices on the market are designed to clean stormwater runoff. Their purpose is to separate oils, sediments, and other toxins from the water before it discharges into its final outlet, such as a river or ocean. Since naturalized solutions are more consistent with the philosophy of sustainable stormwater management and provide a variety of additional benefits, the remainder of this section will be dedicated to summary introductions of various types of naturalized facilities.

URBAN STORMWATER TREATMENT STRATEGIES IN SAN MATEO COUNTY

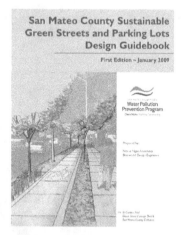

San Mateo County Sustainable
Green Streets and Parking Lots
Design Guidebook

First Edition – January 2009

Water Pollution
Prevention Program

🖱 For more information on this subject please see
www.sherwoodinstitute.org/resources.

In an effort to reduce water pollution caused by stormwater runoff, local governments in San Mateo County, California, decided to develop the *Sustainable Green Streets and Parking Lots Design Guidebook*. The guidebook provides designers, builders, municipal staff, and other interested groups in the county practical, state-of-the-art information on creating low-impact development roadways and parking lots. We collaborated with a team led by the Portland-based landscape architecture firm Nevue Ngan Associates to help create the guidebook. Our staff, notably Robert Dusenbury, PE, provided in-depth local engineering expertise to the guidebook as well as supplemental demonstration projects. The guidebook has proven a valuable model for planners and was awarded a 2009 Outstanding Statewide Planning Award for Innovation in Green Community Planning by the California Section of the American Planning Association (APA).

Figure 4-8 San Mateo County Sustainable Green Streets and Parking Lots Design Guidebook *San Mateo County, Nevue Ngan Associates, and Sherwood Design Engineers.*

Figure 4-9 Choosing stormwater facilities that best fit various urban conditions. (From the San Mateo County Sustainable Green Streets and Parking Lots Design Guidebook.) *San Mateo County and Nevue Ngan Associates.*

	VEGETATED SWALE	STORMWATER PLANTER	CURB EXTENSION	PERVIOUS PAVERS	GREEN GUTTER	RAIN GARDEN
Low-Density Residential	●	● (site dependent)	●	●	●	●
High-Density Residential		●	●	●		
Commercial Main Street	● (site dependent)	●	●	●	● (site dependent)	● (site dependent)
Arterial and Boulevard	●	●	●		●	
Parking Lots	●	●		●	●	●

Figure 4-10 Vegetated swale at Brisbane City Hall, San Mateo County, California. City of Brisbane.

URBAN STORMWATER TREATMENT STRATEGIES

This section offers a brief introduction to the most common types of urban stormwater treatment strategies. It is not intended to be comprehensive, but rather to provide designers with a suite of strategies for integrating LID stormwater management in the urban landscape. A tool for selection of facilities has been provided on page 124.

Vegetated swales are shallow, formalized drainage ways that employ landscaping to stabilize the soil while providing water quality treatment via biofiltration. Also known as bioswales, they are designed to remove silt and sediment-associated pollutants before discharging to storm sewers. Swales can also reduce total stormwater volume if the underlying soils allow for infiltration. Swales are relatively inexpensive, easy to construct, and widely used. The bottom treatment area can be planted in a variety of grasses and rushes, while the side slopes can be planted with shrubs or groundcover. Swales are linear in shape and are ideal for reducing hardscape along the low side of a parking lot or street. Typically, the longer the swale, the greater the level of water quality treatment and potential for infiltration. Where the slope is

Figure 4-11 Urban stormwater infiltration planter. Kevin Robert Perry/City of Portland.

Figure 4-12 Urban planter detail for a project in Taghazout, Morocco. © Sherwood Design Engineers.

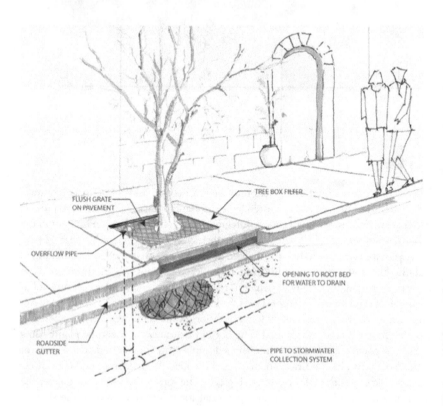

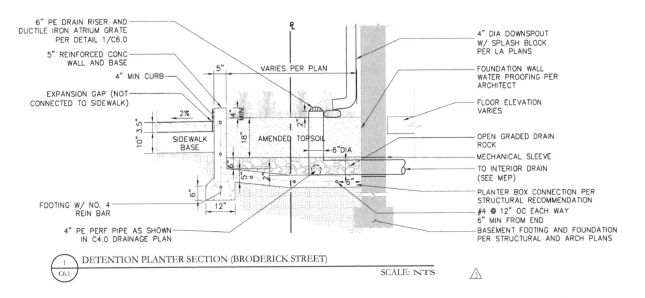

6" PE DRAIN RISER AND DUCTILE IRON ATRIUM GRATE PER DETAIL 1/C6.0

5" REINFORCED CONC WALL AND BASE

4" MIN CURB

EXPANSION GAP (NOT CONNECTED TO SIDEWALK)

2%

SIDEWALK BASE

10" 3.5"

VARIES PER PLAN

5"

4" MIN

2"

18"

AMENDED TOPSOIL

6"DIA

FOOTING W/ NO. 4 REIN BAR

6"

12"

4" PE PERF PIPE AS SHOWN IN C4.0 DRAINAGE PLAN

4" DIA DOWNSPOUT W/ SPLASH BLOCK PER LA PLANS

FOUNDATION WALL WATER PROOFING PER ARCHITECT

FLOOR ELEVATION VARIES

OPEN GRADED DRAIN ROCK

MECHANICAL SLEEVE

TO INTERIOR DRAIN (SEE MEP)

PLANTER BOX CONNECTION PER STRUCTURAL RECOMMENDATION

#4 @ 12" OC EACH WAY 6" MIN FROM END

BASEMENT FOOTING AND FOUNDATION PER STRUCTURAL AND ARCH PLANS

1
C6.1   DETENTION PLANTER SECTION (BRODERICK STREET)

SCALE: NTS

greater than 2 percent, check dams or terraces can be used to help slow water flow and prevent erosion or silt buildup at the lower end.[7]

Vegetated filter strips are gently sloped areas of land with natural or planted vegetation designed to slow stormwater velocity, filter out sediment and associated pollutants, and provide limited infiltration of runoff. Filter strips are excellent choices for receiving sheet-flow runoff from parking lots and roadways and providing pretreatment before runoff enters another detention or filtration facility. The effectiveness of these facilities is enhanced when they receive evenly distributed flow, so a level spreader or equivalent device may be necessary along the upstream edge of the buffer zone.

Stormwater planters are narrow landscaped areas framed in hardscape, often in an urban setting. Their flat bottoms and vertical walls allow for more retention capacity in less space. Planters can be placed in between driveways, trees, and utilities or built into sidewalks. Plants that will grow at least as tall as the planter depth should be selected in order to fill the volume. Planters can either be designed to allow water to infiltrate into the ground on-site, or as flow-through facilities. Flow-through planters have an underdrain system beneath the soil bed. The soil provides detention and filtration before the drain pipes carry the water off-site. These are useful where groundwater levels are high or soil is impermeable or contaminated.[8]

Curb extensions, as the name suggests, are spaces created by extending the existing sidewalk curb out into a roadway. This allows for the conversion of nonessential asphalt into landscape space that can be used for traffic control and stormwater management. The curb extension itself simply provides housing for a street tree, stormwater planter, vegetated swale, or other stormwater feature, depending on the particular site opportunities and constraints. Curb extensions are ideally suited for commercial or residential settings where improved street amenities, access to alternative transportation, traffic control, and stormwater management can be combined into a single street design element.

Figure 4-13 Planter box, Broderick Street, San Francisco. For a residential housing project, Sherwood routed the downspouts into flow-through planters for detention and used native ground cover to reduce sidewalk pavement and maximize treatment in a very narrow sidewalk zone.
© Sherwood Design Engineers.

Figure 4-14 Stormwater curb extensions. Nevue Ngan Associates.

Figure 4-15 Pervious concrete bike lane on R. W. Johnson Boulevard in Olympia, Washington. City of Olympia.

Pervious paving is a very promising technology that is gaining momentum as designers, regulators, and contractors increase their familiarity with how to properly design, install, and maintain it. These paving systems allow water to pass freely through interstitial space engrained throughout the paving matrix, permitting otherwise impermeable surfaces like a driveway or courtyard to absorb water. There are a variety of different pervious paving types and vendors, and they do not all perform equally, so it is important to select a reliable product with proven applications. Here are examples of pervious paving types:

Pervious concrete and asphalt: These products are similar to conventional asphalt and concrete except that they eliminate fines—the tiniest particles in the concrete mix. This makes for a grainier concrete with significant rigid

Figure 4-16 Interlocking permeable pavers installed as a parking surface. © Sherwood Design Engineers.

pore space that allows water to pass through. Pervious asphalt has been used on high-speed roads, where it reduces puddling and the risk of hydroplaning. While pervious asphalt is less expensive than pervious concrete, it is also not as strong and can become worn in areas where vehicle turning is prevalent. For cost-efficient installation, both pervious concrete and pervious asphalt are better suited for medium- to large-scale applications like sidewalks, bike lanes, parking stalls, and alleyways.

Interlocking pavers: Pavers, which are set with sand or another porous material to fill the gaps in between, are a flexible option because they come in a variety of colors and shapes and are easily repaired (by replacing individual pavers). These products are best suited for small- to medium-sized applications including patios, driveways, alleys, and some parking areas.

Reinforced gravel and grass paving: For low-traffic areas, a reinforced plastic grid or other structural material can be filled with small, angular gravel to create a uniform, permeable surface. This can be less expensive than laying concrete or asphalt, though it is not as durable. A paving system with large gaps can similarly be filled with sod to allow grass to grow between the pavers. Grass paving is appropriate for low-traffic areas that have the right soil, drainage, and sunlight conditions to permit growth, like the centerline of a driveway in between the wheel routes. While these products are suited to applications of all sizes, they lack the strength and durability necessary for heavy traffic loads.

Green gutters, as defined in the *San Mateo County Guidebook,* are a hybrid of curb extensions, swales, and planters. Green gutters are a low-cost option for roadways with 2 or more feet of excess outside lane width. Green gutters are

Figure 4-17 Cross-section of a green gutter design (from the San Mateo County Guidebook). Nevue Ngan Associates.

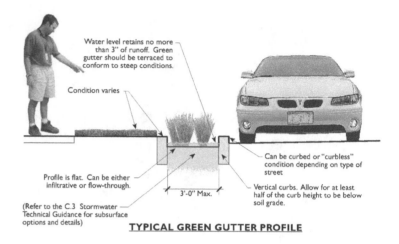

Water level retains no more than 3" of runoff. Green gutter should be terraced to conform to steep conditions.

Condition varies

Profile is flat. Can be either infiltrative or flow-through.

(Refer to the C.3 Stormwater Technical Guidance for subsurface options and details)

Can be curbed or "curbless" condition depending on type of street

Vertical curbs. Allow for at least half of the curb height to be below soil grade.

3'-0" Max.

TYPICAL GREEN GUTTER PROFILE

similar to curb extensions in that they create space for plantings by converting strips of existing roadway into landscaping, with a new curb installed along the roadway's edge. They are similar to swales in their linear form and conveyance function and also similar to planters, with their flat-bottomed treatment areas and curbs on either side. Because they are narrow, green gutters rely on length to be effective. For this reason, they are particularly compatible with streets without on-street parking or frequent driveway interruptions.[9]

Rain gardens are flat-bottomed, landscaped depressions with natural side slopes that can be built to any size or shape, making them a versatile solution for amorphous urban "dead space" that would otherwise be paved over or unlandscaped. For example, they can be built in parking lots, urban plazas, or as landscaped entryways to a courtyard or building. Known technically as bioretention cells, rain gardens are designed to allow water to pond up to several inches so that it has a chance to settle and infiltrate into the soil. Rain gardens reduce the peak discharge rate from a site via detention, but they will only significantly decrease total runoff volume if the soil allows for infiltration. Water quality improvements are achieved through particle settling, nutrient uptake, and filtration as water soaks into the ground. If the native soil has a low infiltration capacity, then the ponding depth should be minimized or the facility should be constructed with amended soil and an underdrain. Rain gardens can be planted with a versatile palette of grasses, sedges, rushes, ground covers, shrubs, and even trees. They have a relatively low installation cost when an underdrain is not necessary.[10]

Green roofs are a good way of managing stormwater on small sites with limited space for more land-intensive stormwater BMPs. Green roofs can either be extensive or intensive. Extensive green roofs typically involve a thin layer of soil and ground cover–type vegetation that is drought tolerant, with very low profiles. The soil layer is typically less than 6 inches thick, and the overall system is relatively light: 10 to 50 pounds per square foot when saturated. Green roofs can also be installed on a slant, making them more flexible.

Figure 4-18 Rain garden in Brisbane City Hall parking lot, San Mateo County, California. © Sherwood Design Engineers.

Intensive green roofs, in comparison, are more like traditional roof gardens. They feature thicker layers of growing media (up to multiple feet of soil, depending on the desired plantings and structural restrictions of the building), with a higher organic material content. Due to the thicker soil layer, a wider variety of vegetation can be supported, but the system weighs a lot more as a result—typically 80 pounds per square foot, and more when saturated. Intensive roofs are much more expensive to construct, because they require greater structural support, more material for the thicker medium, and typically more maintenance, since species planted on intensive roofs tend to require irrigation.[11]

Green roofs are able to store stormwater in the soil medium during rain events, helping to detain runoff. Some of the stormwater will be taken up by the plants' roots, and some will be detained by the soil medium and eventually evaporate, reducing the amount of runoff from the roof. Some portion of the stormwater will run off immediately from the roof drain, as drainage is always required in a green roof to avoid oversaturating the vegetation. The detention and slow release of stormwater decreases sudden flows, which can lead to overflows and flooding during storms. This is an important benefit in cities with combined sewers where overflows are a problem. The retention and detention rates of green roofs vary with the local climate, days between rain events, soil depth and type, and other factors. Many research projects are underway to determine the retention characteristics of different types of green roofs, so designers are advised to find performance information for similar green roof systems in the same region.

Figure 4-19 Constructed wetlands in a residential setting. Colorado Department of Transportation.

EXTENSIVE STORMWATER TREATMENT SYSTEMS

In rural or suburban settings where there is less competition for space and fewer utility conflicts, larger landscape-based solutions become viable options. These more extensive systems may be capable of handling higher volumes of water than the urban strategies listed previously. Additionally, these kinds of solutions can be designed to treat graywater, industrial runoff, or other water sources with higher pollutant levels or treatment requirements.

Constructed wetlands are engineered systems designed to treat and store stormwater by harnessing the functions of natural wetlands. This structure is similar to a regular wet pond (see below, page 119), except that it is shallow, with wetland vegetation planted throughout in order to provide additional biological function and enhanced habitat. Highly engineered systems in more developed settings may not replicate all of the ecological functions of natural wetlands. Due to their shallow configuration, wetlands require a relatively large footprint to treat peak stormwater flows. Multiple wetland cells can be laid out in sequence or terraced to best fit available space and accommodate moderately sloped land. Wetlands are protected by federal and state regulations, so once established they cannot be removed without mitigation measures. A perennial base flow is required to promote and maintain the wetland vegetation through all seasons.

Extended detention ponds (also known as *dry ponds*) are depressions with landscaped side slopes and naturalized pond bottoms that receive runoff and hold the design volume of stormwater for a specified duration—usually between twenty-four and seventy-

Figure 4-20 *Extended detention pond during summer and winter at the Pacific Shores Center, Redwood City, California. Robert Dusenbury, Sherwood Design Engineers.*

two hours—before fully draining. Unlike standard dry detention ponds, which only detain water long enough to reduce the peak runoff rate, extended detention ponds utilize longer detention times to allow particulates to settle and to provide moderate water quality benefits. The structure is normally dry between storm events, but vegetated basins or those with a shallow marsh at the bottom provide greater pollutant and sediment removal.

Extended detention ponds are relatively simple to design and inexpensive to build, and they can be used in almost any soil type, but they are generally only applicable if they are supplied by a watershed of at least 5 to 10 acres. The basin should be configured with a long flow path to maximize sedimentation. To avoid mosquito problems, the pond should be designed to fully drain after no more than three days, and the bottom should be kept out of the groundwater table. These facilities are best suited for residential, commercial, and industrial areas.

Wet ponds are designed to have a permanent pool of water that allows suspended particulates and debris from the current storm event to settle while preventing the resuspension of sediment from previous storm events. Runoff from each rain event remains in the pond until it is displaced by runoff from the ensuing event. Microbiotic and plant activity in the permanent pool assist in biological uptake and the degradation of pollutants. Properly designed wet ponds can achieve both pollutant removal and peak discharge reduction. Where land is available and not prohibitively expensive, wet ponds are often the most cost-effective solution. Similar to extended detention ponds, these facilities are best suited for residential, commercial, and industrial areas. However, they are not recommended in arid climates where supplemental water would be required to maintain the permanent pool.

Figure 4-21 Wet pond. Wisconsin Department of Natural Resources.

ADDRESSING CONSTRAINTS AND BARRIERS TO IMPLEMENTATION

Building in an urban environment is inherently challenging due to the dense programming, limited space, cost of real estate, extensive utilities, and a host of other constraints. The LID stormwater management strategies reviewed in this chapter are specifically designed to achieve holistic water management goals in developed environments. At the same time, they represent a break from conventional stormwater management practices and, consequently, can face significant barriers to implementation. This is especially true in jurisdictions where developers, contractors, designers, and regulatory agencies are still gaining familiarity with LID stormwater management strategies. Addressing these real-world constraints is critical to the success of any project.

In February 2008, San Mateo County, California, invited member municipalities to participate in a survey to determine potential barriers to implementation for green streets and parking lot projects within their respective jurisdictions. The results, which are available in appendix B of the *San Mateo County Sustainable Green Streets and Parking Lots Design Guidebook*, show major concerns in five different areas:

1. Inadequate local resources in terms of qualified designers and construction contractors
2. Cost
3. Physical site constraints
4. Utility conflicts
5. Maintenance burden

⌐ For more information on this subject please see
www.sherwoodinstitute.org/research.

These concerns, described below, are widespread and regularly affect the implementation of stormwater management projects in many cities.

Inadequate Local Resources

Developing the local resources needed to support successful implementation of LID stormwater management practices is an ongoing process nationwide. In some areas of the country, such as Portland, Oregon, it is already common practice. In many smaller municipalities with fewer resources to dedicate to stormwater management, the practice may be completely new or misunderstood. There are, however, a number of valuable guidebooks on this subject that can help designers, contractors, and regulators understand the critical elements of sustainable stormwater management.

Cost

Hiring a design and construction team with practical experience of the strategies discussed in this chapter is likely the best way to control overall costs on such a project. In areas where this method of stormwater management is still new and untried, the key is to identify a high-quality design guide and start simply. For example, the initial green streets project in a commercial district or LID facility in a neighborhood should not be overly complex. By starting small, a design team sets realistic goals and allows all of the involved stakeholders to appreciate the basic principles of an effective sustainable stormwater management plan.

Physical Site Constraints

Some of the most common physical site constraints that restrict the implementation of sustainable stormwater management facilities include the following:

Lack of space: Creating available space should be addressed during the first two stages of design: site preservation and runoff reduction strategies. The San Francisco Public Utilities Commission, for example, has begun a policy that coordinates green street retrofit projects with major sewer infrastructure upgrades. Combining these efforts yields significant economies of scale. Almost all street projects allocate space for landscaping, and facilitating additional stormwater function can be as simple as redirecting runoff from the streets through the landscaping prior to discharging it into the storm drain system. There are additional planting and drainage considerations that need to be incorporated into the landscape plan, but successful projects are as much the result of the design team's determination as their technical expertise.

Steep slopes: Steeply sloping streets can be a challenge when trying to implement LID because of the scouring effect that water has in planted areas under these conditions. There are a variety of design strategies for dealing with steep topography. One such strategy is to fit swales with check dams to slow down and temporarily pond water. Check dams should be approximately 18 inches high and spaced such that the peak of the downstream dam is at the same elevation as the base of the upstream dam. Depending on the underlying soil conditions, some of this water might infiltrate into the native soils along the way. Another strategy is to institute a series of tiered rain gardens or planters at different elevations, feeding from high ground to low. A geotechnical engineer should be consulted about soil stability and infiltration capacity. Infiltration facilities should not be placed at the top of steep slopes.

Poor soils: Poor soils are usually characterized as hard packed, clayey, and not conducive to infiltration. In a soil classification system instituted by the United States Department of Agriculture (USDA), soils are divided into hydrologic soil groups and categorized according to their infiltration capacity into classes A, B, C, and D. Classes A and B have relatively high infiltration rates and are conducive to infiltration facilities. Classes C and D are relatively impermeable and often require the use of imported soil along with an underdrain system. Imported soil with a specified mixture—approximately 50 to 60 percent washed sand, 20 to 30 percent loamy peat, and 20 percent leaf compost—is used to create an amended soil bed; jurisdictional agencies often prescribe their own recommended mixtures. Whatever the mixture, fines should not constitute more than 5 percent of the total weight. As water percolates through the permeable soil bed, it enters the underdrain and is then discharged into the storm drain system or dispersed back into the natural environment. An underdrain is also an effective solution for areas with contaminated soils or a high groundwater table, although the facility should be constructed with an impermeable liner in those instances.

Utility Conflicts

Utility conflicts can quickly add to the cost of a green street or parking lot project, especially if the project is a retrofit and utilities already exist. The urban streetscape is often compressed between utility poles and overhead wires in the air, utility boxes on the ground, and utility mains, laterals, and vaults or valves underground. The best design strategy for dealing with existing utilities is to avoid them altogether. In new development or reconstruction projects, designers should work with utility crews to place utilities in ways that minimize their impact and align them with streetscape stormwater strategies.

In areas of new development, where it is possible to affect utility layout, the following strategies are recommended:

- Utility services should be concentrated into service zones where they cross perpendicular to pedestrian zones to maximize the available space for furnishings and landscaping.
- Primary consideration should be given to methods for locating utilities on nonprimary lot access streets to reduce the impact along the main pedestrian corridors.

- Service access points related to utility services should be located adjacent to the curb (i.e., 12 to 18 inches behind the curb) to maximize the furnishings zone.
- As an alternative to locating the service points within the edge zone, designers should consider using driveways or frontage zones to reduce impacts to the pedestrian throughway and furnishing zones.
- Where feasible, combined service zones for two or more buildings should be considered to further minimize impacts.
- The practice of concentrating services and right of access points within certain defined zones will not only minimize impacts to pedestrian and furnishing zones but also create reliable accessible points for utility workers to repair or use.
- All utilities except major power transmission lines, transformers, switching and terminal boxes, meter cabinets, and other appurtenant facilities should be located underground where at all possible.

Maintenance Burden

One of the largest and most common concerns regarding landscape-based stormwater management facilities is long-term operation and maintenance (O&M). Like any other landscaping, these facilities do require regular maintenance. Here are some typical maintenance activities for landscape-based features:

- *Irrigation* during the first two dry seasons while vegetation is established. Native, drought-resistant plantings should not require regular irrigation following the establishment period, but other plantings might.

Figure 4-22 Stormwater weir trash removal, Staten Island. Easing the maintenance burden starts with good design. This pretreatment filter prevents sticks, leaves, and other items from clogging the system. Dahlia Thompson, Sherwood Design Engineers.

Figure 4-23 Stormwater BMPs. This matrix describes the four major functions of stormwater treatment technologies—conveying water, improving water quality, recharging the groundwater, and reducing water quantity—in the context of the transect zones discussed in chapter 2. As a city becomes denser and more urbanized, the stormwater facilities must fit the available space while providing adequate treatment. Some strategies, like permeable pavement or vegetated streetscapes, will be applicable across a range of transect zones. Others, like channels and swales, can be modified to fit their particular urban context. © Sherwood Design Engineers.

Function	T2	T3	T4	T5
CONVEYANCE	**NATURALIZED CHANNEL** A natural channel is a meandering, vegetated watercourse with natural banks and buffered from development zones by large uncultivated landscape.	**COMMUNITY SWALE** Community swales are similar in size to a natural swale, but more linear in design to conform with the adjacent development zones. i.e. walkways, roadways and buildings.	**URBAN CHANNEL** Urban channels are narrow vegetated or stone lined conveyances framed by vertical stone or concrete banks abutting cultivated landscapes or hardscapes.	**ROAD SWALE** Road swales are shallow paved or stone lined water courses integral with a vehicular or pedestrian circulation route. These conveyances often include intermittent inlets and are underlain by a collection pipe.
	LEVEL SPREADER Level spreaders are structures that are designed to uniformly distribute concentrated flow over a large area. Level spreaders come in many forms, depending on the peak rate of inflow, the duration of use, the type of pollutant, and the site conditions. All designs follow the same principle: Concentrated flow enters the spreader through a pipe, ditch or swale; the flow is retarded, energy is dissipated; the flow is distributed throughout a long linear shallow trench or behind a low berm; water then flows over the berm/ditch, releasing unconcentrated sheet flow.			
WATER QUALITY	**NATURAL BUFFER ZONE** Large uncultivated landscapes which provide separation between development zones and natural resources such as wetlands, streams, ponds, and coastlines.	**FILTER STRIP** Narrower strips of often manicured landscape providing filtration of sheet flow prior to discharge to resource areas.	**GREEN ROOF** Green roofs are multi-beneficial structural components that help to mitigate the effects of urbanization on water quality by filtering, absorbing or detaining rainfall. They are constructed of a lightweight soil media, underlain by a drainage layer, and a high quality impermeable membrane that protects the building structure.	**URBAN GARDENS** Gardens located in pockets throughout urban hardscapes provide opportunities for runoff to be filtered and contaminants removed prior to entering the concentrated stormwater collection system.
	VEGETATED STREETSCAPES The addition of pockets or strip of vegetation within or adjacent to existing or future streetscapes provide a means for runoff to re-enter the aquifer. These spaces also provide filtration of street runoff and ultimate uptake of contaminants by the vegetation.			
RECHARGE	**LANDSCAPE BUFFERS** Vegetated buffer zones adjacent to roadways and paths that allow for shallow unconcentrated runoff infiltration.			
	RIFFLE POOLS Connected landscapes which provide retention of runoff by integrating intermittent vertical drops and daming in a watercourse. The retained runoff is then allowed to infiltrate into the groundwater table.			
	PERMEABLE PAVEMENT Porous pavement is a permeable pavement surface with a stone reservoir underneath. The reservoir temporarily stores surface runoff before infiltrating it into the subsoil. Runoff is thereby infiltrated directly into the soil and receives some water quality treatment and ultimately reduces the increase in stormwater runoff resulting from development.			
	BIORETENTION Bioretention is an up-land water quality and water quantity control practice that uses the chemical, biological and physical properties of plants, microbes and soils for removal of pollutants from storm water runoff. Some of the processes that may take place in a bioretention facility include: sedimentation, adsorption, filtration, volatilization, ion exchange, decomposition, phytoremediation, bioremediation, and storage capacity.			
WATER QUANTITY	**CONSTRUCTED WETLAND** Constructed wetlands are an ideal alternative to traditional detention ponds by providing valuable habitat and water quality improvement in addition to the detention of increased stormwater runoff resulting from development. A wetland system performs a series of pollutant removal mechanisms including sedimentation, filtration, absorption, microbial decomposition and vegetative uptake.		**CULTIVATED WET POND** Wet ponds are generally used where the groundwater conditions, available space or adjacent development do not provide and opportunity for a constructed wetland, while still creating opportunities for habitat development, water quality improvement and temporary detention of stormwater runoff. Ponds generally require a clay liner, deeper water elevations and management.	
	VEGETATED FLOOD PLAIN Flood plains can be integrated with parks, playing fields or unmanaged landscapes. Frequent storm events can be detained by smaller decentralized means, while larger storm events should be directed to non priority vegetated landscapes for temporary detention.			
	URBAN FLOOD PLAIN Urban hardscapes can be used for temporary storage of large storm events. Smaller events should be mitigated by decentralized means, while the larger events can be directed toward non priority spaces which are planned and designed for the temporary storage of stormwater flows.			

- *Biannual inspections* (one following a heavy storm early in the wet season and another early in the dry season) to ensure plant health, nonerosive flow conditions, continued hydraulic capacity, and that no ponding occurs for longer than seventy-two hours. Regrading and sediment removal should be performed as necessary to ensure positive, nonerosive drainage. Weeding can be done during these visits as well.
- *Trash removal.* Depending upon location, appropriate frequency of trash removal may vary from monthly to biannually (as a simple part of the biannual inspection).

OLD MINT PLAZA

The new plaza at the Old Mint Building in San Francisco integrates stormwater BMPs to promote and help establish future development standards for the city and greater Bay Area. Sherwood Design Engineers collaborated with project lead CMG Landscape Architecture to take a nearly abandoned alleyway and transform it into one of San Francisco's hottest spots, with a nightclub, café, and several restaurants extending the vibrancy of the central retail shopping district to the south. The design incorporates several innovative green street strategies, including stormwater infiltration within the public right-of-way, the use of porous pavers, and stormwater conveyance to the infiltration facilities.

The plaza captures the runoff from its 20,000-square-foot surface and has the potential to collect the runoff from the rooftops of many of the historic buildings surrounding this microwatershed. A portion of this runoff is collected in a shallow planted rain garden at the western edge of the plaza for on-site retention and bioremediation. Additional stormwater runoff infiltrates through porous pavers or flows into a slender slot drain that acts as a collection channel. Flow from these channels is then directed to a rain garden with sedges and a native oak tree at the plaza's eastern end prior to overflow into the city's storm drain system. Taken together, the design delays,

Figure 4-24 The Old Mint Plaza incorporates porous paving compliant with the Americans with Disabilities Act (ADA), rain gardens, and subsurface infiltration galleries into a successful urban plaza design. Colin Piper, Sherwood Design Engineers.

cleanses, and retains runoff from most storm events on-site, rather than releasing it to the city's combined sewer system. Larger storm events will also be conveyed through the same cleansing and filtration system prior to discharge.

Because the city's sewage treatment and rainwater management systems are combined, surges in runoff from storms often exceed the capacity of the system, resulting in the direct release of untreated sewage into the bay. To protect the long-term health of the bay and propel San Francisco toward a more sustainable future, several city agencies, including the Department of City Planning and the Department of Public Works, are spearheading the San Francisco Streetscape Master Plan. This plan attempts to incorporate better street design and integrated stormwater management in order to locally treat and retain rainfall prior to its discharge into the combined system. Concurrently with this effort, The city's Public Utilities Commission is working on a citywide stormwater management plan that includes integrated stormwater management considered at a watershed scale.

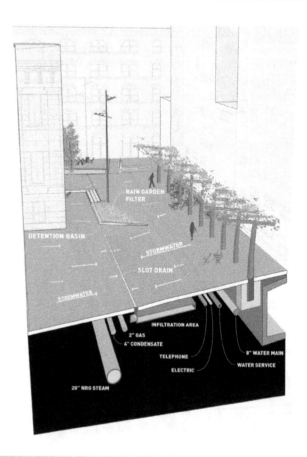

Figure 4-25 Subsurface stormwater utility layout and connections at Old Mint Plaza. CMG Landscape Architecture.

San Francisco's Urban Watershed Planning Charrette

Rosey Jencks, San Francisco Public Utilities Commission, Urban Watershed Management Program

San Francisco's eight major urban watersheds are made up of mosaics of residential, commercial, and industrial lands that are interlaced with parks and natural areas. Each land use is supported by unique topography, hydrology, soils, vegetation, and water resources that create specific opportunities and challenges for drainage and stormwater management. These conditions interface in neighborhoods with unique identities and built forms that can inform where and how to best implement LID throughout the city. LID (or best management practices) refers to the use of strategically placed green stormwater facilities that mimic natural watershed processes. By increasing natural storage and infiltration of rainwater, cities like San Francisco can reduce the quantity and improve the quality of urban stormwater runoff. Examples of green stormwater strategies are rainwater harvesting, green roofs, cisterns, rain gardens, permeable paving, stream daylighting, detention basins, swales, and constructed wetlands.

In September 2007, the San Francisco Public Utilities Commission (SFPUC), the agency charged with managing the city's drainage systems, used an urban watershed planning charrette to convene stakeholders in order to analyze all of these conditions and identify opportunities for basin-scale LID opportunities. The Urban Watershed Management Group, a division of the SFPUC, hosted two charrettes to identify opportunities for stormwater management strategies in San Francisco's eastern watersheds: Channel, Islais Creek, Yosemite, and Sunnydale.

The Charrette as a Game

Charrettes are intensive brainstorming workshops in which a group of stakeholders collaborate to complete a design project in a short amount of time. Approximately seventy participants attended the San Francisco charrette, among them representatives of public agencies, engineering and design companies, nonprofit organizations, and community groups, as well as stormwater experts and unaffiliated San Francisco citizens. Participants divided into watershed teams and developed a set of green stormwater management proposals for their particular basin using the format of a game. The game was played turn by turn, with one group member at a time placing an LID measure (e.g., a cistern, a set of eco-roofs, etc.) on a large map of the watershed and calculating its benefits and costs. Capital costs and peak flow and volume reductions were defined for each LID measure, and each group was charged with meeting specific stormwater reduction targets within a finite budget specific to the conditions of the watershed. At the end of the evening, ideas that were shared by several groups or that were unique were then presented to the entire assembly.

Tips on Charrette Process

The charrette was designed to be both quantitative and visual to enable both technical and nontechnical participants to feel comfortable with the process. For the quantitative participants, the entire game was calibrated to the city's hydrologic models so that each "move" could be used to estimate the impact on the performance of the combined sewer system. For the less technical, participants were given an LID toolkit showing photos of built projects, which allowed people with little experience to visualize the results of their moves.

Because some people find open-ended exercises difficult, the process might have been improved by giving the teams more constraints, like smaller budgets, and directing participants to drainage areas needing more capacity. Doing so might have helped people prioritize their moves.

Results

The SFPUC built on the work of the charrette by further analyzing and prioritizing the most promising projects identified. Some of the proposals analyzed include

- daylighting buried creeks
- installing large-scale stormwater harvesting systems under athletic fields and parks
- partnering with new housing developments to go beyond regulatory requirements
- greening streetscapes
- diverting groundwater from the sewers

Next steps include further prioritizing proposals based on benefits to the sewer system and opportunities for partnerships and creating a priority list for SFPUC wastewater capital improvement projects. Overall, the charrette was a huge success that gained goodwill and buy-in from city staff and the community.

Figure 4-26 Charrette participants discussing potential strategies. Courtesy of the San Francisco Public Utilities Commission.

GRAYWATER TREATMENT AND REUSE

Graywater is typically defined as washwater that comes out of sinks, showers, and laundry facilities. Because it contains fewer constituents (including harmful pathogens), graywater can be recycled more easily than blackwater, which is defined as water from toilets and kitchens. When handled properly, graywater can be an easily available, reliable source of reclaimed water. Reusing graywater on-site saves money and energy by lowering potable water demand and by reducing return flow to the sewage system.

At its simplest, a graywater system might be nothing more than a pipe connected to the shower drain or laundry machine that reroutes the used water to irrigate the garden and recharge the groundwater table. As the number of collection fixtures increases and the scale of the system is expanded, additional elements, such as pumps and advanced treatment devices, might be necessary to utilize the water more efficiently and eliminate health risks.

Graywater treatment is varied and can incorporate natural systems for seepage and filtration, and even living systems for active biological processing and treatment. The standard graywater treatment systems, however, are mechanical or packaged units that can be stored within basements or buried in sump tanks in the landscaping.

Graywater's easiest application is for landscape needs, although advanced applications are beginning to introduce graywater back into the building. Effectively using graywater indoors requires a double-plumbed system within the building to separately handle potable and reclaimed water. The on-site reuse of graywater is an evolving concept that faces an often resistant regulatory environment. Designers, green

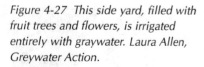

Figure 4-27 This side yard, filled with fruit trees and flowers, is irrigated entirely with graywater. Laura Allen, Greywater Action.

builders, green plumbers, and a variety of water advocacy groups are working to advance sound, sustainable graywater regulations.

In considering a graywater system, it is important to first evaluate whether the amount of graywater available is feasibly balanced with the demand and reuse potential. Then, the system requirements must respond to site characteristics and applicable laws.

Unlike seasonal rainwater, graywater is a water source generated every time we take a shower or wash our hands. This means it is produced daily, in consistent amounts, year-round. Because graywater has application in a variety of settings, it has the ability to be a meaningful solution to problems of water shortage and development impact.

Light and dark graywater: For engineering purposes, graywater is more specifically defined as untreated wastewater that has not come in contact with toilet waste or other highly contaminating discharge. The largest source of graywater is washwater resulting from processes that have the lowest relative concentrations of pathogens and pollutants compared to other sources. This "light" graywater from showers and baths, bathroom sinks, and laundry machines is available throughout the year and is nutrient rich, representing an ideal candidate for on-site reuse, especially to supplement site irrigation demands. Other potential sources, specifically "dark" graywater from kitchen sinks and dishwashers, are available but should be approached with caution, as they tend to be more heavily contaminated. Washwater from these sources has the potential to contain much higher organic content, oil and grease, salts, and corrosive detergents, all of which will be more detrimental to the receiving environment and will require more complex treatment and system maintenance.

Graywater Quality Characterization

Graywater has physical, chemical, and microbial characteristics that have the potential to pose a threat to human and environmental health if a system's characteristics and treatment capabilities are not properly matched to the method of reuse. The constituents of graywater vary considerably, based on the waste streams used and the habits and type of users generating those waste streams, but they will generally include organic material, microbial organisms, chemicals and salts, nutrients, and solids.

Controlling graywater quality at the source is a key element in avoiding potential negative impacts to the local water table and the need for advanced treatment. Responsible practices for controlling the quality of graywater include

- carefully considering all detergents, cleaners, and hygiene products that are used
- choosing natural and biocompatible soaps and cleaners
- using liquid instead of powdered detergents to avoid excessive salt content
- eliminating bleach and other harsh chemicals
- discouraging an "out of site, out of mind" attitude toward pollutants going down the drain

Pathogens, the most serious human health concern, are generally only present if graywater has been contaminated by feces and thus are rarely constituents of light

Figure 4-28 A toilet in a Tokyo hotel incorporates a water spigot, allowing users to wash their hands with fresh water that is then used to fill up the tank for the next flush.
Gavin Anderson.

graywater sources. As a safety precaution, regulations in many areas preclude using water from kitchen sinks and dishwashers for reuse systems because of the potential for pathogens from uncooked food or other disease-bearing contaminants that people were trying to wash away.

The aesthetics of the water, especially if reused indoors, can be important, and untreated graywater is often cloudy due to high turbidity (suspended solids) levels. The chemicals and salts introduced in low quantities of graywater are usually not sufficient to cause negative effects on plants and soil, especially if areas irrigated with graywater are periodically flushed with fresh water or rain. In larger quantities, these elements can be handled by choosing appropriately tolerant plants and augmenting graywater irrigation with rainwater harvesting or other freshwater sources.

Potential as an Alternative Water Source

In 2009, California agreed to allow simple residential graywater systems for irrigation without the need of a permit, in part to conserve water in the face of a statewide drought. Common estimates of the amount of graywater produced by an average household range between 40 and 60 gallons per day, or 30,000 to 60,000 gallons per year. While graywater has been legal in California since 1994, with well over a million systems in place, only 215 permits had been filed.[12]

This proves that graywater reuse is not only valuable where access to potable water is difficult or must be trucked in over long distances, or if additional water rights must be purchased at high costs, but that it is also valuable in urban environments struggling to provide water for expanded populations and in arid climates where local water supplies are scarce and conservation is a pressing issue. Australia

Figure 4-29 A graywater outlet is placed within a valve box in a mulch basin to protect the pipe from becoming clogged with mulch or roots. Laura Allen, Greywater Action.

has been a leader in progressive graywater reuse practices, as have the states of Arizona and New Mexico in the Southwest. The number of installed systems in California is a testament to the safety and success of this practice, as was tacitly recognized by the state when it stopped requiring permits for such systems. Although policy lags behind practice in many places, recycling graywater is becoming more mainstream in many urban environments as water conservation becomes a higher economic and environmental priority.

The method of reuse needs to be carefully matched to the characteristics of the sources and site. The most practical application for graywater is often as a supplement to (or with careful planning, replacement for) the outdoor irrigation water supply. Site landscaping, such as lawns, trees, and ornamental plants, can benefit from the nutrients and degradable organics found in minimally treated water. Subsurface irrigation poses the lowest risk of contact with humans, and the amounts of graywater commonly applied to a landscape do not pose any significant risk of contaminating public water supplies. Fruit trees and other aboveground crops that don't come into contact with the water being piped below the surface to the tree's roots are also candidates for graywater irrigation.

For surface irrigation, and certainly for indoor reuse, disinfection of the water is necessary to ensure that all pathogens and bacteria have been eliminated. Though indoor reuse systems are difficult to permit in the United States, they are regularly installed in Europe and Australia. This is most commonly accomplished by routing bathing water through a treatment unit and then storing the disinfected water for toilet flushing. Reuse of fully treated graywater to wash clothing in laundry machines presents another option; though rarely done, studies have shown that from a hygienic perspective there is likely no difference than washing with potable water. [13]

There are no reported cases of anyone becoming ill as a result of contact with graywater, and it has been shown that the indicator organisms commonly used in sewage to suggest the presence of pathogens do not correlate in the same way to graywater.[14] Health risks associated with a graywater system are most elevated when kitchen sink water is included, as it is the most likely carrier of virulent components, and there is evidence suggesting that households with young children and animals also carry an increased risk of contamination.[15] These risks will be minimized if the system is designed to eliminate any opportunity for human contact with potentially harmful components through the use of subsurface irrigation or disinfection. Detrimental effects to the receiving environment can be minimized by carefully controlling conditions around the source, adequately sizing output to the capacity of the receiving soils and vegetation, and providing a sufficient level of treatment to remove high pollutant loads.

For more information on this subject please see www.sherwoodinstitute.org/ideas.

Graywater Reuse Systems

Graywater systems can range from a simple device that connects the drain of a bathroom sink with the tank of an adjacent toilet to a constructed wetland that serves a whole community. Regardless of their scale and complexity, typical modern graywater systems include the following basic components: collection plumbing, treatment methods, disinfection, and distribution components.

The nature of these components will vary based on the quality of the source water, its intended reuse applications, the volume of water handled by the system, and local regulatory requirements. The most effective and economical approach involves designing the simplest system capable of providing the quantity and quality of water required.

Collection Plumbing

Graywater systems begin with water collection: from sinks, showers, and washing machines. In order to separate the graywater to be reused from other wastewater streams, dual plumbing is installed in new construction or existing plumbing is retrofitted to convey graywater and blackwater to different places. Systems should have the ability to divert graywater flow to the sewer system either manually—such as with a three-way valve—if an inappropriately high pollutant load is anticipated (e.g., from dumping chemicals down the drain or washing highly contaminated clothing) or automatically, in response to treatment or distribution equipment failure.

In most graywater reuse systems, wastewater is diverted to irrigation and landscaping. To ensure that the receiving soil ecosystem has adequate capacity to absorb and process peak flows, surge capacity must be provided to temporarily store water as it dissipates. Deciding whether to install a surge tank is, therefore, an important consideration in terms of collection plumbing. If the system includes treatment devices, filters, pumps, or slow irrigation fixtures, it may not be able to handle a large sudden

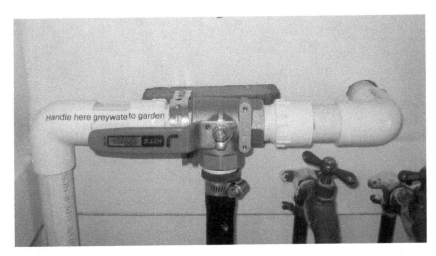

Figure 4-30 A three-way valve placed close to the washing machine allows simple redirection of the effluent from the graywater system to the sewer if necessary. Laura Allen, Greywater Action.

inflow—from, for example, a shower and large washing machine at the same time. This could cause the system to back up or overflow, in which case a surge tank would be necessary. The surge tank will thus need enough capacity for the anticipated peak graywater flow and have its outflow regulated to match the system's processing and distribution capabilities.

Untreated graywater should never be stored for days, as the high organic content in raw graywater will be quickly broken down by bacteria. As these bacteria consume all the dissolved oxygen, the water will turn anaerobic and produce foul odors. In systems with low production, the daily amount produced can be easily matched to irrigation demand, and no storage will be necessary. In systems that produce higher volumes, storage will need to be carefully considered along with appropriate treatment measures.

Treatment Methods

Graywater used exclusively for subsurface irrigation presents a very limited risk of coming into contact with humans or animals. A system with a limited set of users and only small amounts of graywater—like a single-family home—introduces few pollutants to soil and plants and represents little risk of contamination. Such systems typically require minimal or no treatment prior to release underground.

Graywater systems with a greater source water production, such as multiunit buildings or multiple homes, have an increased likelihood of contamination from a wider and more varied set of producers and may require more advanced treatment. In addition, the following scenarios may increase treatment demands in graywater systems:

- Source water with higher levels of pathogens and chemicals
- Systems with reuse applications that come closer to human contact
- Systems that introduce larger pollutant loads to soils and plants
- The need to store water and disperse it through an irrigation network
- More stringent permitting requirements and regulations

Figure 4-31 Basin at the drip line of a young tree to be filled with mulch and connected to graywater distribution. Laura Allen, Greywater Action.

Pretreatment

The pretreatment of graywater may involve either coarse filtration with screens or sedimentation in settling tanks. Properly screening and filtering the water before it enters any of the following treatment methods is invaluable in extending the life and efficiency of a graywater system—especially a more advanced system that includes pumps or other treatment devices that can clog or fail due to large particles or hair.

Mulch Basins

Simple to construct and maintain, mulch basins provide very good natural biological treatment. Mulch is usually made of wood chips but can be composed of a variety of organic materials such as leaves, straw, bark, or yard clippings. By filling a trench or basin with mulch, the graywater is contained at the most useful location and is covered to avoid exposure to humans or animals. Graywater can be discharged directly to the mulch to be immediately absorbed, or it can outlet into buried mulch chambers, providing a higher degree of sanitation.

Media Filtration

Rapid sand filters, which effectively remove larger particles and suspended solids, are an important precursor to more advanced treatment. Their proper operation requires that the graywater be applied evenly at the top of the media, after which it percolates through varying gradations of sand and gravel that physically remove particles. Media filtration also allows for more successful irrigation techniques. Subsurface drip irriga-

Figure 4-32 Ultrafiltration membrane units have a small footprint but provide excellent treatment. Bryce Wilson, Sherwood Design Engineers.

tion is one of the most efficient ways to reuse water, but to avoid clogging the distribution lines it requires water that has been filtered through at least a sand filter. (The filter will need to be regularly cleaned by running water through in the reverse direction.) Off-the-shelf graywater systems that include a surge tank, automatic backwash sand filter, pump and float switch, and supplemental irrigation plumbing can be purchased from a variety of vendors.

Filtration Membranes

Forcing water through filtration membranes possessing very small pores is a more advanced form of physical treatment. Membranes provide excellent removal of suspended solids and turbidity and some removal of organic material, with performance increasing in membranes of lower pore size. The primary concern when using membranes is fouling—the deposition of particles within membrane pores, which limits water flow and cleansing potential. Keeping the membrane clean by filtering the water before it hits the membrane will help limit fouling, but doing so has an effect on system operation and costs.

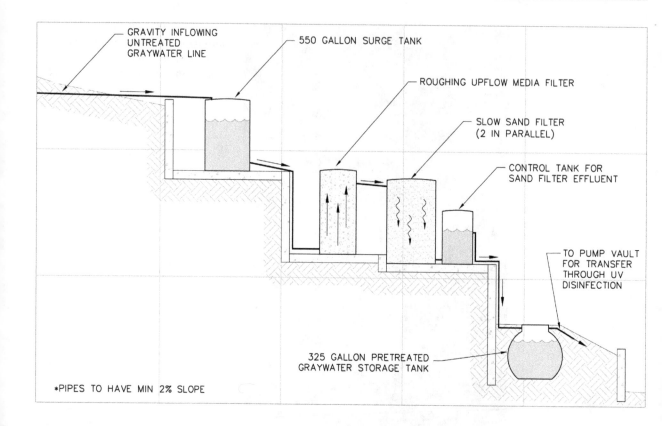

*Figure 4-33 Schematic design of a multistage graywater treatment train, including a media filter for pretreatment prior to slow sand filters that harbor beneficial bacteria for providing advanced biological treatment.
© Sherwood Design Engineers.*

Biological Treatment

The most advanced treatment techniques are those that employ biological treatment. Large-scale applications, such as neighborhood systems, apartment buildings, campuses, and stadiums, will often require the flexibility to store treated graywater for longer periods and reuse it in ways that will result in exposure via surface spray irrigation or indoor usage. Biological treatment provides extremely high removal rates of organic and suspended solid components and varying but generally good rates of microorganism and bacterial removal. In these systems, graywater is exposed to aquatic plants that harbor bacteria that feed on organic material and assimilate contaminants.

Oxygen is an essential ingredient to these systems; it keeps the beneficial bacteria alive and healthy. An electrical aerator component may therefore be required to ensure proper function. There are a wide variety of units that provide biological treatment. The simplest is a slow sand (or soil) filter, which receives a low dose of water that is cleaned as it gradually percolates through the bacteria living in the filtration media. More advanced processes, such as the rotating biological contactor, membrane bioreactor, or aerobic treatment unit, can operate at higher rates and can be designed as small modular units or large-scale processing plants. Biological systems all

Figure 4-34 Constructed wetlands do not have to occupy a large space. They can be integrated into urban environments in a host of different ways. Here, a planter box adjacent to an office wall serves as a treatment wetland for graywater from the building. Kyle Minor.

create a sludge or slime that will periodically need to be cleaned or removed. Biological treatment is typically preceded by a physical filtration stage that increases performance and reduces maintenance requirements.

Constructed Wetlands

A more extensive form of treatment comes in the form of constructed wetlands. As mentioned in the previous section on low-impact development stormwater management (see page 118), wetlands are especially good for the treatment of large flows, since they can be scaled up very easily. In addition to holding stormwater, constructed wetlands can be used to treat graywater to a very high degree with minimal maintenance needs and low operating costs. Wetlands of any type can be used to polish treated water to near-potable levels, but if they are the primary treatment then subsurface-type wetlands may be preferable in order to avoid exposing humans and animals to raw graywater. Biological treatment occurs in the media and root zone, and the production of oxygen by wetlands plants avoids anaerobic conditions and the associated odor. Wetlands are generally not a good choice in dry or arid climates, however, as losses to evaporation can be high and the reuse efficiency low. Furthermore, while the energy and pumping demands of constructed wetlands are lower, they also require a larger land area than other constructed systems. Where applicable, such wetlands provide natural treatment in an environmentally compatible form while creating a beneficial habitat and ecosystem.

Figure 4-35 Ultraviolent water puri-fiers are capable of eliminating nearly all microorganisms. Bryce Wilson, Sherwood Design Engineers.

Disinfection

After water has been treated, it can also be disinfected. This is the most consistent way to provide full and confident microorganism and pathogen removal prior to distribution. Disinfection is an essential step if the treated water is to be reused indoors or aboveground, where it may come in contact with humans. The two most common methods of disinfection are exposure to ultraviolet (UV) irradiation or the addition of a chemical such as chlorine, chlorine dioxide, or iodine. While nonchemical methods can be more expensive, they are generally preferable because the addition of chemicals to graywater can be detrimental to plants and contribute to groundwater pollution.

Distribution Components

In a small graywater system, the collection piping can exit the building and let out directly to the environment without any filtration or treatment prior to that provided by the receiving landscape. In this type of system, the irrigated area must be at a lower elevation than the outlet plumbing so that graywater can be conveyed by gravity. (Existing pumps, such as in the washing machine discharge, can also be utilized to provide limited elevation boost.) For increased efficiency and wider reach, the flow can be split into a branching network of pipes to irrigate multiple areas.

More advanced systems will typically have higher pumping needs for transferring water to and through treatment equipment. In larger systems or those that have an intermittent reuse schedule, there may be a need to store graywater for longer than a day or so to maximize the efficiency of the system. As previously mentioned, the water would then need to undergo more advanced levels of treatment, such as multi-stage or biological, prior to being detained in a tank or cistern for reuse.

Figure 4-36 *Graywater piping for distribution via gravity to mulch basins. Laura Allen, Greywater Action.*

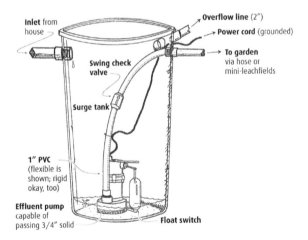

Inlet from house

Overflow line (2")

Power cord (grounded)

To garden via hose or mini-leachfields

Swing check valve

Surge tank

1" PVC (flexible is shown; rigid okay, too)

Effluent pump capable of passing 3/4" solid

Float switch

Figure 4-37 *Drum with effluent pump. Oasis Design.*

If pressurization is required to reach an irrigation area, the simplest system design is to collect the graywater in a surge tank with an effluent sump pump at the bottom. Graywater flows into the tank and water-level float switches control the pump, which discharges water to the distribution system. Designs of this type should include an overflow line leading to a disposal area or sewer system in case the surge tank gets too full or the pump fails.

Figure 4-38 Graywater emitter, placed beneath mulch underground, out of contact and view. Laura Allen, Greywater Action.

There are many ways to assemble the basic components of graywater distribution into the system. Here are some options:

- Direct to landscape via soil absorption
- Direct to mulch basins for minor treatment
- Through a mini-leachfield for treatment
- A low-pressure dosing system with small-diameter perforated pipe in gravel or other media-filled trench
- Subsoil infiltration galleys using infiltrators or box troughs
- Subsurface emitters or drip systems

Keys to the Long-Term Success of a Graywater System

As with all facets of sustainable infrastructure systems, designers will make decisions that best fit the site they are working on, the needs of the users, and the scope of the project. In the case of graywater systems, ensuring that they will be properly operated and maintained is especially critical to their safety and success over time.

Matching the System to the Site

Site soil conditions must be accurately measured before a graywater system is installed. If the soil has a lot of clay and percolation rates are low, the water will not drain quickly enough. This can lead to stagnant water developing odors, or ponding and running off on the surface. If the soil is too sandy and percolation rates are high, then water might not have time to receive adequate natural treatment. In areas with a high groundwater table, this could increase the danger of contamination. Likewise, attempting to construct wetlands in dry, arid environments could lead to system failure. By accurately measuring water tables and soil conditions, systems can be designed to meet treatment needs by controlling the depth and type of media used; adjusting irrigation rates; or adding additional treatment, filtration, or storage capacity. Areas with heavy seasonal rains, snowfall, or lengthy dry spells should be accounted for during site analysis.

Matching the System to the Needs

Just as every site is different, every system is also unique. A variety of criteria can be used to determine the appropriate sourcing, treatment, and distribution methods of a graywater system and to ensure permitting and regulatory compliance. Installing an overly complex system with large energy and maintenance needs but minor reuse potential may likely not be worth the expense involved. Overloading a simple system with high volumes or heavily polluted water could lead to inadequate treatment or system failure. If, for example, the system is designed for a hotel or tourist facility that has seasonal fluctuations in user volume, this should be accounted for in the system's design.

Proper Maintenance and Source Control

Problems can arise anytime a system is not properly maintained. Without proper filtration, drip irrigation systems can clog due to the buildup of solids and natural organisms. A variety of factors can inhibit water movement or shock plants and soils by incorporating overly polluted dark graywater source streams; introducing harsh cleaners or soiled diapers to light streams; allowing the buildup of background pollutants from water-softening systems or pesticides; or introducing chemical salts, oils, and greases into the system. Treatment schemes designed to protect the ecosystem, as well as responsible and constant oversight of what enters the graywater stream and how the system is maintained, are essential and must be well thought out prior to installing a graywater system. Self-sustaining, "hands-off" systems with minimal technical and upkeep requirements may be more expensive initially, but they can pay off over time in reduced maintenance needs. If maintenance responsibilities will be passed on from the system designer to a building manager or new owner, then clear upkeep instructions and schedules should be provided.

BERKELEY ECOHOUSE

The Berkeley EcoHouse is California's first permitted gray-water wetland treatment system for residential use. The system is designed to receive a daily production rate of 75 gallons of graywater (from the home's showers, bathroom sinks, and washing machine), which it treats and reuses to irrigate the backyard. In addition to providing an attractive aesthetic element, this wetland system is estimated to save 20,000 gallons or more of potable water each year.* The system's main component is a subsurface wetland designed according to the EPA manual *Constructed Wetlands Treatment of Municipal Wastewaters*.**

Raw graywater flows from the house through a manual diverter valve into an inlet chamber in the wetland that is surrounded by gravel to distribute the flow and avoid clogs from root growth. The wetland itself is a subsurface type, filled with pea gravel and wetland plants and shaped like a donut: a circle 10 feet in diameter with a 5-foot soil island in the center growing subtropical plants that thrive on large amounts of water. After a two-day retention time, the treated water flows through a branched pipe network to infiltration basins filled with chip bark that irrigate numerous fruit trees and garden planters.

* Paul Kilduff, "Wetland, Gray Water at Berkeley EcoHouse," San Francisco Chronicle, March 17, 2007, http://www.sfgate.com/cgi-bin/article.cgi?f=/c/a/2007/03/17/HOG25OL9DB1.DTL.
** Ecology Center, "EcoHouse," http://www.ecologycenter.org/ecohouse/.

Figure 4-39 a,b The treatment wetland at the Berkeley EcoHouse (a project of the nonprofit Ecology Center), shown here soon after completion (a) and two years later (b), with plants flourishing.
Babak Jacinto Tondre. Designed by DIG Cooperative Inc. A project of the Ecology Center.

HILLSIDE RESIDENCE

Sherwood Design Engineers designed a graywater reuse system that was implemented on a property in Los Altos Hills, California. The system collects all graywater effluent from the showers, lavatory sinks, and laundry washing machines located in the two residential structures on-site. This graywater is routed to a 325-gallon surge tank located underneath the rear deck of one house for treatment and storage prior to distribution to subterranean irrigation fields built into the site landscape.

The surge tank is fit with an inlet screen to capture hair and lint from the graywater. The tank is aerated and ozonated to disinfect the water and prevent septic conditions from developing. A control panel is programmed to receive information from a series of irrigation controllers and float switches to determine when to dose the irrigation field and when to top off the surge tank with municipal water. A submersible pump in the surge tank sends water through a bag filter and then out to the distribution system. When the irrigation needs exceed the available graywater supply, the control panel triggers municipal water to meet the demand.

Due to the new legislation passed in California in 2009, reusing graywater for irrigation became a much simpler proposition from a permitting perspective. The ozonation and underground distribution system are performing above code standards and are extremely efficient, and the ozonation prevents biological growth that might clog an underground drip system.

⌐ For more information on related topics please see www.sherwoodinstitute.org/research.

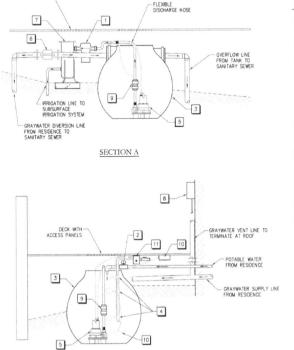

SECTION A

SECTION B

KEYNOTES

1 BASKET STRAINER (SIZE 20 MESH)

2 SOLENOID VALVE FOR SUPPLEMENTAL MUNICIPAL WATER

3 325 GALLON POLYETHYLENE SURGE TANK

4 FLOAT SWITCHES ATTACHED TO FLOAT TREE:
HIGH WATER ALARM – SET TO ALARM WHEN SURGE TANK IS
OVERFLOWING TO SANITARY SEWER
HIGH WATER FLOAT – 50 GALLON DOSE TO SUBSURFACE
IRRIGATION SYSTEM
LOW WATER FLOAT – OPENS SOLENOID TO PROVIDE 50
GALLON POTABLE WATER SUPPLEMENT

5 1.0 HP SUBMERSIBLE EFFLUENT PUMP

6 MANUAL 3-WAY BALL VALVE TO DIVERT GRAYWATER SUPPLY FROM
RESIDENCE TO SURGE TANK OR SANITARY SEWER

7 BAG FILTER

8 CONTROL PANEL

9 CHECK VALVE

10 OZONE GENERATOR WITH DIFFUSER AND OZONE RESISTANT AIR PUMP

11 ELECTRICAL SPLICE BOX

Figure 4-40 Schematic design of graywater surge tank and treatment components.
© Sherwood Design Engineers.

Figure 4-41 Graywater treatment and reuse elements form a significant part of the water resource master plan at the retreat center. © Sherwood Design Engineers.

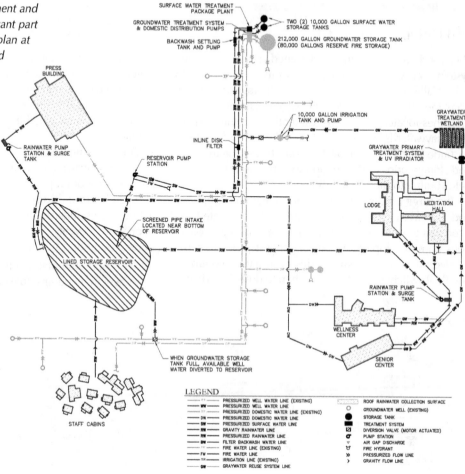

INTEGRATING GRAYWATER INTO A WATER RESOURCES MASTER PLAN

The section of chapter 3 on water balance (see page 68) discussed the first step in Sherwood's work developing an integrated water resource master plan for a retreat center in the United States. On those wet, rolling coastal hills, the two most sustainable sources of water are harvested rainwater and recycled graywater. The various components of that system will now be described in order to demonstrate the different technologies that have been discussed in this book thus far.

Members of the design team from Sherwood recommended a rooftop collection system to augment the site's existing well water, as well as a small reservoir to gather more water from the surrounding hillside. To treat graywater, engineers developed a primary and secondary treatment system, designed a constructed wetland for tertiary treatment, and introduced a storage pond to provide capacity and additional treatment. The living roof on one building acts as a stormwater treatment facility, and water-saving appliances like the ozone laundry help the property tackle one of its biggest water uses. For hot summer days a natural living pool is planned.

System Process and Components

Well water: The limited draw upon well water forms the first component of our system. In place for the prior use of the property, the prior owner's investment in this infrastructure became a foundation for our net-zero water network. Well water continues to be pumped and distributed through its current network connections straight to the existing 212,000-gallon storage tank. The tank stores treated well water in order to distribute potable drinking water across the site; it also stores a fire-protection reserve volume of 80,000 gallons. When the tank is full, a diversion valve sends any available well water to the reservoir directly. Groundwater is treated via manganese filtration and ion exchange and disinfected with UV irradiators before entering the storage tank.

Reservoir: The reservoir serves as the main storage facility for all untreated rainwater on-site. It collects water from the upland collection system, rainwater collection system, and property wells (when the main tank is at capacity). Rainwater used to supplement irrigation receives some filtration before being stored in a 10,000-gallon storage tank. Rainwater used for potable purposes undergoes surface water treatment via media pretreatment filters, membrane ultrafiltration, and chlorine injection.

Graywater treatment: Graywater is collected in a batch-processing tank where it undergoes primary treatment, disinfection, and oxygenation for color. The effluent is then pumped to a wetland treatment system large enough to remove all pathogens. Following treatment, the graywater is stored in a 10,000-gallon tank to be used for irrigation. During peak occupancy in the summer months, a greater volume of graywater becomes available to meet higher irrigation demands.

Constructed wetland: The constructed wetland was designed to expand upon existing wetland habitat occurring elsewhere on the site and to provide passive treatment for the high volume of graywater moving through the site (see figure 4-42). Key components of the treatment wetland include the following:

- An impermeable clay liner to prevent groundwater contamination
- Alternating wetland cells of cattails and bulrushes
- Open water sections to provide reaeration and photodegradation
- Maintenance areas in between each cell
- Swales surrounding wetlands to divert stormwater runoff around the wetland
- Mosquito fish to control insects
- Bypass piping to allow cells to be taken offline for maintenance
- Outlets to an underground temporary storage tank where it is pumped up to irrigation water storage tank and irrigation distribution lines
- Large storm overflow reservoir sized for a one-hundred-year storm (water will be pumped up to the irrigation water storage tank when capacity increases and/or disperses via subsurface trenches)

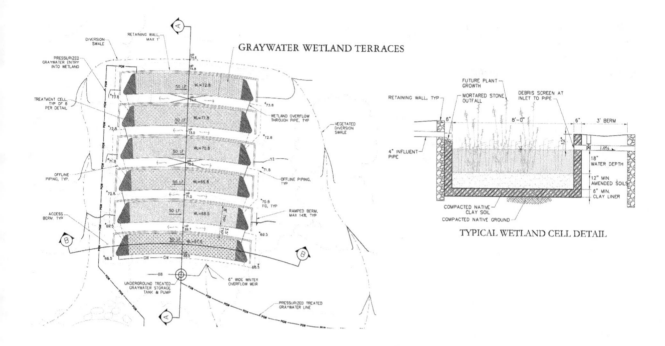

Figure 4-42 Graywater wetland. The reuse of laundry water is a key component of the water supply system. It is treated in a series of wetland cells before reuse, further decreasing the project's energy and potable water demands. (The treatment cells are shown in plan and section.) © Sherwood Design Engineers.

Living roof: One building supports a living roof, which reduces stormwater runoff while supporting native plants. The roof has a variable soil depth to reflect the plant biodiversity of the natural surroundings and further enhance its water absorption capacity. These plants and the roof's growing media filter stormwater, remove potential pollutants, and allow runoff to be reused as supplemental irrigation water.

Living pool: The living pool system is a dynamic natural approach to filtering swimming pool water. More than 7,500 such systems can be found internationally (predominantly in Europe, Australia, and Central America); they are used for both private and public applications. In its pure form, the living pool system uses only plants, gravel, and aeration to remove pathogens. While the water is purified and microbes are reduced to minimal levels using this approach, local agencies require a minimum of 1 part per million (ppm) of chlorine in the swimming water at all times to ensure public safety. To meet this requirement, the pool was designed to operate in three modes:

Biological mode: The wetlands treat water with disinfection prior to its return.
Conventional shock mode: When chlorine is added to the pool, the wetlands are operated as a separate recirculating system to avoid harming beneficial organisms.
Hybrid mode: Residual chlorine is removed as water enters the treatment wetlands; it is reapplied as water enters the swimming area.

Ozone laundry: When the retreat is operating at full capacity, 80,600 pounds of laundry per year is expected. At 3 gallons of water per pound of laundry, this would typically require over 240,000 gallons of water per year; using an ozone-based water recycling system promises a savings of at least 70 percent of that water. This system uses ozonated water as an oxidizer to aid in the cleaning process. The system works on cold water, so it is also expected to save 1,400 therms of water-heating energy per year. It also reduces the need for chemical detergents.

Preparation for heavy storms and drought conditions: To ensure the system would be capable of handling the heavy water flows of winter storms, its response was calculated during five- and ten-year storm occurrences. In order to test the sensitivity of the proposed storage volume, a twenty-five-year drought analysis was also performed and applied to a typical year:

- Monthly rainwater volumes were calculated using local rainfall depth, duration, and frequency records from the Department of Water Resources.
- Statistical derivation of twenty-five-year drought analysis was calculated from historical rainfall information.
- Impacts on design storage volumes were calculated by modeling this data through on-site sources and sinks for a variety of storm- and drought-condition scenarios.

Highly integrated multifaceted water systems are imperative for meeting the water challenges that face designers in the coming years. While every project presents a different set of opportunities and constraints, drawing on the assets of a particular site, the creativity of the design team, and the will to provide sustainable water supply will allow for the right solution to emerge.

BLACKWATER MANAGEMENT APPROACHES

Residential blackwater is any water that comes from toilets. Kitchen water, especially from sinks with a garbage disposal, may be considered blackwater as well, because of its high organic matter content. Blackwater in most urban municipal systems goes to centralized treatment plants that use energy-intensive physical and chemical methods to remove pathogens and disinfect the water. In rural settings, blackwater that is processed on-site is typically disposed of subsurface using leachfields, which allow the water to penetrate slowly through the soil and replenish the water table.

Commercial and industrial blackwater includes water from kitchen sinks and toilets, but depending on the business it can also encompass a much wider array of potential contaminants. A dry cleaner, for instance, may have a number of compounds in its waste stream from chemicals used in the cleaning process. A significant amount of water is used for industrial cooling needs. This water may be considered graywater and be reused multiple times before discharge, whereas water that is exposed to chemicals during the industrial process may require industry-specific treatment. Water is used in a variety of industrial processes, from tanning leather and dying fabrics to the manufacture of paints and stains, and even as a solvent for chemical reactions. In addition, water is used as a cleaning agent in virtually every industrial process, from food production to manufacturing. All of these activities result in a large quantity of water that requires various treatment methods before it can be reused or safely discharged into the environment.

Figure 4-43 Leather refinery sewage outfall in Addis Ababa, Ethiopia. Magnus Franklin.

After proper treatment, blackwater can be used for a variety of purposes. Because of the nature of the contaminants, nutrients, and chemicals within a blackwater stream, the treatment requirements are much more significant than they are for graywater. Passive biological systems as well as a variety of mechanical and chemical treatment systems can, however, bring blackwater up to a high standard.

Finding ways to reuse blackwater on-site can reduce the piping and energy requirements involved in moving blackwater to wastewater treatment plants, the costs of treating it, and the potentially adverse effects of discharging it into local waterways. New York City, for instance, dumps well ove 1 billion gallons of treated water into the rivers and bays surrounding the city every day. The city's largest wastewater treatment plant alone, Newtown Creek, is capable of treating 310 million gallons per day (mgd) for discharge into East River, and is currently being expanded to a capacity of 700 mgd by 2013.[16] This is not only potentially harmful to the marine environment, it is a loss of valuable water that could be reused to recharge aquifers or irrigate urban landscapes. Reusing treated blackwater represents substantial immediate savings; simply using the water twice cuts the energy costs of that water in half.

Blackwater Treatment Levels

Advances in microbiology and hydrology over the last hundred years have given us an increasingly nuanced understanding of how water is treated and moved by natural systems. By taking a resource-based approach to treating blackwater, we can gauge success not on an external purity standard, but by how well the treated water performs in the receiving ecosystem, whether that is a leachfield, an industrial "digester," a constructed wetland, or the local beach.

To match the quality of treated water to its intended use requires an understanding of basic levels and types of blackwater treatment. Water treatment systems and standards vary widely. For the purposes of this book the process has been divided into primary, secondary, and tertiary treatment. These treatment levels correspond roughly to physical, biological, and chemical methods for removing impurities, which are usually handled in that order.

Primary (physical) treatment is the removal of suspended particles by physical means. Techniques include preliminary screening for trash and large objects, filtration for finer particles, and settling tanks that allow particles to sink to sludge at the bottom. Skimmers then remove fats, oils, and grease (FOG) from the surface, while the sludge is scraped and pumped out the bottom. Once the amount of total suspended solids (TSS) has been reduced, the water is passed on to secondary treatment.

Secondary (biological) treatment is further removal of suspended particles and organic matter using bacteria, algae, fungi, and a host of other microorganisms. This process mimics natural systems but is engineered to happen faster and more effectively. Instead of a running stream, aeration tanks pump air through the water to provide oxygen that microorganisms need to survive. As bacteria consume suspended organic material and oxygen, they create larger particles that settle to the bottom and can be removed.

By calculating the biological oxygen demand (BOD) of the microbes living in a water sample, treatment engineers can determine how much organic material the water contains. A pristine river could have a BOD value of less than 1 milligram per liter (mg/L), and a mildly polluted river up to 10 mg/L. Raw sewage could range from 200 to 600 mg/L, depending on the source. Municipal sewage that has been effectively treated ranges near 20 to 30 mg/L.[17]

While some standards calculate the effectiveness of secondary treatment by the BOD level in the effluent, others use a removal percentage. The majority of standard wastewater treatment plants in the United States meet secondary treatment levels defined as removing over 85 percent of the BOD and TSS. Many systems can also perform better than this, with advanced secondary treatment levels of 95 or even 99 percent removal.[18]

Another form of secondary treatment uses anaerobic digestion to treat sewage sludge. This produces methane, which can be used to generate heat and electricity. By creating a localized source of power for treatment facilities and their communities, this method can reduce greenhouse gas emissions and offset the costs of water treatment.

Tertiary (chemical) treatment often uses chemical reactions to either bind toxins with oxygen (creating gases that bubble out of the water) or reactions that precipitate

Figure 4-44 *UV lamps at a waste-water treatment plant play an important role in disinfecting municipal wastewater. Nathan Hewett.*

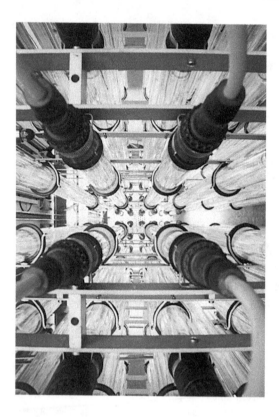

chemicals into heavier compounds that can then be settled out. But tertiary treatment also includes higher levels of treatment that target specific impurities in the water. This can be accomplished via a physical process, like using a membrane bioreactor to push water through very fine membranes; a biological process, such as a treatment wetland, where plants take up the remaining pollutants; or a chemical process, such as denitrification, adding lime to coagulate compounds, or chlorine to disinfect the water.

Disinfection is typically the last step of the treatment process, even if there is no tertiary treatment. Adding chlorine to water is a simple, effective, and widely used method of neutralizing any remaining pathogens in treated water. But because chlorine is harmful to life and dangerous to store and transport, disinfection is increasingly being accomplished using other means. Irradiating treated water with ultraviolet (UV) light can sterilize pathogens without adding any physical chemicals. To be effective, UV radiation requires that the water be highly treated first. And because it requires routine maintenance, including the replacement of its lighting systems, it also adds to costs. Ozonation is another method that is safer than chlorination, though more expensive. This method passes oxygen (O_2) through high voltage, where it bonds with an additional oxygen atom to create ozone (O_3). Because ozone is highly unstable, it oxidizes any organic compounds it comes in contact with and is therefore effective at destroying pathogens.

Treatment Technologies

Wastewater treatment technology design is a complicated field with many subspecialties. The following list, by no means comprehensive, is meant to provide designers and planners with a basic introduction to common technologies and treatment methods used in the field.

Septic System

Although a major contributor to regional water quality problems when they fail, septic system are a very common on-site treatment method used in rural and residential settings; they are found in every state in the United States and in many countries around the world. The system consists of a septic tank and a piping network that filters the water through gravel trenches or leachfields before infiltrating the ground. The septic tank provides a basic pretreatment to the water but requires annual cleaning to remove accumulated solids for further treatment. Water is leached though the ground, which provides natural filtration of organic material, solid particles, nitrogen, and microorganisms, including bacteria and viruses. To properly function, a septic system must be sited where there is adequate slope and proper soils to filter the water. High water tables, shallow soils, clay, or flat terrain may prevent effective treatment by a septic system. In the right conditions, septic systems are a proven method for decentralized wastewater treatment.

Because septic systems are simple, relatively passive, and affordable, they represent a cost-effective method for providing basic treatment and infiltration. When the systems malfunction, however, or in areas of higher density, excessive effluent entering the groundwater from septic systems has negative impacts on water quality. Additionally, compounds increasingly found in residential blackwater, including pharmaceuticals, household chemicals, and cosmetic products, can have adverse affects on receiving ecosystems. The proper maintenance and testing of septic systems is required, especially because they are common in areas that also use well water as a source of drinking water.

Composting Toilet

Composting toilets use very little water and are effective in arid environments or places without access to water or septic systems. Waste is collected in a tank below the toilet and slowly composts into humus. As it dries, the material reduces greatly in volume, making collection easier. Tanks should be sized to hold a year's worth of excreta, which is typically how long a batch takes to fully compost. While processing, the compost can be mixed with soil, lime, or ashes to maintain moisture and aid the composting process. Many systems use two chambers, which can be alternated for continuous operations during removal and cleaning.

Composting toilets are widely used in state parks, public restrooms, and outhouses. They are a low-cost, environmentally friendly, and ancient method of disposing of human excrement. When properly composted, the humus can be used for agriculture.

Figure 4-45 Composting toilet at the Hollenback Community Garden in Brooklyn, New York. Dahlia Thompson, Sherwood Design Engineers.

Careful designs can eliminate the odors often associated with composting toilets. They can also be paired with a reed bed filter or other water garden that captures and treats graywater from the facility.

Sand Filter

Filtration using sand, gravel, or other media is a common step in removing physical particles from wastewater. After preliminary screening and sedimentation, effluent is allowed to seep through the fine grains of the filter. This can provide effective treatment for suspended solids and BOD, but is less effective at removing metals and nutrients. Slow sand filters can harbor a thin film of biological organisms. This biofilm, called a *schmutzdecke* in German,[19] provides a degree of secondary treatment and nutrient removal. While filters are generally gravity fed, they can be pressurized to flow faster or through finer particles, and they must be periodically cleaned or backflushed to prevent clogging. Sand filters are an effective, low-cost method for achieving higher levels of treatment than a septic system, and they can be used in areas where soil conditions are not capable of adequately handling infiltration—places with a high water table or clayey soils, for example.

Sequencing Batch Reactor

A sequencing batch reactor (SBR) processes batches of effluent through several stages of treatment. These systems can be operated in single batches or in sequence

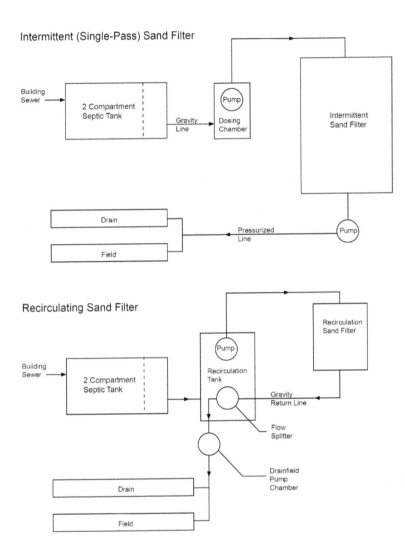

to handle varying amounts of incoming flows. This all-in-one aspect makes SBRs both complex and flexible. Unlike other mechanical systems, which are only economical for large volumes, an SBR can process small batches and still be cost-effective. And unlike natural systems, which require steady flows to maintain their living organisms, SBRs are ideal for hotels or seasonal communities that have fluctuations in their flow volume.

After primary screening, effluent is added to a reactor cell containing microorganisms. During secondary treatment, the tank is aerated and mixed like a conventional flow reactor. The batch is carefully adjusted during the process to maximize efficient digestion. Once digestion is complete, the resultant biomass is allowed to settle out as sludge, and the water flows on for further treatment or disinfection. The complexity

Figure 4-47 Sequencing batch reactor schematic. U.S. Environmental Protection Agency.

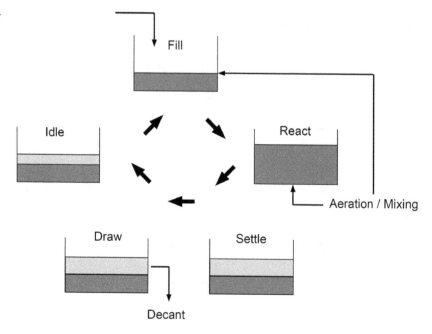

involved in correctly operating the various timers, valves, pumps, and switches means that SBRs require a specialized labor force and relatively high maintenance. Because their treatment can be customized, though, SBRs are easily adapted to handle changes in water quality or new regulations. When operated properly, they are similar to other conventional systems in their level of treatment, achieving BOD removal rates of 85 to 95 percent. SBR manufacturers generally guarantee the systems to produce effluent treated to less than 10 mg/L of TSS and BOD. Sequencing batch reactors can also be modified to be used for nitrogen and phosphorus removal in areas where nutrients in the wastewater effluent are a concern.[20]

Membrane Bioreactor

Many conventional systems use chemicals to coagulate solids that can be settled out and removed from the water. But removing the chemicals requires additional treatment and has other impacts. Biological methods for secondary treatment require maintaining a healthy community of microorganisms and typically require a larger site. The microfiltration membrane bioreactor (MBR) is purely physical: it functions by causing effluent to flow across a fibrous membrane. The pores are large enough to absorb water molecules but small enough to stop anything larger than 1 micron (.001 millimeters). This eliminates virtually all microorganisms, including bacteria and viruses, from the permeated water. The solid material that doesn't permeate the membrane is then ready for secondary biological treatment, and the permeated water is passed on to disinfection.[21]

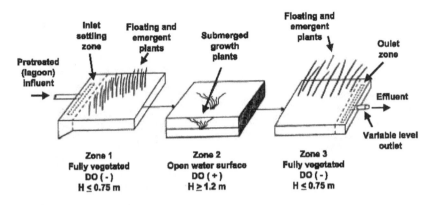

Figure 4-48 Free-water surface constructed wetland schematic. U.S. Environmental Protection Agency.

MBRs are typically more costly than conventional methods but simpler in design than SBRs. They can operate at high volumes and process water quickly and in smaller spaces than other methods. While the membranes are expensive, the smaller size of an MBR installation saves money on construction costs and materials. MBRs require substantial primary treatment to remove particles and heavy solids that could damage the membrane. They have higher energy costs than aeration tanks because the membranes must be scoured with air to keep them clean.

Initially used for smaller treatment systems, MBRs are increasingly widely used and are now applied to larger systems as well. Membranes are also used to treat drinking water, producing over a billion gallons a day worldwide.[22]

Constructed Wetlands

Constructed wetlands were developed to mimic the treatment potential observed in natural marshes. They are relatively low cost, largely passive, and can be constructed from local materials. They are also simpler to operate and require less energy than mechanized systems. Reeds and other aquatic plants native to wetland areas are particularly good filters. With their hollow roots acting as siphons for the water, they draw out large amounts of organic matter, lowering BOD and TSS. Depending on the type of plants and how long the water is detained, wetlands can be effective at removing heavy metals, nitrogen, and phosphorus as well.

There are two kinds of constructed wetlands, referred to as subsurface flow (SF) and free-water surface (FWS). A subsurface flow system is constructed of a gravel bed planted with wetland vegetation. In such a system, the water flows through the roots of the plants but stays below the surface of the gravel. This reduces odors, prevents mosquitoes from breeding, and allows the wetland to perform better in cold weather. As the water flows through the gravel media and the plant roots, the increased surface area of the substrate allows a great number of microorganisms to develop. This permits SF wetlands to treat the same amount of water in a smaller space than a free-water surface system. SF systems are also typically more expensive because of the initial cost of the gravel beds and the increased maintenance necessary to prevent the subsurface media from clogging.[23]

Figure 4-49 An early version of an AEES, the Living Machine, in a greenhouse in South Burlington, Vermont. U.S. Environmental Protection Agency.

Free-water surface (FWS) systems are more supportive of birds, fish, and other wildlife than subsurface flow systems but may require a larger area and have a higher potential for human contact with the effluent. Adding fish to a wetland ecosystem can help control mosquitoes and also provide nutrients and revenue to a community. Two types of plants commonly used in FWS wetlands are duckweed and water hyacinth. Their roots act as a substrate for bacteria and encourage the removal of the wastewater's major contaminants. While water hyacinth grows quickly, it has lower nutrient values than duckweed, which can be sold as fertilizer or animal feed. Both types of plants need to be closely monitored and harvested to maintain the system's proper function.

Advanced Ecologically Engineered Systems

Advanced ecologically engineered systems (AEESs) use advanced biological processes of wastewater treatment that combine many techniques used in more conventional wastewater treatment plants but integrate the use of flora and fauna. AEESs are often installed in a greenhouse for year-round vegetation. They can be accessible to the public, aesthetically pleasing, and provide on-site treatment and reuse for graywater or blackwater. AEESs are considered less expensive than comparably-sized treatment plants for achieving tertiary treatment levels. Because of their attractiveness and versatility, these systems can be designed for community treatment or for large facilities like universities, hotels, or office buildings.[24]

In general, these systems share the following basic components:

Pretreatment tank: At a minimum, this underground tank functions similarly to a septic tank in that it allows solids to settle out, greatly reducing the incoming BOD concentrations.[25]

Anoxic and aerobic reaction: This can occur in a controlled tank using a diffused air system with plants floating in the water to provide odor control and uptake.[26] (Such tanks function similarly to the aeration tanks in activated sludge treatment, but with plants added into the mix.) It can also take place in a subsurface wetland, which could be designed as a park or orchard.

Aquatic cells: After treatment in the subsurface wetlands or control tanks, effluent flows into the surface tanks in the greenhouse. Here the water flows through a series of cells whose unique ecosystems continue treatment using microorganisms, algae, fungi, and clams. An AEES can sustain a wide variety of plants, flowers, crustaceans, and fish.

Ecological fluidized bed: This step provides final polishing using a medium that will capture the sediment and let the water flow through.[27] This can be designed as a sand filter or a vertical flow wetland. After final filtration, the water treated by an AEES can be used for community irrigation or agriculture.

🖱 For more information on this subject please see
www.sherwoodinstitute.org/tools.

Blackwater Reuse Potential

Wastewater has typically been disposed of in two ways: infiltration into the soil or disposal to a body of water. Infiltration is often limited by the type of soil or other site conditions (such as a well located close by), and disposal to a body of water has the potential to create an environmental impact of some kind. It is therefore advantageous to reuse the treated wastewater in a responsible manner rather than discharging it as a first matter of course.

In most locations, reclaimed wastewater is intended only for nonpotable uses, such as the irrigation of landscapes and golf courses, dust control, and fire suppression—and there is controversy about possible health and environmental effects even for those uses. More recently, reclaimed water has been brought into buildings as part of a secondary (dual-plumbed) system used to flush toilets and for cooling water. In some instances, this reclaimed water is indirectly used as potable water, such as at Orange County Water District's Water Factory 21, where reclaimed water is treated and injected into the aquifer systems to prevent seawater intrusion, and extracted later to be used as potable water.

The following is a brief discussion of the reuse, infiltration, and discharge of blackwater:

Reuse

Secondary and tertiary treated wastewater is reused in many places in the United States. In Singapore, it is standard practice to reuse wastewater; in fact, it accounts for 30 percent of the country's water usage.[28] Public perception of reusing treated wastewater is a significant barrier to its being used for potable uses, but Singapore does dilute some of the recycled water into the potable water reservoirs, contributing approximately 1 percent of the country's potable requirements.[29] Before dilution into Singapore's reservoirs, the treated wastewater undergoes microfiltration, reverse osmosis, and UV disinfection, all following conventional water treatment; this produces water quality higher than that of the rest of its potable water resources. Orange County, California, processes treated wastewater in a similar manner,[30] but injects the effluent into the ground and withdraws potable water at a different location nearby, allowing the treated wastewater to mix with the groundwater. In most cases, though, the treated wastewater is treated only to the secondary level and then reused for landscaping irrigation, agriculture, or industry. If human contact is of concern, or the agriculture is for foods for human consumption, then tertiary treatment is recommended.

Reusing treated wastewater for irrigation (on a golf course, for example) is really a form of land application or infiltration, since the water will either be taken up by the plants or drain into the subsurface soils. While reducing irrigation demands is often a goal on projects, using treated wastewater for irrigation is ideal because it replenishes the aquifer rather than transferring the water off-site, and therefore helps maintain a water balance. The nutrients in treated blackwater are also a natural fertilizer.

The major limiting factors in reusing blackwater for subsurface irrigation are solids that might clog the irrigation system and the high levels of nutrients, BOD, and pathogens that may be present in the effluent. Nutrients, typically phosphorus (P) and nitrogen (N), which are found in wastewater, are actually fertilizers. While the presence of nutrients in the effluent could minimize the need for adding fertilizers, it could also lead to increased nutrients in runoff if fertilizer dosing levels are not adjusted to take the nutrients in account. As for BOD and pathogens, the plants may not be affected by them, but if the vegetation is for human consumption, then water-quality restrictions or further treatment may be necessary. Regulations vary from state to state and country to country on this matter, but secondary treatment is usually sufficient for the irrigation of vegetation not for human consumption, while tertiary treatment is required for irrigation of vegetation for human consumption. Secondary treatment in this regard is generally defined as 30 mg/L BOD and TSS, while N and P levels will vary based on wastewater characteristics. Tertiary treatment may be required by local regulations as well, depending on the irrigation methods to be used, even if the irrigation is not being applied to vegetation for human consumption.

Infiltration

If the reuse of blackwater is not an option, or it cannot be used for all of the effluent, infiltration is the next best option. Infiltration involves the reintroduction of treated water to soil systems with the goal of using the land as a large filtration device that slowly sends water down into groundwater aquifers. The land area required for proper infiltration increases as the percolation rate decreases. If appropriate soil conditions are not present or sufficient land area is not available, infiltration may not be a complete solution.

Figure 4-50 A leachfield on Sand Island, Midway Atoll. Forest and Kim Starr.

Discharge

Throughout history, humans have been dumping wastewater into lakes, rivers, and oceans. Although we now have treatment processes in place in many cities, the impacts from discharging effluent are still significant. If potable water is being withdrawn from a river or lake, returning the treated wastewater to that same source can help in maintaining water balance, but if the water is not treated to the required limits, it will impair the water quality of future withdrawals. Unfortunately, this contamination is the reality in many places. Minneapolis's wastewater—as well as that of many other cities along the Mississippi River—is part of New Orleans's water source. As these cities expand, so does their discharge. Without proper reuse strategies, there are invariably negative impacts to the water supply. Often discharge is the only solution, at least during a transition period. It should then be handled in the most sensitive way possible. Treated effluent should be brought up to the highest purity level possible in order to protect surface water quality and downstream users.

Shifting the Water Treatment Paradigm

There is a paradigm shift occurring in the field of wastewater treatment: we are moving away from being solely dependent on large centralized systems and moving toward augmentation or replacement by localized and naturalized treatment systems. This shift is being driven by the high costs of centralized treatment, a recognition of the value and reuse potential of nutrient-rich water, improved methods for naturally treating water, and the auxiliary benefits of decentralized treatment methods. We are treating waste closer to the source and engineering systems that integrate more closely with human communities to provide benefits beyond mere waste removal.

Integrated wastewater planning, or integrated water resource management (IWRM), looks at wastewater not as a distinct function, but as a critical part of a bigger system. The IWRM paradigm takes into consideration the health of the watershed; the water balance in a community; the life-cycle analysis of the materials and energy used to treat water; and a resource-recovery approach to stormwater, graywater, and blackwater. This new paradigm values not only public safety but also the community benefits of integrated water management.

The new approach is a softer path that uses nature's labor and also copies nature's designs. But rather than simply mimic natural systems, we must create smarter, more efficient systems that can accomplish treatment naturally and handle the volumes and speeds that a modern city requires. Techniques like subsurface flow wetlands can shrink the footprint of natural treatment facilities by increasing the amount of water treated per square foot.

Sustainable strategies for water treatment require considering wastewater in conjunction with a community's energy, environmental, and economic goals. The right solution for a particular site or community will often be a blend of strategies or technologies, some more conventional and others more sustainable. Table 4-1 lists the basic characteristics of wastewater treatment methods, with more conventional methods on the left and more sustainable methods on the right. There are advantages and disadvantages to both conventional and sustainable systems, and designers are rarely asked to simply choose one or the other. Instead, we must adapt and integrate new development with existing infrastructure and respond to the unique challenges of each particular project.

Table 4-1 Conventional versus Sustainable Wastewater Treatment Methods.

MORE CONVENTIONAL	MORE SUSTAINABLE
Centralized	Combined centralized/decentralized
Energy-intensive	Land-intensive
Active systems	Passive systems
Mechanical and chemical methods	Natural methods
All water treated to potable standards	Water treated for its intended reuse
Treated water discharged	Treated water reused
Primary goal: public safety	Integrated goals: water quality, reduced footprint, community benefits
Economies of scale	Economy through integration
Treatment cost per gallon	Life-cycle analysis and true-cost accounting
Specialized experts working in silos	Integrated teams design water systems that perform multiple functions
Public management of water	Public and private cooperation in water management
Low community involvement	Greater community involvement in management, jobs, and on-site treatment on private lands

Figure 4-51 Wastewater treatment plant. This plant in Hamburg, Germany, uses huge egg-shaped digesters that reduce the amount of solids to be sent to landfills and provide a power source that can be harvested to help run the treatment plant. Ralf Schulze.

The distinctions between conventional and sustainable treatment methods are, in fact, more of a spectrum than an either-or choice. For example, wastewater treatment systems are often described as either mechanical or natural, but this is not entirely accurate. Many active mechanical systems rely on microorganisms to digest effluent, while so-called natural systems like living machines and constructed wetlands are also highly engineered and carefully operated. Both systems employ natural methods, but mechanical treatment attempts to make nature work faster, often in large, concentrated volumes with chemical additives. For example, a large conventional wastewater treatment plant uses massive blowers for the aeration tanks, complex pumping systems to recirculate the effluent through the system, and giant anaerobic digesters, all of which have very large energy demands. A constructed wetland, by contrast, has minimal energy demands, as such a system is gravity driven.

Given the number of proven conventional systems in operation—systems that offer advantages in crowded environments—cities will continue to use these existing systems for years to come. Nevertheless, sustainable systems—because of their flexibility, reduced costs, and lower impact—are increasingly being adopted.

Life-Cycle Costs and Funding Considerations

Facilities of all kinds are increasingly being asked to account for their full life-cycle costs in energy and emissions. While tertiary treatment levels have improved water quality, they have come at a high energy cost. They have also required additional chemicals and materials that have their own life-cycle costs and carbon footprints. Life-cycle analysis is tipping the scales toward sustainable water treatment systems by fully counting the costs of conventional treatment while increasingly recognizing the auxiliary economic benefits of sustainable systems. Reduced collection costs, increased water savings, and resource recovery allow more sustainable water systems to compete against the large construction, collection, and energy costs of more conventional systems.

Raising capital for a large wastewater treatment system can be challenging politically. The upgrade of Newtown Creek, New York City's largest treatment plant, is currently estimated to cost $2.2 billion.[31] Infrastructure systems that won't be operable for years to come are not usually a high priority for voters. But decentralized systems require less upfront costs to construct and are easier to replace and upgrade with new technologies. Getting zoning approval for them, or achieving community consensus around them, can be much easier than successfully floating bonds for large infrastructure projects. In addition, the infrastructure at a centralized treatment plant has to be oversize to allow for future expansion, something a decentralized system often does not have to take into account. Sewers have to be sized for future flows, and the construction of a sewer system can become very expensive and environmentally intrusive, especially in formerly undeveloped areas.

Development patterns are often determined by available infrastructure, and "sewage-based sprawl" can occur when new housing developments are made possible by extending an existing centralized system. Conversely, decentralization can help preserve local character by restricting incremental sprawl and encouraging cluster development. The flexibility of decentralized systems means that communities are not locked into large infrastructure commitments that require accurate long-range planning around population growth and economic development. If predictions are not met, centralized infrastructure can spur growth artificially to meet its needs or limit growth if the system gets overwhelmed. Decentralized systems can more organically fit a community's needs, instead of acting as a driver or barrier to growth.

Notes

1 United Nations, Millennium Development Goals, "Goal 7," http://www.un.org/millenniumgoals/environ.shtml.

2 Barton Kirk et al., Methods for Comparison of Wastewater Treatment Options, Project No. WU-HT-03-33 (prepared for the National Decentralized Water Resources Capacity Development Project, Washington University, St. Louis, MO, by Ocean Arks International, Burlington, VT), 2005, www.ndwrcdp.org/userfiles/WU-HT-03-33.pdf.

3 Charles Duhigg, "Health Ills Abound as Farm Runoff Fouls Wells," New York Times, September 17, 2009, http://www.nytimes.com/2009/09/18/us/18dairy.html.

4 Wikipedia, "Agricultural Wastewater Treatment," December 12, 2009, http://en.wikipedia.org/wiki/Agricultural_wastewater_treatment.

5 U.S. Environmental Protection Agency, Polluted Runoff (Nonpoint Source Pollution), "Clean Waters Act Section 319: Laws, Regulations, Treaties," http://www.epa.gov/nps/cwact.html.

6 http://www.loudounwildlife.org/PDF_Files/SM_Human_Impacts.pdf

7 Nevue Ngan Associates and Sherwood Design Engineers, San Mateo County Sustainable Green Streets and Parking Lots Design Guidebook (2009), http://www.flowstobay.org/ms_sustainable_streets.php.

8 Ibid.

9 Ibid.

10 Ibid.

11 Greenroofs.com, "Why Does Greenroofs Call Them 'Greenroofs' and Not 'Green Roofs'? 2007, http://www.greenroofs.com/Greenroofs101/faqs.htm.

12 Josiah Cain, principal of Design Ecology, in presentation on "Integrated Water Systems" at West Coast Green, Oct 3, 2009.

13 E. Nolde, "Greywater Recycling Systems in Germany: Results, Experiences and Guidelines," *Water Science and Technology* 51, no. 10 (2005): 203–10.

14 R. Birks and S. Hills, "Characterisation of Indicator Organisms and Pathogens in Domestic Greywater for Recycling," *Environmental Monitoring and Assessment* 129, nos. 1–3 (June 2007): 61–69.

15 Water Conservation Alliance of Southern Arizona (CASA), Residential Graywater Reuse Survey Report 1999.

16 http://www.nyc.gov./html/dep/html/harbor_water/wwsystemplantlocations_wide.shtml.

17 George Tchobanoglous and H. David Stensel, *Wastewater Engineering: Treatment and Reuse* (New York: McGraw-Hill, 2003).

18 Amory B. Lovins, Jeremy Magliaro, et al., *Valuing Decentralized Wastewater Technologies: A Catalog of Benefits, Costs, and Economic Analysis Techniques* (prepared by Rocky Mountain Institute for the U.S. Environmental Protection Agency), November 2004, http://www.rmi.org/rmi/Library/W04-21_ValuingDecentralized Wastewater.

19 EPA Wastewater Technology Fact sheet: http://www.epa.gov/owm/mtb/mtbfact.htm.

20 EPA Wastewater Technology Fact sheet: http://www.epa.gov/owm/mtb/mtbfact.htm.

21 http://www.epa.gov/owm/mtb/mtbfact.htm.

22 San Diego County Water Authority, "Infrastructure: Twin Oaks Valley Water Treatment Plant," http://www.sdcwa.org/infra/cip-twinoakswtp.phtml.

23 Wikipedia, "Constructed Wetland," January 6, 2010, http://en.wikipedia.org/wiki/Constructed_wetland.

24 U.S. Environmental Protection Agency (EPA), "Wastewater Technology Fact Sheet: The Living Machine," (October 2002), http://www.epa.gov/OWM/mtb/living_machine.pdf.

25 Ibid.

26 Ibid.

27 Ibid.

28 PUB, Singapore's National Water Agency, "NEWater," http://www.pub.gov.sg/water/Pages/NEWater.aspx.

29 Wikipedia, "NEWater," November 3, 2009, http://en.wikipedia.org/wiki/NEWater.

30 Groundwater Replenishment System, "Water Purification Process," http://gwrsystem.com/process/index.html.

31 Water-Technology.net, "Newtown Creek Water Pollution Control Plant Expansion and Upgrade, New York, NY, USA," http://www.nyc.gov./html/dep/html/harbor_water/wwsystemplantlocations_wide.shtml.

CHAPTER 5
Energy and Greenhouse Gases

Figure 5-1 Sources of U.S. green-house gas emissions. About 87 percent of U.S. greenhouse gas emissions come from energy production and use. This means the political, economic, and environmental consequences of global climate change directly relate to the way we currently produce and use energy. U.S. Energy Information Administration, Department of Energy.

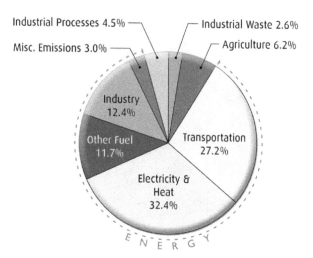

What is energy? This may seem a prosaic question, but it's important to understand what energy is before talking about how best to manage its use. Energy is all around us. The sunlight we depend on for life is energy, as is the heat from this light. Food is packaged chemical energy for our bodies the way gasoline is packaged energy for engines. The rotation of crankshafts on these engines and the movement of our feet when we walk are another form of energy. Even the chirps of a bird or the crashes of a wave are forms of energy. Radiation, both heat and atomic, are energy. A watch spring wound with tension stores energy, as does a bucket of water on a shelf. Even matter itself is energy. Wood may be burned to release stored chemical energy, and an atom may be split to release atomic energy.

These various types of energy are constantly switching forms. Radiant energy from sunlight strikes a plant leaf and is converted into chemical energy that is stored as sugar. This plant might then be eaten by a hamster, which then converts the chemical energy in the plant to mechanical energy on its running wheel. Mechanical energy from the wheel might spin a magnet inside a coil, producing electrical energy. This electrical energy in turn might heat a filament in a lightbulb that, in addition to heat, produces light. In fact, this kind of energy exchange occurs all around us continually, in thousands of different ways. By understanding these constant ebbs and flows of energy, designers can begin to appreciate the complexity of the built environment and learn to make design decisions that optimize the ways we use energy.

The current energy paradigm is massively damaging to our environment—the damage is too varied and extensive to list here. The bottom line is that our current energy strategy is deeply unsustainable. Understanding why allows new solutions to be evaluated through the proper lens. Burning fossil fuels releases dangerous toxins and heavy metals into the air; the "scrubbers" placed on smokestacks to capture these toxins merely shift them from our atmosphere to our waterways. According to a *New York Times* study of U.S. Environmental Protection Agency (EPA) data, power plants

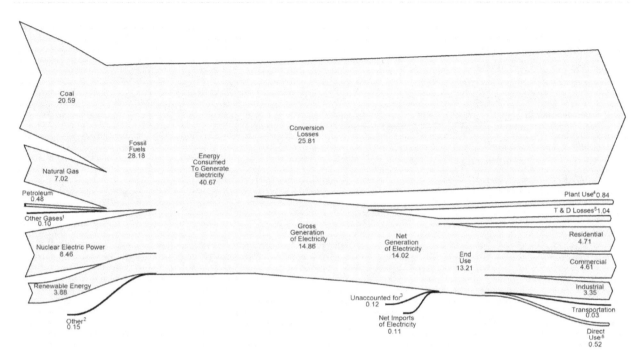

Figure 5-2 Electricity flow, 2008, in quadrillion BTU (quads). In 2008, 40.67 quads of energy were consumed to generate electricity in the United States, yet after conversion, transmission, and distribution, only 13.21 quads of energy were available for use in our homes and businesses—over 26 quads were lost along the way. This means that for every one unit of useful energy produced, over two units are lost in the system. U.S. Energy Information Administration, Department of Energy. Re-created by Sherwood Design Engineers.

are the largest producer of toxic waste in the country.[1] Fly ash from coal-burning power plants is now the second-largest waste stream in the United States, after municipal solid waste, and the EPA reported in 2007 that these pollutants have contaminated groundwater in towns across twenty-six states. Not only will these toxins be extremely difficult to recover, but they will continue to harm people and wildlife for generations. All told, a recent U.S. Academy of Sciences report shows the annual cost of coal power in the United States to be $62 billion from health, recreation, and other effects.[2] In addition to directly poisoning the environment, human combustion of fossil fuels has so significantly altered the composition of the atmosphere that that we are changing the global climate itself, with potentially disastrous implications for civilization as a whole.

But the problems with our current energy systems are not limited to the environmentally damaging sources of our energy or the pollution caused at every step of the extraction, refinement, shipping, and distribution process. Another significant problem is that our entire energy system itself is both fragile and inefficient. Large, centralized power systems lead to systematic overconsumption and large distribution losses. Consider these basic facts:

- More than two-thirds of the fuel energy used to generate electricity is lost before it gets to your house.
- Over 90 percent of the energy dug out of the ground as coal is wasted before it can do any useful work.[3]
- An ordinary incandescent lightbulb loses 90 percent of its energy as heat, using only 10 percent to produce light.

Figure 5-3 U.S. energy consumption and expenditures. United States energy consumption per person has remained relatively stable over the past thirty years; however, the cost of energy has risen sharply as the growing global economy competes for increasingly scarce fossil fuel resources. U.S. Energy Information Administration Annual Energy Review 2008. Re-created by Sherwood Design Engineers.

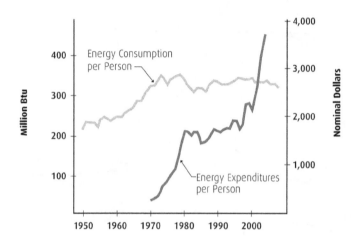

• The gasoline you put in your car loses 85 percent of its energy to combustion, friction, and idling, while only 15 percent of the energy is used to actually move the weight of the car and the passengers.

As Figure 5-2 shows, a majority of the energy we produce is lost along the way as it moves from the source to the end user. This is the result of a tragedy of overabundance: when energy was cheap and plentiful, people were not overly concerned about the inefficiency of getting only 30 percent of the useful energy out of a fuel (as is the case with most combustion engines).

Compounding the inefficiency of our current system is the insecurity of depending on an increasingly limited supply of nonrenewable resources. As a society, we have become entirely dependent on a complex global infrastructure that is both outdated and underequipped for the massive demands placed on it. Shortages, leaks, or breakdowns at any of the many stages of power delivery cause pricing volatility and power outages. Our continued dependence on oil fosters a political dependence on a variety of foreign powers (some unstable regimes) that adds the enormous cost of military support to already skyrocketing energy costs.

Human beings have often changed power sources and dependencies based on climate, technology, and resource availability. Our reliance on oil reserves created hundreds of millions of years ago is relatively recent, but because the complex systems and infrastructure for its extraction and distribution are all in place, it is difficult to transition away from. In effect, the bulk of our economy is subsidized by energy borrowed from the ancient past. (France is one of a few exceptions: there, the majority of electricity generation comes from nuclear power.) The change needed now involves not just our source of energy, but our whole energy system: the way we generate, deliver, and use power.

Shifting the global economy toward one that responsibly uses and produces energy is a daunting challenge. But it is also an enormous design opportunity. It is not enough to just switch to a clean power source overnight; we need to improve the

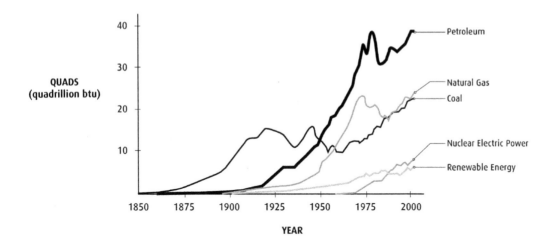

Figure 5-4 The mix of energy production modes is dynamic and continuing to evolve. U.S. Energy Information Administration Annual Energy Review 2008. Re-created by Sherwood Design Engineers.

entire system. We must work to increase efficiency to reduce demand; find ways to optimize power use through smart monitoring systems; and find cleaner, mixed energy sources for locally generated power.

Our need for energy is determined in large part by the way our cities are constructed and how our buildings and transportation systems have been developed. So the transformation of our energy systems is very much a question that designers and architects are dealing with in their work. Doing so requires a series of sequential strategies, from the least costly and most effective demand-reduction measures to more costly system efficiencies and renewable sources of energy.

A successful energy strategy involves the following four steps:

1. Reduce energy demand through design.
2. Use energy efficiently.
3. Select sustainable power supplies.
4. Address climate change and reduce carbon footprint.

REDUCING DEMAND THROUGH DESIGN

The first step toward sustainable energy supply is to reduce the need for energy in the first place. An immense amount of power is wasted through poor or outdated design. In the mid-twentieth century, following the advent of atomic energy, it was widely believed that electricity would soon be so cheap that it would not be metered. Design mentality from that period persists in many products and buildings that were not designed with efficiency in mind. The upside to this embedded thinking is that reducing demand is often quite easy and can offer a quick financial return.

There is a difference between energy conservation and energy efficiency. The former means using less energy, while the latter means getting more use out of the same amount of energy. Amory Lovins of the Rocky Mountain Institute invented the term *negawatt* to calculate the amount of energy a building or project saves due to either conservation or efficiency. Because of the many inefficiencies inherent at all levels of today's system, finding ways to more efficiently use energy is generally far less costly than producing new energy. A McKinsey & Company report has shown that energy productivity investments yield an average 17 percent return, far greater than the average stock market return.[4]

On a small scale, the benefits of energy efficiency can be seen easily. Swapping an incandescent lightbulb for a compact fluorescent will typically pay for itself in a matter of months, and that new bulb will last for many years, continuing to save money every month. Optimizing the energy performance of a large design project can be considerably more complicated than switching out a lightbulb, but reducing energy demand through better design is not only a sustainability imperative, it is a readily achievable design goal with benefits in both reduced costs and improved performance.

Reducing Energy Use in Buildings

Figure 5-5 The major sectors of energy use. Residential and commercial use takes place in buildings, which means buildings account for over 40 percent of the energy we use. Many buildings were built before energy efficiency became a priority. Likewise, transportation systems and industrial processes were often developed without prioritizing energy efficiency. U.S. Energy Information Administration Annual Energy Review 2008.

Buildings are the largest category of energy consumer in the world. In the United States, buildings consume roughly 40 percent of the energy and are responsible for 40 percent of carbon emissions—more than any other sector, including transportation and industry. Yet currently available technologies can make buildings 80 percent more efficient. By incorporating on-site power generation and better design, buildings can be net-zero energy consumers, or even energy producers.[5]

Everything involved in a building's design and use directly affects its energy consumption. Its geographic and topographic location, as well as its orientation and location within microclimates caused by hills, streams, or vegetation, can affect the amount of energy needed for heating, cooling, and ventilation as well as its lighting and pumping requirements for water and wastewater. The selection of building materials affects a similar range of variables. Even its surface treatments matter greatly: a smooth stone or metal surface will exchange more energy with people in

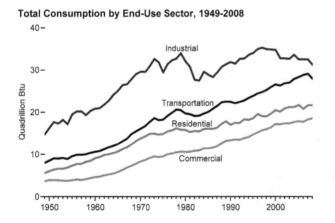

Total Consumption by End-Use Sector, 1949-2008

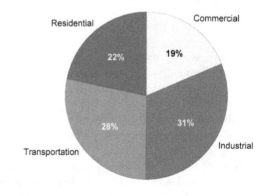

End-Use Sector Shares of Total Consumption, 2008

a room, making the room seem cooler, while rugs and curtains will work to make a room feel warmer.

For the headquarters of a major foundation in California, Sherwood Design Engineers worked on a 50,000-square-foot office building designed to be 100 percent net-zero energy. After extensive energy modeling, the design team recommended 1.5-inch triple-element windows with a heat mirror film in the middle. The increased insulation value of the windows meant the building would require less perimeter heating. Even though the windows cost $75,000 more than high-performance dual-glazed windows, they were efficient enough to allow the mechanical engineer to reduce the size of the building's perimeter heating system, saving $150,000 from the outset. Because the heating system was smaller, it meant less photovoltaics were required to power it, which saved an additional $300,000. But even if a project is not net-zero, significant savings can be had over the life of the building by investing in good design and efficient installations from the start.

Although there are important lessons to be learned from the variety of factors that affect a building's energy use, there is no single solution that works everywhere. To be successful, each building should be tailored to its surroundings, responding to and making use of the local energy flows that optimize health and comfort while maximizing efficiency and minimizing the need for centralized power generation. Everyone involved in a project can make a significant contribution to its success. Better systems allow building managers to keep energy costs down; building occupants need to be taught how to operate their buildings efficiently as well. This means designers need to be conscious not just of the structure and form of buildings but also of the daily functions and habits of the people using the building.

In analyzing the energy systems required for a building, Sherwood begins with passive strategies. Only when those have been exhausted are active strategies considered. (Passive strategies rely strictly on good design and do not require additional energy, while active strategies require external energy input.)

Some of the most effective energy-saving techniques rely on systems that use no energy at all. Examples of passive energy-saving systems include passive solar—lighting and heating a home with sunlight instead of artificial light—or designing windows to capture prevailing breezes for cooling instead of using air conditioners. Many architects have a good understanding of these techniques, collaborating with engineers and other green design professionals to maximize the effectiveness of these solutions. The Passivhaus movement in Germany, for example, has developed very advanced standards and practices for passive design.

Passive Design Strategies

Every site is unique, and it is ultimately up to the site design team to find and tap into the most appropriate energy applications. It is relatively straightforward to design an HVAC system that will drain energy month after month, year after year, to handle heating and cooling needs. And if the site is designed poorly, these systems will have to work that much harder to compensate for the site design flaws. Integrating building and site design can produce a building that is in tune with its surroundings,

Figure 5-6 Gensler's headquarters in San Francisco, California, incorporates extensive daylighting to improve the performance and quality of the interior spaces. Gensler/Sherman Takata Photography.

responds to its environment, and provides more value, comfort, and inspiration for its users.

Reducing the energy demand of buildings and systems involves developing a thorough site analysis, defining a clear inventory of the project's needs and objectives, and then matching that understanding to the available energy opportunities.

At the community scale, street grid orientation, building mass, vegetation placement, and other strategies can use the characteristics of the local environment to maximize comfort and minimize building energy needs. For example, buildings in northern, colder climates can have large south-facing windows to absorb sunlight as well as well-insulated walls and good amounts of thermal mass to buffer temperature fluctuations. This will keep the buildings warm and well lit without the use of any significant mechanical energy systems. In any climate, rooms that are expected to create larger internal gains, such as kitchens, computer server rooms, and laundry facilities, can be positioned in areas with lower solar exposure or high ventilation to balance the temperature in the building without using air-conditioning.

The following are examples of passive design strategies that can improve the energy performance of buildings:

Grid orientation: In temperate or cold climates, orient residential streets so buildings have summertime-shaded south facades in the Northern Hemisphere and north facades in the Southern Hemisphere for maximum solar gain in the winter and to reduce cooling requirements in the summer. The seasonal variation of prevailing winds should also be examined before determining street orientation. In temperate and cold climates, best practice ideally orients main corridors perpendicular to winter winds and parallel to cool summer breezes if possible in order to reduce heating and cooling loads. In hot climates, where cooling needs dominate, orienting corridors parallel to prevailing breezes can provide natural cooling for developed areas.

Microclimates: A neighborhood that is located downwind of a vegetated or wet landscape can experience cooler breezes due to the effects of evapotranspiration. A dense landscape can also provide protection from wind and shield a site from particulate matter from nearby roads or businesses. Strategies such as using parks to break up dense areas, positioning larger buildings to provide shade for smaller ones, and daylighting creeks and streams that have been forced into underground pipes all provide temperature balancing that can reduce building loads.

Tightly sealed building envelope: Use of efficient insulation, sealing, and building materials can reduce the amount of energy needed to heat or cool a space. If used in all construction, properly sealed building envelopes can reduce heating system size and cost by 20 to 30 percent.[6]

Natural ventilation design: Natural ventilation is a whole-building design concept, utilizing wind pressures to supply outdoor air to building interiors for ventilation and space cooling. The goal is to have an airtight building envelope while controlling outdoor air supply through windows that are placed to capture cooling breezes. Many older buildings have windows that face each other on opposite sides of the room. When both windows are open, air currents are naturally drawn between them, providing a current of fresh air. Natural ventilation is also closely tied to improved indoor air quality.

Building design and orientation: A building's orientation and design can make significant contributions to reducing its heating and cooling load. In passive solar design, deciding whether to face a building toward the sun depends on the climate. Using thick walls will increase insulation, while the strategic placement and sizing of windows can provide light and warmth without incurring extra heat loss. Skylights, solar tubing, and light shelves that reflect light deep into a room are all energy-free ways to let more light into a building without using energy. In warmer climates, buildings can be shaded using deep overhangs and awnings or by screening and tinting windows to reduce solar gain.

Figure 5-7 Skylights at Union Station in Washington, DC. Many older buildings were designed in the days before centralized heating, air-conditioning, and electric lights. These buildings often employ passive techniques for lighting, warmth, and ventilation. Peter Griffin.

Thermal mass: Heavy stone walls have been used throughout history in both hot and cold climates as a way to maintain a moderate temperature inside while outside temperatures fluctuate. This works because heat takes longer to travel through stone and other dense materials like concrete, which essentially acts as thick insulation. In the warm months, this element keeps a building cool by absorbing excess heat during the hottest parts of the day and radiating it during the cooler night, while in cooler months it can help warm a building by absorbing and releasing solar thermal energy. The typical walls of many European houses are still more than a foot thick, and the same building idea is utilized in other countries with concrete or other masonry walls. Thermal massing can also be accomplished by allowing a floor slab to pick up solar heat during the day and radiate that heat back at night, helping to keep the entire building comfortable.

Low-emittance windows: Low-emittance (low-e), high-performance windows utilize a microscopically thin coating to either block or retain most of the radiant heat gain that results from exposure to the sun. In a tropical climate, low-e windows allow for large windows and views that would otherwise cause too much heat gain in a building. In colder climates, low-e windows let in light without losing heat.

Radiant barriers: Radiant barriers are installed in the attics of buildings primarily to reduce summer heat gain by reflecting, rather than absorbing, radiant heat. They use thin sheets made of aluminum or another metal, sometimes along with an insulating material. One side reflects heat back to the roof, and the other side stays cool so heat doesn't pass into the attic and heat the building. According to manufacturers, an effective radiant barrier can reflect

Figure 5-8 Simple passive strategies can make a positive impact on energy consumption. White roofs create a distinctive aesthetic while reducing the heat gain of the buildings in Bermuda. © Sherwood Design Engineers.

as much as 97 percent of radiant heat back toward its source, providing substantial energy savings in warm climates.[7]

Reflective surfaces: Light colors reflect heat while darker colors absorb it. Buildings in warm climates like Greece's have been painted white for centuries to keep surfaces cool. Painting roofs white can make an immediate difference in a building's heat gain. And white is not the only possibility: choosing lighter-colored tiles for roofs, courtyards, and sidewalks can reduce the urban heat island effect, which causes cities to be 6 to 8 degrees warmer than the surrounding countryside because of all the black asphalt roads and roofs heating the air.

Vegetation strategies: Using plants and trees to increase shading from the sun is a time-honored technique for keeping buildings cool. Vine-covered terraces and patios have been used for thousands of years in the Mediterranean to shade outdoor areas next to buildings, acting as a deep overhang to prevent sunlight from heating interior spaces. In addition, trees and shrubs act as climate regulators through transpiration, making cool days warmer and warm days cooler. Deciduous trees provide shade from the summer sun, losing their leaves in the fall to allow winter sunlight to warm the building. Nondeciduous vegetation can be planted near buildings in warm climates where cooling is the priority year-round. Plants can also be used to shield mechanical equipment from overheating by the sun, thereby increasing efficiency. Placing landscaping around a building instead of concrete and asphalt can lower the ambient temperatures on-site. Green roofs also reduce heat gain in a building by providing shade, insulating the roof with their soil media and removing heat through evapotranspiration.

Using Energy Efficiently

After implementing passive design strategies, systems and appliances that maximize energy efficiency should be employed in a holistic way, taking into account the overall impacts on the climate of the building and the needs of its occupants. For example, some early attempts at making more energy-efficient buildings used small windows and heavy shading to reduce the amount of heat gained from the hot daytime sun. While this helped to save energy for HVAC systems, it made for unpleasant internal environments and increased the demand for daytime lighting.

Modern green buildings have better insulation, more tightly sealed building envelopes, and high-performing windows that can let in light without losing heat. (Taking full advantage of natural sunlight is a passive strategy discussed in the previous section.) Using daylighting sensors, which detect the light levels in a room, can help make the transition from daylight to electric lighting as night falls and prevent lights from staying on when they are not needed. Combined with occupancy sensors, which turn the lights off when a room is empty, these energy-efficient control systems can reduce a building's lighting demands by 50 percent or more.

Active systems can also be augmented with passive methods in other ways. Water heaters and pipes can be insulated so they retain more heat. HVAC units can be shielded from the sun to further increase their efficiency. Building sensors and remote controls can be used to open skylights or activate shades. These controls require very little energy, but with the right design, they can greatly increase a building's energy performance. As always, the key is to find site-specific solutions that most effectively support the user's needs.

The following are examples of active design strategies to increase energy efficiency:

Energy-efficient lighting: Lighting accounts for 40 percent of the electricity used in commercial buildings and 7 percent of all the energy used in the United States. Improving lighting efficiency offers a major source of potential improvement. Lighting efficiency requirements signed by President Barack Obama in June 2009 represent the single most energy-saving standard ever issued by a presidential administration. The simple act of mandating more efficient lighting will save consumers billions of dollars a year, and obviate the need for up to fourteen new power plants.[8] Lighting technology is continually changing. New compact fluorescent bulbs (CFLs) offer a warmer, softer light than older models, which flickered, hummed, and emitted a harsh light. The price of light-emitting diode (LED) lighting, which is longer lasting and more efficient than even CFLs, is dropping rapidly as new models come on the market and more consumers become aware of the money and energy savings available in high-quality lighting.

Energy-efficient appliances: Energy-efficient refrigerators, washing machines, televisions, and computers can perform as well as or better than traditional models while using significantly less energy. Purchasing more efficient appliances, such as those certified by the Energy Star program, can reduce energy demands. In addition to using less power, many of these appliances also use less water, further reducing a project's power demand through decreased pumping and treatment.

In many homes, the peak power demand is due to the use of a particular appliance, and all electrical infrastructure serving the home is sized to that peak demand. Choosing more efficient appliances can reduce the home's required power rating. Extended to a group of units—replacing a traditional washing machine and dryer, for example, with an efficient ventless washer/dryer combo—can reduce the feeder from the electrical transmission grid by as much as 25 percent. Such savings have substantial cost benefits for a project developer, and a real impact on regional power demand if implemented broadly.[9] In addition to installing energy-efficient appliances, energy-efficient alternatives can complement or replace the same function. Installing ceiling fans, for instance, can reduce reliance on air-conditioning units.

Heat recovery systems: Heat recovery systems introduce an added level of efficiency to existing mechanical systems by capturing heat that is normally lost from these systems as a byproduct. One of the more common heat recovery systems is a coiled pipe that wraps around an effluent water pipe carrying hot water, such as a shower drain. Normally, the heat carried by the hot water would be lost as the hot water travels down the drain, but the recovery process transfers that heat to cool water that runs through the coiled pipe instead. That "preheated" water can then be used in other processes to take advantage of the recycled heat.

Geothermal insulation: Because the temperature of the earth is nearly constant year-round, it can be used to help a building stay warm in winter and cool in summer. Geothermal insulation systems can be highly efficient compared to traditional duct or HVAC systems. They rely on a network of pipes to carry a heat exchange fluid buried underground. The only energy demand comes from pumping the heat exchange fluid, which is much more efficient than circulating air through ducts. These systems are most efficient in regions with wide ranges in annual temperatures.

Interior air exchange: In a tightly sealed building, mechanical air exchange is necessary to bring in fresh oxygen and filter the air. Ohlone College in Newark, California, has installed two "enthalpy machines" that take advantage of the temperature difference between inside and outside air. When the air-conditioning system is running, large fans mix the outgoing cool air exhaust with the warmer incoming air. This precools the hot air before it enters the air conditioner, thus reducing the energy required to chill the air to a comfortable temperature. In the winter, these same machines preheat incoming cold air with outgoing warmer air, thus reducing heating loads. The same concept can be used to regulate humidity as well.[10]

Chilled ceiling/chilled beams systems: Chilled ceilings and beams cool through the process of radiant exchange (heat transfer between surfaces of differing temperatures) and local convection, respectively. In a room served by a chilled ceiling, the surface temperature is normally between 15°C and 18°C, providing a very pleasant radiant cooling effect (with minimal air movement). Chilled beams achieve their cooling effect by using finned elements through which water is passed at around 15°C to 18°C. Chilled ceilings and beams combine radiant cooling systems with conventional overhead ventilation to reduce energy usage, improve comfort levels, and reduce the architectural impact of ductwork and other mechanical systems. These systems are seen throughout Europe but are rarely considered in the United States.

Energy-Efficient Systems for Communities

The energy markets will see many changes in the coming years. Smart grids, electric vehicles, distributed energy generation, combined heat and power, and many other technologies will have an effect on the design of community power systems. Planning for these changes in advance can result in lasting benefits to building occupants, community members, and property owners. Designers and planners can look for opportunities to develop local clean power sources on their projects. Communities can find better ways to use their power utilities. And state and regional authorities can invest in improving energy generation efficiency across the grid.

A typical energy-demand curve for a residential neighborhood shows a peak during the evening hours when heat from the day has built up in the house and families return home from their day and turn on the air conditioners, TVs, computers, and washing machines. All the infrastructure and generation facilities must ultimately be sized for this peak plus a buffer for unusually hot weather, partial system outages, or backup power supplies. Improving efficiencies and balancing these peak loads are important strategies that designers should incorporate into city- and community-scale projects.

Some of the strategies communities can use to improve the efficiency of their energy systems are discussed below:

Combined heat and power: "Waste" heat produced during electricity generation or industrial processes can be used to heat water and make steam. The steam can be distributed through pipes and used to heat buildings or whole communities. In 1984, Copenhagen built a system that supplies hot water to 97 percent of the city by harvesting the heat from local clean-burning biomass plants.[11] Combining heat and power—also known as cogeneration—improves efficiency, since a greater portion of the fuel's energy is being used. Integrating these processes can reduce the need for separate systems, along with the associated greenhouse gas emissions and costs.

District heating: Implementing cogeneration for district heating not only makes power plants more efficient, it also reduces the community's overall demand from the grid. District heating can be very effective in dense communities or neighborhoods where steam does not have to travel far—the heat is lost quickly as the pipe lengths get longer. This is why it is commonly used on college campuses.

New York City has the largest commercial steam system in the world, in part because it is effective in Manhattan's high-density urban environment. District heating can also be used with other heating sources. In Iceland, for example, geothermal resources are used to create a steam network that heats most of Reykjavik. In general, these systems are more practical in a colder climate with higher per unit thermal demand than warmer climates with lower demand.

District cooling: District cooling involves distributing chilled water in pipes throughout dense neighborhoods for the purposes of air-conditioning or other uses. This type of system can be greatly more efficient than single-unit air conditioners for two reasons. As a medium, water transfers heat much more efficiently than the forced air of a typical air-conditioning system. In addition, one large cooling engine is much more efficient than many smaller engines.

Trigeneration is similar to cogeneration, with the addition of an absorption chiller that uses steam to create cool air or water. Trigeneration is primarily used in warm climates, where the demand for cooling is higher than the demand for heating or hot water. The cool air can be used to air-condition the power plant or other nearby facilities, reducing energy costs. Depending on its location, trigeneration could be used to create a district cooling network in a dense community. In some circumstances, such as a hospital or industrial setting, steam production may be added to the mix, replacing one of the other products or adding a fourth output from the same power source.

Smart meters and smart grids: Smart meters provide detailed, real-time reporting of power use and demand. This allows customers to see their electricity rates in real time and set energy thermostats that reduce loads at peak times to save customers money. Integrating smart meters into a community's power distribution system creates a smart grid, or a network capable of syncing power generation and consumption to increase system efficiency and reliability. When people shift their load from peak hours to less expensive ones, it reduces the amount of generation capacity needed systemwide and increases the system's efficiency, because generators can run closer to their ideal set point. This helps reduce the amount of time that older, dirtier "peaker plants" are brought into operation, which reduces emissions.

Many utilities are under mandate to decrease their customers' power consumption in order to reduce carbon dioxide (CO_2) emissions; smart grids are a very promising technology for improving performance, and systems are currently being put in place in California by PG&E; in Boulder, Colorado, by Xcel Energy; and elsewhere.

Smart grids also allow for a greater penetration of renewable electricity into the existing grid by better managing and distributing a variety of power sources. This improves the overall reliability of the power system. It also opens the door to real-time rates and the efficient use of distributed storage, such as electric vehicle batteries. While many of the technology standards and smart appliances are still under development, it is recommended that new construction include provisions for these technologies.

Extending smart technologies to buildings can achieve great benefits as well. Buildings should be constructed with energy monitoring systems so occupants can see the effects of their activities and adjust them. End-use appliances and controls such as thermostats and fans should be able to obtain real-time pricing from utilities and allow users to manage their operation accordingly. Such controls allow buildings to switch to hibernation modes (much like personal computers), reducing all but essential operations.

Accounting for Water as an Energy Use

Energy inputs occur when extracting, conveying, storing, treating, distributing, and using water. Additional energy is then required to collect, convey, treat, reuse, or discharge the wastewater. Pumping water at each of these stages can be the most energy-intensive part of the water cycle. But energy is also needed for transporting chemicals, heating and lighting facilities, electronic monitoring systems, and transportation related to maintenance and monitoring activities. Construction of the infrastructure for these systems also consumes energy. Laying thousands of miles of pipes and building giant hydroelectric dams, sewer systems, and water treatment plants results in large amounts of embodied energy in the water we use.

On-site water sources typically require significantly less operational energy per volume of water produced than traditional municipal water systems. By definition, on-site sources originate close to the end user, and pumping energy demands are therefore minimized. In addition, on-site systems can segregate water sources based on water quality, and each source can be delivered to the appropriate demand with the minimum necessary treatment requirements, facilitating treatment process energy savings.

For more information on related topics please see
www.sherwoodinstitute.org/tools.

The EPA's Water Sense program notes that running water from a faucet for five minutes uses the energy equivalent to leaving a 60-watt lightbulb on for fourteen hours.

Reducing Demand through Transportation Changes

The movement of people and goods is critical to the overall energy puzzle and an important piece to address on any project. In the United States, dependence on automobiles has led to a steady increase in the energy required for transportation. In 2008, transportation accounted for 28 percent of overall energy use, nearly equal to that of industry (31 percent). And while industrial energy use has actually dropped from its peak in the late 1990s, transportation use rose over that same period faster than any other sector, until the economic collapse of 2007 (see Figure 5-5).

But transportation is not synonymous with automobile traffic. Transportation takes many forms, and designers should look beyond the paradigm that establishes automobiles as the standard and all other forms of transportation as "alternative." People will travel using whatever means best meets their needs, and as designers we

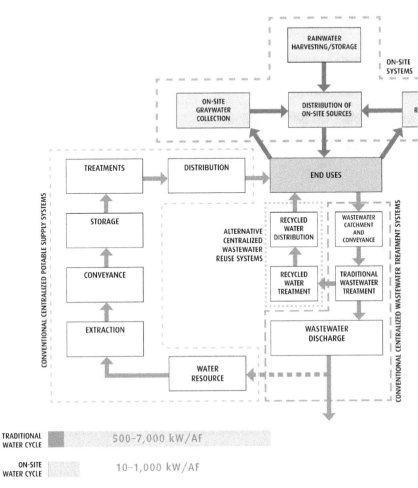

TRADITIONAL WATER CYCLE   500–7,000 kW/AF

ON-SITE WATER CYCLE   10–1,000 kW/AF

Figure 5-9 The water-use cycle and energy use. The lower parts of this diagram illustrate the energy-intensive processes of conventional centralized water supply and wastewater treatment. The net energy required for a project can be reduced through shifting to the upper part of the diagram, which incorporates lower-energy on-site systems for water supply and treatment. © Sherwood Design Engineers.

can greatly impact the energy use of a project by designing energy-efficient forms of transportation as the most effective modes of travel. If we wish to encourage bicycling, for example, we can design bike paths, bike parking, and other bike-friendly facilities. (Strategies for improving transportation and circulation are addressed more fully in chapter 6.)

The Energy Impact of Automobiles

Indirectly, automobiles increase a project's energy demands and capital costs in a number of ways. Most obviously, but perhaps least appreciated, is that they take up space—a lot of it. It is estimated that 38,000 square miles, equivalent to the size of Indiana and 1 percent of all the land in the fifty United States, is road pavement. Twenty-five percent of New York City is road pavement.[12] The ratio for a given project site will

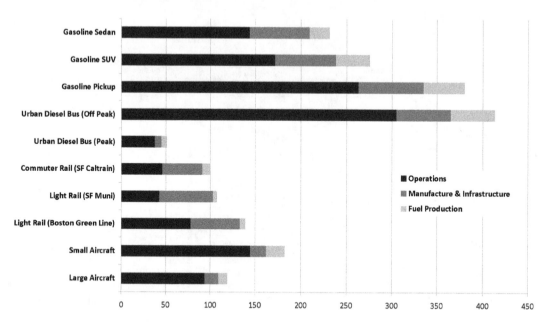

Transportation Greenhouse Gas Emissions

Grams CO2 equivalent per Passenger-Kilometer-Traveled (PKT)

Figure 5-10 Transportation greenhouse gas emissions. Different forms of transportation inherently produce very different levels of greenhouse gas emissions per passenger. Identical forms of transportation can have varying emissions as well, depending on how they are used and their fuel source. A few passengers riding on an urban diesel bus during off-peak hours will have higher per capita emissions than somebody making that same trip in an SUV; those same passengers returning during peak hours when the bus is full will have much lower per capita emissions. Likewise, similar light rail systems, such as San Francisco's Muni and Boston's Green Line, can have markedly different emissions because of the relative carbon emissions of the power grid they run on. San Francisco has a cleaner grid than Boston, so Muni riders have smaller per capita emissions.[13]

range somewhere in between. Pavement is always near buildings. Dark pavement soaks up heat and increases local temperatures, thereby creating the need for more energy to be spent on building cooling. In snowy climates, more roads means more plowing; in general, more roads always means more energy spent on maintenance and repair.

Roads also create the need for a drainage system with embodied energy in its infrastructure, as well as energy demands for pumping and maintenance. The same is true for other infrastructure required by car use, including traffic lights, signage, and gas stations. Roads also create larger home footprints because cars require parking, which usually means driveways and garages.

All told, the energy implications of designing around automobiles stretch far beyond the gallons of gasoline cars consume: sometimes automobiles are the right solution for a project, but the choice should be made with the implications and alternatives in mind.

If car use is to be included in a project, there are opportunities to reduce their impact. Unlike gasoline distribution infrastructure, which is already embedded in our society, adopting alternative fuels is a two-part approach: acquiring vehicles that run on alternative fuels and creating an infrastructure to refuel those vehicles. Creating the infrastructure for alternative fuels, such as biodiesel, electricity, compressed natural gas, and/or propane, can help bring cleaner cars to a site and reduce local pollution and global impact.

Figure 5-11 Electric car charging station in Chicago. Frank Hebbert.

Propane and natural gas burn more cleanly than gasoline, and bio-diesel offers the possibility of a more sustainable fuel source, especially if waste oil is used to create the biodiesel. These fueling systems are particularly applicable for vehicle fleets, including city buses, maintenance trucks, security and emergency vehicles, company cars, or other fleets that have fixed routes and are parked in the same fueling and maintenance facility each night.[14]

DESIGNING SUSTAINABLE POWER SUPPLIES

The need for power is unavoidable. After reducing the need for power as much as possible, the next step is to improve the productivity of the power that is delivered. This is accomplished through a combination of power source selection and new system development.

Nearly all land has energy generation potential that gets overlooked in a typical development, but a sustainable development makes the most of all resources at its disposal, including for energy generation purposes.

Costs associated with on-site energy generation have become more reasonable over time, and given a project's size, context, and available incentives, it may make sense to develop energy generation resources on-site. Proven renewable power sources with reasonable paybacks and possible incentives are the first place to look for energy generation. Solar, wind, geothermal, and biomass fuel are the most vetted energy generation methods on a community scale. However, other renewables, such as microhydro, tidal power, and wave power, might be well suited to the project site.

The characteristics of grid-sourced energy available on-site will impact the extent to which it is desirable to generate power on-site. If the region's source of energy is heavily hydroelectric, for example, as is the case in New Zealand and Costa Rica, the urgency to cover every roof with solar panels is diminished. However, if the source of energy generation is coal or other fossil fuels, then the imperative is greater to ensure that renewable energy is developed on-site.

The expected load characteristics play the central role in determining the appropriate combination of electricity generation. Peaking power sources such as photovoltaics and wind can match the daytime needs of commercial cooling and lighting loads. Baseloads such as industrial processes require sources of electricity that are available twenty-four hours a day. Intermittent power requires storage to cover the troughs, a power grid to exchange with, or more steady supply sources, such as hydroelectric power.

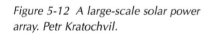

A list of the top twenty on-site green power producers can be found on the EPA's Web site: http://www.epa.gov/greenpower/toplists/top20onsite.htm.

Solar Power

The sun is the driver of virtually all life on the planet and is an essential component of any comprehensive energy strategy. Solar energy is free, falls everywhere, and can generate significant amounts of power even in cloudy, rainy cities. It is estimated that enough sunlight falls on the planet in one hour to power all of civilization for a year. Wind and wave energy are secondary forms of solar energy. Even fossil fuels are simply a form of sunlight stored as decomposed organic matter. The immense solar resource is readily directly tapped locally to provide light, heat, hot water, and power.

Figure 5-12 A large-scale solar power array. Petr Kratochvil.

The most widely available form of solar energy is daylight, and designing streets and buildings to make the best use of natural light is the first step toward reducing the energy required for artificial lighting. The sun's energy can be transformed into electricity in photovoltaic cells, or its heat can be magnified with mirrors for steam-generated electricity. The sun's heat can also be tapped through solar hot water heaters. From simple solar water heating devices used in rural areas to more advanced integrated grid-energy supplying photovoltaic farms powering cities, the use of solar power is rapidly accelerating.

Photovoltaics

Photovoltaics (PVs) turn sunlight into electricity. They can be easily mounted on roofs or set to stand on their own. Building-integrated photovoltaics can be incorporated into windows, skylights, and glass walls. They can be made to look like terra-cotta roofing tiles or other roofing materials. While this technology is continually improving, PV installations are not generally sufficient to supply a building's power needs completely.

Photovoltaic technology is improving at the same time its cost is dropping. Although PVs can still be expensive to purchase, once installed they provide silent, clean energy at no additional cost. When combined with battery storage, energy can be used at night or on cloudy days. PVs are also a very flexible power source: they can be small enough to power simple lights, sensors, or pumps in remote locations, or they can be grouped in large arrays to generate significant amounts of power for a building or community.

Figure 5-13 Solar panels at the civic center parking garage in Santa Monica, California. Outdoor parking lots offer a great opportunity to build solar panel carports that both shade the cars and provide a power source for either an electric car charging station or for nearby office buildings and homes. Omar Bárcena.

Figure 5-14 Students at the Realschule Friesenheim check the orientation of solar panels on top of their school in Friesenheim, Germany. Martin Buttenmuller.

Solar Thermal

By using solar radiation to heat water, solar thermal collectors can provide hot water or space heating. These systems are composed of solar thermal collectors—often black coils on the roof filled with water that heats up in the sun and is then circulated through a storage tank. A typical solar hot water heating system is capable of providing enough hot water to fulfill most needs at the individual home level. This technology is very cost-effective and is common practice in places like Hawaii, which recently passed a law mandating the installation of such a system on all new residences. Solar thermal is a robust and relatively cheap technology that delivers large energy savings because water heating represents a large percent of total residential energy demand. The hot water can also be used to heat swimming pools, provide residential hot water, or for hydronic radiant floor-heating systems.

Large-scale applications of solar power use mirrors or parabolic troughs to concentrate solar rays onto an absorbing tube that carries a heat exchange fluid. This fluid generates steam to run a conventional steam turbine. Solar thermal arrays can be constructed with less expensive components than PVs and built to a very large scale. A key advantage to solar thermal is that solar energy can be stored in its thermal state. Various technologies using phase-change salts and other materials that effectively store and radiate heat back at night are used to balance out the energy generation profile of solar thermal farms.

PS10 outside of Seville, Spain, is an 11-megawatt solar thermal power plant—the first commercial concentrating solar power tower in Europe. It is part of the Sanlúcar la Mayor Solar Platform, which will produce 300 megawatts of energy when complete

in 2013, enough to power the city of Seville.[15] In the United States, Solel is constructing a 553-megawatt solar thermal power facility in the Mojave Desert that will provide power to PG&E.[16]

Figure 5-15 Solar Two concentrating solar panels program in Daggett, California. Sandia National Laboratories.

Wind Power

Wind power is one of the fastest-growing segments of renewable energy. Wind turbines are attractive because of their low environmental footprint. The additional benefits of moving to a secure, localized, clean source of power make wind far more attractive environmentally than coal, natural gas, or nuclear power.

Another significant advantage of wind power is that it does not require water to generate electricity. A Department of Energy study, *20% Wind Energy by 2030: Increasing Wind Energy's Contribution to U.S. Electricity Supply,* found that generating 20 percent of U.S. electricity from wind would

- reduce water use in the electric sector by 17 percent by 2030;
- support 800,000 jobs;
- reduce reliance on natural gas and coal;
- provide electricity at stable prices;
- reduce CO_2 emissions from the electric sector by 25 percent, which would nearly level the growth in emissions from that sector;

Figure 5-16 Wind turbines near Harrogate, United Kingdom Petr Kratochvil.

- provide $1.5 billion additional annual tax revenues and hundreds of millions of dollars to rural landowners;
- lower fuel costs by $155 billion.[17]

Building-scale wind or microturbines have a small footprint, allowing for multiple uses of land or roof spaces. They generate clean power (even if only in small amounts), and they make use of a natural resource that in some areas is quite abundant. As technologies improve, they will become more capable of significant energy generation and become more cost-effective.

Geothermal Systems

There are several ways the heat of the earth can be used to generate electricity. Conventional geothermal power plants harness energy from hot water or steam created by geothermal activity deep beneath the earth's surface. Dry steam plants take steam out of fractures in the ground and use it to directly drive a turbine that spins a generator. Flash plants take hot water (usually at temperatures over 200°C) out of the

Figure 5-17 A geothermal facility in Beijing taps warm water beneath the city to power a campus and provide water to a hot springs resort.
© *Sherwood Design Engineers.*

ground, allow it to boil as it rises to the surface, then run the steam through a turbine. In binary plants, the hot water flows through heat exchangers, boiling a fluid that spins the turbine. Geothermal power plants require subsurface geothermal activity and substantial financial investment; they may be an appropriate source of renewable energy in certain locations.

A promising new technology known as enhanced geothermal systems, or EGS, is a deep-rock geothermal heat-extraction process that utilizes the natural heat in the earth's crust to create power. The technology works by first drilling down to the bedrock at depths sufficient to tap the heat of the crust. Using a process called hydrofissuring, water is injected into the rock to create a network of cracks and veins in the hot underground rocks in order to increase surface area. Water is then circulated through these veins, heated rapidly, and returned to the surface as steam to turn conventional power-generating turbines. Because the water is cooled and reused in a closed loop, the systems are very efficient. Since the earth's crust is suitably thin in many places, EGS offers the promise of very clean, reliable baseload power that can be located in areas with otherwise poor renewable power potential.

According to a 2007 Massachusetts Institute of Technology study, *The Future of Geothermal Energy*, with enough investment, EGS has the potential to generate 10 percent of U.S. power demand at competitive prices within fifty years. This is one reason it was one of the first investments that Google made under its RE<C program to generate renewable energy cheaper than coal within five years. While the deep drilling necessary is expensive, it is not as difficult as the deep-sea drilling now being done to find increasingly scarce oil reserves. EGS could potentially offer oil companies a lucrative clean energy business that utilizes their skills and technology in a more sustainable way.[18]

Figure 5-18 Heat exchangers in a Beijing geothermal facility are arranged in series to meet all heating and some power needs for the associated buildings. © Sherwood Design Engineers.

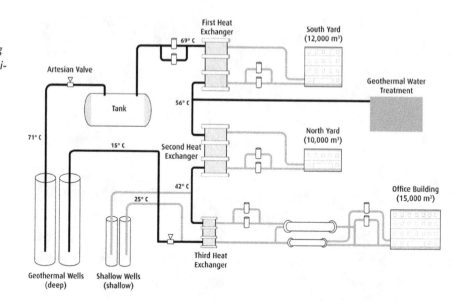

Biomass

Burning wood for fire is the oldest example of using vegetation as a fuel source. Biomass fuel source, which refers to use of organic leftovers from forestry and agriculture, is a more advanced form of the same principle. Corn stovers, rice husks, wood chips, and pressed sugar cane can all be used to generate energy. Fast-growing "energy crops" like willow and switchgrass can be grown specifically for biomass power generation. These materials can be treated in different ways to produce electricity or clean-burning fuels for vehicles. They can be burned like fuel, fermented into fuels, digested to produce methane gas, or heated to make clean-burning gas. Biomass plants can be large, producing over 50 megawatts of power annually, and are used to supply communities with power in Denmark, Sweden, and Germany.

Designers can encourage pairings of industries where the waste of one can fuel another. For example, the wood chips from a furniture manufacturer could provide fuel for a neighboring biofuel power plant. In turn, the waste heat from the plant's combustion process could heat water for a neighboring laundry facility. A mutually beneficial relationship such as this provides cheap, local resources for one business and turns a costly waste product into a revenue source for another. Other benefits include direct energy savings, diversion of solid waste from landfills, lower transportation and fuel costs, and financial savings. This concept should be analyzed at the programmatic level and is especially applicable to sites that have industrial or artisanal components.

Biogas

Using the gaseous byproducts of the anaerobic decomposition of plant and animal waste is an effective way to both reduce emissions and take advantage of a ready fuel source. The gobar gas methane system, for example, may be built for around $400 in materials and will produce about 1 cubic foot of gas from 1 pound of cow manure. In a year, a single cow can produce the energy equivalent of 50 gallons of gasoline.[19]

Municipal landfills are another source of methane that can be harnessed to generate energy. While this can offset the environmental impacts of existing landfills, this form of waste-to-energy production should not be used as a reason to justify the creation of new landfills. Municipal landfills are a significant source of methane and other gases from decomposing garbage. These gases can be trapped and used to generate energy or provide natural gas for home heating and cooking. This can reduce natural gas demand, lower greenhouse gas emissions, and supply baseload electricity.

Stockholm is producing biogas from anaerobic digestion in its wastewater treatment plant and using it to run biogas ambulances. "We can run this ambulance thanks to what is flushed down the toilet," says health-care worker Tomas Buxbaum.[20]

Water Power

While hydroelectric power is often considered a renewable energy source, large dams interrupt the natural water cycle and often have negative impacts on the environment. Dams stop the flow of water and nutrient-rich sediment down to the valleys where they are needed to regenerate the soil; they also inhibit the passage of fish and other animals. But dams are not the only way to extract energy from moving water. The next generation of hydrokinetic technologies won't alter the natural movement of water; they generate energy from the movement of waves, currents, rivers, and tides. Many people are experimenting with a variety of new ways to generate energy from water. Some of these strategies are listed here:

- *Microhydroelectric installations* take advantage of the energy in moving water to create electricity without completely damming rivers.
- *Wave energy* extracts the energy of waves through buoys, hydraulic motors, or turbines.
- *Vortex-induced vibration (VIV)* captures energy from very slow-moving currents.
- *Tidal power* works by using submerged turbines, buoys, or holding tanks to extract energy from the movement of the tides.
- *Ocean thermal energy conversion (OTEC)* utilizes the temperature difference between deep and shallow waters to run a heat engine for power generation.

These and other technologies are spurring a resurgence in water-based energy production globally and hold promise of providing sustainable untapped resources for the future.

ADDRESSING CLIMATE CHANGE AND REDUCING CARBON FOOTPRINT

One of the leading threats of our time, climate change should be addressed in some manner by every new project. Climate change is caused by a series of gases with heat-trapping properties that act on the earth's atmosphere much as a greenhouse acts on the air within it. Emissions of these substances are important to manage in their own right, but because of the interrelationships between water, energy, materials, and people, emissions levels can also serve as a general indicator of other environmental issues. Thus, tracking and reducing a project's carbon footprint, for example, is a good way to reduce its overall environmental footprint.

The first step in reducing a project's carbon footprint is to reduce energy demand and provide cleaner, more efficient sources of energy, as previously discussed. But it is also important to calculate a project's overall carbon footprint and work to reduce it. There are three steps to mitigating impact: (1) measure the carbon footprint, either through design modeling for an intended project or actual measuring for a built project; (2) work to reduce that footprint; and (3) offset the rest. Dividing the total carbon footprint by the project area's population can provide a per capita value for direct comparison with other properties as well as an effective metric for setting goals or policies.

Measuring a Project's Carbon Footprint

A carbon footprint attempts to quantify the cumulative impact a project is having on the climate. Typically, the carbon footprint is reported in CO_2 equivalents (CO_2e), meaning that methane, nitrous oxide, and other greenhouse gases are included in the analysis but are tracked as an equivalent carbon tonnage based on their global warming potential. Methane, for instance, has 23 times the global warming potential of carbon dioxide, which means that 1 ton of methane emissions is equivalent to 23 tons of carbon dioxide emissions.

A project's carbon footprint includes its direct emissions and the emissions caused by the electricity the project consumes. The carbon footprint also includes the emissions embodied in the materials used on the project, those caused by transportation to and from the project, and the emissions generated by the project's waste stream. These embodied emissions also include the impact of the water used on the project, as well as the effect of land cover changes like deforestation. All these factors must be included for an accurate accounting of a project's carbon footprint. Methods for calculating the footprint of these common project components are discussed below.

Energy

The greenhouse gas emissions from electricity use, fuel use, and other energy sources can be converted to CO_2 equivalents. The term *emission factor* refers to the average emission rate of CO_2 for a given utility relative to the energy used—for example,

ENERGY GOALS AND STRATEGIES

CARBON NEUTRALITY FOR OPERATIONS

75% ON SITE RENEWABLE POWER

50% ENERGY REDUCTION FOR GARAGE

- A net balance of carbon generation or carbon neutrality for park operations will be achieved to eliminate all green house gas emissions related to the operations of the Park and its facilities.

- Carbon sequestration will occur on site by natural vegetative uptake of CO_2 in the acres of new landscape.

- On site renewable energy generation to power 75% of park facilities and offset its carbon footprint.

- 50% Garage Energy Demand Reduction will be accomplished by installing high efficiency mechanical systems and sensors.

- The café and other minor structures will be LEED certified buildings and include high efficiency mechanical systems to significantly reduce their energy demand.

- Photo voltaic panels will be installed on the rooftop of new buildings, the existing Union Station, and integrated into shade structures throughout the Park to generate power for park operations and maintenance.

- Vertical axis wind turbines which take advantage of the significant prevailing winds and can adapt to variable wind direction will be installed in the landscape to offset power for park operations and maintenance.

- LED lighting will be installed throughout the site and parking garage, where practical, in place of standard bulbs, reducing energy demand by approximately 50%.

CARBON BALANCING

	Source	CO_2 (tons/yr)
DEMAND	Fountains	140
	Lake Recirculation	58
	Buildings	49
	Ice Rink	39
	Site Lighting	15
	Irrigation	4
	Total 305	
OFFSET	Solar Arrays	200
	Wind Turbines	45
	Landscape Sequestration	25
	Total 270	
	89% Carbon Offset	

Figures 5-19 and 5-20 For a large urban park project in Oklahoma City, Sherwood's carbon balance looked initially at energy and balanced offsets with the park's operational demands. Renewable energy generation and carbon sequestration through the landscape allowed this project to achieve a carbon balance.
© Sherwood Design Engineers.

pounds of CO_2 per megawatt hour (MWh). The emission factor can be calculated based on an electricity provider's energy portfolio and the CO_2 emissions for each energy source (e.g., coal, natural gas, hydroelectric, nuclear, solar, wind, etc.).

Emission factors vary widely based on energy sources, portfolios, and locations. The Energy Information Administration has made data available for regions of the United States, as well as for nations around the world, regarding average carbon, methane, and nitrous oxide emissions per megawatt hour of electricity consumed. These national averages vary greatly depending on the combined methods of energy production. For instance, France uses mostly nuclear energy, so it produces 0.083 metric tons of CO_2 per MWh of electricity. Poland, which uses coal as its primary energy source, produces 0.730—nearly ten times as much CO_2 per MWh of electricity.[21]

If the heating source for a home or community is natural gas, then 0.0001304 lbs CO_2 per Btu is used. One gallon of heating oil is equivalent to 26.04 lbs CO_2; 1 gallon of propane is equivalent to 12.68 lbs CO_2. These figures may then be converted to tons per MWh or other values for comparison.[22]

Water

The carbon footprint of a project's water use is closely tied to the amount of energy required to treat and transport the water as well as to the method of producing that energy. A solar-powered pump will have a smaller footprint than one powered by a diesel generator; a gravity-fed graywater irrigation system will have a much lower footprint than running a sewage line to a municipal treatment plant. Thus the first step in calculating the carbon footprint of a project's water and wastewater requirements is to determine the energy use of both the potable and wastewater systems. When the details for various water resources have been determined, the carbon footprint can be calculated by multiplying by the emission factor for the electric provider.

Travel

Travel to, from, and within a project site is often a significant, if not the largest, contributor to greenhouse gas emissions. Travel can be calculated using vehicle miles traveled (VMT), flight miles, or in island conditions, by fuel sales. There are many readily available calculators for converting miles to CO_2 equivalents. Carbon emissions for automobiles are calculated using a conversion factor of 19.56 lbs CO_2 per gallon of gasoline. For air travel, it can be calculated at 0.64 lbs CO_2 per mile traveled, though this will vary considerably depending on the type of plane used, the altitude, route, wind speed, and direction.[23] The emissions for electric vehicles and public transportation will vary depending on how the electricity is being generated.

Materials

While harder to quantify, materials have a large impact on a project's carbon footprint. The energy used to create and transport materials to the site is referred to as their embodied energy. On previously developed sites, when bricks, wood, plastic, metals, and other materials are dicarded, the embodied energy it took to produce them is no longer being used. Deconstructing and reusing these commonly demolished materials can greatly reduce a project's carbon footprint. For example, concrete requires a lot of energy both to produce and to transport. Reusing materials like concrete on-site can therefore significantly reduce a project's carbon footprint. For new construction, using local materials or building supplies with lower embodied energy can also help reduce the project's carbon footprint. When purchasing new materials, manufacturers can provide information regarding the carbon footprint of their products. Finding more efficient transportation methods for construction crews and material can also play a role in reducing carbon emissions.

Waste

CO_2 equivalents for waste will depend on the type of waste management the community employs. Emissions associated with landfills are ~40 g CO_2 and 20g methane per pound of trash, 450 g CO_2 and 0.2 g methane per pound of compost, and 447 g CO_2 and 0.56 g NO_x, among other pollutants, per pound of trash incinerated. However, incineration can also provide an energy source, in which case it can offset greenhouse gas emissions from another source. To be comprehensive, the transportation emissions associated with waste management must also be taken into account.[24]

Land-Cover Changes

Converting vegetated land to a developed or urbanized condition both releases the CO_2 stored in the plants and soil and prevents the future uptake of carbon dioxide. These impacts must be measured. Land-use change is also hard to quantify, since it can be highly dependent on the type of existing or new vegetation, the age of the existing vegetation, and the climate. The Intergovernmental Panel on Climate Change (IPCC) estimates the value of 350 to 900 tons CO_2 avoided per hectare of deforestation prevented. Each project should carefully evaluate the existing conditions in order to establish the appropriate metric for this component. Several guides are in development that provide direction on this issue and should be sought out for each project.[25]

⌐ For more information on related topics please see
www.sherwoodinstitute.org/tools.

Reducing a Project's Carbon Impact

The design strategies covered in this chapter are intended to provide a roadmap to reducing a project's energy consumption as well as the impacts and embodied energy of its materials, water, transportation, and land use.

Efficient monitoring of mechanical systems and water systems, for example, will improve performance, stop leaks, and reduce waste. All of these measures will simultaneously serve to reduce a project's carbon footprint. Likewise, purchasing sustainable materials, reducing transportation requirements, and increasing green space will reduce carbon while improving a project's health benefits and environmental quality.

But even when all these steps are taken, it is still rare for a project to be truly carbon neutral, and further steps are often required to mitigate the project's impacts. These can take the form of additions to the site plan itself or efforts taken elsewhere to sequester an amount of carbon equivalent to what the project produces.

Sequestering Carbon

One option for reducing impact is the sequestration of atmospheric carbon dioxide on-site. The simplest means of doing this is the establishment or growth of vegetation that absorbs CO_2 from the atmosphere. To achieve a carbon balance, an equivalent amount of carbon and greenhouse gases need to be removed from the atmosphere. Areas of reforestation or other planting act as carbon sinks, offsetting a project's carbon emissions. On-site planting can be designed to provide additional local benefits such as habitat cooling, water and air filtration, noise reduction, shielding buildings from roadways, improved aesthetics, or even producing cash crops.

For an eco-resort development in Costa Rica, Sherwood prepared an overall carbon sequestration enhancement plan that combined different natural sequestration methods. Most notably, the strategy of land management included the reforestation of hundreds of acres of existing cattle-grazing lands and riparian areas. The growth of the tropical dry forest was the single largest on-site opportunity to sequester carbon and had the synergistic effect of restoring the natural ecosystem as well.

Carbon Sequestration Alternatives

Communities in more dense and urban settings will likely not have sufficient area on-site to sequester much carbon. Instead, they may be able to utilize methods to raise funds to purchase off-site sequestration lands or fund other programs. Depending on the project, designing or contributing to community-scale carbon sequestration may be more efficient and beneficial than concentrating solely on on-site carbon sinks. In areas of degraded ecosystems, communities can set aside large areas of open space for reforestation. Revegetating cleared areas will have many benefits beyond merely reducing carbon in the atmosphere.

In addition to developing carbon sinks for a project, small finance charges on guests, residents, students, homeowners, or other project users can fund carbon reduction efforts. An energy conservation fund can be established that invests in reducing the project's overall energy consumption; this fund can also contribute toward the education of users about energy conservation. Another option is to establish an alternative energy development fund that receives contributions from users to invest in the development of renewable energy sources like solar, wind, or biomass power generation. Such a fund helps to wean the project off fossil fuel dependency and fosters the long-term goal of improving the local use of renewable energy.

In a hotel or resort environment, many guests come from far away, arriving by plane. To offset these emissions, the resort can offer guests an easy way to mitigate their travel through carbon offsets or by contributing a small percentage of their bill to local programs that would restore the local ecology.

Carbon Credits and Offsets

If it is not feasible to develop an on-site or local carbon mitigation strategy, carbon offsets can be purchased from a variety of vendors who will invest the money in renewable energy generation projects or other environmental mitigation efforts that act to remove carbon from the atmosphere. The market for offsets is growing rapidly, but it is still mostly unregulated, so it is important to verify the source of the offsets and the end use of the contributions. When choosing carbon offsets, make sure that they are new or supplementary—not merely carbon reduction efforts that are already underway. They should be tangible and verifiable as well.

The following is a brief overview of the steps to take in implementing a comprehensive carbon management plan.

Developing Carbon-Neutrality Management Plans

Developing a carbon-neutrality management plan or achieving net-zero carbon development is a complicated effort that involves tracking all potential carbon-emitting aspects of a development. Begin by coordinating all of a project's key players and providing a comprehensive roadmap for balancing carbon sources and sinks. It is best to implement this roadmap early in a project and to involve as many team members as necessary to be comprehensive in this effort. There are many ways to structure such a plan, and the approach will vary from project to project. Below is a checklist of items that should be included.

Step 1: Defining Scope of the Plan

When determining the greenhouse gas impacts in a given project, the project boundary should include the project site as well as all activities and parcels of land that support the site. All phases of the project should be counted, including design, planning, construction, operations, occupancy, and maintenance. For each project phase, select the items that will be measured. The primary sources of greenhouse gases on a project should always be included. Secondary and tertiary sources should be included in projects striving for a higher level of sustainability.

Greenhouse Gas Sources

- Primary
  - Land-cover changes
  - Solid waste emissions
  - On-site power production/consumption
  - On-site fuel use
  - Fugitive emissions (HVAC equipment, fuel depots, etc.)
- Secondary
  - Customer and employee travel to and from the site
  - Design team and other consultants (Calculate by multiplying total project emissions by the fraction of time spent on the project.)
  - Importation of goods and materials
  - Off-site power production (including transmission and distribution losses)
- Tertiary
  - Embodied energy of materials production
  - Embodied energy of food production
  - Embodied energy of water production

Step 2: Mitigating Greenhouse Gases

There are many ways to mitigate greenhouse gases and sequester carbon, as discussed in the previous section. Here are some opportunities to look for:

- On-site vegetative sequestration
- Off-site vegetative sequestration
- Off-site green energy projects
- Off-site energy conservation projects
- Carbon credit purchases

Step 3: Implement Program Management

Ongoing calculation and verification of the carbon reduction strategies is necessary to determine the project's footprint over time and to establish whether the project is meeting its carbon-reduction goals. Here are three steps to support that effort:

1. Utilize funding from a percentage of all on-site property sales and resales in perpetuity.
2. Create an annual sustainability report, including a full carbon accounting, goals, and metrics.
3. Certify all claims of carbon neutrality by a reputable third party.

Figure 5-21 Carbon emission reduction plan. This graph illustrates a successful carbon neutrality plan. The area between the two arrows for base case emissions and engineered case emissions represents reduction strategies such as switching to solar power, increasing appliance efficiency, and mandating that all suppliers be carbon neutral. These strategies are put in place by engineers and perpetually improved by the foundation that runs the project. The vertical bars represent the strategies employed each year to offset the remaining emissions. Over time, this may shrink to zero as the project ceases to produce emissions. © Sherwood Design Engineers.

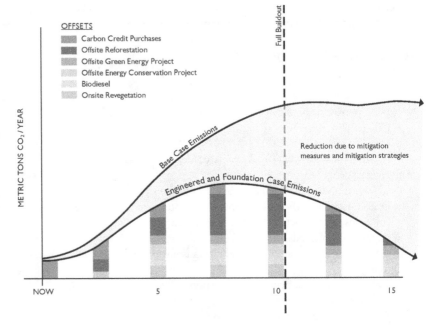

Step 4: Improve Long-Term Outlook

After a carbon management plan is put in place, long-term strategies can be developed to bring the project's net emissions to zero. The summary plan for one of Sherwood's projects in Latin America was as follows:

Over the long term, ongoing operations will be offset with a mix of on- and off-site vegetative sequestration projects, off-site green energy and conservation projects, and carbon offset purchases. This will be mixed with an investment in carbon reductions on-site, with the goal of eventually needing no offsets or external projects. Examples included the

- installation of additional renewable energy
- installation of additional energy-efficient equipment
- selection of carbon-neutral transport companies
- selection of carbon-neutral products, goods, and services
- mandate and successful enforcement of carbon-neutral travel to the site
- successful cessation of all nonrecirculative waste disposal

POLICY MEASURES FOR INCREASING ENERGY SECURITY AND EFFICIENCY

Policy strategies may be implemented at any scale but are generally used by governments, regional organizations, or sometimes property associations and stakeholder groups. The purpose is to set up rules, incentives, or penalties to advance positive energy practices. There are several tools available; the following is a brief overview.

Setting Caps

Setting thresholds for energy usage is a powerful means of sending a signal about proper consumption levels and recouping costs of developing new energy systems. In a typical system, a cap is set for a given resource, such as electricity consumption, and users are penalized for use beyond the cap. In some water-short regions, groundwater withdrawals are capped and new development may not take place unless a builder finds a way to purchase or free up water rights from elsewhere. The same can be true for energy; in fact, many utilities charge tiered rates that rise as energy use increases.

Net Metering

Typically, this is a state-level policy that requires utilities to purchase electricity surpluses generated by small, grid-connected renewable electricity at the retail rate. *Net* means consumers still purchase electricity from the grid at times when they are not generating enough electricity on-site to meet their load. Net metering is typically applied to rooftop photovoltaics, which generate a surplus during the day and run a deficit at night. The utility then essentially acts as a storage bank, providing electricity when it is needed and only charging for the net amount of electricity purchased from the utility. Utilities without a net-metering policy mandate do not pay for net surpluses or pay only wholesale rates. The advantage to the utility is that it reduces peak loads as well as dependence on more carbon-intensive forms of fuel.

The use of net metering encourages people to invest in renewable energy even if they are not off grid or are able to supply only a portion of their energy needs through a renewable system. By encouraging distributed sources of energy generation that do not suffer from distribution losses, net metering increases overall energy efficiency. In tandem with two-way smart meters that allow the utility to adjust individual power needs, the integration of on-site renewable energy to the larger grid permits sophisticated energy management that can shave peak loads, reduce costs, avoid blackouts, and reduce the need for excess generating capacity. Additionally, net metering may pave the way for widespread use of plug-in electric vehicles that act as distributed storage devices—the same way rooftop photovoltaics provides distributed generation.

Renewable Energy Certificates

Renewable energy generates power, but it also generates a climate benefit by offsetting the dirty fossil fuels that would otherwise be needed to supply that same amount of energy. To quantify and trade this environmental service, renewable energy certificates (RECs) were developed as a form of currency that can be bought and sold just as power is. This allows renewable energy generators to sell not only the electricity they produce but also the environmental benefits of that electricity to other users who wish to offset their own emissions, or their dependence on CO_2-emitting forms of energy. Purchasing RECs allows a project or company to reduce its carbon footprint overall despite, for instance, airplane travel or other carbon-emitting activities. RECs can be purchased from a variety of vendors, but they should be verified by a reputable third party such as Green-e.[26]

Green Power Programs

Utilities may choose to install centralized renewable energy in addition to other generation schemes in place. Customers can choose to support renewable energy by enrolling in the voluntary program, effectively purchasing RECs. For example, the Los Angeles's Green LA program lets customers sign up online to offset anywhere from 10 to 100 percent of their power with renewable wind and solar power, thus helping to fund the communities' development of those resources.

Incentive Programs

The use of pricing incentives or disincentives can encourage renewable energy investment or conservation measures. There is a strong economic argument for this, as the full life-cycle costs of standard energy production are often shifted away from the utility onto neighbors, nearby waterways, and the environment at large. Placing a penalty on standard energy generation can make cleaner alternative sources more attractive. Alternatively, incentives can be geared toward the production of clean energy or toward the installation of energy-efficient features. Taken further, home-builders could be given refunds if their buildings required substantially less infrastructure or used fewer harmful materials.

Utilities can offer customers that own on-site photovoltaic systems an incentive based on the size and expected performance of their systems. Fees can be paid either to the customer or directly to a solar installer. Up-front costs are shouldered by individuals; in return, individuals are guaranteed a return on investment at higher rates than normal retail costs of electricity. Incentives can also include a tax credit for some portion of the purchase price of a renewable energy system, effectively lowering the purchase point for the consumer.

Regional Power Purchasing Agreements

A power purchase agreement (PPA) is a long-term contract between a customer and the owner of a renewable energy installation. The customer agrees to host the installation (by allowing their roof space to hold photovoltaics, for example) and purchase electricity from the owner at a fixed, discounted rate. In return, the owner finances, maintains, and insures the project. This is an opportunity for a project to pursue renewable energy with lower up-front cost and financial risk. It allows the project to guarantee a long-term, environmentally friendly, fixed-cost source of electricity for its residents and businesses while handing off planning, installation, and financing tasks to a specialized third party.

Building-Scale Financing Options

Many third-party companies offer PPAs that install photovoltaic systems at no up-front charge to the building owners. The company finances, installs, and maintains the system while charging the building owner for the electricity used over the life of the contract. Often this price will be equal to or lower than what the owner previously paid for power, resulting in a win-win situation. Financing makes photovoltaic systems less risky and more accessible for residential or commercial sites. This removes financial hurdles and maintenance responsibilities.

After a successful demonstration program in Berkeley, the State of California passed Assembly Bill 811, which calls for the foundation of community financing districts to allow homeowners to pay for renewable energy and efficiency upgrades with low-interest loans attached to their mortgages. These property-assessed clean energy (PACE) financing districts are being set up on a county or regional basis to provide financing at a large scale and help the state achieve its climate change mitigation goals.

Utility Profit Decoupling Strategies

Decoupling a utility's profits from the amount of energy purchased by its consumers can help realign incentives toward energy productivity and help justify investments in renewable energy, smart meters, and efficiency programs. In this model, revenue targets are created in partnership with a municipality and trued up or down at the end of the year. This puts an emphasis on utilities meeting their expected loads instead of increasing sales. It removes obstacles to efficiency programs and reduces overall energy consumption. Some states have already adopted decoupling plans.[27]

Efficiency Incentives and Requirements

Many utilities and third-party companies offer energy audits that examine HVAC systems, building envelopes, and fixtures to identify recommendations for energy savings or enforce necessary upgrades. Most of the time, these upgrades offer financial savings or rewards. In some instances, utilities can impose excessive energy use penalties, further incentivizing component upgrades. Information about usage patterns and education can also help the users understand how to reduce their energy impact.

Benefits include financial incentives for lowering energy demands. Strategies include efficiency retrofitting; utility decoupling (financial rewards for lower usage; as well as building dashboards, procuring usage information from utilities, and education.

⌁ For more information on related topics please see
   www.sherwoodinstitute.org/tools.

DESIGN GUIDELINES AND PERFORMANCE STANDARDS

Efficiency Programs and Standards

Efficiency is the cheapest, cleanest energy resource. Increasing efficiency saves money, reduces emissions, and frees up generating capacity on existing energy grids. For these reasons, many state, federal, and local programs are offering financial incentives for customers who implement efficiency measures. On the other hand, regulatory agencies are also implementing minimum efficiency standards for lighting, buildings, and new development, or costly rate tiers for energy-intensive customers. When designing a project, its energy performance is an increasingly important indicator of overall cost-effectiveness and economic viability. Up-front investments in better windows, lighting, or more efficient appliances can easily pay for themselves when their increased efficiency is considered in the context of overall energy budgets.

Performance Standards

As opposed to a design guideline (which tends to be more prescriptive), a performance standard gives designers a target to reach without telling them how exactly to get there. Performance standards, if in place at a district or city level, can ensure a utility provider expected loads and reduce the overall energy requirements. Performance standards can also be used to set and achieve specific metrics (e.g., watts per square foot, or kilowatt hours per capita). With specific metrics in place, a program's success can be more easily monitored.

✍ For more information on performance standards please see
www.sherwoodinstitute.org/ideas.

Notes

1 Charles Duhigg, "Cleansing the Air at the Expense of Waterways," *New York Times*, Oct 12, 2009, http://www.nytimes.com/2009/10/13/us/13water.html?_r=1.

2 Brian Merchant, "Coal Plants Do $62 Billion of Damage a Year to U.S. Environment," Treehugger, October 19, 2009, http://www.treehugger.com/files/2009/10/coal-62-billion-damage-us-environment-year.php.

3 World Business Council for Sustainable Development, "Making Tomorrow's Buildings More Energy Efficient," June 26, 2006, http://www.wbcsd.org/plugins/DocSearch/details.asp?type=DocDet&ObjectId=MTk1MjU.

4 McKinsey & Company, "The Case for Investing in Energy Productivity," February 2008, http://www.mckinsey.com/mgi/publications/Investing_Energy_Productivity/.

5 U.S. Department of Energy, "Recovery Act Announcement: Obama Administration Launches New Energy Efficiency Efforts," *EERE News*, June 29, 2009, http://apps1.eere.energy.gov/news/progress_alerts.cfm/pa_id=194.

6 Tony Woods, "The Next Big Energy Savings Frontier: Airtight Building Envelopes," Building Envelope Forum, http://www.buildingenvelopeforum.com/pdf/airtightbuilding.pdf.

7 "Radiant Barrier Benefits," RadiantGuard, 2010, http://www.radiantguard.com/.

8 U.S. Department of Energy, "Recovery Act Announcement."

9 Keith Lane, P.E., "Washing Away Electrical Costs," CSE live. July 1, 2006, http://www.csemag.com/article/177643-Washing_Away_Electrical_Costs.php.

10 Ohlone College, "Newark Center Sustainability Green Building Information," December 3, 2009, http://www.ohlone.edu/org/newark/green/renewableenergy.html; Ohlone College, "Ohlone College Newark Center Realizes Unprecedented Energy Conservation in First Year of Operation" (press release), 2009, "Why Waste Heat?" International District Energy Association. December 10, 2009. http://www.pitchengine.com/free-release.php?id=37592

11 "Benefits of Water Efficiency," EPA WaterSense. March 22, 2010, http://www.epa.gov/watersense/water_efficiency/benefits_of_water_efficiency.html; http://www.reuters.com/article/pressRelease/idUS113607+03-Jun-2009+BW20090603; Michael Kanellos, "Generating Heat from Thin Air" (article and video), GreentechMedia, August 6, 2009, http://www.greentechmedia.com/articles/read/video-generating-heat-from-thin-air.

12 "Porous Pavement: A Win-Win Stormwater Strategy," *Building Green*. September 1, 2004, http://www.buildinggreen.com/auth/article.cfm?fileName=130901a.xml.

13 Mikhail V. Chester and Arpad Horvath, "Environmental Assessment of Passenger Transportation Should Include Infrastructure and Supply Chains," *Environmental Research Letters* 4, (June 2009), http://www.sustainable-transportation.com/.

14 http://www.greentechmedia.com/articles/read/mitsubishi-expands-ev-lineup-beyond-i-miev; http://www.mitsubishi-motors.com/special/ev/; http://www.mitsubishi-motors.com/corporate/e/corporate_tagline/index.html.

15 "Solar Tower, Seville, Spain," Power-Technology.com. http://www.power-technology.com/projects/Seville-Solar-Tower/

16 PG&E, "PG&E Signs Agreement with Solel for 553 Megawatts of Solar Power" (press release), July 25, 2007, http://www.pge.com/about/news/mediarelations/newsreleases/q3_2007/070725a.shtml.

17 US DOE, "20% Wind Energy by 2030 Report". October 2008, http://www.20percentwind.org/20percent_wind_energy_report_revOct08.pdf.

18 AltaRock Energy Inc., "Engineered Geothermal Systems (EGS): The Energy Under Our Feet," http://www.altarockenergy.com/egs.html; U.S. Department of Energy, Geothermal Technologies Program, *The Future of Geothermal Energy*, 2007, http://www1.eere.energy.gov/geothermal/future_geothermal.html; National Geographic, "Geothermal Energy: Tapping the Earth's Heat," http://environment.nationalgeographic.com/environment/global-warming/geothermal-profile.html; http://geo-energy.org/ - Geothermal Energy Association.

19 MotherCow.org, "Gobar Gas Methane Experiments in India," http://www.mothercow.org/oxen/gobar-gas-methane.html.

20 Ida Karlsson, "Environment: Swedes Going Green in Emergency," Inter Press Service (IPS), July 28, 2009, http://www.ipsnews.net/news.asp?idnews=47844.

21 International Energy Agency (IEA), "2007 Energy Balance for France," http://www.iea.org/Textbase/stats/balancetable.asp?country_code=FR; IEA, "2007 Energy Balance for Poland," http://www.iea.org/Textbase/stats/balancetable.asp?country_code=PL; U.S. Department of Energy, Energy Information Administration, "Voluntary Reporting of Greenhouse Gases: Appendix F. Electricity Emission Factors" (Form EIA-1605 (2007), http://www.eia.doe.gov/oiaf/1605/pdf/Appendix%20F_r071023.pdf.

22 SafeClimate, "How Was This Calculated?" http://www.safeclimate.net/calculator/ind_calc_how.php.

23 Ibid.

24 Integrated Solid Waste Management Report for Pedro Gonzalez Island by Norton Engineering, March 2009, Appendix B1.

25 Nabuurs, G. J., O. Masera, K. Andrasko, P. Benitez-Ponce, R. Boer, M. Dutschke, E. Elsiddig, J. Ford-Robertson, P. Frumhoff, T. Karjalainen, O. Krankina, W.A. Kurz, M. Matsumoto, W. Oyhantcabal, N. H. Ravindranath, M. J. Sanz Sanchez, X. Zhang, 2007: Forestry.

In Climate Change 2007: Mitigation. Contribution of Working Group III to the Fourth Assessment Report of the Intergovernmental Panel on Climate Change [B. Metz, O. R. Davidson, P. R. Bosch, R. Dave, L. A. Meyer (eds)], Cambridge University Press, Cambridge, United Kingdom and New York, NY, USA. , http://www.ipcc.ch/pdf/assessment-report/ar4/wg3/ar4-wg3-chapter9.pdf, p550.

26 U.S. Environmental Protection Agency (EPA), Green Power Partnership, "Renewable Energy Certificates (RECs): What Is a REC?" http://www.epa.gov/grnpower/gpmarket/rec.htm.

27 Progressive States Network, "Utility Decoupling: Giving Utilities Incentives to Promote Energy Efficiency," *Stateside Dispatch*, September 10, 2007, http://www.progressivestates.org/content/671/utility-decoupling-giving-utilities-incentives-to-promote-energy-efficiency.

CHAPTER 6
Sustainable Site Planning, Built Systems, and Material Flows

Civil engineering has typically been characterized as the transformation of natural environments for the purpose of meeting the needs of evolving and expanding civilizations. In the last century, the art and design of civil engineering have given way to a more technocratic approach to building infrastructure. The fact that landscape architecture is conventionally separated from the design of engineered systems is symptomatic of an engineering approach that focuses on conforming to agency standards and codes, with the role of the site design itself as a secondary consideration. This emphasis on function by engineers—while architects are left to focus on form—is now gradually being displaced by the interdisciplinary collaborations that characterize sustainable design.

In nature, form and function are never separate. Each form has multiple functions, and each function takes many forms. Every site we develop begins with considering unique living system functions. The better we understand the complexities of the systems we build upon, the more we can harness natural energies, flows, and materials. This allows designers to incorporate more living infrastructure in their projects, using the technical properties of soil, water, sun, and biological systems to accomplish design goals that are not based on written codes but rather emerge from the individual landscape of each site.

This chapter discusses the natural patterns of ecology, water, wind, and climate. It identifies the way we interact with these elements, assess their value, and enhance them or protect them through the development process. Looking at human patterns of development can help us target inefficiencies and make improvements so that our cities will be more productive and fulfilling. To protect, create, and improve these environments, we establish methods for understanding the relationships between these elements and identify the complementary pieces. When combined, these pieces create and enhance the value that could not be achieved by viewing an individual element by itself. Where development patterns or features are in opposition to each other or to a natural pattern, appropriate transitions and buffers between them are suggested. Finally, chapter 6 focuses on the materials used to create and maintain these systems, establishing strategies for responsibly sourcing, using, reusing, and disposing of these materials in a way that emphasizes the concepts of integration and balance.

SUSTAINABLE SITE PLANNING

Baseline studies must be conducted on a site in order to understand its past and present influences. Civil engineers are familiar with the idea that topographical and utility surveys establish a baseline of physical features and existing infrastructure. And it is easy to understand that the more accurate the survey, the better the building will fit the land. In just the same way, ecological baseline studies result in built systems that better fit the local ecological system. This includes an accurate understanding of natural systems such as watersheds, rainfall, solar and wind patterns, geology, soils, flora, and fauna. In sustainable site design the land, its hydrology, and the complex diversity of living systems are interdependent and cannot be isolated from the design process.

Figure 6-1 Fisherville, Tennessee. The existing ecological framework on a project may be complex and overt or subtle and hidden. Understanding the systems in place and the broader ecological context of a site is an important starting point. © Sherwood Design Engineers.

Understanding a Site as a Living System

A design approach that views each site as a living system necessitates an understanding of the ecological ingredients, native inhabitants, and natural patterns of the land. We must understand what they are, why they are important, how they work together, and the ways they change over time. No two sites are alike, even if they are only a block apart. So creating truly sustainable design means never designing the same thing twice. For our projects to become healthy components of their environment, each design must be unique; each must also be developed from the common principles that support the diversity of life forms always present in healthy ecosystems.

To keep the ecosystems we design healthy, we need to know what makes them thrive, and if they are struggling and degraded, we need to know how to make them whole again. We begin this process of "learning the land" by taking inventory, measuring biodiversity, and doing baseline analyses at regional and local scales to understand the ecological context we are building in and its relationship to past and future human impact.

Understanding Natural Patterns

Look beyond single indicators such as vegetation type, soils, or current usage to observe the connections and relationships among a site's natural systems. Understanding these patterns is the key to creating a more successful built environment, because the loss or isolation of one vital element in an ecosystem will have a negative affect on the others.

Natural patterns often reach far beyond a single plot of land and its place in the region. Migratory pathways, ocean currents, and prevailing winds, for example, promote unique patterns of seed dispersal and habitat growth. Similarly, natural cycles occur in seasonal rhythms that must be taken into account. A thorough understanding of local weather patterns, water movements, plant blooms, and temperature differentials will not be gained from a few site visits or a traditional topographic map: it requires a deeper investigation. Integrating our designs more effectively into each site requires understanding a broader range of ecological patterns.

Analysis: Performing Contextual Background Studies

To do a contextual analysis of the physical and living systems present on a site, as well as the external factors—both natural and human— acting upon that site, engineers begin by making inventory maps. Using geographical information systems (GIS), various systems are mapped in order to see how natural patterns interact. By combining related physical assessment maps, zones for protection, development, or restoration can be drawn out. These maps are helpful for greenfields, brownfields, and even suburban or urban landscapes.

Useful assessment maps for a baseline analysis may include

- topography and land analysis (slope, aspect, elevation);
- current and historic land cover (vegetation);
- current and historic ecological communities;
- current and historic land management zones;
- infrared maps to identify current and historic drainage patterns of a watershed area;
- wetlands and riparian corridors;
- soil surveys (from the Natural Resources Conservation Service or elsewhere);
- flood plains (from the Federal Emergency Management Agency or elsewhere);
- historic maps showing old roads, development patterns, and other infrastructure;
- surveys including property boundaries, roads, and utilities;
- personal accounts of longtime residents about high flood marks, historic forest lands, and so on.

By combining and layering this information in relation to the program design criteria, a series of planning maps can be created that inform the physical layout of the various systems, both natural and man-made. These maps can then be tailored to show both the constraints that limit development and the opportunities for where and how it may be most appropriate to develop a particular site.

Conducting Inventories of Natural and Built Systems

Just as a biologist would conduct a biological inventory to understand the biodiversity of a forest, the design team should conduct an inventory of a site's natural systems. This includes internal systems and regional systems—particularly those regional systems that affect the project site in some way. The conditions that support vital ecosystems such as forests and wetlands should be identified, including plant and animal types, endangered species, hydrologic systems, soil systems, native plant requirements, topography, temperature, and the influence of adjacent ecosystems.

The following are short descriptions of important natural system resources that should be identified at the site or regional scale. These component elements should be evaluated for their overall health and relative value to adjacent systems. Comparative analysis of these resource systems can then inform strategies for the conservation and restoration of natural systems as well as for their integration with built infrastructure systems.

This book deals more extensively with natural systems inventories than built systems inventories. This is because surveys of built systems are more widely used and generally understood, while surveys of natural systems are more complex and often incomplete or underemphasized in planning and design projects.

Geological Inventories

Understanding local geological conditions is necessary for comprehensive site design. Expensive construction delays and time-consuming design alterations can be avoided by completing geological surveys and a geotechnical soils report. Basic geological conditions will provide a designer with the locations and depths of bedrock and soil bearing capacity for the construction of structures, roads, and other systems. This information becomes an important tool in identifying the appropriate siting of these features. These inventories clarify the depth of groundwater and its variability, which can inform opportunities for wetland creation and restoration as well as limitations on excavation for structures and utilities.

A complete geological inventory will expedite many areas of design, including drainage, earthwork, retaining structures, and keyways. If not performed adequately, the repercussions can become a significant liability for the project. For example, the premature siting of a building may result in the design of cut slopes in areas of bedrock, thus resulting in expensive excavation and increased energy output.

A good geotechnical report includes these basic components:

- Subsurface soil and bedrock conditions
- Groundwater table fluctuations
- Soils subject to expansion, settlement, and liquefaction
- Soil infiltration potential/percolation rates
- Stability (slumps and slides)
- Seismic design parameters

- Construction requirements
  - Earthwork and grading parameters
  - Foundations
  - Pavement sections
  - Retaining walls
  - Drainage and subdrainage
  - Setbacks to top/toe of slopes
  - Pond/reservoir recommendations

Soil Health Inventories

Soils supply life to all terrestrial ecosystems. Our consideration of the natural environment often ends with plants and animals, but soil nutrients, root structures, and microorganisms in the soil support all flora and fauna. Healthy topsoil is necessary to support the plants and animals that grow, decompose, and sustain new life. Soils require a delicate balance between continual growth and decay to maintain the cycles that supply nutrients to the biosphere aboveground.

A comprehensive soil assessment can identify the presence of contaminants that may need to be removed or stabilized. In many previously developed areas, these studies yield the presence of fill materials, which may compromise bearing capacity and potential use. Topsoil depth, the percentages of loam and sand present, and the permeability of that loam and sand will all inform the potential to introduce wastewater and stormwater systems on-site.

Understanding local soils is necessary for designing stormwater controls and deciding which plantings are suitable to a site. Maintaining a stable and dense growth of vegetation, especially in areas where it is exposed to rainfall runoff, will prevent erosion and displacement of the soil and its valuable nutrients. Whether the soil is acidic or alkaline, clayey or sandy, north or south facing (as well as a number of other factors) determines the future health of vegetation. Soil testing is often performed to determine which plants will grow most successfully on a site. Aligning a native plant palette with the proper soil conditions helps to sustain plant growth and build healthy soils that will support future growth.

Hydrological Inventories

All surface and subsurface water systems within a site or region should be considered, including springs, streams, lakes, rivers, intermittent streams, groundwater tables, aquifers, wetlands, tidal bodies, estuaries, oceans, and any other indicators of water sources. A professional hydrologist, engineer, or wetland expert should be retained to provide a detailed understanding of the whole hydrologic system.

Wetlands/Hydric Soils

Wetlands provide some of the most diverse habitat of any natural system and can be functional under both seasonal and permanent conditions. The restoration or creation of wetlands requires proper implementation, but given the correct conditions,

Figure 6-2 Lake Merced, California. The restoration and enhancement of wetlands, as well as their reestablishment as habitat, can often come into play on development projects. Seen in this image, the wetlands around San Francisco's Lake Merced survive despite the loss of nearly 90 percent of the lake's watershed to urbanization and stormwater diversion. © Sherwood Design Engineers.

wetlands are feasible in most development types. The presence of hydric soils, high groundwater, natural depressions, low topography, and flood plains are all indicators of historic or potential wetland areas that might be successfully restored. Initial planning of potential land uses should include the identification of these factors in addition to existing wetlands and naturally buffered areas. Once these systems are identified, zones suited for more appropriate land use can be delineated.

Open Water Bodies

Open water systems such as intermittent or perennial streams, marine systems, lakes, and pond habitats are the delicate and exposed arteries transporting, cleaning, and maintaining one of the most valuable resources to all living systems. Site design must identify and treat these systems with extreme care. The identification of current stream corridors—or closed or relocated waterways—indicates the potential for conservation or restoration during site design. Open water bodies, or flowing waterways, are often desirable on a site, but they require a source and specific geological conditions. With a careful reading of the landscape, it is possible to restore or create natural water bodies that will be more successful, sustainable, and cost-effective than relying on pumping to maintain healthy water bodies.

Riparian Zones

Water bodies evolve with an upland buffer at the water's edge, generally known as the riparian zone. These buffer areas create diverse, unique, and highly valuable ecosystems that control flooding, filter runoff, prevent erosion, and provide habitat.

Figure 6-3 Butterfly Bay, New Zealand. Despite the great distance to the nearest city, this remote portion of Northland, New Zealand, was faced with environmental challenges. A century of ranching patterns had deposited considerable volumes of silt in historically productive oyster beds. Linking land use and marine system function is critical for sustainable coastal land management. Hart Howerton.

Protecting or restoring healthy riparian zones during a site's development is vital in avoiding the degradation of water quality and loss of habitat.

Biological Inventories

A biological expert should be retained to help understand the flora and fauna of the site. Flora includes all the plant species within a region, such as a forest or wetland. Conditions such as climate, latitude, and land formations affect the natural landscape and thus the local flora. The island of Bali, for example, has tropical forests at sea level but pine forests at the higher elevations on the slopes of its volcanoes.

Fauna includes all the animal life in a region. In the past, humans have been biased toward protecting the big creatures that we consider majestic or beautiful, but the unseen tiny organisms are equally important to a properly functioning environment. These include the insects that act as pollinators as well as the bacteria and microbes that act as decomposers. Legislation enacted to protect endangered species has caused developers significant frustration when their projects are shut down to protect a rare plan or animal. But it is not those species in isolation that are so important. Rather, it is the role they play in keeping the entire ecosystem healthy. As designers, we can communicate the ecological values beyond "species protection" and that it is the ecosystem as a whole, and the services it provides, that we must work to protect.

Figure 6-4 Butterfly Bay, New Zealand. Studying infrared and color aerial photography is a valuable starting point for gaining an understanding of vegetation patterns and biological connectivity. Sherwood Design Engineers and Cerulean.

Native Vegetation

Zones of native vegetation are an excellent place to start when identifying areas to be protected or restored. In most city settings, however, nonnative habitat defines the majority of the land cover. Certain invasive species can be viewed as detrimental to the ecosystem, but in many urbanized systems, the nonnative vegetation has found a balance and simply changed the composition of the habitat to create a different and

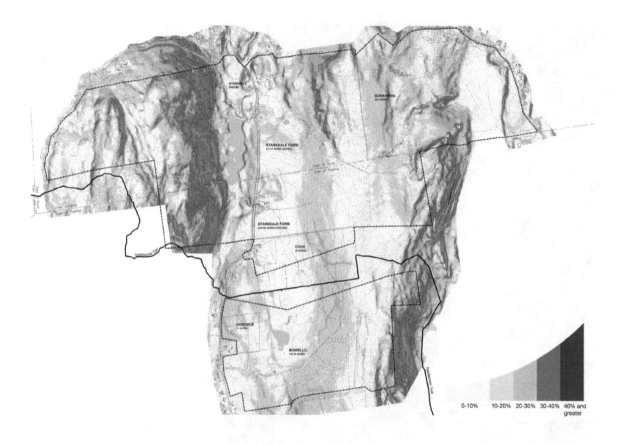

0-10%   10-20% 20-30% 30-40% 40% and
greater

Figure 6-5 Slope maps are useful tools in determining the potential impacts of development on the landscape and to help organize an appropriate design response. © Sherwood Design Engineers.

valuable resource. These growth patterns should be identified: successful species that have adopted a healthy relationship with the local habitat may be promoted even if they are nonnative. However, removing unsuccessful or invasive nonnative species and replacing them with native habitat can yield more resilient, site-appropriate landscapes in many cases.

Topography and Land Analysis

Designers understand the value of assessing the land on which they develop; however, it is critical to achieve a more complete understanding of the land and its connectivity to regional ecosystems than can be gleaned from topographic maps alone.

Landform: The shape of the land's soils, slopes, and bedrock is formed over time by external influences such as rain, wind, and groundwater moving through and over the surface. And just as the landscapes are formed in adaptation to their surroundings, the land's shape itself also determines the paths of shade, wind, and water. By learning from the land, designers can understand the forces that will act on built structures. Mimicking natural land forms through design can minimize these external forces and will create a longer-lasting built environment.

Slopes: A slope analysis measures the incline of a surface as a percentage from the horizontal. A typical analysis is broken down in ranges from 0 to 5 percent, 5 to 10 percent, 10 to 20 percent, 20 to 30 percent, and so on, where 100 percent is equal to a 45-degree slope. A slope analysis helps identify environmentally sensitive land, erosion potential, developable land, and the corresponding cost implications.

Elevation: An elevation analysis aids in comprehending topography and the three-dimensional relationship between various positions on the site. It is useful for understanding view relationships and corridors as well as the placement of infrastructure such as water tanks at high points and pump stations at low points. This analysis is generated from surveyed points, contour lines, aerial imagery, and/or satellite imagery. It is broken into elevation bands to clearly illustrate slight elevation changes.

Aspect: An aspect analysis depicts the direction land faces. This valuable tool allows planners to identify solar orientation and preferred building zones, and design using passive solar strategies or when taking key view orientations into account.

Protection of viewsheds, hilltops, and ridgelines: The identification of existing and future viewsheds is a valuable asset in the early stages of the planning process. A viewshed analysis helps to identify building sites that minimize visual impact to others while maximizing views from the site. This is an important study when identifying areas where obstructions may occur or the views are of high value. Just as the value of protecting water edges for public enjoyment is recognized, hilltops and ridgelines should be considered a protected zone when conducting site layout and grading studies.

Building placement should minimize the impact to the site itself, as well as to those who view the site from afar. In addition to hilltops themselves, the land immediately adjacent to the top of the ridgeline should be protected with setbacks. This will help promote slope stability and erosion control, important concerns for developing on hilltops and ridgelines.

Solar orientation: Using a site's latitude and longitude, topography, and orientation, it is possible to measure the incident solar radiation, or insolation, of a precise location. Insolation measures the intensity of the sunlight over time and is usually expressed in kilowatt hours per square meter per day. This data, paired with climatic data (including sun path studies), helps identify opportunities for solar hot water systems, solar power generation, and the reduction of heating and cooling loads through passive solar design.

Open space: We often perceive dense tree cover or forests as the healthiest form of natural habitat. As we design, however, it is important to balance and integrate forests with other open-space systems like meadows, deserts, prairies, and wetlands, as each offers unique value to ecosystems. Agricultural fields, large and small parks, community gardens, and yards are all examples of open spaces with potential ecological value. Requirements for site greenways and open space are increasingly being mandated, either directly by

Figure 6-6 Open space defines the edge of development in Calgary, Alberta, Canada, and provides a tranquil counterpoint to urbanization. © Sherwood Design Engineers.

applicable codes or indirectly by land designation for things like stormwater management, groundwater well and treatment facility setbacks, right-of-way designations, and building envelope setbacks. The thoughtful design of open space can greatly benefit a site as a whole, as well as adjacent public areas.

As climate change comes to the forefront of our minds when considering building system and infrastructure design, so too should it when we consider sustainable site and open space design. Building up the resistance and resilience of a site's ecosystems by increasing its biodiversity is integral to its ability to adapt to climate change and the corresponding changes in natural resource flows. When designing for open space, the following tenets are paramount:

- Keep existing habitat intact (the larger the area, the better).
- Maintain buffers to habitat ("working" buffers such as agricultural lands are better than none).
- Provide for connectivity between core protected areas (narrower is better than none).
- Keep waterways and riparian corridors intact (headwaters are critical).

Climatological Analysis

Understanding the major climatological variables at work on a site is important for successful systems optimization. The air, water, heat, and light flowing through a site should be thought of as valuable resources that can be captured and utilized through good design. A full study of each sector should be conducted during the early planning process to evaluate climatological factors.

Wind: Wind patterns provide a variety of opportunities and constraints on a site, affecting major systems, including human comfort, through evapotranspiration rates and building heating/cooling patterns, as well as seed dispersion, air quality, and energy potential. Understanding the patterns of local wind speed, direction, force, and quality can greatly influence design decisions.

Solar: Solar orientation is one of the most important siting considerations. Apart from its impact on the built environment, solar exposure can either destroy or promote healthy vegetated systems. Ideally, these impacts would be identified in the design phase, before construction begins.

Shade: Shade is a valuable resource for passive cooling, minimizing water loss, and controlling temperature. If designed properly, shading can greatly buffer the energy inputs for building cooling or decrease the heat island effects.

Precipitation: Rainfall and stormwater runoff are valuable resource flows within a site. In addition to opportunities associated with harvesting rainfall for irrigation and potable water offsets, precipitation is a critical element in species selection and vegetation establishment.

Air: The air quality on a site affects all aspects of ecology, health, and human comfort. Air contamination can contribute to urban heat island effect or exacerbate asthma, for example. Assessments of pollutant loads, dust, allergens, and other air contaminants should be undertaken, as should efforts to improve air quality through planting, ventilation, building placement and orientation, shading, and other site design decisions.

Flood plains: It is important to assess seasonal flooding and historical floodplain and floodway levels before building near the water. Designers should consult local flood maps early in the process to make sure they have a complete understanding of minimum elevation requirements. Flood plain data may not always be readily available, but reviewing the watershed in context will provide a clear view of natural patterns for water movement and potential flooding. Available data should also be critically reviewed relative to topography and actual records of flooding, as most data was created at a scale much larger than the one at which a site designer reviews an individual parcel.

The factors causing any flooding identified—such as excessive development, poor soil conditions, groundwater depth, or historic streams and ponds—should be well understood. That understanding will improve the effectiveness of planning and design. Given global warming and the associated impacts on rainfall patterns and sea levels, designing more conservatively when it comes to minimum elevations and buffers to waterways is recommended.

Built Systems Inventories

Figure 6-7 Shanghai. In urban environments, the haphazard placement of utilities can result in a tangled mass of overhead wires and cables. Where possible, utility design should be coordinated to reduce the visual and physical impact on public spaces. © Sherwood Design Engineers.

For the purposes of planning, *gray infrastructure* is generally considered to be human-built habitat that provides a functional benefit exclusively to humans. A summary of gray infrastructure systems is an important part of baseline contextual studies.

Transportation: Transportation networks are one of the most invasive systems on the planet due to their exclusively human uses and their segmentation of the natural environment. These corridors are nonetheless necessary for human development. By identifying and understanding existing natural patterns, their impact on surrounding ecosystems can be reduced. Like all corridors, human transportation routes have a destination and an origin. These change over time, however, allowing us the opportunity to reconsider dimensions and alignments that can better serve both the purposes of the natural environment and the needs of human activity.

Utilities: Utility corridors are another exclusively human system with large impacts on the natural environment. Therefore, each system should be reviewed for redundancy and purpose. Oftentimes these corridors are vestiges of previous land use patterns and are no longer necessary or are improperly located. In addition, each utility corridor provides a potential opportunity for combined use with transportation, other utilities, or surface easements that can serve as habitat. It is not uncommon for a utility corridor to preserve a natural surface condition over a long and navigable route that can provide circulation for fauna. Identifying these opportunities and enhancing these spaces will maximize the benefits to both the natural and built environment.

Water and wastewater infrastructure: Water collection, treatment, and distribution systems have a large impact on the ecosystem yet are essential to human settlement. The capacity of these systems and their potential costs, both environmental and economic, inform the limits of the land for development as much as any other factor. Understanding the availability and feasibility of introducing these systems provides an indication of the settlement pattern's viability and sustainability. The source of potable water should be reviewed in the context of the resources depending upon it and its ability to recharge, and thus be a sustainable source. Wastewater discharge methods and locations must be understood to identify opportunities and constraints for improved efficiencies, reuse opportunities, environmental degradation, and land consumption.

Synthesis: Interpretation and Response

The individual assessment of each opportunity and constraint should be preceded by a comprehensive comparison of each discrete component to identify the synergies and mutual benefits lying between them. Mutual benefits will reinforce individual patterns and deemphasize others, providing a clear set of priorities for the planning process.

This process of synthesizing opportunities and constraints requires the designer to contrast similar and dissimilar site conditions. Resource areas for habitat, such as wetlands and coastlines, often overlap with the built environment, and design opportunities can be found by considering infrastructure and habitat corridors together. The placement of a piece of infrastructure such as a transmission line or access easement may present an opportunity for complementing or improving local ecosystem connectivity.

Beyond integration, the adjacency or relationship of one land use to another can compromise or enhance the viability of the other. The context of all systems should be clear so we can identify where buffers and transitions are necessary, and what form these buffers should take. Temporal transitions can be challenging to determine but are necessary to accommodate. The natural evolution of a forest or the change in use of a neighborhood will have significant effect on the viability of the adjacent spaces. Providing flexibility in the planning of site systems—natural and synthetic—will allow the landscape to adapt and thrive to its evolution.

Protection vs. Restoration

Maintaining a clear picture of the land in its context is essential. Natural ecosystems operate at a variety of scales, so correctly interpreting baseline ecosystem maps means looking closely both at the specific site and at how the site fits into the larger regional systems. Mapping environmental systems at both local and regional scales is important in correctly determining which areas or ecosystems need to be protected and which can be developed with minimal disturbance to the larger systems.

Maps should not be oversimplified to merely represent *where* to develop. The careful interpretation of constraints and opportunity plans during the sustainable design process shows designers *how* to develop. For instance, they may show opportunities for the restorative development of land that needs recovery. In this process, emphasis is put on understanding the natural systems at work on the land prior to siting, and then programming site infrastructure in a way that will promote balance by minimizing the impact of human systems while buffering and promoting the natural systems.

Mapping Blueways

Blueway systems are water systems that form the hydrological cycle. Blueway mapping is used to integrate these layers, including streams and rivers, intermittent streams, runoff patterns, wetlands, hydric soils, elevations, and any other natural feature that can be used as an indicator to highlight current or past water systems. Blueway systems are the lifeblood of the land and should be preserved or restored whenever and wherever possible.

A blueways map can tell the designer about

- existing waterways that should not be impacted
- potential zones of restoration to historical waterways that have been drained for development or agriculture
- waterways with hydrologic or hydraulic connectivity potential

Mapping Greenways

Greenway mapping is a useful tool that integrates natural ecosystem layers such as trees, vegetation, grasslands, soils, species habitat, migratory pathways, farmlands, and any open space or parklands. Connecting these critical areas within a site or between sites creates green corridors, or greenways.

Figure 6-8 Habitat priority map, Florida. As part of a large planning project, Sherwood synthesized GIS data from the state of Florida and supplemented it with site-specific data to better understand the larger ecological systems in the context of the project. This map helped to develop an understanding of mammal movement patterns within the region. State of Florida.

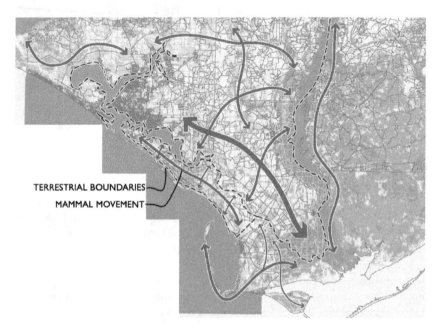

TERRESTRIAL BOUNDARIES

MAMMAL MOVEMENT

A greenways map tells the designer about

- current open space or green space patterns
- current urban forest
- opportunities for connection of open and green space
- opportunities to define, create, or restore green corridors
- opportunities for restoration of disturbed areas

Once the blue and green infrastructures are connected, built gray infrastructure can be responsibly interwoven into these natural systems. Some of the keys to finding restoration opportunities, and properly knitting natural and human infrastructure together on a site, include the following:

- Value and protect land that is providing ecosystem services.
- View endangered or damaged landscapes as an opportunity for active restorative development.
- Restore areas that reconnect a broken ecosystem.
- Develop with a density in context to the adjacent gray infrastructure.
- Develop to diversify and make a functional edge between gray, blue, and green systems.

Connectivity

Connectivity to other similar and interdependent ecological systems, such as open water systems, is important for the survival of many flora and fauna, because that connectivity can affect migration, food sourcing, and propagation. Because the built environment often creates obstacles and impediments to flora and fauna, it is crucial for development to provide connectivity between sites so ecosystems can function properly. This requires maintaining and restoring habitat, individual flora and fauna species, and the regional links between these systems. As past development has shown, disturbing any one element in an ecosystem can throw off the balance of the entire system.

Development needs to provide habitat for an ecosystem to exist, a place where connections can happen and individual species can find the resources they need for life. Development should also provide connectivity to surrounding communities through planting, grading, and water management strategies to ensure continuity and prevent disruption of natural evolutionary processes. Past and ongoing research in the field of biodiversity has shown that even narrow and marginal corridors are critical to keep plant and animal gene pools evolving (and surviving) across regions with the ever-changing global environment.

Buffers and Edges

Conserving, restoring, or creating healthy and functional buffer zones between natural and synthetic systems is necessary to the sustained health and value of the whole system. For example, the value of wetlands is directly affected by the provision of functional upland areas and buffer zones. The form of a buffer can be anything from a strip of natural grassland to a wooded riparian corridor to an active agroforestry operation. These systems not only complement the habitat they buffer but can also support other interdependent ecological systems. The interaction of blue, green, and gray infrastructure creates an edge that promotes diversity of habitat and ecology. Their influence on one another should be considered during the design of multifunctional and integrated systems. The need for these transitional zones presents many opportunities for creative and sustainable open space design.

Land-Use Succession

In conventional land planning, each site tends to be viewed as a snapshot of current conditions at the time of development; the natural succession of a landscape is generally not considered. But because meadows become forests, streams meander, sand dunes move, and species migrate, the succession of the landscape is an important factor in ecologically sound planning. This leaves planners with two important considerations: how to develop now and not compromise the land for future uses, and how to reclaim currently disturbed landscapes for human development rather than impacting currently healthy landscapes. Fortunately, succession also means that in time, a landscape can recover, healthy prairies can return after the tractors and pesticides are withdrawn, and forests and marine wildlife can regenerate if we allow them to take their natural course.

Designers can help direct the form and pace of this recovery by choosing development patterns that restore a balance, one that is agreeable to both human use and ecological function. Establishing connective corridors by allowing select woodland to grow back, restoring a missing section of wetland, or protecting buffer zones between ecosystems are all choices that can promote the healthy evolution of the landscape. By designing for the succession of the land, we can make designs that evolve in time and in tune with the natural landscapes.

⤒ For more information on related topics please see
   www.sherwoodinstitute.org/casestudy.

GREEN STREETS AND TRANSPORTATION NETWORKS

Streets have always been more than just a way to move people and goods from one place to another. Streets also provide an open space—a communal area for markets, gatherings, social interaction, and civic functions. Many streets in modern cities have lost these additional functions and have been reduced to sections of pavement dominated by automobiles. Some streets are designed solely for automobile traffic and parking, losing any shared public space, and in many cases losing all pedestrian-based furnishings.

Sustainable street design focuses on pedestrian orientation and green streets in an attempt to reallocate street space for more enhanced pedestrian and ecological system integration while still providing for the movement of vehicles and goods necessary for modern society. There are many ways to create community-oriented sustainable streets, including the addition of walkable areas, bicycle lanes, street trees and other plantings, pervious surfaces, gathering spaces, and traffic calming controls. When all of these functions are integrated into the public right-of-way, we have streets that perform a variety of valuable functions for their communities, from reducing pollution and managing stormwater to promoting healthy activity and community interaction.

Taking an integrated approach to land-use and transportation planning that incorporates complete street and green street elements has a cascade of benefits. Developing multiple modes of transportation reduces overall car travel demand, which reduces traffic congestion and vehicle miles traveled (VMT). The benefits of these reductions include reduced energy consumption, reduced carbon monoxide generation, and reduced greenhouse gas emissions. Likewise, green streets contribute to urban air quality; help establish ecological corridors; sustainably manage stormwater; provide shading and cooling for the urban environment; and contribute natural, seasonal elements to urban scenery.

Incorporating green streets elements can redefine a street's use and traffic patterns, giving it a new position within the surrounding street hierarchy. Reassigning the hierarchy of streets within an entire neighborhood through sustainable street retrofits can change the way the community or city functions. Shifting a network of streets from automobile-focused to pedestrian-focused circulation patterns keeps the majority of vehicular traffic on arterials, allowing pockets of local streets to form pedestrian-oriented zones.

Ultimately though, for streets to become more sustainable, the urban fabric in which the streets are found also needs to become more sustainable. Improving the street to encourage walkability is a necessary step toward changing behavior, but people still need a destination that is within walking distance. Redesigning our streets at a human scale will not be effective unless we also rethink our approach to community and city development, making it essential that we prioritize

- transit-oriented development
- New Urbanism/traditional development
- clustered development
- urban renewal
- urban infill
- retrofits of existing neighborhoods

A comprehensive discussion of these various approaches to urban planning is beyond the scope of this book; however, this section does discuss how designing better streets can support the goal they all share: creating more livable, sustainable communities and cities. Designers must get beyond traffic studies and instead create plans for mixed modes of transportation designed to move people rather than vehicles, taking into account denser cities with a diversity of transportation options—from bike lanes to bus rapid transit, from neighborhood light rail to regional high-speed rail.

In thinking about sustainable transportation, planners and engineers often focus on how to design a greener roadway. But the roads themselves are a symptom of an unsustainable, auto-centric approach to urban planning. In many U.S. cities cars are the overwhelmingly predominant means of travel because these cities lack convenient

Figure 6-9 Streets should be designed for multiple modes of transportation, with safe and efficient interaction between them. © Sherwood Design Engineers.

transit systems, bicycle lanes connecting to the commercial and recreational centers, and comprehensive sidewalk networks.

Taking a street design approach that integrates multiple modes of transportation in a way that is both useful and attractive to people *and* improves community connectivity and ecological function can make streets an important contributor to a healthy urban landscape. The focus here is on designing complete streets, which encourage a diversity of transportation systems, and green streets, which fit naturally into the landscape, promote ecological connectivity, and provide stormwater management.

Complete Streets

At the city scale, transportation policies significantly influence how transportation infrastructure is established and designed, which greatly determines people's overall travel behavior. Planners use roadway classifications, such as arterial, collector, and local streets, to delineate roadway functions. This approach often yields a highly auto-oriented city. A newer approach is to treat all streets as "complete streets," designed with diverse users in mind: drivers, transit riders, pedestrians, bicyclists, as well as older people, children, and people with disabilities. These policies have been adopted by several states, including Oregon, Florida, and South Carolina.

The complete street approach classifies streets according to their primary transportation role, rather than their size. This helps create linkages between bicycle-oriented or pedestrian-oriented streets, for example, ensuring that bike routes are not cut off by freeways and that pedestrians have safe sidewalks and crosswalks on the routes connecting common destinations. Linking streets by their usage helps create networks through the city and greatly amplifies the effectiveness of multiple modes of transportation.

TYPICAL STREET TYPES AND USES

- *Auto-oriented streets* are those designed primarily to accommodate automobile traffic to and from an activity center. Auto-oriented streets should also have convenient and safe sidewalks and crosswalks.
- *Transit-oriented streets* are designed primarily to accommodate large volumes of transit vehicles. These streets should have exclusive bus lanes (center or side); signal priority for buses; and convenient bus stops with amenities such as shelters, benches, and LED displays of arriving bus times. For center lane–running transit systems like light rail, a median will be an integral element, providing opportunities for streetscape treatments like pervious paving or vegetated stormwater elements.
- *Pedestrian-oriented streets* have significant pedestrian activity and thus warrant wide sidewalks,

crosswalks with pedestrian crossing signals, corner or midblock bulb-outs, scramble pedestrian signals, pedestrian-scale lighting, and streetscape treatment.
- *Bicycle-oriented streets* are streets with bicycle lanes, and preferably bicycle signals, as well as facilities like bicycle locker boxes and bicycle parking and/or storage areas.
- *Pedestrian malls* are outdoor, pedestrian-only streets from which vehicular traffic is prohibited. They can be fitted with landscaping and seating areas and reserved for farmers' markets, festivals, and other public events. Temporary pedestrian malls can be created by closing a street to traffic on certain days and using the street space for pedestrian-centered events like markets, festivals, and parades.

Figure 6-10 A pedestrian-oriented street in Paris is temporarily coverted into a street fair. Note the pedestrian function typically occupies 50 percent of the street width. © Sherwood Design Engineers.

Traffic Calming

The term *traffic calming* has been used by transportation engineers for several decades in reference to methods for reducing vehicle speeds and creating a safer streetscape condition. These methods have a common thread: reducing the space or changing the geometry where vehicles can travel. Drivers thus perceive that a higher speed of travel is unsafe and are therefore less inclined to travel over the speed limit. Bringing nonvehicular components of the streetscape closer to the travel way creates driver awareness of their context. Reduced lane widths, radii, sight lines, and close proximity to landscape features and pedestrian spaces are all common methods of traffic calming.

The methods of traffic calming are constantly evolving and have produced multiple benefits. The aesthetic and desirability of the streetscape is often improved by adding landscaping, variable materials, and more pedestrian space. The addition of vegetated landscape provides opportunities for stormwater management. Reduced vehicle speeds and improved pedestrian space promote nonvehicular activity and comfort. Reduced speeds and alternative travel corridors, such as bike lanes, promote alternative transportation.

Figure 6-11 Paving materials and patterns in a French town delineate various street uses in a shared street. © Sherwood Design Engineers.

Depending on a street's classification, appropriate traffic-calming methods can be used to create a shared circulation space where pedestrians and bicyclists feel comfortable alongside vehicles. Most traffic-calming strategies rely on some combination of horizontal or vertical deflections in the flow of traffic and narrowing the street to slow vehicles down. The following is a list of traffic-calming practices and their benefits:

Road Narrowing

Road narrowing can be applied in many different ways. Creating features that take up a portion of the shoulder or parking lane can make the road appear narrower and influence drivers to slow down without actually taking away width from the travel way. Removing a lane or utilizing narrow lanes can also slow vehicles down. Using a narrow road section must be approved by governing fire departments, as emergency vehicle access must still be maintained in all cases.

For low-volume streets in commercial or residential neighborhoods, narrowing a street can effectively reduce traffic flow and speed. A narrow street can deter vehicular traffic from entering a street and force traffic to slow down to negotiate in a tight area; it can also convey to drivers that a street is a pedestrian-first zone—that although automobiles are allowed, they must yield to pedestrians.

Woonerfs and Shared Streets

Woonerfs are a type of shared street developed in the Netherlands. The design concept involves removing traditional street elements like lanes, curbs, and road signs. This encourages drivers to be more aware of the people and buildings around them and creates a space that is safely shared by pedestrians, cyclists, and vehicles. By removing the lane lines from the center of a street, a broad expanse is created that gives pedestrians and cyclists more space. While it would still be wide enough for two vehicles to pass each other, drivers will use more caution if there is no line or barrier dividing them from oncoming traffic. Within the landscaping exist opportunities to add green street elements for stormwater management integration. Permeable pavement may be used in *woonerfs* with lighter traffic loads and lower speeds, particularly in parking areas.

Shared streets are designed to accommodate pedestrians, bicycles, and vehicles. Sometimes this involves creating dedicated bike and bus lanes to separate cyclists from vehicular traffic. Shared streets where very low-speed vehicle traffic mixes freely with pedestrian and bike traffic is also standard practice. Traffic-calming devices such as special paving types or speed bumps can help keep speeds low and discourage unnecessary traffic.

Integrating Bicycles

Modifying striping and lane configurations can serve as an effective and inexpensive method to expand bike use by providing increased safety for cyclists. As a first phase in improved circulation within Manhattan, New York City officials painted

Figure 6-12 Designated bike lanes. Drawing cyclists out of the regular lanes of traffic reduces accidents and allows traffic to flow more efficiently. A. Mannle.

green bike lanes on surface streets to encourage cycling by making it more visible and safer.

Copenhagen's extensive bike network has encouraged more people to ride bikes than drive automobiles during rush hour. There are separated bike lanes on some lower-speed streets, but other streets feature open lanes where long-term parking, pedestrians, and bike traffic are separated by a physical barrier from the vehicular traffic. Two-way biking is allowed on some low-speed one-way roadways to help speed up bike travel in the city. On bus-priority roadways, efforts are made to ensure bus stops are set back from the intersection so that the bus stop does not hinder visibility for the cyclists.[1]

Traffic-Calming Design Elements

Traffic-calming design elements aim to reduce vehicular traffic and speed while adding beauty to the shared environment, thus creating more pedestrian- and bicycle-friendly communities. These elements can be designed as green space, creating an ideal location to reinforce broader ecosystem restoration and stormwater management goals. Strategies include the following:

- *Curb extensions:* Used to narrow streets and widen sidewalks, curb extensions increase pedestrian safety by reducing crossing distances on throughways and vehicular speeds.
- *Medians:* Medians divide large throughways and provide area for landscaping, stormwater management, and pedestrian refuge. When used in multilane boulevards, medians can break auto-dominated areas into shared spaces with the addition of reduced-speed local access lanes and green space.
- *Chicanes:* These streets with S-shaped deviations located within the right-of-way to calm traffic consist of curb extensions or medians. Having these "obstacles" in the street deters vehicles from speeding.
- *Intersection treatments:* Vehicular speeds and volumes can be reduced by raising the intersections and adding speed bumps, traffic-calming circles, and curb extensions to the intersection design. At crosswalks, changes in pavement and street texture can be applied to deter vehicles from speeding.

Emergency Vehicle Access Accommodation

Emergency vehicle access (EVA) is often the most restrictive design component in the streetscape. Designing for large vehicles with wide wheelbases and large turning radii can force street sections and intersections to be much larger than desired, compromising the planned pedestrian-oriented streetscape.

Sherwood's engineers have successfully addressed this condition by meeting with regulatory agencies directly (including the fire marshal), presenting the design intent, and suggesting alternatives to the standard large streetscape dimensions. If a design provides for appropriate access routes and maneuverability, the details are often flexible. Some of Sherwood's more successful strategies include the following:

- Reinforced roadway shoulders, often made of permeable material, to provide a drivable surface wide enough to allow emergency vehicles to maneuver, park, and pass.
- Low (2- to 4-inch) curbs that allow larger emergency vehicles to mount them but maintain a narrower traveled way or intersection radius for passenger vehicles. These are combined with reinforced shoulders.
- Reinforced landscape consisting of a standard road base material capable of handling large vehicle loading but covered with a shallow layer of topsoil to allow grass or other short ground cover to grow. These zones provide exclusive emergency access routes passing through an otherwise pedestrian landscape, lawn, park, or yard.

For more information on related topics please see www.sherwoodinstitute.org/resources.

IMPLEMENTING A *WOONERF:* SANTA MONICA BORDERLINE

In the Borderline neighborhood (so-called because it is sandwiched between Venice Beach and Santa Monica) in the Los Angeles area, Sherwood worked with transportation planners Nelson\Nygaard Consulting Associates, Blackbird Architects, and landscape architects and planners Van Atta Associates to turn a low-traffic residential street into a shared street connecting a neighborhood park with the local commercial district.

Several blocks were narrowed from 40 feet of pavement to an 18-foot-wide drive aisle flanked by landscaped planters and parking areas and driveways of permeable pavers. The intersecting thoroughfares were also narrowed based on

their traffic volumes. This shared street zone gives priority to pedestrians and forces automobile traffic to slow down and yield the right of way, creating a safer zone for all users.

The street was narrowed by working with the local fire department to ensure emergency vehicle access throughout the project area. Additionally, the utilization of permeable pavement and landscape areas reduced impervious surfaces by 45 percent, allowing stormwater to infiltrate into the groundwater. By utilizing on-site treatment of stormwater, the project is working to restore the health of Santa Monica Bay, which has been impaired due to historical stormwater management practices in the region.

Figure 6-13 Creating a woonerf *on a neighborhood scale in Santa Monica, California, exemplifies a movement of street redesign around the United States to reclaim public space from cars. This application creates a flexible space for the movement of cars, bikes, skaters, and pedestrians. Blackbird Architects/Van Atta Associates.*

Figure 6-14 (far right) Smart-growth streets involve creatively and attractively using trees and plantings to capture and treat polluted runoff. Jack Coyier Photography.

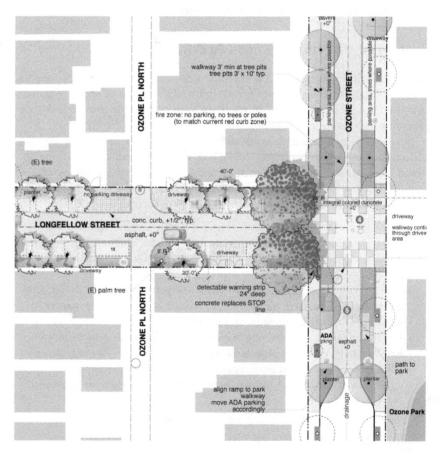

IMPLEMENTING SMART-GROWTH STREETS
Balancing Movement, Ecology and Community
Clark Wilson, U.S. Environemental Protection Agency, Smart Growth Division

While watching the evening news one night, I saw five stories reported in succession: flooding in Iowa, wildfires in Southern California, the worsening mortgage crisis in the Southwest, rising gas prices nationwide, and an epidemic of diabetes and obesity in children. Although these topics vary widely, as an urban designer it occurred to me that they are all consequences of how and where we build.

Dealing with climate change, energy costs, public health, polluted waterways, and crumbling infrastructure in a way that is real, understandable, and readily affects our day-to-day life may seem an overwhelming challenge. But that is our responsibility as urban designers. Increasingly, we are finding solutions by working with natural processes instead of against them, and specifically by rethinking how we design our streets. Streets in most of our towns and cities represent roughly 30 percent of our public open space. While this is an enormous amount of land area, at the street level that space is highly constrained. Designing smarter streets requires asking the obvious question: how do we fit everything into this finite amount of right-of-way?

How can communities redesign their streets from being merely conduits for vehicles to places that are, in the words of Danish urban designer Jan Gehl, "sweet to the pedestrian" (pedestrians being the "indicator species" of a healthy urban environment)? How can natural elements like street trees and planters go from being simple ornamentation to vital pieces of infrastructure?

These exact questions were the premise for the 2009 Environmental Protection Agency (EPA) research paper *Implementing Smart Growth Streets*. The paper identified and described nineteen street design projects in communities across the country that are valuable examples of good design, construction, and management. The technical definition established was, "Smart Growth Streets are roadways designed and operated to support compact communities while promoting least-polluting transportation performance and preserving environmental resources within and beyond the right of way."* More simply, these are streets that are

walkable, bikable, and transit friendly. They are streets that creatively and attractively use trees and plantings to capture and treat polluted runoff. And they effectively connect places to one another while themselves becoming the places where people want to be. In summary, they balance movement, ecology, and community.**

* Undertaken by the Smart Growth Division with contractors ICF International and Ellen Greenberg, AICP.
** Terminology originally developed by Ellen Greenberg, "Sustainable Streets: An Emerging Practice," *ITE Journal* (May 2008).

For more information on related topics please see www.sherwoodinstitute.org/casestudy.

Green Streets

Green streets can serve a community by managing stormwater, supporting landscape treatments, and promoting alternative surfaces within the public right-of-way. Green streets improve water quality, air quality, temperature, aesthetics, and safety. They promote local ecology and provide cost-effective, low-maintenance infrastructure designs for cities and communities.

Chapter 4 discussed urban stormwater management strategies. Applying those tools in the design of new and existing public rights-of-way allows us to steer away from traditional piped solutions. The public right-of-way provides decentralized opportunities for community space very well suited for stormwater collection and treatment. Green street programs can also be used to create extensive networks of stormwater design features, which can work together to handle larger flows of stormwater. By capturing stormwater, green streets can impact sewer design and allow for increased green space in the urban setting.

Integrating Stormwater Programming into Street Design

Stormwater facilities can be incorporated into streets, corridors, open space, or retrofitted urban "found" spaces. When opportunities are discovered during an opportunities and constraints study, it is the responsibility of the designer to determine the needs of the community as well as the requirements of the municipality to achieve multifunctional green infrastructure improvements. The final design of stormwater facilities are based on a site's contextual land use and the various constraints that each site presents.

Naturalized systems like bioswales and vegetated channels can detain and convey stormwater safely off city streets. They absorb the water, reducing runoff rate and volume and recharging the groundwater. Naturalized detention structures collect, temporarily hold, and slowly release stormwater runoff. As pollutants settle during the detention period, water quality is enhanced. Permeable pavement, rain gardens, planters, infiltration trenches, and wetlands are detention practices that can be integrated into a streetscape design.

Many of the stormwater best management practices (BMPs) discussed in chapter 4 can also be used for the retention of stormwater in a green streets application. Retention strategies, which offer long-term collection and storage for stormwater reuse or groundwater recharge, can further reduce stormwater runoff volume and peak flow rates.

Incorporating these landscape-based stormwater management techniques into street design reduces the need for additional infrastructure by focusing on a decentralized system of features that capture and treat precipitation where it falls, more closely mimicking natural systems. This approach is often referred to as integrated because it seeks to incorporate several forms of naturalized or structural stormwater management systems into the urban landscape.

Rain gardens, for example, which are a replacement for manufactured plastic and concrete stormwater treatment systems, use soils, native plantings, and aggregate for the treatment, attenuation, and reduction of site runoff. The rain gardens are placed in low-lying natural drainage collection areas within the site. With proper placement and use of native plantings, the gardens can be seamlessly integrated into the landscape.

Vegetated swales reduce the need for piping and man-made treatment systems when designed for biofiltration. When used in conjunction with existing infrastructure, swales convey runoff from impervious areas to drainage structures and other stormwater treatment facilities. These low-impact development (LID) stormwater systems provide a more sustainable alternative to traditional, centralized stormwater treatment systems.

Green street designs also reduce the impact on underground stormwater infrastructure by reducing the impact from peak flows entering the system. Fewer or smaller piping and drainage structures will be required for green street projects that incorporate natural stormwater treatment facilities. There is also less wear and maintenance on existing infrastructure. Adopting a stormwater management approach to street design extends beyond just green infrastructure. Curb extensions, medians, and other hardscape elements can also help provide obstacles to reduce peak flows or be designed to feed water into swales or rain gardens for treatment.

Optimal stormwater management systems focus on reduction of runoff and simplicity of design. There is a mutual dependency between the quality of stormwater runoff and the health of resident ecosystems; therefore, natural solutions are typically preferable to constructed alternatives.

Impervious areas directly connected to storm drainage systems are the most critical to managing the quantity, rate, and pollutant loading of runoff. Proper planning allows landscaping to incorporate areas for shallow ponding and infiltration, overland flow through vegetated areas, and the reduction of stormwater flowing into the storm drainage system. In areas requiring stormwater detention for peak flow reduction, it is best to combine the treatment and detention measure in one feature.

Reinforcing Urban Forest Fabric with Green Streets

The network of trees and ground-level landscaping that results from the addition of green street design concepts helps to form an urban forest. There are many opportunities within the public right-of-way to develop trees and landscaping, which can perform important ecological functions such as stitching together broken pieces of habitat or reviving the water cycle. An urban forest can also be reinforced along wide boulevards; in tandem with stormwater management facilities like rain gardens; and within pocket parks, green roofs, or commercial street frontages. The urban forest acts to reduce the urban heat island effects, provide stormwater management, and increase biodiversity of habitat.

Green Streets Design Opportunities

Several areas within the streetscape provide ideal locations for green street elements:

- *Driveways:* Permeable pavement or materials can be incorporated into driveways, which handle relatively low traffic volumes.

- *Curbs:* Curb cuts and flush ribbon curbs provide an entrance for stormwater flow into nearby rain gardens and swales that may be located within pocket parks, planting strips, and medians. The curb cuts located at crosswalks and driveways can be used as entrances for runoff, and cuts can often easily be designed and installed midblock on both new and retrofit projects.
- *Traffic calming circles:* These can be placed within large intersections. They offer areas for trees, landscaping, and permeable pavement, all of which can incorporate stormwater treatment.
- *Irregular intersections:* Such intersections often contain unusable pavement with great potential for pedestrian-friendly uses. The pavement can be used for green street items such as curb extensions, planting areas, and pocket parks.
- *Sidewalk planters:* Sidewalk planting areas are suitable for most development densities and are commonly used as streetscape improvements. They are easily integrated into existing developed lots and are especially effective in very high-density residential neighborhoods.
- *Pocket parks and planting strips:* Planting strips can be used for natural drainage along neighborhood green corridors. Pocket parks are most appropriately used along sidewalks in high-density areas lacking other public open space. They can help integrate landscaping into a multiuse space that cannot be fully vegetated, such as along widened sidewalks, extended corner curb extensions, portions of parking lanes, and medians.

CHICAGO GREEN ALLEYS PROGRAM

Alleys provide unique opportunities for green street design elements because they have low traffic volumes and are often considered semiprivate space by local residents. It is sometimes possible to close all or part of an alley to vehicular traffic; where access must be provided for service uses or garages, alleys can be narrowed or made greener:

- *Permeable paving:* Alleys with infrequent traffic can be retrofitted with permeable paving to effectively decrease the paved area and restore the natural hydrologic cycle by allowing water to infiltrate into the ground. Permeable paving is generally best suited for areas of low traffic volume.
- *Planting strips:* In wide alleys, pavement can be reduced by adding planting strips on the side of the alley. In neighborhoods where alleys border on backyards, this effectively extends yard space.

In tighter urban areas, a thin planting strip can create a vegetated border between the alley and the buildings.

- With over 1,900 miles of alleys, Chicago has more miles of alleyways than any city in the world, according to mayor Richard Daley. As an alternative to connecting these alleys to the sewer system, Chicago instituted its Green Alleys Program to help manage stormwater, prevent flooding, and reduce the urban heat island effect. The benefits of the Green Alleys Program are described in the *Green Alleys Handbook* prepared by the Chicago Department of Transportation. These include:
- *Stormwater management:* By repaving alleys with permeable pavement, up to 80 percent of the rainwater that falls on them can pass through to the earth below. This reduces flooding while filtering

and recharging groundwater. By reducing the flow of stormwater into the city's combined sewer system, the use of permeable pavement also saves city taxpayers the cost of treating that additional stormwater.

- *Heat reduction:* By using alley pavers that are a lighter color and more reflective than asphalt, Chicago's Green Alleys absorb less heat and help the city stay cool. This in turn reduces air-conditioning costs and saves energy.
- *Material recycling:* By building the alleys with recycled construction materials like concrete aggregate, slag, and ground tire rubber, the city can reduce the amount of waste hauled to landfills. This cuts pollution while saving energy, money, and natural resources.
- *Energy conservation and glare reduction:* By using new energy-efficient light fixtures in the alleys, the city can reduce glare and light pollution while saving energy and maintaining a safe, well-lit urban environment.

Figure 6-15 a,b An alley retrofit project showing the positive effects of a permeable paving application; before (left) and after the retrofit (right.) Chicago Department of Transportation.

CITY OF PORTLAND GREEN STREETS PROGRAM

In April 2007 the Portland (Oregon) City Council approved a green street resolution to promote and incorporate the use of green street facilities in public and private development. The primary goals of this resolution as stated on the city's Web site are to

- reduce polluted stormwater entering rivers and streams;
- improve pedestrian and bicycle safety;
- divert stormwater from the sewer system and reduce basement flooding, sewer backups, and combined sewer overflows;
- reduce impervious surface so stormwater can infiltrate to recharge groundwater and surface water;
- increase urban green space;

- improve air quality and reduce air temperatures;
- reduce demand on the city's sewer collection system and the cost of constructing expensive pipe systems;
- address requirements of federal and state regulations to protect public health and restore and protect watershed health;
- increase opportunities for industry professionals.

There are already numerous built examples of green streets in Portland.

Source: Portland Bureau of Environmental Services, "Portland Green Street Program," 2010, http://www .portlandonline.com/BES/index.cfm?c=44407.

Figure 6-16 a,b Southwest Twelfth Avenue, Portland, Oregon. Flow-through planters allow for street retrofits that include significant stormwater management without changing the physical grades of the streets and sidewalks. City of Portland.

WORKING WITH THE LAND

The natural form of a landscape is the product of an intricate system that integrates soils, rock structures, groundwater dynamics, complex slopes, and varying pockets of living systems across its topography. Understanding what is shaping a site's existing landscape before beginning development is important because the same forces of gravity, water flow, wind, soil traction, and plant growth will continue to influence the site during and after development.

The landforms found in nature are a result of an equilibrium achieved over their geological life span. These forms are for the most part stable and resistant to erosion. Their geometries include slopes that gradually flatten as they approach the bottom and regularly spaced drainage valleys along their faces. Vegetation follows the flow of surface and subsurface water patterns, and its roots help to hold slopes in place.

In conventional land development, the earth is moved to accommodate buildings and roads, prioritizing the design of the facilities. This type of development favors flat building sites, simple slopes, and straight drainage channels. While this approach may result in the maximum level area around a building site, it also disturbs a much larger piece of land. This is a very time- and energy-intensive process, with a large carbon footprint. Likewise, straight drainage channels cause erosion and require networks of drainage systems. Building sites cut into hillsides also require networks of subdrains to prevent erosion.

This section describes various strategies for integrating built systems into the landscape. It discusses ways to work with nature and allow designs for roads, buildings, and site grading to blend in a more harmonious way with nature.

Sensitive Streetscape Design
Conform to the Natural Patterns

A designer's main goal in designing a street is to create a safe condition for all users that fits into the natural landscape as seamlessly as possible. A fundamental objective in street design should be to avoid developing new streets in undisturbed, natural areas. Increasing the density of already developed areas or redeveloping areas that have already been disturbed can help minimize the environmental impacts of new streets. Whenever new streets are being planned, sensitive responses to the topography and underlying ecological systems are a primary concern for sustainable design.

A road whose geometry matches its landscape will fit more seamlessly with the terrain and minimize the disturbance to the environment (see figure 6-16). Achieving this goal requires integrating the topography, the existing vegetation, and the subsurface conditions with the project's master plan to determine the least impactful routing and design for the street.

Street Alignment

In order to best accommodate the surrounding landscape, a street's horizontal and vertical geometries should be designed together. Curves and slopes should influence each other as the street rises and falls with the landscape. This will often naturally align the user with views of major natural features, creating an experience that makes users feel a part of the land in which they are traveling, offering a more pleasant walking, biking, or driving experience. Vertical geometry also affects drainage design; keeping streets moving with the natural topography allows drainage design to mimic the site's preexisting drainage patterns.

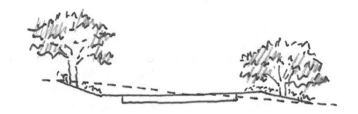

Figure 6-17a Cut to fill on a gentle cross slope. The ideal placement of a rural street depends primarily on the steepness of the terrain and the desired earthwork balance. On a gentle cross slope, a cut-to-fill situation is ideal: when viewed in cross section, the street's centerline will be at grade, with one side in slight cut and the other in slight fill. This typically yields a close balance between cut and fill. © Sherwood Design Engineers.

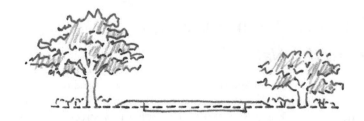

Figure 6-17b Cut to fill on a flat cross slope. On extremely flat cross slopes, cut to fill can be achieved by placing the centerline of the street slightly above grade to account for the material generated by placing the base course of the street. © Sherwood Design Engineers.

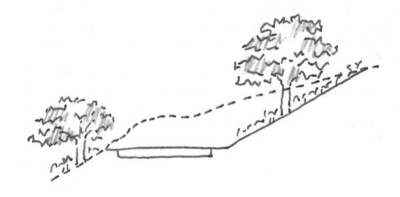

Figure 6-17c Pinned at edge. On steep cross slopes, it is advisable to pin the downhill shoulder at the existing grade and cut into the hillside. This avoids sliver fills—fills that contain a small volume of material spread out over a large area. Sliver fills are difficult to build and unnecessarily disturb an excessive area of existing vegetation and soil. © Sherwood Design Engineers.

There are many instances where cut or fill is necessary, and there are a few where they are even desirable. For instance, an exposed rock face cut at a steep slope can be quite attractive, depending on the material and the excavation technique. Cases such as these should not be ruled out, but they are often the exception. Also, a project may have a surplus or deficit of material in other locations, and the street construction can address that imbalance.

Minimize Street Width

One strategy Sherwood has employed to reduce impact to the existing landscape is to define street hierarchies that incorporate bike paths and cart paths, restricting conventional automobile access. Removing automobiles and replacing them with bikes or modified golf carts has many benefits. Carts often run on alternative fuels or electricity, reducing greenhouse gas emissions. Because the carts are narrower, the streets themselves can be narrower than a conventional street. And the carts can frequently allow the streets to be steeper. These two benefits can drastically reduce the extent of areas disturbed by street construction on steep slopes. Cart paths often still need to provide emergency vehicle access, so they are required to meet standards for EVA, typically defined by the local fire department. EVA requirements can still be met with narrower street designs, however, through the use of pullouts and/or separations constructed at specific locations.

Figure 6-18 Sample street sections. By managing vehicular types and access within projects, street sections and corresponding impacts can be minimized. For a project in Costa Rica, Sherwood decreased street sections by up to 10 feet in golf cart–only neighborhoods, allowing for drastic reductions in cuts and creating a more pedestrian-friendly neighborhood. © Sherwood Design Engineers.

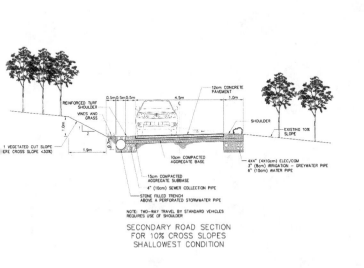

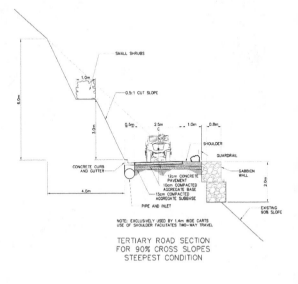

SANTA LUCIA PRESERVE STREET DESIGN PROCESS

The Santa Lucia Preserve, which includes some of the most beautiful landscape of Northern California's coastal region, represents an innovative model for combining development and conservation. This 20,000-acre watershed is both a functioning nature conservancy and a residential community where homeowners act as invested stewards of the land. Extensive resource mapping was completed prior to the planning process to identify the most important resource areas on the site and, more importantly, identify areas where development and access roadways would not have a significant adverse impact upon the environment. As part of the project's commitment to the environment, we worked hand in hand with the project landscape architect to design the optimal road-

way and trail network from a preservation standpoint, creating a network that melds with the natural conditions—protecting trees, preserving natural slopes, following the contours of the land, and promoting site aesthetics.

During the planning phase we used aerial photography, topography, constraint mapping, site reconnaissance, and the latest design software to ensure that the concept design was as accurate as possible. During the design documentation phase we walked the roads with the client, explaining impacts and design considerations, and we worked collaboratively with the general contractor to make adjustments where necessary to ensure an end product that protected vegetation, sensitive habitat, rock outcrops, and water resources.

Sensitive Site Design
Conforming to the Existing Patterns

Carving up the land to create flat building sites is a large contributor to unbalanced landform design, which increases the amount of earth that must be hauled to or off of a site. To cut costs, one common practice is to spread out the extra dirt over a large area to help balance the site earthwork. Unfortunately, doing so increases the disturbed area while burying and compacting native soils. This makes it more difficult for the soil to drain and for plants to grow—both of which contribute to erosion.

In contrast, sustainable development requires an approach to land forming that mimics natural forms and works in tandem with natural forces. Sensitive site design works to attenuate site flattening, minimize graded areas, protect existing soils and vegetation, and implement designs that work with the natural slopes of the landscape instead of against them.

By considering the local topography, hydrology, and planting, we can design landforms that have greater long-term stability, require less upkeep, and fit more naturally into their surroundings. Since earthwork is one of the more expensive and energy-intensive parts of construction, substantial savings can result from a design that conforms to the constraints of the existing topography.

Another method for reducing the impact of earthwork on a project is balancing the cut and fill on-site. This is accomplished by designing the grading so that the amount of material from cut sections roughly matches the amount of fill needed to establish a desired surface. The placement of structures on an existing topographical landform usually results in unbalanced earthwork. Frequently, this leads to an excess of material that requires disposal.

Balancing earthwork means integrating a variety of important design decisions, including building location, finish floor elevation, foundation and wall construction methodology, and geotechnical factors, as well as grading and drainage patterns. Although designing more integrated and complex landforms can present new challenges for designers, it can also bring considerable value to a project by making the landscape more aesthetically pleasing, environmentally responsive, technically functional, and cost-effective. Cooperation and coordination among engineers, ecologists, and land planners from the start of a project produces better results than much current practice, which often decouples environmental land planning and engineering.

Grading to Mimic Natural Drainage Patterns

The final design must achieve proper drainage and conveyance of surface runoff to avoid trapping water or disturbing the original drainage routes. The design must also take into account possible geologic hazards and potential subgrade issues.

Replicating the natural drainage of a watershed system is one of the more challenging design objectives we face as engineers. Once stormwater is collected, conveying it to a safe downstream discharge point becomes an engineering problem. Mimicking the natural drainage patterns within land-forming designs can avoid or reduce the amount of collection points and subsurface networking required.

Opposite page, clockwise from top left:

Figure 6-19a Before construction of a rural neighborhood roadway, the alignment was staked in the field, then reviewed and adjusted with an arborist to minimize the impact on trees. © Sherwood Design Engineers.

Figure 6-19b During construction we worked to carefully grade the roadway into the landscape and to soften the cut and fill slopes to blend in with the landscape. © Sherwood Design Engineers.

Figure 6-19c After six months, the rains fostered the regrowth of the ground cover. The roadway sits effortlessly in the land and looks like it has been in this location for decades. © Sherwood Design Engineers.

Figure 6-20 The road design process at the Santa Lucia Preserve. Road design was viewed as an art as well as a science. From planning through construction, careful attention was paid to the form of the land and local ecology. Great care was taken to design a road network that blends into the natural surroundings and maintains the physiographical function as close to predevelopment conditions as possible. Hart Howerton.

Figure 6-21 Pelican Court, Sea Ranch, California. The principle of living lightly on the land is a fundamental part of the philosophy at Sea Ranch, one of the West's early sustainably designed communities. Preservation of the coastal meadow habitat and wildlife corridors was of primary importance in the planning for this remote coastal residence. Earthwork disturbance was minimized by close coordination with the architect, enabling the house and driveway to be integrated into the existing topography. Nick Noyes Architecture/ JD Peterson Photography.

Opposite page:

Figure 6-22 (top left) The numbers on this plan reveal the difference between the existing topography and the proposed design: +4 requires a 4-foot fill to meet the design, while -3 means a cut of 3 feet. By balancing the cuts and fills, the need to haul dirt to or from the site can be limited. © Sherwood Design Engineers.

Figure 6-23a (bottom), b (top right) This diagram shows two proposed design placements for a property at California's Santa Lucia Preserve. The grading analysis determined that Alternative B was more balanced from an earthwork perspective, allowing us to guide the development toward a more sensitive design. © Sherwood Design Engineers.

As we plan our landscapes, we must maintain the natural water patterns of runoff with respect to volume, rate, and discharge location as closely as possible; mimicking their undeveloped conditions will prevent ecosystem degradation within—or even beyond—the area of development. Typically, as we build upon previously undeveloped land, the natural conduits for recharging and maintaining groundwater levels in the soil are blocked and reduced. A more sustainable development approach compensates for this by designing for the retention of rainfall on-site to facilitate infiltration to the local groundwater and minimize development impacts.

The drainage infrastructure of an undeveloped site typically consists of soils that allow the water to infiltrate and natural drainage paths, streams, and rivers that convey the overland runoff as well as base flows. To minimize the amount of new drainage infrastructure required, these natural drainage systems should be maintained as much as possible when developing a site.

Minimizing drainage infrastructure can be accomplished by

• incorporating and utilizing the existing drainage routes into and out of the development;
• ensuring that no water is trapped, such as behind a building on a slope;
• creating saddle points so that no drains are required;
• avoiding compacting well-draining soils during construction;
• minimizing the impact to existing established vegetated growth at the edges of development.

BALANCING EARTHWORK USING GRADING ANALYSIS

A particular site design might optimize an energy-saving strategy like daylighting a building, but if that building placement requires significant site grading, it may counteract those energy efficiency gains. By modeling the grading effects of a proposed site layout, we can input that data into our design process.

We develop a grading a plan for finished floor elevations for the building and then model that against the existing surface to show where the cuts and fills are required for a given design. By tallying the total cuts and fills, we can determine how to adjust the plan to achieve a balanced earthwork scenario with that particular design configuration.

When sensitive site design is incorporated with integrated energy and water management, it allows engineers to have less impact on the land and minimize the amount of energy devoted to constructing our projects.

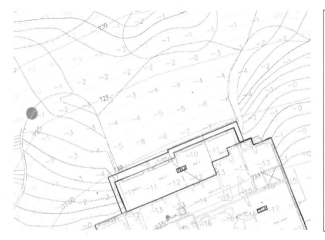

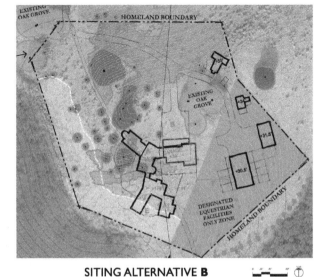

ALTERNATIVE EARTHWORK ANALYSIS

	Cut	Fill	Net
ALTERNATIVE "A"	3809	23	3786 (C)
ALTERNATIVE "B"	1633	590	1043 (C)
PROPOSED CURRENT LOCATION	4630	3150	1482 (C)

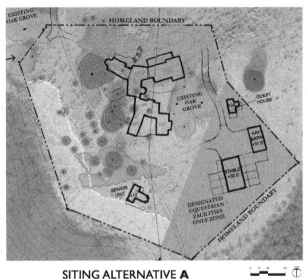

SITING ALTERNATIVE A

SITING ALTERNATIVE B

MATERIAL AND WASTE FLOWS

So far, much of this book has focused on strategies for better design, better configurations of common systems, and strategies for thinking about resources differently. This section delves into the physical makeup of the infrastructure we design and the implications these choices have on overall sustainability.

Materials impact the functionality of the systems that they comprise, and they also embody the energy, materials, and environmental and social impact of their manufacture. Accounting for and reducing these impacts is an important part of the sustainability picture.

A key component of design analysis is the consideration of the materials selected for the projects we build, with a primary focus on materials used in construction. However, the ongoing material flows of project operations also have significant environmental implications. It is beyond the scope of this book to talk about ongoing materials use—in building operations and maintenance, for example—but similar principles apply. This section discusses life-cycle analysis and material footprint calculations as tools for choosing sustainable materials. These can be helpful in selecting materials at any stage of a project's ongoing operations as well.

Designing durable infrastructure with low maintenance requirements should be a primary consideration when choosing materials. Aging infrastructure is an expensive and dangerous liability in dense urban areas, where failure can immobilize transportation and supply networks. Failing infrastructure can cause electrical fires, flooding, or power outages. Extreme examples of infrastructure failure include tunnel and bridge collapses. Less extreme failures cost taxpayers in the form of bond measures for infrastructure upgrades and emergency repairs to water and sewer lines. It is also important to consider the environmental impact of the failure of an infrastructure system. Lower-quality designs might appear to cost less in terms of developer or taxpayer money and potentially reduced installation times, but a failure in a water piping network can compromise foundations, streets, and slopes; generate more leaks and inefficiency; and possibly create public health problems.

Evaluating the Environmental Impact of Infrastructure Materials

What follows is a discussion of how to complete a materials assessment and how to establish a materials footprint, two tools often used on projects as part of a sustainable materials strategy. Materials assessments and footprints allow designers to analyze the relative environmental impacts of materials on a project, as well as the environmental impact of the project as a whole. These tools can help designers make better materials decisions by better communicating the full energy and environmental costs of the materials used on a project. A life-cycle assessment (LCA) is a further evaluation of a material in terms of its environmental impact over the course of its entire life span: from the extraction of the raw material to its final disposal or end use. International standards have been developed for evaluating LCAs by the International

Organization for Standardization [ISO] and ASTM International [originally known as the American Society for Testing and Materials], but a discussion of these is beyond the scope of this book.

Questions to Consider during a Materials Assessment

A material's environmental impact is a combination of a number of factors and can be defined in various ways. The following questions will help a designer to assess the environmental impact of construction materials over the life cycle of a project:

Production

* How much energy and water are used to extract the raw material and manufacture the material?
* Is the product extracted in a deleterious manner (such as strip mining or clear cutting)?
* What is the environmental impact of production, accounting for raw materials, additional ingredients, and waste associated with the manufacturing process?
* Does the material contain recycled content or wastes from other materials?
* How much packaging is used? Does the manufacturer provide minimal or reusable shipping methods?

Toxicity

* Is the product nontoxic? Does it leach toxins into the environment during any stage of its life cycle? (See the sample Materials Red List sidebar on page 248.)
* Have manufacturers or suppliers been consulted about possible toxic materials within their products? Can material safety data sheets, which contain a complete listing of ingredients in materials, be requested?
* Has the source of the material been investigated to determine whether toxins are involved in its manufacture?

Durability

* Does the material have the strength or flexibility needed to ensure a longer life span than a comparable material?

Performance, Maintenance, and Operations

* How well does the material perform?
* Does it require frequent and careful maintenance to ensure an efficient working condition?
* Does the lifetime maintenance require a high amount of resources (e.g., labor, energy, water, additional materials)?
* Are there secondary effects on other systems within the project (such as increased heat gain, decreased water use, etc.)?

For a more detailed list of the variables related to a life-cycle analysis of construction materials, refer to Meg Calkins, *Materials for Sustainable Sites: A Complete Guide to the Evaluation, Selection, and Use of Sustainable Construction Materials* (Hoboken: John Wiley & Sons, 2009).

End of Life

- If the infrastructure the material was used for were abandoned, what would happen to the material?
- Can it be easily disassembled for reuse?
- Is the material homogeneous and able to be recycled (material characteristics are unchanged) or downcycled (material characteristics are degraded)?
- Will it biodegrade to become a useful part of the natural environment?

Regional Issues

- Does the material perform well in a given region in response to heat, humidity, freezing, or seismic conditions?
- Is the material regionally available? (Repairs can be delayed if replacement parts are too specialized and difficult to obtain.)

Agency Requirements

- Do state, county, or city agencies require or ban the use of specific materials within their jurisdictions?

MATERIALS RED LIST

Projects should refrain from using any of the following materials or chemicals:

- Cadmium
- Chlorinated polyethylene and chlorosulfonated polyethylene*
- Chlorofluorocarbons (CFCs)
- Chloroprene (neoprene)
- Formaldehyde (added)**
- Halogenated flame retardants[†]
- Hydrochlorofluorocarbons (HCFCs)
- Lead[††]
- Mercury[‡]
- Petrochemical fertilizers and pesticides
- Phthalates
- Polyvinyl chloride (PVC)[‡‡]
- Wood treatments containing creosote, arsenic, or pentachlorophenol
- Endangered wood species
- Materials extracted from a critically endangered species habitat

* High-density polyethylene (HDPE) and low-density polyethylene (LDPE) are excluded.

** A temporary exception is made for glulam beams made using phenol formaldehyde.

[†] Halogenated flame retardants include polybrominated diphenyl ethers (PBDEs), tetrabromobisphenol A (TBBPA), hexabromocyclododecane (HBCD), decabromodiphenyl ether (decaBDE), tris (2-chloroisopropyl) phosphate (TCPP), tris(2-carboxyethyl)phosphine (TCEP), Dechlorane Plus, and other retardants with bromine or chlorine.

[††] An exception is made for solder and grid-tied solar battery systems only.

[‡] A temporary exception is made for low-mercury fluorescent lighting.

[‡‡] A temporary exception is made for PVC in wiring applications where it is mandated by code or where it is a small part of a larger component.

Source: Adapted from the Living Building Challenge. http://www.cascadiagbc.org/lbc-old/member/living-building-dialogue/materials/prerequisite-five

🖰 For more information on this subject please see www.sherwoodinstitute.org/resources.

*Table 6-1 Qualitative Material and Product Evaluation Template.**

EVALUATION CATEGORIES	EVALUATION CRITERIA DESCRIPTIONS	QUESTIONS TO ASK	YES/NO/ UNKNOWN	COMMENTS
HEALTH AND POLLUTION	Free of hazardous chemicals	Is the product free of hazardous chemicals such as PCBs, bromines, formaldehydes, and other substances on the Red List?		
	Avoids use of hazardous chemicals	Does the product avoid the use of hazardous chemicals such as degreasers, special cleaners, or other additives?		
	Manufacturing avoids hazardous chemicals	Does the manufacturing process avoid the use of hazardous chemicals? Does the manufacturing process avoid the production of hazardous wastes?		
	No leach/off-gas potential	Does the product *not* leach or off-gas compounds such as formaldehyde, plasticizers, or volatile organic compounds (VOCs)?		
	Health enhancement	Does the product enhance the health and well-being of those who encounter or use it (e.g., a bicycle- powered information display)?		
	Resource efficiency	Is the product energy efficient (Energy Star rated or similar)? Does the product minimize water and other resources used (WaterSense rated or similar)?		
ENVIRONMENTAL RESOURCES	Raw material content	Is the product made from 25 percent postconsumer recycled materials or salvaged materials (percentage by weight)? Is the product made from rapidly renewable materials such as cork, birch, or bamboo? Is the product made from sustainably harvested materials (e.g., is it Forest Stewardship Council [FSC] certified)?		

Table 6-1 Qualitative Material and Product Evaluation Template.* (continued)

EVALUATION CATEGORIES	EVALUATION CRITERIA DESCRIPTIONS	QUESTIONS TO ASK	YES/NO/ UNKNOWN	COMMENTS
ENVIRONMENTAL RESOURCES	Resource efficiency during manufacture	Does the product produce positive environmental gains during its manufacture and use (energy, water, air)?		
	Recyclability	Can the product be fully disassembled? Is the product fully recyclable?		
	Post-use	Does the manufacturer have a program to recycle or take back the product?		
	Transport costs	Where are the product's raw materials harvested/extracted? Where is the product manufactured? Where is the product's distributor?		
	Packaging	Does the product avoid excessive packaging?		
	Local impacts	Does the product provide habitat or enhance local ecosystems? Does the product positively impact the local microclimate/ environment (e.g., heat island effect)?		
	Fair wages	Is the product produced using fair-wage labor? Is the product produced in a shop that allows labor organizing?		
	Safe workplace	Is the product produced in a safe workplace? Are safety compliance documents in place for manufacture or fabrication?		
COMMUNITY AND SOCIETY	Safe products	Is the product safe for users and maintenance personnel?		
	Transparency	Are the companies manufacturing and distributing the product transparent in their business practices? Does the manufacturer have a written environmental policy?		

EVALUATION CATEGORIES	EVALUATION CRITERIA DESCRIPTIONS	QUESTIONS TO ASK	YES/NO/ UNKNOWN	COMMENTS
COMMUNITY AND SOCIETY	Social change	Does the product produce positive social change in its manufacture and use (e.g., employ homeless, produced locally, etc.)?		
	Effectiveness and usability	Will the product effectively meet the long-term needs of the project? Is the product currently in use on-site? If so, is feedback positive?		
	Aesthetics	Is the product aesthetically appropriate?		
	Life-cycle cost	Does the product have a favorable long-term cost, including all maintenance, utilization, and disposal? What is the product's cost per square foot (unit cost)?		
HUMAN VALUE	Service	Is the product well serviced and guaranteed by the manufacturer and/or vendor?		
	Local economy	Is the product made in the United States?		
	Recommendations	Is the product recommended in any green product databases such as the EPA's Environmentally Preferable Purchasing (EPP), the California Integrated Waste Management Board's list, GreenSpec, or Oikos Green Building Source?		

* This product evaluation template was designed as part of Sherwood's work with a Department of Energy laboratory. It was used to compare and contrast various materials and products for use within this growing laboratory from the perspective of sustainability. © Sherwood Design Engineers.

The footprint—or environmental impact—of the materials used on a project is a combination of several factors, including the material's toxicity, life span, manufacturing process, cost, weight, and reusability, as well as the distance to its extraction and/or manufacturing source. By combining these factors into a single number, the footprints of the different materials used on a project can be compared, and the material footprint for the project as a whole can be calculated.

For the Pearl Island project in Panama (discussed more fully in chapter 8) Sherwood engineers worked with designers from Hart Howerton to develop a unique formula for calculating material footprint. This formula helped to guide design decisions and communicate the benefits of the proposed design solutions. The equation's waste component encourages locally sourced items, doesn't punish compostable or organic items, and imposes an exponential weight on plastics and toxic items. In the case of products generated on the island (foods, flowers, and craft items), the material footprint will be quite small, effectively encouraging local industry.

Choosing Environmentally Appropriate Materials

The previous section discussed methods for evaluating the environmental impact of materials used on a project. The next section covers the range of different materials commonly used by civil engineers and site designers. It is meant as an introduction to selecting environmentally appropriate materials and understanding how they can be used more sustainably (or replaced with sustainable alternatives).

Materials commonly used for site elements and infrastructure include

- pavements and surfacing materials
- piping materials
- structural materials
- erosion and sediment control materials

The selection of materials for these elements can have a great impact on the overall environmental footprint, as well as on a project's performance.

Alternative Pavements and Surfacing Materials

Pavement is more than just the visible surface. Below it are layers of pavement buildup, aggregate base, and subbase, often with subdrainage pipes. The pavement surface area should be minimized to reduce negative impacts such as urban heat island effect and contaminated stormwater runoff. Overall impact can also be reduced by choosing better asphalt and aggregate materials, alternative pavement surfaces, less energy-intensive production methods, and alternatives to petroleum-based materials. The following list describes ways to improve the environmental performance of materials commonly used in road construction.

Asphalt, which accounts for the vast majority of pavement construction, is formed by combining heated petroleum-based asphalt cement with coarse

aggregates (gravel), fine aggregates (sand), and water. This mixture is placed over an aggregate base sprayed with an asphalt emulsion. A few modified asphalt options are more sustainable: recycled asphalt pavement; warm and cold mix asphalts; and asphalt with recycled content including used tires, glass, and other materials. These serve to reduce the asphalt cement quantity, reduce the pollution from the cement, or reduce the virgin aggregate quantities.
Aggregates are composed of crushed stone or other materials that are components of asphalt or concrete pavement mixtures. They are also used to provide a compacted structural base below pavement, and can be used as a drainage section beneath porous pavements or engineered site backfill. Using recycled aggregates is the primary means for reducing the ecological footprint of aggregates. For large projects, recycled aggregate can be produced on-site from the demolition of existing pavements or existing concrete buildings. Smaller projects can request recycled material from a local quarry or centralized recycling facility.

If the source material comes from a construction site and has mixed or unknown gradation properties, testing and approval overseen by a geotechnical engineer are required. When using recycled aggregates, additives may also be required to ensure proper binding performance. Additional opportunities to reduce environmental impacts when using aggregates include: looking for local sources in order to minimize transportation distances; avoiding aggregates that are mined in fragile ecosystems such as river beds; and using a structural element such as geogrid to reduce the thickness of a given application.
Chip seal is a street surfacing option that can also be used for creating light-grade streets. A layer of coarse aggregate is applied over a proper subbase and then topped with an asphalt sealant. This construction technique is ideal for parking lots, bike paths, private driveways, and other lightly trafficked areas. Its life span is less than pavement, but it is less expensive and uses fewer resources and less energy. It is also a traditional surfacing material used to extend the life of existing asphalt streets. Chip seal can be replaced with natural emulsifiers (see "stabilized soils and natural pavement surfaces," below).
Concrete pavement, which is formed by combining cement with coarse and fine aggregates and water, has negative impacts resulting from the energy-intensive production of cement. This impact can be reduced by replacing some of the cement with cementitious industrial waste products (such as fly ash), by replacing virgin aggregate with crushed concrete from demolition, and by using porous concrete where appropriate.
Rubberized asphalt, also known as *crumb rubber* or *asphalt rubber*, uses ground-up rubber tires as part of the aggregate. The technique was pioneered in Phoenix, Arizona, and has been proven to provide distinct environmental benefits. By recycling tires, a large source of material waste that is otherwise costly and difficult to dispose of is turned into rubberized asphalt. This technique creates a quieter road surface. Because rubber doesn't gain heat like asphalt, cement, and rock, rubberized asphalt also lowers urban heat gain.
Warm mix asphalt allows asphalt to be mixed at lower temperatures than traditionally required. Using chemicals with lower binding temperatures can

*Figure 6-24 A natural pavement sur-
face at a retreat center in Sonoma,
California. © Sherwood Design
Engineers.*

*Figure 6-25 This resin-stabilized bike
path in Los Angeles is a good example
of a strategy to introduce alternative
paving materials. A. Mannle.*

save the significant amounts of energy required for heating during asphalt installation, thus reducing the overall impact of street construction. Using nontoxic binders in place of the conventional, toxic variety can also reduce the environmental impact of street construction.

Stabilized soils and *natural pavement surfaces* can provide an alternative to asphalt-based pavements. Stabilized soil emulsifiers can be used for private driveways, paths, trails, patios, and parking lots that are flat or gently sloping. The emulsifiers are typically resins or a combination of proprietary polymers and wax or other biodegradable materials mixed or sprayed into a prepared base. When applied, the emulsifier binds to the soil particles and either coagulates or is compacted. The stabilizers can be tree-based or other proprietary resins (the finished surface is sometimes slightly dusty) or a combination of polymers and wax (creating a firmer, dust-free surface). This technique was originally used in the construction industry for controlling dust on temporary access drives or other unpaved streets. In recent years, the array of stabilizer and emulsifier technologies has advanced; they are now capable of providing a variety of diverse and reliable finishing surfaces. These stabilizers are often used in conjunction with decomposed granite, which comes in a variety of colors.

Pavers can be created from a variety of materials such as concrete, dimensioned stone, or brick. They can be mortared together or have the spaces between them filled with a permeable material such as sand or gravel to promote stormwater infiltration. Pavers made of porous materials can be specified to decrease the impacts of impervious surfaces. Mortared bricks are easier to reuse if lime mortar is used instead of cement mortar. No mortar may be needed for paving sections contained with a restrained edging.

Modular pavement consists of individual paving stones, as opposed to smooth slabs, and is used in many applications of sidewalks, streets, and plazas. Using modular paver or pavement material simplifies maintenance for below-grade utilities, because pieces in the immediate area of work can be easily removed, set aside during the repair, and then replaced. If an impermeable surface is

Figure 6-26 Bricks have been reused to pave this driveway in Culver City, California. The brick driveway requires no mortar, so it absorbs water and allows plants to grow between the bricks. A. Mannle.

Figure 6-27 Turning concrete into recycled paving stones for reuse on a project can reduce material production and transportation costs. A. Mannle.

Figure 6-28 Modular sidewalks allow for straightforward repair of below-ground utilities. © Sherwood Design Engineers.

required, the joints between them can be mortared with a material weaker than the modules themselves. During the utility repair, only the mortar will need to be replaced. This practice, widely used throughout Europe, retains durable natural paving stones, thus reducing material replacement costs as well as keeping the embodied energy for extraction and transportation low.

Piping Materials and Installation

Piping networks supply urban environments with many of our most vital resources. These include water pipes for drinking, irrigation, and fire protection; conduits for gas, electric, and communications cables; and pipes to convey sewage and stormwater. Each of these networks is a combination of pipes and junction boxes to allow changes in direction and access for maintenance. The environmental footprint of a piped network is determined by the piping materials—typically concrete, metal, and plastic—as well as the energy and impact involved in installing the network itself.

Pipe installation is most often performed by one of two methods: trenching and boring. Trenching is the most common method, but it can be a disruptive process at the surface. If the trench is over several feet deep, it will require a wider benched cut, with an increased footprint, or shoring, which can be expensive, time-consuming, and unsafe.

Trenchless technologies involve boring, jacking, or tunneling pipes underground between two aligned open pits or manholes. This technique reduces the amount of heavy earth moving, minimally disturbs the surface, and allows aboveground traffic and businesses to operate as usual. Some small conduits can be safely bored under large sensitive trees, allowing for the protection of landscapes. Boring, however, is considerably more expensive than trenching and can be difficult where pipe crossings are involved.

The materials used for backfilling trenches can have a significant impact on a project's sustainability measures. The use of native (local) soils for utility trench backfill is almost always desirable due to cost and energy savings, but they are not always available (or adequate). A newer backfill technique using flowable fill material is useful in tight construction areas or sections with multiple piping connections that prevent proper compaction. This cement-enhanced material flows like a liquid, hardens quickly, is self-leveling, and does not require compaction. A flowable fill mixture can be modified to include more recycled content (such as fly ash or slag) or to have lower strength, enabling it to be easily excavated in the future, if necessary.

Structural Materials

The many materials used in site construction should all be evaluated to find the most environmentally responsible choices. Because these materials—including metal, wood, concrete, and earth—are very heavy, using local materials can significantly reduce impact. However, as these are also durable materials designed for long-term use, they can often be recycled, repurposed, and reused on-site. Designing for deconstruction (see p. 261) can greatly improve the reusability of these common structural materials:

> *Metal* is used to reinforce concrete slabs and walls, and as edging for some pavements and paver stones. Metal has a very high embodied energy because it is difficult to extract, and some metals exist in limited quantities worldwide. Metal should be used only where necessary and specified with recycled content. Fortunately, reclaiming and recycling metals is becoming a standard practice in construction.

Figure 6-29 The recycled content of metal is rapidly rising in materials available for the construction industry, improving the environmental footprint of this material choice. A. Mannle.

Figure 6-30 FSC-certified wooden beams are specified to reduce the extraction of nonrenewable forest products. A. Mannle.

Wood is used in concrete formwork; to create site retaining walls; to jack up houses or other structures under construction; as framing material for a large proportion of residential construction; as well as for decks, fences, and furniture. The quantities of wood used for construction can be reduced through careful design. Reusing wooden beams and wood used for concrete forms can also reduce the need for fresh wood. In place of using large logs, particleboard plywood, framing materials, and particle I-beams are now being used in construction. These can be constructed from wood scraps and fast-growing woody crops that reduce waste and unsustainable logging practices. Sustainably harvested wood, such as that certified by the Forest Stewardship Council (FSC), has become an increasingly available resource. Designers should avoid wood treated with toxic content if possible, due to its inability to biodegrade or be recycled.

Masonry is used as a basic construction material for buildings, walls, and other site features. Typically an energy-intensive building unit due to both its weight and manufacture method, masonry can be made more sustainable by producing it locally. At a development in Loreto Bay, Mexico, bricks for residential construction were manufactured on-site from local materials. The final product was then transported less than a mile to the buildings under construction. The result was dramatic savings in transportation costs for a heavy construction material. And local labor was used in both the manufacturing and construction, thereby creating jobs through a new industry.

Figure 6-31 a,b On-site brick manufacturing in Loreto Bay, Baja California Sur, Mexico. © Sherwood Design Engineers.

POST-TENSIONING IN CONCRETE STRUCTURES

Post-tensioned reinforcement is considerably more sustainable than traditional reinforcement techniques for larger structures, be they bridges, foundation slabs, or building slabs. Significant benefits include the following:

- Reduced use of concrete through thinner slabs
- Reduced use of steel through more efficient use of reinforcement
- Reduced use of wood through a reduction in formwork
- Reduced corresponding carbon footprint (20 percent CO_2 emission reduction)

- Lower construction costs due to materials savings and shorter construction cycles
- Lower cost of ownership through reduced cracking and maintenance
- Material reductions typically include 25 percent for concrete and 65 percent for rebar. Overall materials cost savings of 10 to 20 percent are typically realized.[*]

Florian Aalami, "Economics of Post-Tensioned Construction," ADAPT Corp., 2008.

Figure 6.32 Material and cost savings gained by using post tensioning (PT) as the primary reinforcement in concrete. ADAPT Corporation.

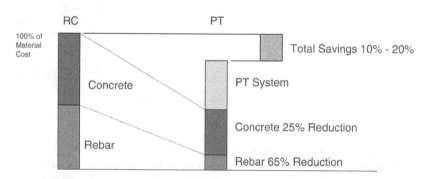

Erosion and Sediment Control Materials

Temporary erosion control measures help protect a site's environmental integrity by preventing the loss of soil during construction activities until the exposed earth can establish a new protective cover of vegetation. Some of the more common materials used include erosion control blankets, geotextile fabrics, wattles, silt fences, hydroseeding products, mulches, and rock.

Erosion control products can be made from natural or petroleum-based materials. Materials designed to remain in place should be made from biodegradable materials like jute netting made from coconut fiber, which will be absorbed by the environment once natural vegetation has been established. Synthetic products that do not break down should be avoided for long-term stabilization efforts, but have certain reusability benefits for sequential short-term applications. Whenever possible, local materials should be used when installing permanent erosion control measures. This can be accomplished by using site materials during clearing and grubbing activity to create stick or brush wattles placed on contour, mulch to cover exposed areas of soil, and tree-protection fencing from branches.

Construction Methods and Management

A project's construction phase is critical because it affords the opportunity to implement sustainable practices. From construction planning and addressing in-field changes to ensuring green ratings and managing waste, construction needs to shape design decisions throughout the project development process.

General Contractor Involvement

The early involvement of a construction contractor and a clearly communicated plan can play a pivotal role in the successful design and implementation of green infrastructure projects. A contractor's early involvement is as important as that of an engineer or landscape architect. A sustainable design needs to be easily constructible, and in many instances, local contractors have deep knowledge about local conditions, labor, and materials.

Engineers and architects should involve a contractor in the process as early as possible in order to flag design elements that may not be as constructible as originally believed and to provide the contractor with a clear understanding of design goals and criteria. A contractor's experience and input may allow for simpler designs that achieve the same goals—and decisions made in the field can actually improve the design's performance.

Design Infrastructure for Deconstruction

The Environmental Protection Agency quotes U.S. Census Bureau data that indicates the annual demolition of approximately 245,000 residential units and 45,000 nonresidential units generates 74 million tons of debris.[1] When building materials are demolished en masse as opposed to being disassembled by smaller machinery or by hand, the materials are crushed into one another, and they cannot be reused or recycled easily. Creating a deconstruction plan in place of the conventional demolition plan presents an opportunity to address this problem before construction begins. A deconstruction plan identifies material suitability for reuse, both as part of the existing conditions as well as the future condition of the proposed development. Some of the benefits of a deconstruction plan are reduced embodied energy, revenue from salvaged materials, reduced soil and vegetation disturbance, less noise and dust, and job creation.[2]

Green Certification Programs

A significant component of earning a rating from a green certification program is the documentation of what was actually done during the construction phase. The general contractor must be made fully aware of both the attention to detail and the extent of documentation required of both his or her company and any subcontractors. Prior to starting construction, it is imperative that a member of the design team hold a pre-construction meeting with the contractor and subcontractors dedicated to detailing the project's sustainable documentation strategy for the purpose of meeting these green rating requirements. (This is often done by the member running the certification process.) Whether it is cost, weight, or distance traveled, materials and products often need to be recorded in a manner not presently typical in the industry.

Developing a Project Specifications Manual

Directions for determining which materials to use for each element of a design should be explained in detail in the project specifications manual. This document is typically submitted along with the construction documents, though smaller projects often use a notes sheet instead. The manual lists the materials, models, and manufacturers that have been approved by the design team for every infrastructure system included in the project, as well as their installation procedures. It may also include specific procedures for deconstruction, site clearing, and earthwork. Specifications should list local suppliers whenever possible, and contractors should keep this list in mind when choosing alternate suppliers and manufacturers. If a certain material cannot be found or the contractor believes another material would be equivalent, contractors must seek the designer's approval for such a change. Careful development of the specifications is crucial in ensuring sustainable materials are used and installed properly and that low-impact construction methods are implemented throughout the construction process.

Addressing in-the-Field Challenges

Changes in the field are one of the major areas where sustainable design elements can, and often are, eliminated from a project. Designers can be faced with the challenge of supporting the cost of a more environmentally friendly approach or product when construction budgets reach limits and value engineering becomes necessary to meet the owner's and contractor's financial constraints. In-field changes need not, however, take away from the sustainability of a design. Clear communication is essential before, during, and after the construction phase to ensure that the project meets the targeted design goals and detailing. The contractor must understand the importance of minor design details that may be constructed with new twists on traditional construction methods.

Here are six useful steps to ensure designs are being built as intended:

1. Conduct frequent site visits during construction to ensure that the integrity of the design is carried out. Include these costs in the budget.
2. Discuss alternate material and method approval processes with the design team and contractor at the preconstruction kickoff meeting.
3. Make the contractor aware of the project's goals so everyone is on the same page.
4. Have the contractor submit material specification sheets, or "submittals," to the designer for approval prior to making a purchase. (The designer must then respond quickly in order to not delay the construction process.)
5. Make sure the general contractor communicates all of the above to all subcontractors.

6. Ensure the documentation of what was built (as-built drawings) as well as the creation of operation and maintenance manuals. (These are necessary to facilitate efficient maintenance in the future.)

Construction Waste Management Plans

From the outset of construction, a waste management and/or construction-debris recovery plan should be put into place so that reusable, recyclable, and toxic materials are not commingled in dumpsters. This can save on disposal costs and potentially generate revenue while reducing the project's environmental impact.

Handling toxic or dangerous materials on-site should also be addressed, so paints, cleaning supplies, nails, and so on do not contaminate the landscape. Dust, debris, concrete, asphalt, and moved earth should all be transported and stored safely so they do not degrade the site or erode into neighboring sites.

Sustainable Employee Travel and Housing

Despite choosing the most environmentally friendly materials, excessive transportation for material deliveries and construction workers can add significantly to a project's embodied energy and carbon footprint. If a local construction company is not awarded the project and employees must travel hours to and from the job site every day, it may make sense from both a cost and environmental standpoint to provide housing accommodations. Another option for reducing the vehicle miles traveled (VMT) on a project is to modify the work schedule, adopting one with fewer days with longer hours. Working four 10-hour days instead of five 8-hour days can reduce VMT by 20 percent. No matter what the distance, workers should be encouraged to carpool to the job site.

Solid Waste Management

Understanding a project's sources of waste—as well as the final destination of those waste products—is essential for developing an integrated solid waste solution to promote sustainability. Landfills and incinerators are often the centerpiece of solid waste management, with significant adverse impacts to the environment. To minimize the use and impact of landfills and incinerators, projects at all scales can encourage solid waste reduction as well as efforts to change the general perceptions of solid waste and find ways to use it as a resource.

Although all projects, regardless of their size, require a solid waste program to manage and dispose of waste, the primary objective of any materials strategy should be to minimize the production of solid waste in the first place. By avoiding excessive or environmentally unfriendly products, and by significantly reducing the demand for excess materials through construction and operational efficiencies, waste materials can be avoided at the outset, thereby commuting a financial benefit to the developer and an environmental benefit to the region.

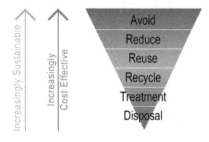

Figure 6-33 The waste management hierarchy. Hart Howerton.

The following techniques and opportunities, in order of priority, should guide the design and operation of an integrated solid waste management system.

1. Reducing material consumption
2. Reusing and recycling materials
3. Composting biodegradable materials
4. Transporting excess solid waste to one of three types of processing facilities (in order of preference):
   a. Sanitary landfills
   b. Incineration with energy recovery
   c. Incineration without energy recovery

For more information on this subject please see www.sherwoodinstitute.org/ideas.

The city of San Francisco has a waste-diversion rate of 75 percent, in part because of its aggressive composting program, which accepts many paper products that would otherwise be sent to a landfill. The San Francisco Department of the Environment collects food scraps and yard trimmings citywide from homes, restaurants, and hotels. Every day, 300 tons of compostable material is sent to Jepson Prairie Organics, where it is converted into nutrient-rich compost and sold to farms, nurseries, landscape contractors, and vineyards. Numerous vineyards in the nearby Sonoma and Napa valleys use this organically certified amendment to recondition their soil after the harvests. The wines produced from these grapes are sold to San Francisco restaurants, thus closing the loop on the material flow cycle.

Composting involves the aerobic decomposition of organic materials into a biologically stable material that can be used as a soil amendment. Today, community composting programs include food scraps, food-soiled paper, and compostable food containers. Similar to reusing and recycling, composting diverts waste from landfills and incinerators. Recycling yard trimmings kept 25 percent of municipal solid waste out of disposal facilities in 2006.[3] The controlled biodegradation of yard wastes, food scraps, and paper mulch by microorganisms produces nitrogen-rich compost that can be used to recondition soil, thus reducing the use of petroleum-based fertilizers. Depending on the project site and scale, various composting programs can be integrated into the solid waste management system at the community or individual building scale.

Notes

1 Alyse Nelson, *Livable Copenhagen: The Design of a Bicycle City*, Center for Public Space Research, Copenhagen, and University of Washington, Seattle, http://www.sightline.org/research/sprawl/res_pubs/Livable_Copenhagen_reduced.pdf.

2 U.S. Environmental Protection Agency (EPA), "Deconstruction: Building Disassembly and Material Salvage, NAHB Research Center, http://www.epa.gov/waste/conserve/rrr/imr/cdm/pubs/decon_br.pdf.

3 EPA, "Municipal Solid Waste Generation, Recycling, and Disposal in the United States: Facts and Figures for 2006," http://www.epa.gov/waste/nonhaz/municipal/pubs/msw06.pdf.

PART III

DESIGN
APPLICATIONS

The application of our design work occurs at various scales and in various forms. Ultimately, however, our work has three goals: to design projects that make sustainable use of our resources; to provide for basic human needs in ways that also promote positive human and ecological development; and to foster positive interactions and integration with the larger and smaller systems they are nested within.

The resource systems discussed in part II, from water to energy to material flows, are directly impacted by a project's footprint. We are living within a global environment whose finite resources we depend on. Solutions to the threats surrounding these global resource systems are being developed in rapidly changing ways all over the world, using new tools and strategies but also new alliances, economic models, and policies. At this scale we must not think of our work as a blueprint, a project with an identifiable end, but rather as a roadmap to how human communities can more sustainably interact with our natural environment. And although we must push to be sustainable in what we do, we must look further for opportunities to apply solutions that regenerate these natural systems as well. From mapping to analysis, planning to construction, we must keep an eye on both the larger and more intimate ecological systems we are designing within.

As engineers working within this new paradigm, designing projects that are sustainable in terms of global resources and ecological systems is often seen as our primary goal. At the most fundamental level, however, it is humanity that we must keep paramount in our design. If our buildings and projects don't promote healthy, vibrant human communities, then they cannot meet the challenge of sustainability. Clean air, good light, and public spaces that promote positive social interaction are some of the many attributes we should be designing for. The greenest building in terms of material and natural resource flows does not provide real and sustainable benefit if it is unoccupied or does not support the human community in a meaningful way.

This section offers examples and case studies for projects at the city (chapter 7), community (chapter 8), and site scales (chapter 9). While these are intended to demonstrate applicable solutions for each scale, it will be up to each designer to develop a palette of strategies for his or her particular project. Additionally, these scales are nested within each other. Communities are made of individual sites, and cities are made of diverse communities. Achieving optimum design requires understanding the full context of a project—what is happening within at smaller scales as well as how it connects to the larger city or region of which they are an integral part.

CHAPTER 7
City-Scale
Approaches

Cities are humanity's largest creations. They contain our most powerful social, political, and technological systems. In the twenty-first century, they have also become, for the first time, home to the majority of our species. Reshaping our cities will transform how we see the world. Cities are our hope for the future, because without fundamentally reimagining and re-forming our cities, we will never evolve into a sustainable global civilization.

As cities struggle with pollution, economic instability, resource depletion, and increased population, the redevelopment and adaptation of old cities is ongoing and inevitable. Taking advantage of this massive reinvestment in our cities is the perfect opportunity for a paradigm shift—and quite feasible, given a city's unique ability to effect meaningful change. The U.S. Conference of Mayors Climate Protection Agreement, for instance, has currently been signed by over one thousand mayors from cities large and small across all fifty states in America. These mayors, representing over eighty-six million Americans, have pledged their cities' commitment to meet the Kyoto Protocol and are urging state governments, Congress, and federal agencies to do the same.[1]

Cities have a recognized responsibility and an increasing ability to make positive change. This recognition is shifting priorities, goals, and policies at a scale where the changes being made are significant and measurable. Using interagency teams, such as New York City's Office of Long-Term Planning and Sustainability, integrated sustainability plans that set comprehensive goals are being developed by cities around the world. A number of cities are leading by example, providing real projects for others to study and learn from.

Today, most work being done at the city scale is happening through the reimagining of existing cities. Strategies such as shifting away from the automobile through congestion pricing, multimodal transportation systems, bicycle networks, and bus/rapid-transit programs are changing urban circulation systems. Because cities manage large amounts of our natural resources, they can reap huge savings by implementing efficiency and conservation measures. Cities are saving energy through combined heat and power programs and improving water efficiency through leak detection practices, ongoing upgrades and maintenance of aging systems, and smart metering. All these actions contribute to this necessary transformation.

Implementing city-scale initiatives for sustainable infrastructure would be impossible without engaging with policy makers and funding agencies. Technical expertise alone cannot transform our cities. Chapter 7 builds on the strategies discussed in part II by examining implementation approaches at the city scale.

This chapter highlights the integrated nature of this work and how all these approaches are being combined in large-scale projects in China. It discusses the Tianjin Eco-City being designed by Gensler and Sherwood Design Engineer's own ongoing work with Skidmore, Owings & Merrill (SOM) of sustainability master planning for Guangzhou and the Pearl River Delta.

Experiences from Sherwood's work in the San Francisco Bay Area are also discussed, and the chapter addresses working with municipal stakeholders, designing projects in cost-effective ways, building demonstration projects, and finding creative funding mechanisms. While it is impossible to cover all the exciting advances being made, green streets and stormwater management are a vital part of the larger network of strategies that contribute to urban sustainability, and an important aspect of the work we discuss.

It is also important to think beyond the city, to the region—in particular, to the regional watersheds that supply a city with water. The approach New York is taking as part of PlaNYC's commitment to protecting the city's water quality and promoting sustainable stormwater management is examined. The importance of a watershed-based approach is highlighted by public artist Cliff Garten in a discussion of his work in Canada designing a public art plan for the expressive potential of infrastructure.

New cities, while far less common, can showcase sustainable designs and provide models for a variety of systems and operations that older cities can learn from. Whether these cities are energy independent, carbon neutral, economically stable, or ecologically integrated into their surroundings, they provide designers a vital laboratory for testing the sustainability of urban environments.

GUANGZHOU: CITY-SCALE TRANSFORMATION IN CHINA

The city of Guangzhou is located in southern China, within the Pearl River Delta. It is the capital city of Guangdong Province and is an important commercial center, with the largest harbor in southern China. The Pearl River Delta is the second-most populous area in China, and one of the most densely populated areas of the world. It is also one of China's main engines of growth and a hub for export processing. However, its economic prowess has come largely at the expense of the environment.

The city of Guangzhou is literally bursting with people. Rapid economic development in China has created a rural-to-urban migration so rapid that cities are being turned virtually inside out as they try to accommodate the massive influx of people. Preserving affordable housing is one of the most pressing concerns for managing this wave of urbanization, because low-wage workers are the backbone of the manufacturing industry.

Historically, Guangzhou was a fortress on the high ground adjacent to the Pearl River. For centuries, beyond the walls of the fortress city, there existed just a handful of fishing villages that occupied the relatively higher ground in the massive estuary of the Pearl River Delta. With the exploding population and urbanization, these fishing villages have rapidly been transformed into midrise neighborhood centers with extensive commercial and industrial uses. The population doubled in the 1990s to over ten million people by 2001, and estimates in 2009 were as high as seventeen million for the combined Guangzhou-Foshan, cities that have essentially merged.

As Guangzhou develops rapidly, it is introducing and experimenting with sustainable infrastructure on a massive scale, simultaneously developing several neighborhood- and district-scale projects. The California-based firm Heller Manus Architects has developed the master plan for the innovative Pearl River New Town project, within which SOM's Chicago design group conceived of the iconic Pearl River Tower, which rises prominently. The tower was designed to funnel wind through the center of the building, driving wind turbines that supply clean electricity. This project exemplifies the opportunities to integrate sustainability into the urban fabric, and the city of Guangzhou has adopted it as a symbol for China's efforts to improve the sustainability of its urbanization in the twenty-first century. Looking across the Pearl River from the New Town Project, SOM has developed an extensive and ambitious masterplan with the help of Sherwood Design Engineers, Hargreaves + Associates, and others. This 36-square-kilometer plan reconceived the idea of urban sustainability by advancing highly integrated ecological systems with urban sustainable development. This project is introduced below.

For more information on Guangzhou, China, please see www.sherwoodengineers.com/book/26.

Figure 7-1 An existing promenade along the Pearl River, Guangzhou, China. © Sherwood Design Engineers.

Baietan Area Master Plan, Guangzhou

The Baietan Area Master Plan in Guangzhou is an effort to transform 36 square kilometers of heavily industrialized land in the city—property that was once the home of one of the world's largest steel mills, among many other large-scale heavy-industry facilities. The new master plan will facilitate Guangzhou's transition from its industrial past into a city of the future that exemplifies a focus on service industries and serves as a model for ecological regeneration of the urban environment.

The master plan involves creating 50 percent of the land as open space. (The project area is nearly fully developed and paved over.) The open space will consist of a network of greenways and blueways. The city will incorporate advanced wastewater management, streetscape stormwater integration, and a new canal network for water circulation.

The grid orientation developed minimizes the heat island effect, optimizes cooling and power generation, and reduces solar gain to the built environment. Guangzhou Baietan is complementing the open space

with a housing strategy of high-density, mixed-use infill development, with an integrated transportation plan that includes high-speed rail, a modern subway system, bus rapid transit, and extensive networks of pedestrian and bicycle pathways.

The comprehensive sustainability plan for Guangzhou Baietan is aimed at establishing standards for the entire project area. Guidelines were established to set aggressive targets for achieving globally exceptional levels of economic development, quality of life, and environmental responsibility. A collection of resources vital to the health of Lingnan culture (the locally defined identity) and the prosperity of Guangzhou were identified as goals and targeted for optimization:

- Restoration of natural systems
- Balanced water cycle
- Energy independence
- Cradle-to-cradle materials management
- Revitalized air quality

Specific strategies were developed to accomplish these overarching goals. These strategies were selected for their efficacy and appropriateness within the existing cultural, climatic, and regulatory context of Guangzhou, as well as

Figure 7-2 Integrated treatment wetlands, waterways, and canals define and complement the new high-density, mixed-use commercial district.

Figure 7-3 The 36-square-kilometer planning area of Guangzhou Baietan creates in detail an exceptionally large-scale new international model of sustainable development.

IDENTIFY
GOALS
确定目标

Environmental   Social   Economic

QUANTITATIVE
OUTCOMES
定量效果

QUALITATIVE
OUTCOMES
定性效果

Restoration of
Natural Systems — Balanced Water Cycle — Reduce Energy Dependence — Regenerative Materials — Improved Air Quality — Health & Prosperity — Celebrate Lingnan Culture

DEVELOP
ACTION PLAN
开发实施计划

Brownfield Remediation — Open Space Plan — Habitat Restoration — Engineered Water Sys. — Integrated Water Mgmt. — Water Reclamation — Water Use Reduction — Renewable Energy — Energy Efficiency — Heat Island Mitigation — Waste Management — Sustainable Materials — Public Transit — Reduce Car Use

Figure 7-4 The action plan for master plan implementation stems from a comprehensive system of goals and projected outcomes for urban regeneration. © Skidmore, Owings & Merrill LLP 2009, with Sherwood Design Engineers. All rights reserved.

Figure 7-5 Open space plan for Guangzhou Baietan. A web of restorative open spaces complements the urban development. These open spaces are primarily comprised of ecologically regenerative plantings that filter and cleanse water along with the reintroduction of habitat that has been destroyed through rapid urbanization. Hargreaves Associates.

for their benefit to economic growth, environmental restoration, and energy savings. When implemented, they will translate into the following outcomes:

- Significant long-term savings in infrastructure requirements
- Secure long-term water and energy supplies
- Improved citizen and tenant satisfaction
- Reductions in environmental pollutants such as greenhouse gas emissions
- Resuscitated native populations of aquatic and terrestrial species

Guangzhou Baietan as a Global Leader

As Guangzhou Baietan transitions its economic base from traditional industry to high tech, establishing itself as a leader in green development will attract the type of businesses needed to support that evolution. Implementing this sustainability plan will create unique infrastructure systems to underpin a modern, high-tech business center. Green buildings and public facilities that serve as a living example of the modern technologies promoted by Guangzhou's new businesses will support Guangzhou Baietan's overall redevelopment vision.

The Guangzhou Baietan redevelopment project supports the June 2007 national climate change plan.* That plan sets 2010 targets of increasing renewable energy to 10 percent of total energy consumption and reducing energy intensity per unit of gross domestic product by 20 percent. The plan also targets an increase of renewable energy to 15 percent of energy consumption by 2020. China's president Hu Jintao has committed to taking several additional steps toward greener development:

- Reduce carbon dioxide (CO_2) emissions per unit of gross domestic product by a "notable margin" by 2020, compared with 2005 levels
- Increase forests by 40 million hectares
- Work to develop a green economy

The country is facing the cataclysmic threats of sea level rise and desertification, making it critical to face the issue of global warming head on. China alone accounts for more than 20 percent of global carbon emissions.**

Economics of Infrastructure

The infrastructure systems supporting the Guangzhou Baietan redevelopment project will serve as the backbone of social and economic prosperity in the decades and centuries ahead. These infrastructure systems are designed to spur economic growth in leading industries, improve quality of life for the citizens, and restore the environment to resuscitate native populations of aquatic and terrestrial wildlife.

Energy

In 2006, China surpassed the United States as the global leader in CO_2 emissions.[†] It is therefore critical that China adopt energy-efficient development standards. Through the use of building-scale energy-efficiency measures and smart-grid technologies, Guangzhou can drastically reduce its carbon footprint while saving on infrastructure costs. The energy conservation and efficiency measures recommended for Guangzhou Baietan have the potential to reduce power demand by approximately 500 megawatts within the redevelopment area. Based on the $10.2 billion cost for the new 6,000-megawatt Yangjiang nuclear power plant currently under construction in Guangdong Province, reducing Guangzhou Baietan's power demand by 500 megawatts would result in saving approximately $850 million in additional power plant construction costs.[††]

Potable Water

In the coming years, China will face a severe water shortage. According to its Ministry of Water Resources, the annual shortage will peak at 40 to 50 billion cubic meters by 2030.[‡] There is currently a major water diversion project underway to redirect 3.5 million cubic meters per day from the West River in (Xijiang) to Guangzhou to serve as source water for three of the city's potable water plants. As part of the Guangzhou Baietan Master Plan plan, conservation and efficiency measures are expected to reduce potable water demand by 32 percent across the project area, which will save the government money by reducing the size of the water treatment plants needed to support the project area. Based on the cost of upgrading the water treatment plant, cost savings of $8.1 million will be realized in foregone drinking water plant expansion costs.

Figure 7-6 Sunlight and shading studies are overlaid on the three-dimensional urban form to determine strategies to optimize passive energy design and reduce demands on the city's power infrastructure. © Skidmore, Owings & Merrill LLP 2009. All rights reserved.

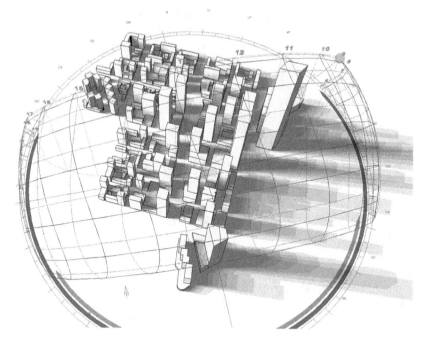

Figure 7-7 An integrated water system introduces extensive water recycling and reuse in order to bring the size of water and wastewater treatment facilities down and to reduce the systems' vulnerability in the future. © Sherwood Design Engineers.

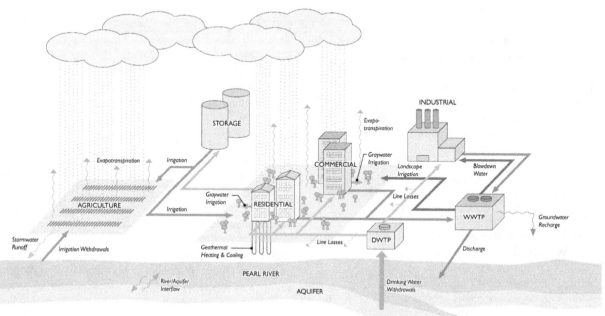

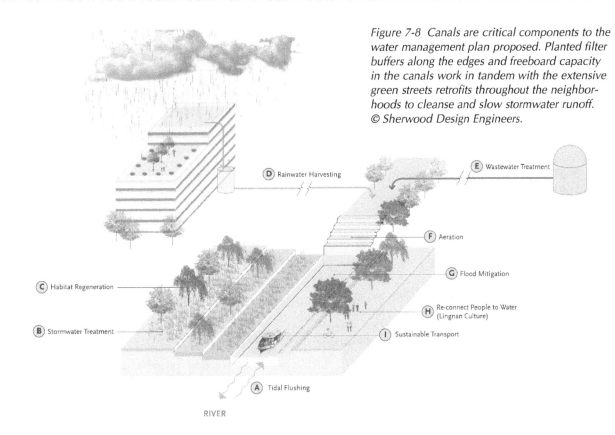

Figure 7-8 Canals are critical components to the water management plan proposed. Planted filter buffers along the edges and freeboard capacity in the canals work in tandem with the extensive green streets retrofits throughout the neighborhoods to cleanse and slow stormwater runoff. © Sherwood Design Engineers.

D Rainwater Harvesting

E Wastewater Treatment

F Aeration

G Flood Mitigation

C Habitat Regeneration

H Re-connect People to Water (Lingnan Culture)

B Stormwater Treatment

I Sustainable Transport

A Tidal Flushing

RIVER

Water recycling is anticipated to reduce overall water demand by another 20 percent, which will save an additional $5 million in foregone infrastructure costs, for a total savings of over $13 million.

Wastewater

Reducing water consumption also decreases the amount of wastewater produced. Reduced wastewater production results in a savings of $10.5 million in equivalent wastewater treatment plant expansions, based on the cost of the nearby Chongqing wastewater project.

Integrated Stormwater Management

Stormwater is currently combined with wastewater throughout the project area. This leads to regular sewer overflows and makes it extremely difficult to manage the water quality in the rivers that surround the site. The Baietan Master Plan proposes a series of measures to cap-

ture, treat, detain, and recycle stormwater. These measures will reduce localized flooding and improve the broader water quality problems in the delta.

Internationally Recognized Models/Evaluation Systems

There are several primary steps in adopting a comprehensive system of sustainability standards. Guangzhou Baietan Master Plan has put forth customized set of policies and requirements to guide development by the private and public sectors, so that the government can create the internal framework to implement and enforce these new standards. At the same time, the redevelopment project seeks acknowledgement from an internationally recognized sustainability rating system in order to maximize marketing potential and attractiveness to developers and businesses by

- providing a comprehensive sustainability framework to establish green building and development standards for Guangzhou Baietan
- developing an implementation plan to create the institutional framework for enacting the comprehensive suite of policies and standards established by this sustainability plan
- receiving Leadership in Environmental and Energy Design for Neighborhood Development (LEED-ND) verification and accreditation to gain recognition and bring prestige to Guangzhou Baietan as a certified world leader in sustainability

Sustainability Framework

The Master Plan benefitted from a customized sustainability framework to account for the unique cultural, geographic, climatic, and economic conditions within the city and the opportunities that those conditions afford. The Framework incorporated the tenets of the One Planet Living (OPL) program, which is administered by the group BioRegional and fosters the customization of sustainability targets for individual projects. The process of establishing these targets incorporates appropriate metrics established by other green building and development standards, as appropriate, including LEED-ND, LEED-NC (new construction), and China's Green Star program.

OPL is based on the principle that the world's population must consume natural resources at or less than the rate that the earth is able to regenerate those resources. Globally, we are currently consuming resources 30 percent faster than the planet can regenerate them. China is currently consuming natural resources at a pace 10 percent above the sustainable rate; therefore, China is living just above its sustainable biological footprint. Due to China's rapid rural-to-urban migration, that footprint will increase by several orders unless sustainable policies and practices are adopted in tandem with further development.

Implementation Plan

The most comprehensive and thorough sustainability plan will not be successful without an equally well thought out implementation plan. Success is dependent upon an enormous collaborative effort among leaders in the governmental, professional, academic, and civilian communities.

The city of Guangzhou will be making a significant commitment to the fulfillment of this plan, including budget allocations and the assignment of enforcement responsibilities to appropriate city and provincial agencies. An implementation plan outlining the responsibilities, critical steps, milestones, and budget commitments will likely be developed to guide this plan to success.

Third-Party Verification and Accreditation

For immediate recognition and marketing value, Guangzhou Baietan should seek third-party verification and accreditation to certify its development as a world-class model of sustainability. Taken together, the sustainable measures proposed for the Guangzhou Area Master Plan would allow the project to pursue a high level of certification from a recognized green building rating system. (In fact, the redevelopment project will be designed to achieve superior performance under the four LEED-ND categories of this United States Green Building Council–tracked rating system for urban development.)

Building Institutional Capacity

Guangzhou Baietan will need to build its institutional capacity to implement and enforce citywide sustainability measures. These responsibilities must either be assigned to existing agencies, or new agencies must be created to fulfill the role. Progress will only be made if there are responsible agencies in place to champion the policies, standards, and requirements set forth in the sustainability plan because new policy, code, or government agencies will be required to support critical elements of a city-scale plan. The creation and implementation of the following instruments was recommended to the government so the institutional capacity necessary to support our proposed sustainability initiatives could be built:

- Pearl River Delta Conservancy
  - Monitor the health of the river and maintain central repository of relevant data, activities, and projects.
  - Prioritize protection and restoration projects for implementation.

- Ecological commissioning
  - Provide long-term management strategies.
  - Establish research stations.
  - Establish scalable demonstration projects.
- Green building standards
  - Establish policies and standards governing private development.
  - Establish policies and standards governing the construction of public infrastructure.
- Distributed energy and net metering
  - Allow for the generation of site- or neighborhood-scale energy when derived from clean fuels or renewable resources.
  - Allow for net metering so that small-scale generation can sell excess energy back to the grid.

These steps, combined with the implementation of the Baietan Area Master Plan, with its planned population greater than the entire city of San Francisco, will create a nucleus of change critical for this next chapter of evolution in China.

* *China's National Climate ChangeProgramme*, prepared under the auspices of National Development and Reform Commission People's Republic of China, June 2007.
** United Nations Statistics Division, Millennium Development Goals Indicators: Carbon dioxide emissions (CO_2), thousand metric tons of CO_2, collected by CDIAC.
† John Vidal and David Adam, *China overtakes US as world's biggest CO2 emitter*, www.guardian.co.uk, June 19, 2007.
†† *Nuclear Power in China*, http://www.world-nuclear.org/info/inf63.html, updated 15 February 2010.
‡ Chinese Ministry of Water Resources, *Report on the program for water supply sources for those main cities in shortage of water.*

Tianjin Eco-City Master Plan

BY ERIN CUBBISON/GENSLER

Summary

Based on the values of people, planet, and profit, Gensler completed an innovative, sustainable master plan for the Sino-Singapore Eco-City near Tianjin, China. The site is a 40-hectare area about 45 kilometers east of Tianjin's central business district. The team developed design guidelines, organized by six key principles: place-making, open space, transportation, architecture, water cycling, and energy. Gensler's approach was to closely integrate sustainability analysis tools into the urban design process. The plan achieves a compact mix of uses, including residential, commercial, retail, and institutional, with specific attention paid to the integration of green space and sustainable infrastructure.

Site Analysis

The project began with an analysis of the site, including existing topography, natural features, climate, transportation infrastructure, surrounding land uses, and cultural context. The site is undeveloped, slopes slightly from south

Figure 7-9 Tianjin Eco-City Master Plan. Gensler.

to north, and is located between two important water elements, the Jiyunhe River to the northwest and the Bohai Sea to the southeast. During summer, the climate is hot and humid with winds from the southeast, and during winter, cold with winds from the northwest. Annual rainfall is approximately 56 centimeters, more than half of which falls during July and August. The soil is extremely saline and supports very little vegetation.

The existing, newly constructed transportation arteries are on an approximately 400-meter grid and were set 45 degrees off of a north-south and east-west alignment. A major passenger rail line is being planned to connect the site with cities to the north and south. The line runs through the southern portion of the site and will have one stop within the site. A university is currently being built adjacent to the site to the northwest, and a large employment center is planned for the area adjacent to the site to the southeast.

Analysis of the cultural context is also critical to developing an appropriate and successful master plan. In China, the use of public spaces, connection of the dwelling unit to the outdoors, and access to southern sunlight are essential considerations in designing the built environment. The acceptable walking distance from home to amenity or transit stop is much greater in China (fifteen minutes) than in the United States or Europe (five minutes). And while the bicycle has historically been the dominant form of transportation, it is rapidly being replaced by the automobile as many areas urbanize. To provide a reference for the project, the team found that the number of cars per person in nearby Tianjin would nearly double between 2008 and 2010. The growing presence of the automobile is a significant challenge to sustainable development in China.

Goals

This project was a competition and joint venture between the governments of Tianjin and Singapore to create an eco-city. The site was meant to be a model and catalyst of sustainable development for the region.

The control targets given by the client were eco-environmental health, social harmony and progress, economics and efficiency, and regional coordination. For each target, several areas of focus were specified:

- *Eco-environmental health:* air quality, surface water, tap water, noise reduction, carbon, wetlands, green building, local vegetation, and public green space
- *Social harmony:* water use, sustainable transportation, neighborhood amenities, accessibility, affordable housing, and waste generation, collection, and management
- *Economics and efficiency:* economic development in renewable energy and nontraditional water sources, technological innovation in research and development, and an overall balance in housing and employment
- *Regional coordination:* safety and health, pollution control policy, cultural elements, developing a recycling industry

Strategies

After performing various analyses of the site, the team evaluated the potential for both passive and active design strategies and integrated them into the development of the master plan. It researched both proven and cutting-edge sustainable technologies as well as eco-city precedents within China and around the world in order to establish a benchmark for design performance. Autodesk's Ecotect simulation software allowed the team to target specific bioclimatic design strategies and provided the optimum building orientation, which is about 5 degrees east of south. The team then needed to balance the goals of optimum building orientation and harmony with the existing road network. It rotated the roads toward the optimum orientation as much as possible, while still creating reasonable intersections.

The team used Gensler's own sustainable performance assessment tool to determine the overall impact and design implications of energy, water, and waste management strategies. Specifically, these included resource conservation, renewable energy strategies (such as geothermal, photovoltaic, solar thermal, and biogas), and water-cycling strategies (such as segregated water supply, on-site graywater treatment, and blackwater digesters). The team incorporated biological wastewater treatment systems into the design for distributed water treatment. It located one facility within each block, based on system capacity, parcel distribution, and its ability to be phased in over time.

Figure 7-10 Tianjin Eco-City Perspective Rendering. Gensler. Rendering by Shanghai Crystal Information Technology.

As a guiding vision that unites the development in the region, the team designed an urban agricultural spine atop the regional underground transit line. This feature is linked to the rest of the development via two axes: a main street corridor and a green space corridor. The main street corridor is an active mixed-use zone providing a variety of public spaces, sustainable transportation modes, and a connection between the nearby university and the regional transit line. The green corridor provides significant habitat for the ecosystem as well as the opportunity for recreation and connection to nature for the human occupants. The green corridor is designed as a compound, or stepped, channel, which integrates usable recreation space with stormwater treatment and infiltration.

PlaNYC: An Integrated Stormwater Approach

New York City has invested billions of dollars in programs that will enhance its wastewater treatment system by processing larger volumes of stormwater while simultaneously greening the city. Alternately known as source controls, green infrastructure, low-impact development (LID), or best management practices (BMPs), they are all aimed at capturing stormwater at its source using naturally vegetated installations.

The city's Sustainable Stormwater Management Plan is described in the *PlaNYC Progress Report 2009* as "the first comprehensive plan in the country to analyze the location and feasibility of source controls in a dense, ultra-urban environment on a citywide basis, specifically targeting impermeable surfaces such as rooftops, roadways, and sidewalks."*

The stormwater plan was the result of an interagency best management practices task force led by the Mayor's Office. Taking an interdisciplinary approach has led to stormwater management guidelines being incorporated into other city planning manuals. For example, the Department of Transportation's (DOT) *Street Design Manual* will promote stormwater-capturing strategies, including landscaped medians, expanded sidewalk bulb-outs, roadside swales, and the use of permeable materials. The Department of Design and Construction's (DDC) *Sustainable Urban Site Design Manual* will offer strategies

Figure 7-11 As part of the water quality initiatives outlined in PlaNYC, New York City has implemented a variety of green initiatives to control stormwater and improve the urban environment. PlaNYC Sustainable Stormwater Management Plan.

Table 5: Benefits and Limitations of Source Control Techniques

Benefits and Limitations	Biofiltration (water is infiltrated into the ground)	Retention (water is retained on site for other use)	Detention (water is held before going to treatment facility)
Reduces CSOs	X	X	X
Reduces Treatment Costs	X		
Reduces Potable Water Consumption		X	
Reduces Flooding	X	X	X
Reduces Sewer Backup	X	X	X
Reduces Separate/Direct Discharges	X	X	
Reduces Strain on Sewers	X	X	X
Provides a Community Asset	X		
Improves Air Quality	X		
Reduces Urban Heat Island Effect	X		
Limited by High Groundwater and Bedrock	X		
Higher Capital Expense	X		
Higher Maintenance Expenses	X	X	

Figure 7-12 Implementing innovative water management techniques must be evaluated within the context both of water costs born by customers and that of the infrastructure system savings overtime that these facilities replace. On-site stormwater management strategies can be more cost-effective per gallon over time than centralized infrastructure treatment systems. PlaNYC Sustainable Stormwater Management Plan.

Table 3: Costs of Source Control Technologies

SOURCE CONTROL	INCREMENTAL CAPITAL COST (PER SQ. FT. OR UNIT)	NET PRESENT VALUE (PER SQ. FT. OR UNIT)	LIFESPAN (YEARS)	COST PER YEAR	GALLONS* (PER SQ. FT. OR UNIT)	COST TO CAPTURE GALLON	ANNUAL COST PER GALLON
Blue Roof (2-inch detention)	$4.00	$4.00	20	$0.20	1.25	$3.21	$0.16
Rain Barrel (55-gallon tank)	$200	$200	20	$10.00	55	$3.64	$0.18
Sidewalk Biofiltration	$36.81	$39.68	20	$1.98	8.60	$4.61	$0.23
Porous Asphalt Parking Lane	$8.13	$10.33	20	$0.52	2.18	$4.74	$0.24
Porous Concrete Sidewalk	$6.83	$8.67	20	$0.43	1.82	$4.77	$0.24
Swale	$18.73	$22.50	40	$0.56	1.82	$12.39	$0.31
Blue Roof (1-inch detention)	$4.00	$4.00	20	$0.20	0.62	$6.42	$0.32
Cistern (500-gallon tank)	$3,700.00	$3,700.00	20	$185.00	500	$7.40	$0.37
Greenstreet	$42.67	$62.79	30	$2.07	5.24	$15.81	$0.53
Sidewalk Reservoir	$98.48	$110.41	20	$5.52	3.74	$29.52	$1.48
Green Roof	$24.45	$62.39	40	$1.56	0.47	$133.37	$3.33
REFERENCE CASES	**INCREMENTAL CAPITAL COST (PER SQ. FT. OR UNIT)**	**NET PRESENT VALUE (PER SQ. FT. OR UNIT)**	**LIFESPAN**	**COST PER YEAR**	**CSO GALLONS (PER SQ. FT. OR UNIT)**	**COST TO CAPTURE GALLON**	**ANNUAL COST PER GALLON**
Newtown Creek Tunnel	$1,299,000,000	$1,300,000,000	50	$26,000,000	40,000,000	$32.50	$0.65
Flushing Bay Tunnel	$1,038,000,000	$1,039,000,000	50	$20,800,000	25,000,000	$41.56	$0.83

to maximize vegetation and better manage stormwater. And the DDC's *Water Conservation Manual* will promote methods of reducing potable water use.

PlaNYC's water quality efforts extend beyond the city itself to the watersheds and wetlands that supply and treat the city's drinking water. By investing in watershed protection, the city has avoided tens of billions of dollars in water treatment costs. The filtration avoidance determination

program quantifies the natural filtration capability of the Catskill and Delaware watersheds and allows the city to invest in upstream water protection rather than downstream water treatment.

Instead of building larger treatment facilities, the city acquired thousands of acres of protected lands, developed a forest management plan for those lands with the U.S. Forest Service, installed hundreds of pollution control practices on rural farms in the watershed, funded the repair of failing septic systems, and improved stormwater control projects for small towns in the watershed. This decentralized, watershed-based approach to water quality protection represents an important shift in integrated water management.

To further improve the ecological side of the water cycle, the city has acquired and protected over 5,000 acres of wetlands, including the Staten Island Bluebelt system, and installed eel grass and oyster bed restoration projects as part of the Jamaica Bay Watershed Protection Plan. In January 2009, it issued a report on filling regulatory gaps that leave small wetlands unprotected and began exploring ways to create better wetland maps, develop wetland restoration funding efforts, and study the effect of sea-level rise on wetlands and other critical infrastructure.

Comprehensive integrated water management programs such as that taken on by New York City serve as a model for rapidly developing or developed cities elsewhere in the world. Taking a watershed approach to stormwater management, environmental restoration, and water supply can serve to benefit citizens, city finances, and the quality of open space alike.

*PlaNYC Progress Report 2009, www.nyc.gov/html/planyc 2030/.../planyc_progress_report_2009.pdf, p. 17.

For more information on this subject please see www.sherwoodinstitute.org/resources.

Figure 7-13 The Staten Island Bluebelt. Dahlia Thompson, Sherwood Design Engineers.

SAN FRANCISCO CITY GREENING INITIATIVES

This section discusses a handful of plans and projects through which San Francisco is implementing an integrated approach to wastewater treatment, stormwater management, street greening, and community revitalization. The growing awareness of ecological principles among city residents—and their demands that the principles be integrated into public space design—has been one of the major drivers behind this transformative thinking. Regulatory requirements for cleaning stormwater running off parts of the city constitute another driver. Additionally, holistic thinking adopted by key individuals in the Mayor's Office, the Planning Department, the Public Utilities Commission, the Department of Public Works, and elsewhere has helped focus these ideas on distinct plans and guidelines that will yield multiple benefits to the city. Eight of the plans are covered below:

1. San Francisco Better Streets Plan
2. Urban Forest Master Plan
3. Stormwater Design Guidelines
4. Sewer System Master Plan
5. Mission Streetscape Plan
6. Cesar Chavez Green Street Corridor
7. Old Mint Plaza
8. Pavement to Parks Initiative

While these efforts are specific to San Francisco, similar plans can be adopted by any city to improve the health of its watershed, reduce water treatment costs, and promote long-term sustainable development. Although seemingly disparate at first, the variety of plans and projects shown here all tackle a common challenge: stabilizing the hydrological cycle that has been disrupted by the rapid urbanization of the area over the past 160 years. Stormwater management and appropriate street design operate in tandem; urban forestry and water quality go hand in hand. And all of them work toward the common goal of improving the quality of life for San Francisco residents.

1. SAN FRANCISCO BETTER STREETS PLAN

The San Francisco Better Streets Plan was developed to create a unified set of guidelines and strategies for improving public streets. The intent was to classify all streets using a variety of typologies and to offer a toolkit for integrating design strategies into street improvements. The Better Streets Plan promotes the coordinated redevelopment of streets in a way that integrates ecological function into a more pedestrian-friendly, less auto-dominated city. The toolkit shows ways to integrate stormwater management, landscaping, traffic calming, and street greening into streetscapes ranging from neighborhood and commercial streets to alleyways. Each different street type merits a response that allows for individuation based on neighborhood and community input, while the overall plan fosters citywide cohesion.

The San Francisco Better Streets Plan

- helps retain families in San Francisco;
- supports Muni (the city's transportation agency) and a transit-first city;
- helps promote public safety;
- helps to minimize impact on global climate change and local air pollution;

- helps to minimize sewer/stormwater overflows into the San Francisco Bay;
- decreases the likelihood of pedestrian injuries and fatalities;
- increases accessibility for all street users;
- supports the city's local shopping districts and small businesses;
- provides open space in areas that are lacking;
- support neighborliness, civic interaction, and identity;
- enhances the everyday quality of life for San Francisco's residents.**

The Better Streets Plan represents an important step forward in citywide planning. It also forms the basis for deeper green streets implementation. As such, the Better Streets Plan itself is only one of a suite of strategies that work synergistically to improve the urban landscape. The seven other plans and policies described below represent efforts that directly complement or build on the Better Streets Plan.

**Adapted from "Better Streets Plan Goals and Objectives" (DRAFT_BSP_Goals-4-5-07.pdf), http://www.sf-planning.org/ftp/BetterStreets/about.htm (accessed 3.18.10).

Figure 7-14 San Francisco Better Streets Plan. San Francisco Better Streets Plan, San Francisco Planning Department.

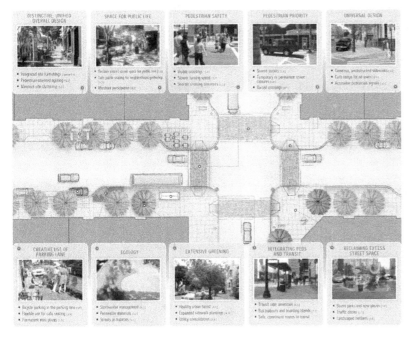

Figure 7-15 The Better Streets Plan identifies opportunity sites for streetscape improvements and integrated stormwater management for the full spectrum of streets found in the city of San Francisco. San Francisco Better Streets Plan, San Francisco Planning Department, Community Design + Architecture (CD+A).

2. URBAN FOREST MASTER PLAN

The Urban Forest Master Plan, contributed to by AECOM Design + Planning (formerly EDAW) and Sherwood Design Engineers, is a San Francisco Planning Department project. It reinforces the Better Streets Plan and other policies by seeking to comprehensively stitch together fragmented areas of open space. Extensive areas of open space within the city are currently used as auto-centric streets. The Urban Forest Master Plan identifies priorities for ecological connectivity, aiming to use open space to connect the city's existing and future ecological zones. By informing street design with an understanding of the historical natural assets underlying the city fabric and identifying opportunity areas for restoring and enhancing those assets, future design efforts can be focused on enriching neighborhood habitats.*

The plan's key objectives include the following:

- Develop a set of best practices for tree selection, purchase, installation, and care that include creative adaptations and establish high standards for all public and private projects.
- Protect the urban forest from and during the development process, on public and private property.
- Establish a goal of no net loss of trees. (When a tree is removed due to development, whether public or private, the responsible party should be required to replace it in kind, either through new planting or fees.)
- Institute a comprehensive reforestation program for aging stands in city parks and public institutions.
- Allocate and secure funding for planting and maintenance from public and private sources.

- Establish citywide goals for the urban forest and monitor results on an annual basis. (Possible examples include providing one street tree for every five residents and raising the canopy coverage to 15 percent.)
- Update the list of recommended trees to reflect availability and horticultural advancements and to be consistent with the identity and local character of the city.
- Engage the leadership of the city to implement major tree-planting programs targeting underserved neighborhoods in order to achieve greater environmental equity and accessibility.
- Engage the San Francisco Unified School District, parent-teacher associations, and community groups to develop tree programs at schools.

*http://www.sf-planning.org

3. Stormwater Design Guidelines

This booklet was developed as part of a compliance plan for the National Pollution Discharge Elimination System (NPDES) permit for the uncombined sewer areas of San Francisco. The design guidelines provide comprehensive tools for integrating stormwater management into the urban environment, including harvesting rainwater, designing bioswales, and implementing rain gardens. These tools are available for projects citywide in San Francisco but have a regulatory driver behind them in those parts of the city where the sewer is uncombined. The San Francisco Green Building Ordinance has a LEED-NC stormwater requirement that takes the implementation of these guidelines to the city scale for new development projects. This is a groundbreaking green building code with respect to stormwater integration, and the Stormwater Design Guidelines provide accessible tools for meeting these new requirements.

⌨ For more information on this subject please see www.sherwoodinstitute.org/tools.

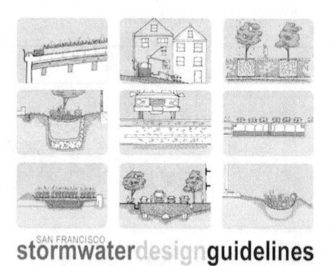

Figure 7-16 San Francisco Stormwater Design Guidelines San Francisco Public Utilities Commission.

4. Sewer System Master Plan

The San Francisco Public Utilities Commission (SFPUC) is the city's single most important agency responsible for proposing and implementing green street and stormwater strategies. The SFPUC is responsible for treating the city's sewage and stormwater and managing the regulatory permits that allow the city to discharge treated sewage and stormwater, as well as permits regarding combined sewer overflows into San Francisco Bay and the Pacific Ocean. A significant portion of the water and sewer rates collected by the agency goes toward managing stormwater.

Over the past century, the sewer system master plans for San Francisco have been revised several times (every forty years on average). The initial plan of 1899 was revised in 1935 to include the city's first wastewater treatment plants. In 1974, the master plan concentrated on improved and expanded treatment to meet the demands of the Clean Water Act. Currently, the plan is undergoing yet another major planning effort to address the growing needs of the city, new methodologies and technologies, and the increasing impact of water pollution.[2]

In the next hundred years, the city will significantly reshape its stormwater management practices. The City is investing over $4 billion in near-term infrastructure improvement projects, of which nearly 20 percent will be dedicated to developing long-term strategies for decentralized sustainable street greening, rainwater harvesting, and retention facilities distributed throughout the city's watersheds.[3] This plan supports the community aspiration for the widespread implementation of LID strategies. Wherever possible, LID will be implemented as a substitute to the hard infrastructure improvements needed to clean the water that is ultimately discharged into the Pacific Ocean and San Francisco Bay.

Using a watershed-based approach to stormwater management will significantly change how the SFPUC funds the wastewater system's operation and maintenance. Shifting the infrastructure from belowground pipes and pumps to the aboveground urban forest, streets, and distributed stormwater harvesting measures requires a corresponding shift in expenditures and positions the city's residents to reap the many benefits from adopting this approach.

5. Mission Streetscape Plan

Shortly after the completion of the Better Streets Plan, the San Francisco Planning Department used the Mission Streetscape Plan to examine opportunities to introduce districtwide integrated bike paths, street narrowing, shared streets, stormwater management, and ecological corridors. The Mission District is a historically underserved yet vibrant and culturally diverse community in the heart of San Francisco, and the Mission Streetscape Plan is the first project to incorporate the suggested outcomes of the Better Streets Plan on a district scale.

The Planning Department's City Design Group describes the goals and outcomes of the plan:

The goal of the Mission Streetscape Plan is to reimagine Mission District streets as vital public spaces that serve the needs and priorities of the community. The outcome will be a system of neighborhood streets with safe and green sidewalks, well-marked crosswalks, widened sidewalks at corners, creative parking arrangements, bike paths and routes, close integration of transit, and roadways that accommodate automobile traffic but encourage appropriate speeds. The Mission Streetscape Plan designs will improve pedestrian safety and comfort, increase the amount of usable public space in the neighborhood, and support environmentally sustainable stormwater management.*

Highlights of the plan include

- new gateway plazas and a temporary public plaza as part of the Pavement to Parks initiative
- traffic-calming suggestions for residential streets
- flexible parking strategies for reclaiming urban space for community gathering and outdoor seating uses
- green connector streets and a "living alley" network for smaller residential streets

*http://www.sf-planning.org/ftp/CDG/CDG_mission_streetscape.htm (accessed 3.18.10).

Figure 7-17 Mission Street: existing streetscape conditions. Sherwood Design Engineers.

Figure 7-18 Mission Street: proposed conditions after revitalization strategies are implemented. Sherwood Design Engineers.

6. Cesar Chavez Green Street Corridor

Figure 7-19 The sewer main that runs beneath this proposed planter (currently all asphalt) needs to be replaced. Instead of simply replacing the pavement surface over the newly buried pipe, the street will be rebuilt with this significant addition to the urban forest. San Francisco Planning Department, City Design Group.

Sherwood worked with San Francisco's Planning Department, Municipal Transportation Agency, Public Utilities Commission, and Department of Public Works to implement a plan that transforms a heavily industrialized street with dangerous intersections into an integrated street that accommodates bike lanes, shortens pedestrian crossing distances, and creates rain gardens for stormwater management in bulb-outs at each intersection.

This section of Cesar Chavez Street occupies the same low ground that historically was Islais Creek. The Creek now runs in a 6-foot diameter combined stormdrain-sewer pipe. As part of a replacement project for the failing 6-foot sewer main that runs down the length of the street, a new median with street trees and other plantings will be created to reduce stormwater runoff. We are depaving a large portion of the street, reintroducing planting, allowing water to run through landscaped areas, and putting in signage about the historical watershed and the creek that now runs underground.

Because of the highly urbanized setting, full creek daylighting was deemed inappropriate. But the naturalized stormwater infrastructure elements being installed will slow water down, allowing it to infiltrate to the groundwa-

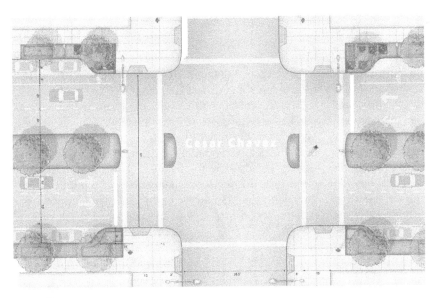

Figure 7-20 Bulb-outs and stormwater planters will be included at each intersection to reduce the crossing distance for pedestrians, and to decrease the volume while increasing the quality of stormwater runoff. San Francisco Planning Department, City Design Group.

ter table; provide habitat for insects, birds, and pollinators; and improve the air quality on the street. In other words, through engineered solutions, we are restoring as much of the ecological functionality once provided by the creek as possible in the same location.

In this way we tied the redevelopment of a roadway to a stormwater project that includes educational features about the history of this particular place in the city. By honoring and interpreting the historic creek, we are creating public awareness about the broader vision of watershed-scale planning being implemented in the community.

7. Old Mint Plaza

One of the success stories of the city's new approach to planning can be seen in the Old Mint Plaza, where we worked with a team led by CMG Landscape Architecture to turn a blighted inner-city alleyway into a vibrant urban plaza that performs environmental function and creates a great new space for the public. By closing the space to traffic, we have reclaimed a piece of the urban landscape and improved its environmental performance by designing it to reduce stormwater runoff and recharge groundwater. At the same time, we created an urban gathering space that quickly became home to four new restaurants and a gourmet coffee shop. The plaza supports street fairs and other cultural activities, and will serve as the entryway to the new museum at the Old Mint.

Figure 7-21 The plaza at the Old Mint is designed to filter and infiltrate stormwater to the groundwater table, reestablishing a broken hydrological link in one of the city's most developed neighborhoods. CMG Landscape Architecture.

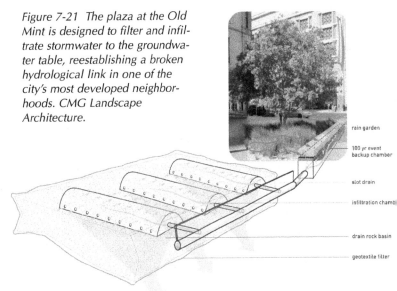

rain garden

100 yr event backup chamber

slot drain

infiltration chamb

drain rock basin

geotextile filter

8. Pavement to Parks Initiative

San Francisco's Pavement to Parks (P2P) initiative is a collaboration among the Mayor's Office, the Department of Public Works, the Planning Department, the Municipal Transportation Agency, and several community groups. The program was inspired by New York City Department of Transportation efforts to reclaim sections of Broadway near Times Square through low-impact, "temporary" measures that have transformed the street. San Francisco has followed suit, placing protective barriers along the street and setting out temporary seating and landscaping to create instant plazas. Painting or treating the asphalt creates new bicycle lanes and pedestrian areas.[4]

This approach short-circuits the extensive, slow, and cumbersome process of permanently taking a vehicle lane out of the street. It creates a temporary condition that allows the community to get used to the transformation or decide how to change it to make it work long term. In San Francisco, where streets and public rights-of-way occupy 25 percent of the city's land area, under-utilized sections of streetscape exist as a result of past

Figure 7-22 a,b Log planters in Guerrero Park, a Pavement to Parks project in San Francisco's Mission District. © Jane Martin/Shift Design Studio.

planning efforts or changes in city circulation patterns. These underutilized areas are gradually being converted into community gardens and public open space that also detain and slow down stormwater runoff. If the community likes the temporary solution, steps can then be taken to make it permanent.

Guerrero Park is an interesting example of a Pavement to Parks project that transformed a dangerous intersection into a public plaza. The signage for the park explains the unique constraints of the program:

> In keeping with the temporary nature of the P2P program, the project had three main parameters: no asphalt could be removed, most materials used must already be in the city's possession, and the project must be able to be built by city workers. The funding for this low-budget project was covered by private donations.

> Jane Martin, founding director of Plant*SF and principal of Shift Design Studio, wanted a park that was in keeping with the story of the place. She created plantings on the open asphalt inspired by the landscape design of William Hammond Hall in Golden Gate Park.

> Without disturbing the pavement, these "temporary" gardens harbor a biologically diverse collection of native and nonnative lupines, succulents, bamboo, and apple trees. The Pavement to Parks initiative is a very low-cost example of effectively reclaiming an important urban space for the community.

As described by Shift Design Studio, these are some of the significant sustainability features of Guerrero Park:

- Nearly 100 percent of the materials are from waste-stream diversion.
- The logs are from the Golden Gate Park compost yard.
- The stainless steel planters represent the reuse of rejected construction material from an unrelated project.
- The log chocks are made of used redwood posts.

- The materials are nearly 100 percent natural.
- The interpretive signage is made of recycled-content and fully recyclable aluminum.
- The soil and mulch are made locally from waste material (not stripped topsoil transported from a distance).
- The planters and islands slow and absorb stormwater.
- Many of the plants are self-propagating.
- There are no annuals—only perennials—among the plantings.
- The plantings are biologically diverse.
- The plantings have habitat and forage value for birds and pollinators, including butterflies, bees, and other insects.
- Among the plantings are eighteen native species: lupine, juncus grass, red fescue, chokecherry, cow parsnip, penstemon, white sage, Cleveland sage, blue-eyed grass, yellow-eyed grass, sticky monkey flower, fuchsia, coffeeberry, artemisia, carpenteria, erigeron, dogwood, and galvezia.
- There are also more than forty nonnative, drought-tolerant species, including flax, protea, hebe, sedum, leucadendron, aloe, agave, dodonaea, and geranium.
- There are two species of edible (not ornamental) apple trees and three species of bamboo, which are evergreen, self-propagating, and provide harvest value.
- The purchased items support local business—with the exception of the play equipment, all were sourced regionally.
- The concrete removed was recycled into aggregate for new concrete (diverted from landfill by law in San Francisco).
- The LED streetlight conversion saves energy and maintenance labor.

Guerrero Park is a model for rethinking lost urban spaces. It performs the missing function in this place of community-building as it is designed for all ages and has explicit ties to the history of the site and to the vicinity.

THE EXPRESSIVE POTENTIAL OF INFRASTRUCTURE

Cliff Garten's work uses integrated design elements to enhance the public's understanding of urban spaces in terms of their ecological context, and the infrastructure that sustains them. When the Canadian city of Calgary asked him to design a public art program, he turned to its watershed as a source of inspiration and information for designing the program.

A Public Art Plan for the Calgary Watershed

CLIFF GARTEN, CLIFF GARTEN STUDIO AND VIA PARTNERSHIP

> What is a watershed? It is "that area of land, a bounded hydrologic system, within which all living things are inextricably linked by their common water course and where, as humans settled, simple logic demanded that they become part of the community."
> —John Wesley Powell, explorer of the
> Colorado River, 1869

In 2005, the city of Calgary's Public Art Program, in conjunction with its Utilities and Environmental Protection Department (UEP), determined that due to the complex and often hidden nature of UEP infrastructure projects, a comprehensive public art plan was necessary. The Public Art Plan for the Expressive Potential of Utility Infrastructure was intended to engage artists, engineers, city government, and local communities in a dialogue about engineering, ecology, water infrastructure, and public education. Proposals were solicited, and the team of Via Partnership, Cliff Garten Studio, and CH2M Hill were awarded the contract.

We immediately proposed that the plan be based on the watershed of the Bow River, which flows through the center of Calgary and is the city's water supply. The public art plan would celebrate two aspects of the watershed:

1. The geomorphology and hydrology of the landscape
2. The built infrastructure that mediates the water from that landscape

The simple logic of gravity and the flow of water provided the concept of the plan as a series of linked public art projects along the course of the river. The subject of the artists' work for the public art plan would be the UEP's expansive engineered system—pump stations, dams, reservoirs, treatment plants, runoff catchments, and culverts—whose forms mediate water resources for the city's population. Our intention was to bring poetry to these highly engineered systems in a way that would render them legible to the public and allow the infrastructure to give the public a visually engaging system of information about the resources that the infrastructure delivers.

The team used geographic information systems (GISs) to map the UEP utilities in the landscape and the urban patterns of the city against the patterns of the watershed. This effort resulted in a compelling vision of the intersection of the natural watershed with the man-made watershed.

The mapping began with a picture of the Bow Glacier and the Bow River running through Calgary, but included the more global downstream concept of that same water running through Saskatchewan and into Hudson Bay. These maps accurately depicted the watershed's hydrologic patterns and the location of its infrastructure; more importantly, they were a way of presenting the big idea of a public art plan that used the watershed as its imaginative and conceptual armature. The power of bringing these 40 x 60-inch maps into a city or community meeting cannot be underestimated. They fixed the literal notion of where people live to the imaginative scale of the landscape and provided a way for city managers and community groups to renegotiate and celebrate the jewel of their city with the poetic promises of the public art plan.

Long days of meetings and interviews, as well as a large-scale community workshop, allowed the team to use the maps as a way to leverage funds and zero in on the most important sites for public art along the Bow River. The mapping and the big idea of the watershed was the sounding board for the community's imagination. We wanted this collective imagination to be the key ingredient of the planning process. By combining interdisciplinary thinking and artistic engagement with the geology, hydrology, and ecology of the riparian zone, we also placed science and engineering in the realm of imagination. The goals of the art projects will be to shape public places, advocate for change, and engage the community around water rights and responsibilities.

The Visual Language Project is the cornerstone of the UEP's public art plan. It provides a cohesive and elegant visual system for UEP infrastructure by creating a visual strategy that encourages citizens and UEP staff to expand the way they think of their relationship to water resources. Through the creative use of literal and cognitive mapping, artist teams are creating a unified, iconographic and symbolic language that will educate users about the systems managed by the UEP and about the larger context of the natural watershed as well. Using graphics and sculpture, this three-dimensional visual language will become part of the everyday vernacular for water utilities and promote user recognition of UEP infrastructure. This presents an unprecedented opportunity for artists to influence a major infrastructure system by engaging in everything from the graphic design for the department to writing code for future infrastructure projects.

🖱 Further information on the UEP Public Art Plan can be found at www.calgary.ca/publicart/.

Portions of this material originally appeared, in slightly different form, in the Public Art Review, *no. 40.*

Notes

1 U.S. Conference of Mayors, "U.S. Conference of Mayors Climate Protection Agreement," http://usmayors.org/climateprotection/agreement.htm.

2 http://sfwater.org/mto_main.cfm/MC_ID/14/MSC_ID/120/MTO_ID/676.

3 "On Thursday, March 18, 2010 in Fremont, the San Francisco Public Utilities Commission (SFPUC) together with Alameda County and City Officials will kick-off three major water infrastructure projects that are part of the $4.6 billion SFPUC's Water System Improvement Program to upgrade and improve the region's aging water system. "Press Release: "SFPUC to Break Ground on First Phase of $332 Million Bay Pipeline & Tunnel Water Construction Projects" Published: 03/17/2010. Updated: 03/17/2010. Published By: Communications and Public Outreach. http://sfwater.org/detail.cfm/MC_ID/18/MSC_ID/114/C_ID/4955. Accessed 3.23.10

4 San Francisco Planning Department, "Pavement to Parks San Francisco," http://pavementtoparks.sfplanning.org.

CHAPTER 8

Applications for Sustainable Communities

The next layer of sustainable infrastructure design is at the community scale. Communities have always redefined themselves by responding and adapting to dynamic conditions. In the twenty-first century, our challenge is to protect and enhance existing ecosystems while designing sustainable infrastructure that builds on the wisdom of natural systems for cleansing air, recycling water, and providing energy. We must embrace technological advances that allow us to apply clean, regenerative systems in our work, from remote developments to dense urban redevelopment.

This chapter presents applications for designing sustainable systems at the community scale, each with its own conditions, climate, resources, and requirements—and all calling for a unique and sensitive response. For an island off the coast of Panama, a comprehensive strategy applies the five pillars framework to community development. On the banks of the Roaring Fork River in Colorado, a plan for developing a mixed-use community reduces sprawl and uses stormwater management techniques to *improve* the quality of the water that runs off into the river. And in the center of Los Angeles, a new park is being designed as a catalyst for environmental restoration and community revitalization.

These projects reference strategies and frameworks introduced earlier in the book and demonstrate how to apply and integrate sustainable infrastructure solutions for their communities.

ACHIEVING A PERFECT BALANCE: PEARL ISLAND, PANAMA

A collaboration by Zoniro Panama, Hart Howerton, Sherwood Design Engineers, and Atelier Ten

Islands have always been sources of innovation, and have often promoted sustainable patterns of settlement and living. Historically, island cultures show patterns of resource use—in materials harvesting, water collection, energy generation, and food production—that reflect maximally efficient responses to their distinctive environments. Therein lie many more general lessons for how to live sustainably, in "perfect balance."

To achieve sustainability, it is therefore useful to think of every project as an island. On an island, it is easy to see the effort (cost, time, energy, etc.) involved in bringing in goods and materials. Resources are often transported hundreds or even thousands of miles. On an island, one sees the trash piling up, or the fouling of the ocean with non-biodegradable plastics. Our global ecosystem is just as delicate as an unspoiled beach. Until we learn to design all our communities as if they were on a beautiful, remote island, we risk fouling the global "island" we all share.

Isla Pedro Gonzalez in the Gulf of Panama is known locally as Pearl Island. It is an island of unique natural beauty and environmental diversity, with a settlement history that dates back nearly five thousand years. With an area of 4,225 acres, Pearl Island is the third largest of the islands in its archipelago. Except for the small fishing village on its northern coastline, the island is virtually uninhabited. Its coastline is a combination of pristine white sand beaches—some used by turtles and marine birds for nesting—cliffs, rocky formations, and mangroves. The color of the water varies from the clear turquoise along protected beaches to a deep blue below steep rocky shores. Numerous coral reefs surround the island, with significant populations of fish typical of the Gulf of Panama.

Classified as a moist tropical forest, the island has suffered significant deforestation over the last several decades, caused mostly by slash-and-burn agriculture. This has diminished the diversity of animal and plant species, and contributed to the excessive stormwater runoff impacting the coral reefs surrounding the island.

The existing village of Pedro de Cocal is a cluster of very modest one-story buildings with metal roofs and deep over-

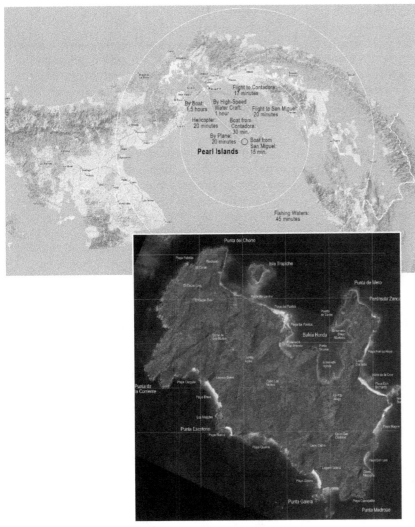

Figure 8-1 Access to Pearl Island from within the Gulf of Panama. Hart Howerton.

Figure 8-2 Aerial image of Pearl Island. Zoniro Panama.

Figure 8-3 Isla Trapiche, looking toward Pearl Island. Hart Howerton.

hangs sitting on a regular north-south grid of narrow pedestrian streets. The layout follows the topography, providing views and ventilation while creating an orderly pattern. The village has very limited infrastructure, with electric power provided for about four hours per day and wastewater discharges directly to the bay. Although it is a fishing village, docking and dockside support facilities are limited.

At Pearl Island, our assignment was to develop an islandwide sustainable development strategy as a member of an interdisciplinary design team led by Hart Howerton and including environmental design firm Atelier Ten. The project was managed by Zoniro Panama, a joint venture of international equity firm Dolphin Capital and local partner Grupo Eleta. Zoniro's commitment to sustainable resort development is evident in their comprehensive planning process and their ongoing implementation locally of environmentally and socially sustainable measures. As part of this commitment the Smithsonian Institute has been working on the island since 2008, performing coral biodiversity surveys and archeological digs.

The master plan we developed for Pearl Island outlines a development strategy for limited residential and eco-resort development aimed at supporting a vibrant and attractive island community in harmony with the setting's natural beauty. On an island, especially one located fifty miles from the nearest commercial center, construction and operations costs can average 50 to 500 percent higher than on the mainland. Reductions in demand from infrastructure, buildings systems, consumables, and transportation—matters at the core of any sustainable development strategy—are necessarily at the heart of cost-effective development on an island.

Designing for Unique Island Conditions

Sustainability is achieved through careful, intelligent decision making throughout a project and at all scales. Embedded in the master plan for this project are decisions about the land, appropriate patterns of development, and multifunctional, integrated systems that take advantage of the particulars of the setting and the development program. The overarching design drivers follow:

- *Maximize ecological connections* by working with the natural contours and slopes, protecting and connecting biologically rich zones, and designing a development program with consideration for the island's carrying capacity.
- *Establish development patterns that match appropriate density to the land* by respecting sensitive ecological areas, concentrating density into walkable neighborhoods, considering synergistic land uses to encourage positive social interaction among residents (reinforced by a transect model for development), and integrating human and natural ecologies.
- *Build integrated systems that reinforce development patterns* by including high-performance infrastructure and high-performance buildings; creating an interconnected biological open-space and park network; setting up intelligent transportation links and offset measures; developing low-carbon circulation systems; establishing education, employment, health and wellness, and recreation programs; and mixing uses, including commercial, industrial, and residential.
- *Work with the land's natural features* by introducing intelligent arrangements of density, maximizing the benefits of the climate, and employing vernacular and passive systems.

Analyzing Critical Climate Factors

The first portion of our work was a study of the local environmental conditions based on an analysis of the climate. The extent to which a building needs to provide shelter, and how the requirements for shelter change over the course of the day and year, directly influence the optimal design of the building and its systems. Critical climate factors are air temperature, humidity, rainfall, solar radiation, and wind speed. These variables are directly tied to the ecological regeneration strategies as well.

Identifying Critical Habitat Factors

Creeks, lagoons, wetlands, and mangroves represent critical habitat areas that influence design decisions. An understanding of solar aspect, elevation, slope, and views influenced initial decisions about the land, including determinations of appropriate densities, road alignments, and lot sizes and types. Areas of mature forest growth were carefully avoided. Similarly, avoiding excessively steep slopes minimizes the disturbance to the forest cover required by road and building construction, and diminishes the costs of retaining walls and foundation systems as well.

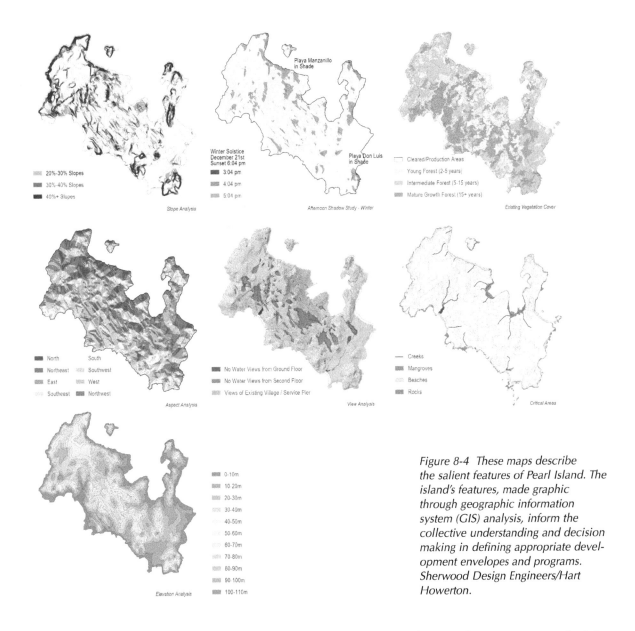

Figure 8-4 These maps describe
the salient features of Pearl Island. The
island's features, made graphic
through geographic information
system (GIS) analysis, inform the
collective understanding and decision
making in defining appropriate development envelopes and programs.
Sherwood Design Engineers/Hart
Howerton.

The Master Plan

The master plan focuses on the seamless integration of
man-made and natural environments. Narrow street
widths maintain habitat connections across them.
Stormwater strategies restrict destructive sediment from
reaching the surrounding network of coral reefs. Buildings
and public spaces draw on the energy potential of the
equatorial sun and the cooling potential of natural
breezes. Organic farms and agroforestry areas reaffirm a
focus on locally grown foods; the composting areas that
serve them demonstrate a closed-loop approach to supply
and waste streams.

Figure 8-5 The illustrative master plan. Hart Howerton.

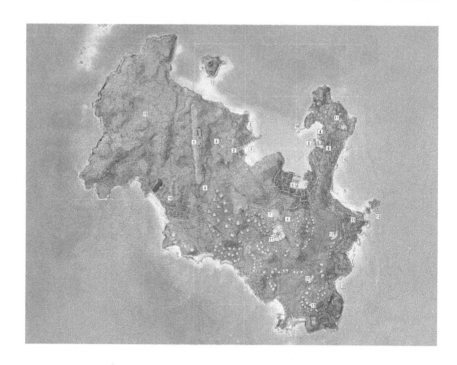

Figure 8-6 Collector street, including existing and potential plant species. Hart Howerton/Sherwood Design Engineers.

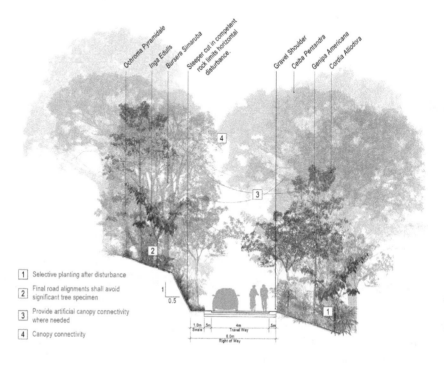

Circulation

The streets on Pearl Island are essentially civic spaces. The network of streets is conceived as a pedestrian-focused, highly landscaped, multipurpose environment, safely mixing together people, bicycles, cars, and stormwater management and other utility infrastructure. Residential streets are designed to slow traffic and promote pedestrian activity, comfort, and safety. Across the island, streets are sized according to the density of development along them, making them no wider than necessary.

Sustainable Development Framework

The five pillars framework, the sustainable development framework used at Pearl Island, examined development and operational activities. The project goals for each of the five pillars are summarized here:

Community: Provide continual support and investment in the local community. Enhance quality of life for guests, residents, and employees through human-dimensioned development strategies, with ongoing and measurable programs.

Ecology: Mitigate the impacts of development on local and regional ecosystems while capitalizing on the value-rich diversity of flora and fauna. Ecological concepts influenced the design of the master plan, including the preservation and conservation of critical habitat areas. The project dedicates 1,133 hectares to a land preserve to be managed in perpetuity by the Pearl Island Foundation.

Water: Achieve on-site water balance through demand reduction, reuse strategies, and low-impact solutions to stormwater management. Potable water demand for the project can reasonably be reduced by 51 percent, reducing costs for wastewater and energy systems while positively affecting the island's aquifer and natural systems.

Energy: Significantly reduce Pearl Island's dependency on imported energy through demand reduction, system synergies, and on-site generation. With comprehensive design strategies, energy demands will be lowered by 36 percent from baseline, with additional cost and energy savings available through the

	BASELINE	25% REDUCTIONS	50% REDUCTIONS	NET ZERO
COMMUNITY	• No Investment in Surrounding Communities • Project Design Isolates Residents and Requires Vehicles for Connectivity	• Investment in Local Community Facilities (Education, Health Care, Housing, Parks, Infrastructure Improvements) • Project Encourages Walking, Bicycling and Social Interaction	• Active Involvement in Local Community (Job Skills, Women Empowerment and Literacy Programs, Job Training, Community, etc.) • Regional Transportation	• New Marketplace Opportunities (Jobs, Financing, Grant Assistance) • Active Partnership with Local Community (Community Development Services, Childcare Access, etc.)
ECOLOGY	• Native and Nonnative Plantings with Significant Irrigation Demands • No Intentional Habitat Plans	• Protect Existing Vegetation and Wetlands • Remove Non-Native and Invasive Species • Create Ecological Corridors • Protect Marine Ecology	• Monitoring Program for Flora and Fauna, Air Quality, Biodiversity Index • Contribute to Regional Conservation Programs and Reforestation	• Reestablished Forest Cover and Bio-Diversity Index On-Site • Regenerative Native Systems • Partner with Academic Groups; Sponsor Research
WATER	• Imported Water or Desalination • Traditional Septic Tank	• Dual Plumbing and Water Conservation Fixtures • Permeable Hardscape (Max. 0.5 Runoff Coefficient) • Graywater Systems	• Rainwater Harvesting • Predevelopment Water Quality Levels for Runoff • Package Treatment On-Site	• On-Site Water Balance • Aquifer Recharge • All Wastewater Managed On-Site with Low-Energy Treatment
ENERGY	• All Imported Diesel Generation • Gasoline-Powered Transportation • Minimal Insulation Values for Building Envelope and Windows	• Advanced Framing, Shading, and Overhangs to Limit Solar Gain • Energy Star Appliances • On-Site Solar Energy Generation (Solar Thermal)	• On-Site Solar Energy Generation (Photovoltaics) • Electric Vehicles • Low-E IG Windows • R-30 to R-40 Building Envelope • Advanced Bldg. Controls	• On-Site Energy Balance • Solar Absorption Cooling • Extensive Distributed Photovolatic Panels for Peak Mitigation
MATERIALS	• Off-Site Municipal Solid Waste Program • No Material Sourcing Restrictions	• Recycling of Construction Waste and Materials • Minimize Use of Packaged Goods • On-Site Composting & Recycling	• Recycling and Reuse • Waste to Energy Incineration Systems • On-Site Agriculture and Food Sourcing	• On-Site Material Balance • No Use of Packaged Goods • Produce 100% of Food On-Site

Optional Level of Commitment

Cost Prohibitive in Current Market

Figure 8-7 A range of sustainable objectives and potential levels of commitment are summarized in the sustainable opportunities matrix. Hart Howerton/Sherwood Design Engineers.

SUSTAINABLE COMMUNITY DEVELOPMENT RESEARCH & STRATEGY AREAS

LIVELIHOOD & CAPACITY BUILDING

- Job Training for Range of Skills
  - White-Collar Workers (management, sales)
  - Blue-Collar Workers (maid service, porters, janitorial)
  - Visitor-Direct Workers (concierge, spa, transport, guides)
  - Physical Labor (landscape, construction) *
  - Farming, Livestock & Agroforestry
- Commuting/Transportation Plans & Financing
- Financing for Microenterprise
- New Marketplace Opportunities
- Grant Development Assistance
- Local Organization Development
- Childcare Access

SUSTENANCE & HEALTH

- Access to Variety of Fresh Foods
- Clean Drinking Water *
- Adequate Health Clinics & Transport to Emergency Care

EDUCATION & CONNECTIVITY

- Primary & Secondary Education (with free lunch)
- Foreign Language Skills Development
- Adult Literacy Programs
- Women's Empowerment/Skills Organizations
- Public Internet Facilities

INFRASTRUCTURE & CIVIC PRIDE

- Sewer, Waste & Stormwater Improvements & Education *
- Infrastructure Repair and/or Development *
- Housing for Key Individuals (i.e., teachers)
- Cultural & Environmental Asset Education
- Individual Residence Aesthetic Improvements
- Neighborhood Landscape & Lighting Upgrades
- Local Public Buildings, Parks & Other Improvements
- Transparent Community Master Plan
- Development and Environment Guidelines
- Disaster Management Plans

** Programs Already Underway*

Figure 8-8 Sustainable community development research and strategy areas. Hart Howerton.

increased use of renewable sources such as solar thermal and photovoltaic (PV) production.

Materials: Monitor and minimize the project's carbon footprint during construction and its long-term operation; maximize locally sourced materials. The strategies provided here are a road map the project will follow for sustainable construction methods, material sourcing, operations, and farm-to-table programs.

The following sections discuss in more detail how each of the five pillars was applied to Pearl Island.

Community Strategies

Throughout the project, the objective was to determine the mix of ingredients that would foster dynamic interaction in daily public and private life. Successful communities are places where these ingredients—private spaces, public spaces, economics, underlying infrastructure and systems, and land—come together seamlessly in both the short and long term.

Community strategies for Pearl Island fell into two categories:

1. Integrating new development into the existing ecological, social, and economic structure of Pearl Island
2. Designing Pearl Island to maximize aspects of community—people in public spaces, productive social relationships, and a high degree of civic pride

See Figure 8-8 for ongoing and proposed community development strategies.

Ecology Strategies

The key components of the plan— being light on the land, preserving and enhancing areas of the island, and maximizing ecological connectivity—influenced the location, density, and configuration of development. Within these development bubbles, a variety of strategies further soften the impact of development on the natural surroundings:

- Critical ecological areas (bird and turtle nesting, riparian areas, steep slopes) were avoided altogether or given extensive setbacks.
- With limited developable areas and no allowable fences, conservation lots act as biological sieves for plant and animal movement.
- Larger, lower-density lots act to buffer smaller, higher-density lots from biological corridors and patches. Smaller lots will employ stilt construction to minimize permanent ground and vegetation disturbance.

For more information on this subject please see www.sherwoodengineers.com/book/29.

Index of Ecological Importance

The index of ecological importance was developed as a starting point for understanding the relative value of the green infrastructure system at Pearl Island. The index summarizes these conditions and opportunities, identifying areas as **most critical** (no development allowed) and **critical** (employ envi-

ronmentally responsive design techniques) and establishing a general framework for biological connectivity to the remainder of the island.

This index is a primary component of the opportunities and constraints plan and has guided decision making throughout the master planning process, focusing development with greater impact away from critical habitat areas. As the team's understanding of the island's ecosystems improves, the index will be updated.

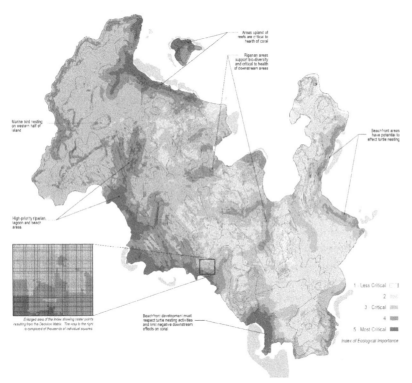

Figure 8-9 The index of ecological importance analysis allows for the emphasis of development in appropriate areas while preserving sensitive land. The darker the tone, the more critical is resource protection. Sherwood Design Engineers/Hart Howerton.

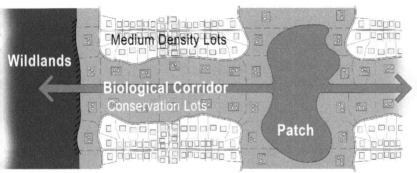

Figure 8-10 Real estate and biological corridors: conservation and connectivity are principles that frame the spatial relationship of the master plan's components. Hart Howerton.

The decision matrix assigns relative value to specific known physical and ecological conditions of the island. The slope analysis, vegetation survey, existing development, and waterways, as well as the mapping of critical bird, turtle and reef habitats, have been included in the weighting system. These seven sets of ecological data were weighted by relative importance and layered to form a single map. Figure 8-9 translates this decision matrix into physical space, providing a relative comparison of ecological value to inform decisions about the placement of buildings and infrastructure.

The following is a list of the criteria with relative weightings and range of influence:

8: Proximity to turtle habitat: 50 to 250 meters
7: Proximity to coral reef: 100 to 300 meters
6: Proximity to pelican habitat: 50 to 3,500 meters
6: Proximity to freshwater: 30 to 200 meters
4: Land cover type: agriculture/clearing to mature mangrove
2: Proximity to existing village: 0 to 1,000 meters
2: Terrain slope: 0 to 40+ percent

Using these weightings, land near streams that is also close to habitat for turtle and bird nesting and surrounded by mangrove, for example, is viewed as highly sensitive. Development will be avoided in these areas. An area with no significant habitat, where trees have recently been cleared for agriculture and that is proximate to the existing town, is most appropriate for high-density development.

Water Management Strategy

Water is a limited resource and is vital to the function of ecological and human systems. It is also energy intensive to obtain, treat, and transport—making its efficient use important to both the health of the island and the strength of the economy.

A comprehensive water management plan was put in place to meet the long-term demands of the population and mix of uses by capturing, cleansing, and utilizing stormwater; converting wastewater into a resource; and sustainably drawing on the island's natural aquifer. Long-term water sustainability—a zero water balance—is achieved through efficient water usage, sensible irrigation strategies in harmony with the island's native landscape palette, and the reuse of treated effluent for irrigation and nonpotable uses.

Specifically, the water strategy at Pearl Island

• detains, slows, and cleanses stormwater runoff to recharge the aquifer and minimizes particulate matter that reaches the ocean in storm events;
• achieves zero discharge of wastewater to the ocean;
• uses low-energy, low-maintenance biological systems to process wastewater distributed appropriately across the site according to density;
• utilizes rainwater harvesting to supply potable water, thereby minimizing potential impacts on the fresh water aquifer.

Water Usage

In order to a establish a balanced water system, the baseline water usages across the island were modeled. The use rate for the model are

• 80 gallons per capita per day for residences in Pedro de Cocal and the multifamily and townhouse buildings at the marina village

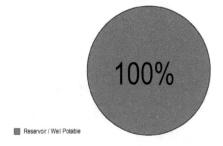

Figure 8-11 Baseline residential water demand by source. Sherwood Design Engineers.

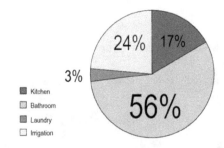

Figure 8-12 Baseline residential water demand by use. Sherwood Design Engineers.

- 100 gallons per capita per day for all other residential units
- 120 gallons per capita per day for hotel rooms

These assumptions are derived from Panamanian standards and are inclusive of all standard water demands associated with a neighborhood, including reception for the hotel, community facilities, retail, and so on.

Water Balance

A water balance is a decision-making tool that allows stakeholders to examine the full spectrum of water use on the island. A comprehensive water balance incorporates historical climate data, seasonality (wet and dry seasons), the evapotranspiration rate of the island, anticipated water demand for irrigation, building and service uses, and expected occupancy rates into a formula that balances the amount of water used and reused—and thus required—to operate independently of any external supplies such as desalination. The goal of the project was an on-site water balance, which, based on our analysis, is a reasonable and

achievable goal. Figure 8-13 illustrates the various components of a balanced water system for Pearl Island.

🐭 For more information on this subject please see www.sherwoodinstitute.org/tools.

Potable Water

Potable water will be made up by a mixture of rainwater, surface water, and groundwater. The following design hierarchy was used for the potable water systems:

1. Reduce demand/loading through conservation and efficiency.
2. Reuse water throughout the project wherever possible, including rainwater, graywater, and treated blackwater.
3. Maximize the efficiency of the water infrastructure.

The hydrogeologic study concluded that surface water needs to be the primary potable water resource for this project. Given the abundant rainfall and limited terrestrial water resources, rainwater harvesting will be a significant

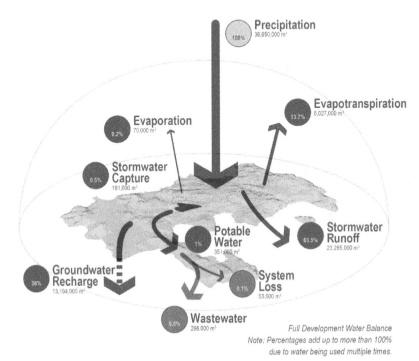

Figure 8-13 Full development water balance. Hart Howerton/Sherwood Design Engineers.

Full Development Water Balance
Note: Percentages add up to more than 100% due to water being used multiple times.

component of the island's water system. Due to the long dry season and seasonality of many of the surface water resources, groundwater resources or storage will need to be developed prior to full project build-out. subsurface investigations have indicated scattered groundwater resources within rock fractures below the island's streams, which may offer a renewable supply water during the dry season.

Rainwater is plentiful, and clean. Captured on-site for use in potable systems, it will provide a critical water resource for Pearl Island. Rainwater has the added advantage of being desirable for both laundry systems (because it reduces detergent needs and softens clothes) and for showering. All single-family homes will be required to harvest rainwater for potable use. Although it may not be required to, a single-family home could store sufficient rainwater to meet its annual potable water demands.

The amount of rainwater storage required to meet all potable demands is a function of roof area and number of bedrooms. This relationship is based on homes being able to provide approximately 80 percent of their annualized domestic water demands through rainwater harvesting. A typical four-bedroom home requires a 21,000-gallon cistern to provide 100 percent of its potable demands during an average rain year. (These calculations were made using standard residential assumptions based on U.S. Environmental Protection Agency [EPA] guidelines and assume rainfall capture from 75 percent of the estimated 297-square-meter roof area of a conservation lot.) Overall, harvested rainwater is estimated to satisfy 57 percent of the final potable demand.

Alternate Sourcing

To further reduce demand for limited potable water resources, the use of reclaimed (treated) graywater and blackwater will be employed across the site. In residential uses, blackwater is the water from toilets and kitchens, while graywater makes up the remainder of the water. The treatment and reuse of these water sources provides a safe, local, and energy-efficient substitute for potable water where the end use does not require drinkable water. Graywater and blackwater are acceptable for toilet flushing, the irrigation of ornamental plants or crops, mechanical system makeup, and other nonpotable needs.

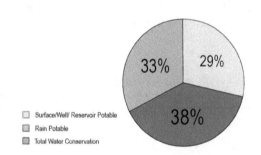

Figure 8-14a Domestic water use by source. Sherwood Design Engineers.

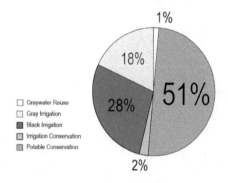

Figure 8-14b Domestic water conservation by source. Sherwood Design Engineers.

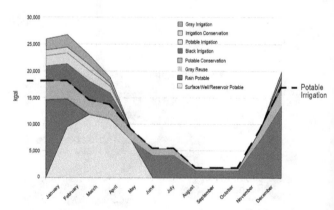

Figure 8-14c Monthly engineered water use by source. Potable uses are shown above the heavy dashed line, and irrigation uses are shown below it. Sherwood Design Engineers.

Reducing Demand

In residential buildings, water-conserving fixtures and appliances can reduce the amount of potable water required; these include low-flow showerheads, faucets with aerators, dual-flush and low-flow toilets (which may be fed with lavatory water), high-efficiency front-loading washing machines, and high-efficiency dishwashers. Commercial facilities will employ these strategies and others, including the capture and reuse of HVAC condensate, efficient water-use practices for applicable commerce and industry, and prohibiting water sweeping and other water-wasting activities. In aggregate, this is projected to reduce overall potable water demand by approximately 24 percent compared with baseline conditions: from 596,300 to 453,190 gallons per day.

Consistent with customary practice in the region, irrigation with potable water will be prohibited, reducing the total residential potable water demand by an estimated 24 percent as measured against a comparable project.

Maximizing Infrastructure Efficiency

The remaining water demand will be fed through a series of interconnected community systems and backed by a centralized reservoir or potable water wells. These systems will be optimized for water and energy efficiency, minimizing leaks and other water losses as well as the energy required to deliver each gallon. Water storage tanks will be located at high points in the neighborhoods, providing distribution via a gravity system. The footprint of the reservoir will be minimized to reduce the environmental impacts of reservoir construction.

Irrigation Strategy

Irrigation needs for both agriculture and landscaping will be met nearly entirely by nonpotable sources. Agroforestry areas will be supplied by treated wastewater from the wastewater treatment plant at Pedro de Cocal. Edible crops will be irrigated with harvested rainwater or surface water resources rather than reclaimed wastewater. Landscape irrigation demands will be met through the use of treated wastewater or graywater collected on-site. The use of potable water for landscape irrigation will be prohibited.

Appropriate planting (primarily xeriscaping and native plantings, with select areas of ornamentals) and preventing irrigation from potable water sources through the development and enforcement of design and performance guidelines are anticipated to reduce demand 25 percent.

Stormwater Management Plan

The highest priority of the island's stormwater management plan is to avoid disturbing established vegetation. In areas where there has been significant disturbance over the last ten to twenty years, the goal will be to return the land to preexisting runoff conditions and to restore tree growth, soil characteristics, and aquifer function to presettlement conditions. Development design guidelines will also be used to decrease new impervious surfaces and integrate built stormwater management facilities with the natural environment.

The following are the three components of a stormwater management plan for Pearl Island:

1. *Erosion and sedimentation control:* Designed to meet or exceed EPA standards, the erosion and sedimentation control plan will be a part of all development projects on the island. Stormwater best management practices (BMPs) that promote groundwater recharge will reduce the amount of runoff as well as the total volume of solids present in the runoff. This will allow the water to infiltrate into the island aquifers and help to prevent saltwater intrusion while providing a potable water source.
2. *Water quality:* Water quality treatment will be provided by directing runoff to the landscape to allow for natural treatment via biochemical reactions and infiltrative processes. This will protect marine ecosystems.
3. *Water quantity:* Stormwater runoff from the site will be maintained at or below the island's presettlement levels for a 2-centimeter, twenty-four-hour storm. This management requirement will help restore the hydrologic cycle to its natural state. By directing stormwater to water-quality treatment areas or discharge points at velocities that will not cause additional erosion or flooding, water quality will also be improved.

Determining Density and Use

The critical objectives of sediment control, water quality management, and water quantity conveyance will be executed differently across the island, depending on the density of development and the existing vegetation.

In village areas, where there is little green space relative to hardscape, streets will be designed to incorporate stormwater treatment facilities within the right-of-way. These landscape-based treatment facilities reduce stormwater pollution and volume on-site, with the ancillary benefits of improved greenery, place-making, and other aesthetic and quality-of-life improvements. Treatment facilities will include permeable paving sys-

tems, flow-through and infiltration planters, swales, rain gardens, channels and runnels, and infiltration and soakage trenches.

Along the village waterfront, mechanical stormwater separators will be utilized to ensure that only water with acceptable quality is discharged to the ocean. Detention within streetscape management elements and under paving will minimize flows and the size of these mechanical separator units. Water in higher-density areas will be conveyed through above ground channels that join into water features where possible, showcasing the movements of water across the site.

In less developed areas, roadways are designed to incorporate natural vegetated swales. Periodically interrupting these swales, check dams allow for settling and infiltration, while bioretention areas and level spreaders with filter strips disperse stormwater in a decentralized manner.

Figure 8-15 Streamside forest buffers play an active role in stormwater management and erosion control practices. Sherwood Design Engineers/Hart Howerton.

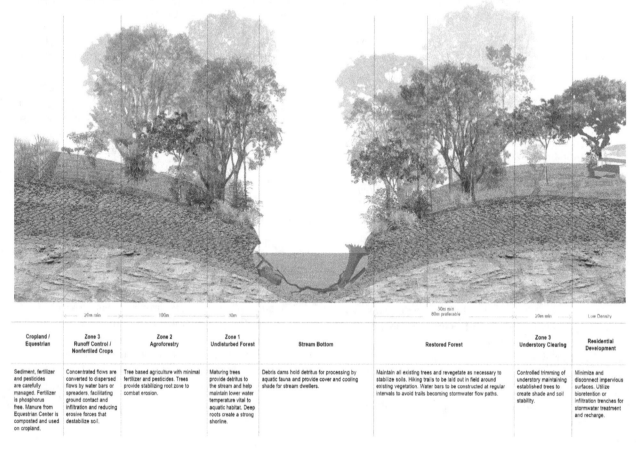

Cropland / Equestrian	Zone 3 Runoff Control / Nonfertiled Crops	Zone 2 Agroforestry	Zone 1 Undisturbed Forest	Stream Bottom	Restored Forest	Zone 3 Understory Clearing	Residential Development
Sediment, fertilizer and pesticides are carefully managed. Fertilizer is phosphorus free. Manure from Equestrian Center is composted and used on cropland.	Concentrated flows are converted to dispersed flows by water bars or spreaders, facilitating ground contact and infiltration and reducing erosive forces that destabilize soil.	Tree based agriculture with minimal fertilizer and pesticides. Trees provide stabilizing root zone to combat erosion.	Maturing trees provide detritus to the stream and help maintain lower water temperature vital to aquatic habitat. Deep roots create a strong shoreline.	Debris dams hold detritus for processing by aquatic fauna and provide cover and cooling shade for stream dwellers.	Maintain all existing trees and revegetate as necessary to stabilize soils. Hiking trails to be laid out in field around existing vegetation. Water bars to be constructed at regular intervals to avoid trails becoming stormwater flow paths.	Controlled trimming of understory maintaining established trees to create shade and soil stability.	Minimize and disconnect impervious surfaces. Utilize bioretention or infiltration trenches for stormwater treatment and recharge.

Within the existing heavily eroded stream channels, rock wall check dams will be constructed of nongrouted native stone. These features will keep sediment from entering the surrounding ocean waters. Sediment from these facilities will be collected on a regular basis and mixed with compost to create fertile soil for landscaping and agricultural uses.

Wastewater Master Plan

Low-energy, low-maintenance biological systems will be used at Pearl Island to process wastewater, generating a total of approximately 0.385 million gallons per day [mgd], 85 percent of the potable demand. These systems will be distributed across the island's six sewer sheds according to density. As density increases towards the urban core, individual lots and buildings shift towards connection with the centralized treatment facilities. In areas of extreme low density, wastewater treatment will be handled entirely on individual lots. Medium-density areas will employ pretreatment systems on-site to provide primary treatment, with secondary and tertiary treatment provided at a centralized plant. The highest-density areas will rely entirely on a centralized treatment plant.

Treated effluent will be used to satisfy irrigation demands in the dry season. In the wet season, that effluent will be treated to a higher level and ground applied. A wastewater irrigation system allows for significant demand reductions on the water supply system and experiences reduced flows in the wet season because of lower occupancies. In addition to the mechanical treatment systems described in this section, two treatment wetlands are proposed at the headwaters of primary creeks on the east side of the island. These wetlands will provide treatment through natural low-energy processes that will simultaneously enrich the biology of the island.

Technology Selection

Typical drivers of a wastewater treatment solution include footprint area, initial costs, ongoing maintenance costs, effluent quality, environmental impact, and energy requirements. At Pearl Island, there is sufficient space for a variety of treatment systems in most areas. While effluent quality is of great concern, secondary treatment will typically be sufficient because the effluent will be primarily reused for irrigation. Thus, up-front costs, energy requirements, and effluent quality drove the selection of a treatment plant technology.

A low-energy plant will help decrease up-front capital costs associated with energy generation infrastructure as well as long-term operational expense. High-quality effluent will help to maintain both healthy terrestrial and marine ecosystems and subsurface water quality. Figure 8-16 illustrates how some common treatment technologies compared over a range of criteria.

For Pearl Island, we recommended using recirculating sand filter technology, which provides a high-quality effluent similar to that of a sequencing batch reactor or a rotating biological contactor while having very low energy demands and a much smaller footprint than a traditional sand filter. This type of technology is also well suited to make use of solar pumps during daylight hours, further minimizing demand for grid-supplied electricity.

This system will be phased in over time and is easily sized to the community's needs. It is composed of a series of pods connected by high-density polyethylene (HDPE) piping. A large recirculation tank, sized for one-and-a-half times the daily flow, is located at the headworks. As new

Figure 8-16 Wastewater technology comparison matrix. Sherwood Design Engineers.

	Worst			Average				Best
Footprint / Size	Evapotranspiration	Wastewater Treatment Wetland	Rapid Infiltration	Algal Ponding System	Living Machine	Activated Sludge Treatment	Sequencing Batch Reactor (SBR)	**Media Filter**	Membrane BioReactor (MBR)	Moving Bed BioReactor (MBBR)
Initial Cost	Membrane BioReactor (MBR)	Sequencing Batch Reactor (SBR)	Living Machine	Moving Bed BioReactor (MBBR)	Evapotranspiration	Algal Ponding System	Activated Sludge Treatment	**Media Filter**	Rapid Infiltration	Wastewater Treatment Wetland
Maintenance / Upkeep Costs	Membrane BioReactor (MBR)	Moving Bed BioReactor (MBBR)	Sequencing Batch Reactor (SBR)	Activated Sludge Treatment	Living Machine	Wastewater Treatment Wetland	Evapotranspiration	Rapid Infiltration	**Media Filter**	Algal Ponding System
Effluent Quality	Evapotranspiration	Rapid Infiltration	Algal Ponding System	Activated Sludge Treatment	Living Machine	**Media Filter**	Sequencing Batch Reactor (SBR)	Moving Bed BioReactor (MBBR)	Wastewater Treatment Wetland	Membrane BioReactor (MBR)
Energy Requirements	Membrane BioReactor (MBR)	Sequencing Batch Reactor (SBR)	Activated Sludge Treatment	Moving Bed BioReactor (MBBR)	Algal Ponding System	Living Machine	Rapid Infiltration	**Media Filter**	Evapotranspiration	Wastewater Treatment Wetland

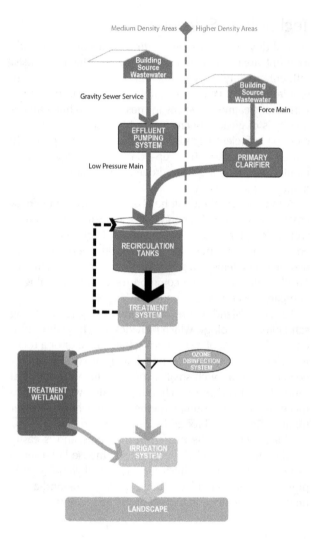

Figure 8-17 Wastewater treatment process flow schematic.
Sherwood Design Engineers/Hart Howerton.

be below 10 milligrams per liter during normal operating conditions. In the rainy season, when occupancies and irrigation demands are low, effluent will be of the highest quality when it is applied, as the saturated ground has slower absorptive capacity. Two tertiary treatment wetlands are proposed to handle wastewater from the higher-density areas of the island, including hotels and the village center. These wetlands will facilitate increased biological activity while minimizing energy usage.

Energy Management Strategy

The energy system on Pearl Island will not only account for the power generated for transportation and to operate buildings but will also be mindful of the environmental impacts of the power generation itself. By designing to minimize imported fuels and the emission of carbon dioxide and other detrimental greenhouse gases, short-term infrastructure and long-term environmental costs borne by the project will be substantially lower than they would with conventional (baseline) systems.

Without appreciable wind speeds, plentiful year-round sun, or sufficient elevation change for hydropower, there is no silver bullet for renewable energy to take the project off the grid cost-effectively. Accordingly, the proposed energy system employs a series of coordinated strategies that, taken together, will deliver reliable, cost-effective, environmentally friendly power to residents and guests.

The energy strategy is comprised of five key elements:

1. Demand reduction
2. Peak shifting/mitigation
3. Distributed renewable generation
4. District cogeneration and trigeneration systems
5. A central biofuel-ready generation facility

At full build-out, using baseline development practices, the project will have a peak electrical demand of 14.3 megawatts, with additional propane required for hot water and cooking demands and additional gasoline needed to power personal and project vehicle fleets. Through a comprehensive, whole-systems approach to engineering and infrastructure design, the energy burden on a centralized power production facility will be reduced by 36 percent, to 9.1 megawatts. In doing so, much of the cost of an islandwide power system will be deferred to home buyers and hospital-

homes or neighborhoods are brought online, pods can easily be added to the system to accommodate increased demand. The system will be designed to recirculate approximately five times before overflowing to the irrigation distribution system. However, in periods of low occupancy, the water will recirculate many more times, improving water quality with each pass, up to a point.

Effluent loadings of TSS and BOD [Total Suspended Solids and Biological Oxygen Demand] are expected to ity providers, while the carbon emissions generated by the project will be significantly reduced through the use of renewable energy sources, electric vehicles, and demand reductions. The 9.1-megawatt electrical demand includes the operation of an all-electric vehicle fleet, eliminating the need for the storage, sale, or distribution of gasoline for automobile use. Lastly, the reduced power demand will also significantly reduce the quantity of propane required by the island.

Renewable Energy Generation

In lower-density residential and hotel areas, homes and hotel units will benefit greatly from renewable energy generation. Through enhanced construction techniques, these units can be designed to be net zero or even energy positive. Nonetheless, for master planning purposes, we assumed that all homes and hotel rooms would be connected to the islandwide power grid. At a minimum, each residence and hotel room in low- and mid-density areas will have sufficient solar thermal panels to supply 100 percent of domestic hot water, with propane backup and cooking fuel supplied by localized propane tanks serviced via delivery as required. Additionally, equipping a home with four to sixty-one roof-mounted photovoltaic solar panels (6.5 to 78 square meters) can provide 8 to 100 percent of that home's total power needs, appreciably affecting base power demand for the island, providing a good level of long-term energy security, and making a substantial positive impact on the project's overall carbon emissions. Cooling and dehumidification will be supplied by high-efficiency units for each building. Dehumidification may be separated from cooling where advantageous.

In higher-density residential and hotel areas, 100 percent of the domestic hot water demand will be supplied by solar thermal panels, with propane backup. With lower roof area-to-unit ratios, buildings in the village and Pedro de Cocal will need to rely more heavily on the islandwide electrical grid. Where possible, photovoltaic panels will be integrated to augment peak daytime power needs. The density of the villages and hotel cores facilitate a district cooling system supplied by a chilled water distribution loop fed from a centralized chiller unit. Dehumidification may be supplied via fan-coil unit or by a solar-regenerated desiccant unit located in each building.

The service pier provides an opportune area for a large-scale photovoltaic array. The project will explore this

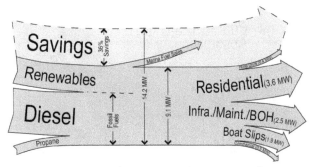

Figure 8-18 Proposed start-up conditions energy flow breakdown for Pearl Island, Panama. Hart Howerton/ Sherwood Design Engineers/Atelier Ten.

opportunity during later phases. Where feasible, photovoltaic panels will be added to the roofs of covered infrastructure works (booster pumps, wastewater treatment facilities, water tanks, etc.) to further reduce overall electrical demand.

Costs and Financing

The financing and structuring of the project's infrastructure offered many opportunities. Because of the high price of on-site generation and the strong commitment to sustainable development, extensive use of solar technology was

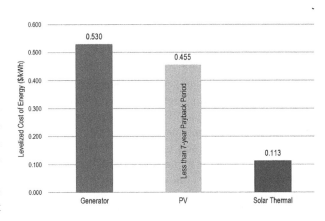

Figure 8-19 Levelized cost of energy. The true costs of a diesel generator are much higher than that of solar thermal and marginally higher than that of photovoltaics. Renewable technologies are profitable if the system's up-front costs are properly financed or if the costs of fossil fuel–based energies increase over time. Atelier Ten.

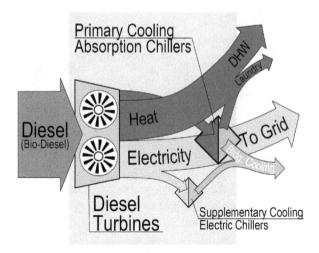

Figure 8-20 Schematic diagram of the trigeneration central plant proposed for the service pier. Hart Howerton/Atelier Ten/Sherwood Design Engineers.

recommended. The estimated payback for a detached single-family home that installs solar photovoltaic panels on this project will be under seven years.

Overall power demand projections will be aggressively tracked throughout the project's design and construction. A reduction in overall infrastructure can help to offset any onetime cost increases for more efficient systems. Long-term energy savings are also a means of cost recovery.

Central Generation

Given the island's size and the environmental challenges of distributing and storing fuel, we recommended a central plant located adjacent to the service pier and boat dry-storage facility. The generation capacity will be brought online in stages, decreasing up-front capital costs and providing strong incentives to maximize conservation and distributed generation technologies. The central generation facility, which will initially operate on diesel fuel, will be capable of utilizing biofuels such as biodiesel when they become commercially viable in the Panamanian market-place. The generation facility will also be able to operate in conjunction with cogeneration and trigeneration schemes in the higher-density areas.

Trigeneration systems are highly efficient and provide many services at once, greatly reducing overall resource demand and cost. Employing a trigeneration system for the central power plant could efficiently provide islandwide power as well as building cooling and hot water. It could also enable a highly efficient laundry facility to be colocated with the power plant.

Distribution

Power will be distributed across a modern distribution system built in accordance with Panama City electrical grid standards, matching those of the United States and enabling simple use of electronics from many countries. All power lines will be located underground in joint utility trenches along primary rights-of-way. The system will be designed to allow distributed generation and resale of distributed power (produced at individual homes and buildings) back to the grid.

District Systems

A series of district systems are proposed in higher-density core areas. In the village and Pedro de Cocal, centralized chiller units will provide chilled water for district cooling systems. A combination of conventional electrically powered centrifugal chillers and solar-powered absorption chillers are expected to achieve cooling demand savings of 71 percent (19 percent total energy demand savings) within each district.

Peak Shifting

Large-scale power systems are often built to accommodate peak demand (at the most energy-intensive time of the day or year), resulting in power plants that are oversized or inefficiently operated for much of the rest of the time. Through the introduction of solar photovoltaic and solar thermal technologies, as well as by exploring smart-grid and smart-meter technologies, the daily peak energy demand will be reduced. Additionally, by designing a sophisticated power plant, efficiencies and fuel savings will be achieved by only engaging the necessary generation capacity.

Materials Strategy

Materials—foods, furniture, sunscreen, napkins, beer bottles—will find their way to Pearl Island from all over the

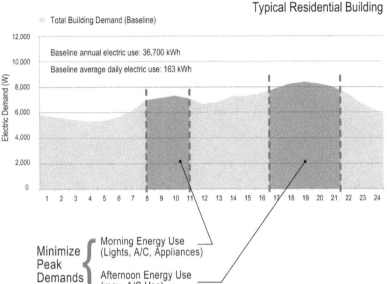

Figure 8-21 Hourly electric demand for a typical residential building. Atelier Ten/Hart Howerton.

Capitalizing on Peak Reduction or Shifting Opportunities Would Enable the Central Plant to Operate at Reduced Levels and Potentially Allow the Overall Plant Size to Be Reduced.

world. Some will require massive expenditures and amounts of energy to procure; some will be especially harmful to the ecology. Those that are grown locally will provide nourishment to the regional economy. The project has the opportunity to direct the means and methods by which these all things arrive on the island, impact its ecosystem, and are disposed of.

Every pound of material not brought to Pearl Island is a potential savings realized by the constructor and operator. Every mile not traveled by construction materials and furnishings is a direct carbon savings and an investment in the regional economy. Every contaminant not brought to Pearl Island is a benefit to the flora and fauna that surround and inhabit the island. And food that is grown on Pearl Island and served at the tables of restaurants and residents is fresher than imported food and enhances the health and wellness of the island, its residents, and its guests.

Below are outlined objectives for materials programs at Pearl Island, which focus on three key components:

1. *Sustainable construction practices,* which utilize regionally produced nontoxic building materials, optimize transport and workforce flows, and minimize waste generated on-site.
2. *Sustainable operations and material sourcing guidelines,* which encourage local crafts and products while restricting certain products known to be harmful to the environment or not easily handled by the solid waste disposal program.
3. *Farm-to-table guidelines,* which stimulate the local economy of the Pearl Island Archipelago by furnishing every resident and restaurant at Pearl Island with locally grown meats and produce.

Underlying each of these objectives is a commitment that only nontoxic, certified, sustainably produced goods be tolerated on Pearl Island, contributing to the overall healthfulness of the project while diminishing its net ecological footprint.

Figure 8-22 Ninety-five percent of construction materials are to be procured within 500 miles. Hart Howerton.

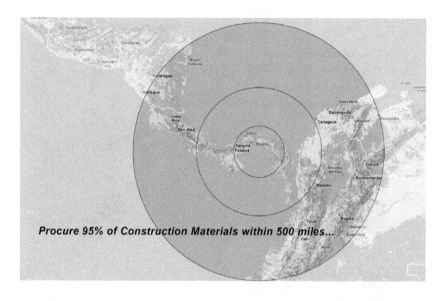

Procure 95% of Construction Materials within 500 miles...

Figure 8-23 Seventy-five percent of construction materials are to be procured within 100 miles. Hart Howerton

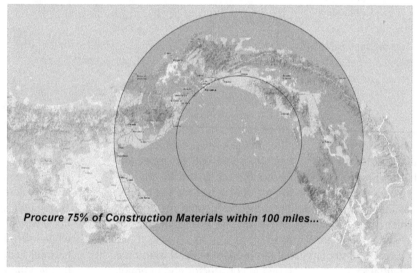

Procure 75% of Construction Materials within 100 miles...

Material Use Guidelines

To ensure that the project's long-term goals for sustainable materials use are adhered to, the following project guidelines were recommended:

Pearl Island Sustainable Construction Methods Guidelines: In collaboration with industry experts and the primary general contractor for the project, comprehensive guidelines were produced prior to the start

of construction activities to govern construction methods and practices. These modes of practice will be furnished to all prospective contractors at the request for proposal (RFP) stage and assumed for all proposals for work on the project. Throughout the entire construction process, an International Organization for Standardization (ISO)–trained appointee of either Pearl Island, the primary developer, or the general contractor will be tasked with enforcement and compliance, records of which will be kept on permanent file. These guidelines will help determine the savings—both environmental and financial—associated with sustainable construction practices.

Pearl Island Material Sourcing and Operations Guidelines: In collaboration with regional experts on the availability and transport of goods and services, as well as industry leaders in sustainable hospitality and marina operations, Pearl Island will enact a set of comprehensive guidelines to govern materials used on the island as part of the ongoing operations of Pearl Island, including commercial, hospitality, and residential programs. These operations guidelines will minimize the burden placed on the island's solid waste and wastewater infrastructure, minimize transport and fuel expenditures, and ensure that no environmentally harmful products or chemicals come into contact with Pearl Island's sensitive ecosystems.

Pearl Island Farm-to-Table Opportunities and Guidelines: Pearl Island will cultivate a farm-to-table culture that encourages residents and hospitality operators to source locally grown organic foods. Pearl Island will promote locally based agriculture through education, community outreach, and networking. Farm-to-table programs enhance the local character of the island's restaurants and markets, encourage the local farming and fishing economies, are a source of local employment, preserve agricultural traditions, and further an understanding of the links among farming, food, health, and local economies. Firm project-wide commitments to health and wellness will translate to positive marketing and brand strength for the development.

Limiting Harmful Products

Retail outlets and hospitality operators at Pearl Island will encourage the sale and distribution of only environmentally friendly products. Given the sensitivity of the surrounding reef and marine ecosystem, product awareness is uniquely important. There are downstream effects to many everyday products we come in contact with. Similarly, transporting hard-to-process waste off-island is cost prohibitive. An example of restricted products that harm marine wildlife are petroleum-based exfoliating scrubs. These scrubs contain thousands of tiny polymer granules that, when washed downstream, find their way into the stomachs and breathing apparatus of marine life and eventually into the birds and larger mammals that eat them. Instead, only 100 percent natural exfoliants—those using seeds, shells, sugars, or salts—will be used on the island.

By limiting the presence of harmful products and materials on Pearl Island (or encouraging the use of alternatives to them), we diminish the risk of contaminating these sensitive ecosystems through their use and disposal.

GOING BEYOND ENGINEERING: SHARING STANDARDS FOR SUSTAINABILITY

As clients and collaborators, the Ocean Foundation has worked with Sherwood Design Engineers to advance the inclusion of legacy institutions and government capacity-building tools in order to extend the value of development projects far beyond the limits of conventional practice. Mark J. Spalding presents his perspective on these items below.

Mark J. Spalding, president, the Ocean Foundation
Sustainable development practices meet the needs of the present without compromising the needs of the future by leveraging four components: environmental protection, social equity, aesthetic beauty, and economic returns. Sustainable design

- returns to a design for climate, culture, and place;
- integrates design solutions among all the design and engineering disciplines;
- reduces or eliminates negative environmental impact;
- saves energy and water;
- reduces operating costs;
- promotes health;
- maximizes local resources before importing materials or talent;
- embraces environmentally sensitive and appropriate technologies that require fewer resources, are easier to maintain, and have a lower overall cost.

Sustainability is not a differentiation point any more. It is a necessity. And it is a necessity for all types of tourism. The Ocean Foundation's unique mission is to support ocean environments around the world. Green resorts and coastal developments depend on conservation and the protection of natural resources to attract visitors and maintain a competitive edge.

Resorts sell natural amenities: beaches, coral reefs, dive sites, surf breaks, sailing and marinas, bird-watching, sportfishing, scenic vistas, culture, and lifestyles. These natural amenities are more important than golf courses, cruise ships, or large hotels. For example, a beach produces more revenue than a golf course, and it doesn't have to be bought, designed, built, or operated. But it does have to be protected.

Our resort partnership model supports local conservation, sustainability, and long-term positive community development with 1 percent of the proceeds from coastal and island developments. We work with developers who incorporate best practices for the highest levels of sustainability during planning, construction, and operation.

Ideally, many pristine coastal properties identified for resorts would not be developed. Understanding that government approval for strategic tourism development has already occurred for a particular site of great natural beauty and value, it is our goal to ensure that any development provides lasting benefit to the local community and to the natural resources on which the success of the development depends, now and in the future.

We design a resort partnership fund to provide a long-term predictable revenue stream that enables both grant planning and independence from transitions in political and developer leadership. As such, the foundation fully retains its transparency, credibility, and value as a partner for the developer, the developer's clients, the local community, and the government. We thus ensure a process that is as independent from political and economic pressures as possible.

In addition to providing economic sustainability, we also work to develop standards to guide and ensure the sustainable development of coastal environments and communities.

Coastal Sustainable Development Standards

The Villages of Loreto Bay, Mexico, represent a model of well-executed sustainable development, and the Loreto Bay Foundation is our effort to provide for the long-term sustainable health of the people and the place. Loreto's future depends on preventing it from becoming another Cancun—a town with unsustainable, out-of-scale, high-rise resort developments that ignore the local resources, culture, and vistas.

To avoid creating an island of sustainability amid more traditional development, we have pursued the creation of coastal sustainable development standards in partnership with the Baja California Sur state government and Sherwood Design Engineers. The standards were drafted to address the most common concerns about coastal development, including

- the further degradation and overuse of resources;
- the scale of development versus the scale of the existing community;
- the impact on affordable housing, the job market, and so on;
- the impact on local culture, historic legacy, and so on;
- funds to meet local needs beyond those necessary to address the influx of outside workers, tourists, and others;
- how to engage visitors in community;
- how to meet the need for independent monitoring and conflict resolution.

As part of a process to create these standards, we started in 2006 with a guiding document that set context and acknowledged the need for standards, informed intended reviewers and users on types of standards, and explained the process of developing standards as well as how to approach and use the document. The outstanding result: we have now developed a clearinghouse for methods and sustainable technologies that are tailored to Baja California Sur that address

- project siting and program;
- potable water;
- built environment and energy;
- wastewater;

- access and transportation;
- landscape, irrigation, and nonbuilding structures;
- grading and drainage;
- solid waste management;
- construction procedures;
- watershed restoration;
- golf course design;
- marina design and construction.

The guiding document and a draft of the standards (in English and Spanish) were circulated for comment throughout the nongovernmental organization (NGO) community, the foundation community, and to private clients. The Spanish draft was then edited and provided to the state government for review. We then supported a workshop with the Baja California Sur Dirección de Planeación Urbana y Ecología (Division of Urban Planning and Ecology). As part of this workshop, we identified relevant Mexican law at multiple levels, recognized points of overlap between standards and existing law, and developed a strategy for implementation.

In May 2009, we fulfilled the request of the Dirección de Planeación Urbana y Ecología for a guide for developers. While educating developers, it creates an approach-able review process and provides the state government with a legally relevant metric to evaluate projects. We also expect to use the guide and the standards to inform urban development plans and ecological ordinances. When adopted into existing development laws, coastal developments, including tourism resorts, will be required to incorporate sustainable practices that protect natural resources and those who depend on them.

In the end, if this project to develop and implement standards is successful, the map will show a mosaic of pristine, relatively undisturbed areas and vital, well-planned, and viable urban development that is highly profitable and low impact, and has a small ecological footprint.

This is about the future, and it is about wellness. We must have healthy coasts and oceans so that we can have healthy communities that depend on them (including hospitality guests). It is also about being green to increase net revenues via the cost savings inherent in more energy-efficient buildings, renewable energy, and waste reduction processes.

For more information on this subject please see www.sherwoodinstitute.org/ideas.

INTEGRATING STORMWATER STRATEGIES INTO THE TRANSECT AT THE COMMUNITY SCALE: CATTLE CREEK, COLORADO

Water rights in the western United States have a long and storied history. At present, the rights to all of the water that enters the Colorado River watershed are owned. If a rain-drop falls in Aspen, one-seventh is owned by the state of California, and complex mathematical formulas are used for determining annual water allowances. This means that someone living on the Roaring Fork River is not allowed to harvest rainwater unless it comes from a well outside a municipal water system. At Cattle Creek, we worked with lead master planner Hart Howerton to develop a stormwater strategy that integrated with the community plan, as it cleansed the water within this upper reach of the Colorado River watershed.

As architect Eron Ashley from Hart Howerton recalls,

It's a great site, right on a beautiful, protected river, with a creek running through it. The whole valley is glacial till—essentially cobblestones—on top of a layer of very hard rock, so water picks up toxins from the built environment and runs off the site very fast. Our strategy was not to reclaim water but to cleanse it before it hits the river.

Where there are plants, runoff happens slowly, so rivers don't get overburdened. We wanted all of the water running off to be cleaner than a river or stream. Rather than a mechanical or chemical cleaning treatment and holding ponds, we set up distributed swales and other stormwater treatment methods. These methods slow down the water by hours and hours before releasing it into river.

The engineers worked with us to tell a story about how stormwater worked at different densities. Water that falls on the lot itself can be managed in low-density areas. As density increases, more of the burden of water falls in the public realm—streetscape, park space, rights-of-way, and so on.

To help organize our response, we set up a transect. In low-density areas, most of the treatment is done on the lot, with some amount of street treatments (bioswales and so on). Most of these look very natural, with soft edges. As one goes toward downtown, they get harder edges and look more engineered, but they treat more water. These measures were a selling point with the community, which understood that even with no moving parts, the water would be cleaner than if there were no development.

🖰 For more information on this subject please see
www.sherwoodinstitute.org/tools.

Restorative Development at Cattle Creek

The Cattle Creek site is a series of sloping topographic benches on the eastern edge of the Roaring Fork River. When the project began, much of the land was stripped of topsoil after it had been graded for a golf course by the previous owner. The Cattle Creek riparian corridor, which bisects the site, is home to a protected wetland area within the Roaring Fork Conservancy easement. The existing riparian vegetation (such as cottonwood and box elder trees) that thrives along the riverbank is also protected by the Roaring Fork Conservancy easement. The Roaring Fork Transportation Authority (RFTA) regional trail runs along the eastern edge of the site, providing an opportunity for pedestrian connections.

Figure 8-24 Soils and hydrology. Many existing natural and man-made features of the site influenced the team's vision for the development. Cattle Creek, the protected Roaring Fork Conservancy easement area, the RFTA regional trail, existing sink holes, and soil composition, as well as the natural river bluffs and mountain views, all helped to shape the design of the Cattle Creek community. Hart Howerton.

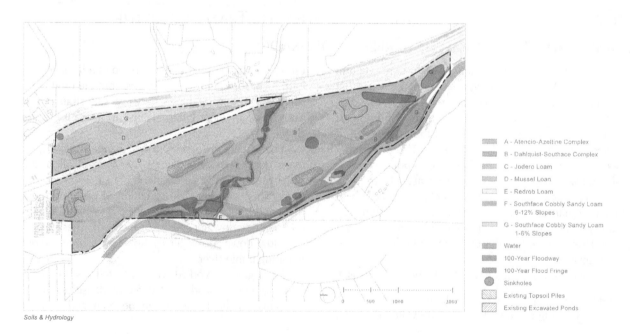

A - Atencio-Azeltine Complex
B - Dahlquist-Southace Complex
C - Jodero Loam
D - Mussel Loan
E - Redrob Loam
F - Southface Cobbly Sandy Loam 6-12% Slopes
G - Southface Cobbly Sandy Loam 1-6% Slopes
Water
100-Year Floodway
100-Year Flood Fringe
Sinkholes
Existing Topsoil Piles
Existing Excavated Ponds

Soils & Hydrology

Figure 8-25 Looking south along the RFTA corridor to Mount Sopris and the Glenwood Ditch at Cattle Creek. Hart Howerton.

An old railway corridor running through the heart of the site has been converted to a regional trail that serves as a pedestrian spine through the community. The RFTA trail forges a walkable or bikable connection between each neighborhood and the elementary school, the village core, and a proposed transit hub and park-and-ride just north of the property. Neighborhood streets lined with shade trees, landscaping, and sidewalks create a comfortable, pedestrian-friendly street landscape.

Community Framework

Cattle Creek, Colorado, includes neighborhoods that range from low to high density; the highest concentration of population is focused around the greatest concentration of activities and amenities. The diagrams that follow illustrate the transect zones at Cattle Creek. Each transect zone is an area with similar densities and related neighborhood character. Within each density transect is a variety of housing products and corresponding open spaces.

At Cattle Creek, the interconnected network of streets were conceived as pedestrian-focused, highly landscaped, multipurpose environments, safely mixing together people, bicycles, cars, and stormwater management and utility infrastructure. Residential streets are designed to slow traffic and promote pedestrian activity, comfort, and safety. Traffic-calming measures—such as short residential block lengths, variable pavement types, raised intersections, narrow pavement widths, reduced building setbacks, and managed parking—encourage slower driving speeds. Where the residential densities are higher, alleys access garages, eliminating driveways, garages, and a wall of parked cars from the streetscape. Throughout the project, streets are sized according to the density of the buildings along them, making them no wider than necessary.

Integrated Stormwater Management

A comprehensive set of stormwater best management practices (BMPs) help efficiently manage stormwater while protecting the environmental integrity of the existing wetlands and improving the water quality of Cattle Creek and the Roaring Fork River. System components including rain gardens, bioswales, naturalized channels, landscape buffers, riffle pools, permeable pavement, bioretention, cultivated wet ponds, and vegetated flood plains make it possible for the development to function harmoniously with the surrounding ecology. The routing of all wet and dry utilities has been designed to minimize the negative impacts of infrastructure, including strategies for reducing heat island effect and environmental impact, improving performance and lifecycles, maximizing utility-free planting zones, and minimizing the disturbances required for maintenance over time.

Figure 8-26a The transect for real estate product at high, medium, and low densities. Hart Howerton.

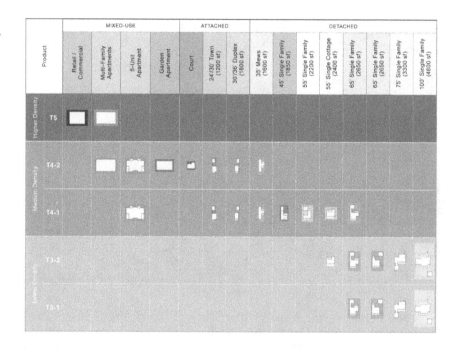

Figure 8-26b Varying densities within the core of the development are identified by different shades of gray. Hart Howerton

Figure 8-26c Urban pattern and subsequent infrastructure system
design response varies from neighborhood to neighborhood.
Hart Howerton.

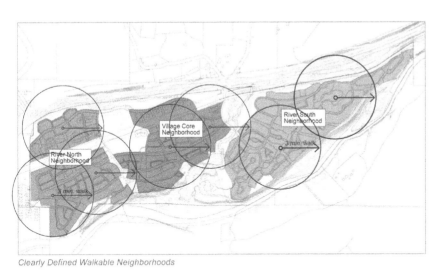

Clearly Defined Walkable Neighborhoods

Figure 8-27 Clearly defined walkable
neighborhoods. These interconnected
neighborhoods are designed to
encourage residents to walk instead of
drive within the community. The elementary school and Market Square
commercial area are located in the
heart of the community adjacent to
the densest neighborhoods, affording
easy access. Parks and open spaces
are located throughout each neighborhood, within walking distance from
each residence. Active and passive
recreation opportunities throughout
Cattle Creek link residents to an
extensive system of parks and trails.
Hart Howerton.

Cattle Creek shows how a collaborative approach can shift the developer
paradigm toward a regenerative state with simple, effective integrated design
strategies. These concepts, and the underlying approach, are highly transferable
to other projects of this type.

Figure 8-28 Local streets and connector streets in plan and section view showing vegetated zones that double as decentralized stormwater management and traffic-calming measures. Hart Howerton/Sherwood Design Engineers.

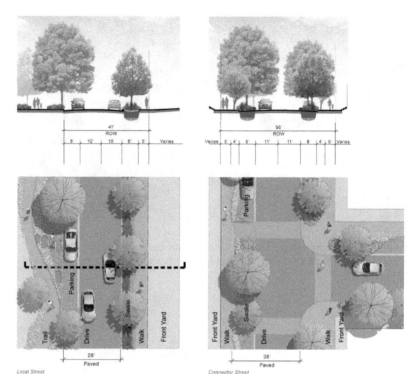

Figure 8-29 High-performance infrastructure. By designing each neighborhood as a distinct watershed, stormwater is routed into the naturalized infrastructure of neighborhood stormwater BMPs. The water flows through swales and parks and is detained and cleansed on-site before emptying into the creek. Hart Howerton/Sherwood Design Engineers.

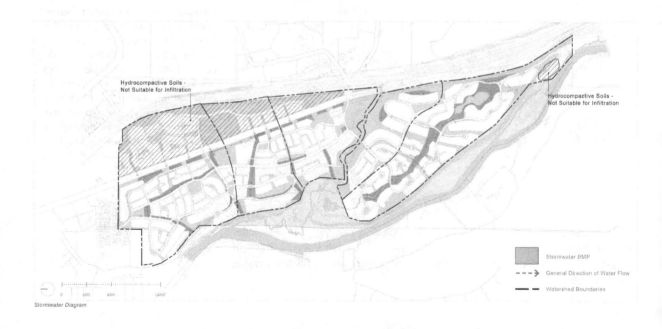

STITCHING TOGETHER LOST CONNECTIONS WITH GREEN INFRASTRUCTURE
Los Angeles State Historic Park

Jacob Petersen, Hargreaves Associates

The Los Angeles River Master Plan has set the stage for the restoration of a vast watershed that is home to one of the world's largest urban environments: the greater Los Angeles metropolitan area. This master plan recognizes the environmental value that the river once provided and the need to reconnect the urban population to this lost asset. Much of the river and its tributaries have been put into pipes and concrete channels and hidden beneath industrial users and behind chain link fences.

Sherwood Design Engineers has been working with Hargreaves Associates of San Francisco on one of the most significant planned projects that is bringing the master plan to life. A major site that sits between the Los Angeles River and downtown Los Angeles is being transformed from a polluted, nearly abandoned wasteland into a vibrant park, ecology center, and river restoration project. Jacob Petersen, principal at Hargreaves Associates, describes this project and what it means to the community and to the reorientation of Los Angeles to its ecological past.

The 32-acre Los Angeles State Historic Park occupies the historic Union Pacific Rail Yard between the channelized Los Angeles River and the expanding downtown core of the city. Surrounded by several diverse downtown neighborhoods, the park's design expresses many of the interwoven histories and the multicultural significance of this site while satisfying a broad range of year-round recreational opportunities. Los Angeles State Historic Park includes the re-creation of more than 10 acres of natural habitats in the heart of the city that vanished long ago. It also establishes a major public open space with a plaza, performance space, café, ecology center, and water features.

Community and Ecological Elements

At the heart of the park is a 5-acre multiuse lawn and performance venue, oriented toward a stage built upon the remaining foundations of the historic rail yard. A raised pedestrian bridge spans the width of the park, reconnecting the site to adjacent communities that had been separated for decades by rail infrastructure. As a modern interpretation of

Figure 8-30 The 32-acre Los Angeles State Historic Park seen in plan view, bracketed by the Los Angeles River to the right and the Chinatown light rail station to the left. Image credit: Hargreaves Associates conceptual image used with permission of California State Parks.

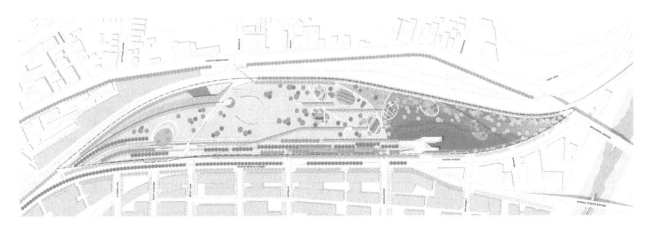

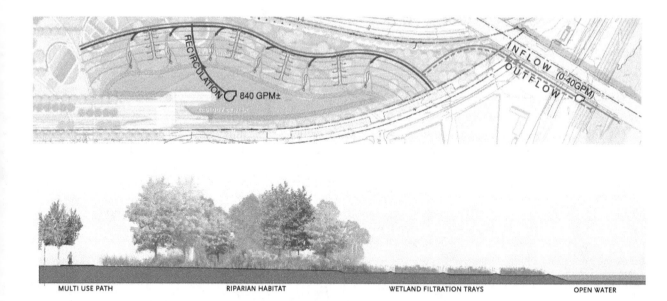

MULTI USE PATH   RIPARIAN HABITAT   WETLAND FILTRATION TRAYS   OPEN WATER

Figure 8-31 The new wetlands at Los Angeles State Historic Park will treat water from the Los Angeles River and return it back to the channel in a purer form. The wetland cells are shown here in plan (small arrows indicate where water is introduced into wetlands) and in cross-section. Hargreaves Associates conceptual image used with the permission of California State Parks.

the historic trestle bridge that previously spanned the rail yard, a "fountain bridge" will create a field of "rain" along its length, providing a whimsical interactive water element for children and refreshing relief from the hot Los Angeles sun. The fountain bridge will also be a dynamic backdrop for the central performance venue, further dramatized by the downtown skyline beyond. The rail yard plaza, which extends the length of the park frontage, features a linear garden environment that incorporates on-site parking and flexible plaza areas for special events, markets, and festivals.

The river end of the park boldly celebrates the Los Angeles River as the historic lifeblood of the city and the center of local biodiversity, with 5 acres of re-created wetland and riparian habitats and an additional 5 acres of transitional and upland habitats. These wet and dry ecologies will allow visitors to experience the incredible biological richness of the historic river corridor. Working in concert with these re-created habitat zones, an ecology center will facilitate public access to a wide range of indoor/outdoor interpretive, educational, and community programs that explore the region's complex ecological history as well as civilization's role in transforming ecologies at different scales. The ecology center will be home to a range of ongoing interactive science projects ranging from water and energy conservation to biogeographic mapping of indigenous flora and native and migratory fauna. Beyond tying the park into the larger ecosystem of the Los Angeles River basin, this center provides a context for learning about the much larger history of California and its environment.

Figure 8-32 The team has worked with federal and state agencies to allow for the physical connection of the park to the river. Shown here, the bank of the river (foreground on both sides of the train tracks) has been naturalized to serve as floodplain and habitat. Hargreaves Associates conceptual image used with permission of California State Parks.

Sustainability

The park's materials, systems, and mechanics are designed with sustainability as their foundation. Major landscape sustainability elements include the collection, detention, filtration, and storage of all stormwater within bioswales, constructed wetlands, and below-grade cisterns; the use of reclaimed water (and captured stormwater) for all irrigation; and an emphasis on drought-tolerant and native plant materials throughout the park, to create a landscape that is appropriate to the site as well as one that will conserve California's limited water supply. Constructed wetlands will remove pollutants from the adjacent Los Angeles River by diverting river water through the park's off-channel constructed wetlands. The wetland water conveyance system will be powered by microturbine generators installed within the river channel, in essence allowing the negative aspect of river channelization (i.e., the embedded energy of fast-flowing water) to provide the energy needed to move the water through this filtration process.

All buildings on the site will be minimum Leadership in Energy and Environmental Design (LEED) Silver certified and are specifically designed to integrate systems, technology, and form, allowing them to reflect the park's larger environmental goals while achieving energy self-sufficiency. Oriented along the east-west axis of the park, and with dense shading along their southern faces, the buildings are designed to minimize solar heat gain to interior spaces. All rooftops will accommodate photovoltaic cells and will be designed to collect rainwater for reuse within the structures.

Figure 8-33 In the foreground is that portion of the park that tells the story of its agricultural history. Further back is the ecology center (folding roof), native habitat, lake, and wetlands. Hargreaves Associates conceptual image used with permission of California State Parks.

Interpretation

A series of interpretive paths and gardens thread throughout the park. They offer visitors a variety of portals for learning and reflection that reveal the overlapping flows of natural, cultural, industrial, agricultural, and water-related histories that have shaped Los Angeles. In its full composition, the park seeks to acknowledge the past and yet find the universal qualities that will create new frames of reference and new windows of understanding for the future. The park is thus "an observatory" of the past, present, and future, and provides a lens for seeing—and a new language for expressing—our culture, our nature, and ourselves.

For more information on this subject please see www.sherwoodinstitite.org/casestudy.

CHAPTER 9

Building-Scale
Sustainable Infrastructure

Buildings have important connections to the community and environment they occupy as well as the infrastructure supporting their systems. Just as the architect and landscape architect make design decisions based on the surrounding built and natural environments, so must design engineers study on-site and off-site opportunities for optimizing building location, site access, water, and energy. The greatest synergies between design elements are gained when buildings are fully integrated into the sites they inhabit and the design team seeks to optimize that integration.

A collaborative approach implemented early in the design process creates great potential for systems integration, energy efficiency, and water conservation—which can pay for the up-front investment many times over during a building's life cycle. A water strategy that integrates site drainage and mechanical, plumbing, and irrigation systems can use water multiple times, dramatically increasing water efficiency. An energy strategy that integrates site design, building performance, and renewable power generation will yield significant savings in money, energy, and carbon emissions.

Understanding the opportunities and constraints for developing sustainable systems at the building scale means analyzing climate data, the local utility context, client receptiveness to nontraditional design scenarios, and code and permitting compliancy issues. During the concept design stage of any project, these opportunities and constraints should be documented in a simple format so the project team can use them to start building consensus and setting design objectives.

This chapter looks at designing more efficient buildings and high-performance sites. It discusses the highly acclaimed Academy of Sciences, designed by architect Renzo Piano with a sloping green roof that functions as a piece of San Francisco's living infrastructure. The basic principles for designing more energy-efficient buildings are also discussed in the context of Sherwood Design Engineers' work on Pearl Island, Panama, as well as in the design of the award-winning Chartwell School in California. The Sustainable Sites Initiative developed by the American Society of Landscape Architects is examined, and integrated site design from Sherwood's own work—a demonstration project for the Brisbane City Hall in California—is offered as an example.

Two highly innovative building designs are also showcased: the Stanford University Green Dorm in Palo Alto, California, a living laboratory of sustainable engineering; and Pearl River Tower in Guangzhou, China, one of the most environmentally responsive buildings in the world, designed to funnel wind through the building to generate electricity.

These are examples showing how site ecology can be enhanced through the design of a building. Establishing a connection between the built environment and local natural systems is the first step in looking for restoration or regeneration opportunities.

THE CALIFORNIA ACADEMY OF SCIENCES, SAN FRANCISCO, CALIFORNIA

In 1999, the California Academy of Sciences invited a number of top architects to present ideas for renovating the historic science museum in the heart of San Francisco's Golden Gate Park. Five of the finalists came in with impressive presentations and carefully prepared models. The final candidate, Italian architect Renzo Piano, came in with a sketchpad and a green pen. Instead of presenting his own vision, he had the academy staff sit in a circle, and he began to ask them about their own vision for the museum.

For several days he engaged in a dialogue with the staff and walked through the park. He wanted to understand how the park fit into this famously hilly city and how the museum could fit into the park. After seeing the view from the roof of the existing building, he realized that the building—as a science museum dedicated to nature—could become a living part of the park. When Piano finally presented his design to the staff, it was a simple drawing: an undulating line that has become the new living roof of the California Academy of Sciences, as well as a prime exam-ple of the collaborative design process and the principle of fitting our designs into the landscape.

> Golden Gate Park is one of the most beautiful parks in the world—it's filled with life and nature. And of course the academy is a natural science museum that is all about nature. These are two things that should belong to each other. And so I decided that the roof should be like a piece of the park flying—as if you cut out a piece of the park, lifted it up, and slid the museum in underneath.
>
> —Architect Renzo Piano[1]

As part of the team that helped develop this vision, architect Brett Terpeluk worked with the Renzo Piano Building Workshop to see the design through to its implementation and reopening as a world-class museum. Terpeluk describes the workings of this extraordinary building below.

Figure 9-1 The California Academy of Sciences, as seen from above, includes a 2.5-acre green roof. Tom Fox, SWA Group.

CREATING THE NEW ACADEMY

Brett Terpeluk, Studio Terpeluk

Envisioned as a physical extension of nature and science, the California Academy of Sciences is defined by both its historical legacy and its immersion in Golden Gate Park. The vegetated roof is a metaphorical section of park lofted 36 feet into the air and draped over the building's rectilinear and spherical volumes. Populated by 1.7 million native drought-resistant plants, the roof's 2.5-acre area represents one of the largest swaths of native vegetation in San Francisco, contributing significantly to the region's ecology. Its organic diaphragm acts as both a thermal insulator and an ecological sponge, absorbing water while attracting wildlife and migrating pollinators. Its steel and glass perimeter provides canopy shading and 213,000 kilowatts of photovoltaic-generated power annually; 3.6 million gallons of stormwater are collected in subgrade recharge chambers, which allow percolation back into the local aquifer. The round portholes that punctuate the roof allow for the daylighting of tropical exhibits while exhausting heated air. The roof is also a living public exhibit of ecological experimentation as well as the nerve center of the building, monitoring the wind speeds and directions, sunlight, and rainfall that drive the matrix of active systems below.

Site Manipulation

Using the renovated historical building volume as a site datum, the new building components were distributed to accommodate a net floor area increase with a reduction in footprint. These competing objectives necessitated an excavation two stories below grade to house five levels of research and collection spaces. The site landform was laid back from the excavated portions of the building, permitting 90 percent of these occupied areas access to daylight, views, and natural ventilation. The slopes were planted with native ferns while native tree species were reintroduced in the adjacent landscaping, thus stitching the site back into its natural surroundings.

Figure 9-2 The two cross-sections shown here illustrate the undulating roof forms that support the green roof and create interior spaces housing a planetarium, a tropical rainforest, and other uses. Renzo Piano Building Workshop.

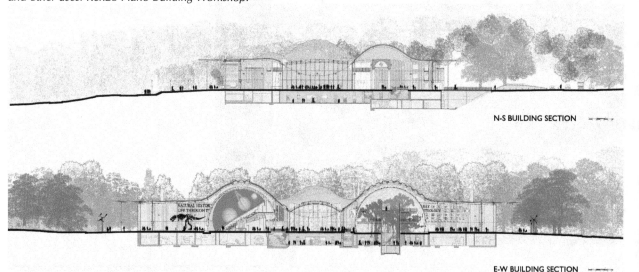

N-S BUILDING SECTION

E-W BUILDING SECTION

Energy and Thermal Comfort

The academy can be viewed as a container of diverse ecosystems, each requiring precise control of temperature, humidity, and lighting levels. The project's primary energy conservation challenge was to balance the vitality of these extreme habitats with the demands of thermal comfort in a naturally ventilated environment. The coastal siting of the building allows for the exploitation of westerly winds off the Pacific Ocean, which are pulled through the 430-foot-long, 47,000-square-foot exhibit hall. The volume and velocity of airflow is calibrated by an array of operable windows, while the large opening in the center of the building acts as a giant lung, inhaling or exhausting fresh air depending on climatic conditions and pressure differentials. The operable skylights distributed at the upper extremities of the domes capture the higher wind velocities, driving a continuous stack effect for the rising hot air.

The spherical nature of both the rainforest exhibit and the planetarium allow for smooth, laminar air circulation throughout the exhibit hall. The rainforest is a contained ecosystem within the exhibit hall with an independent air supply and exhaust capacity. Condensation typically associated with tropical environments is eliminated by the use of registers that push cool air along the inside face of the spherical glazing. Outside the sphere, the adjacent skylights exhaust the heat buildup from 250 kilowatts of life-support lighting. Given the temperature and humidity fluctuations associated with a naturally ventilated space, smaller-scale environments contained and displayed on the exhibit floor rely on localized climatic controls, thus minimizing the heating and cooling demands on the building's system.

Reduced building energy usage—35 percent lower than code requirements—is achieved by a computerized building management system that regulates airflow, radiant heating and cooling, exterior retractable sunshades, carbon dioxide (CO_2) sensors, and dimmable lighting. Extensive daylighting, HVAC heat recovery systems, and reverse osmosis humidification systems also contribute to energy efficiency, while the thermal mass of the living roof reduces the building's cooling load. The sixty thousand photovoltaic cells generate 5 percent of the building's annual energy needs.

Material Use and Reuse

Working closely with the contractor, our team carefully salvaged 90 percent of the demolition debris, refurbished existing building components, and specified a range of both regional and recycled materials. Historically significant building components were seismically upgraded and renovated

Figure 9-3 The building form allows for smooth air circulation through the interior spaces. The large opening in the center takes in or exhausts air, depending on climatic conditions and pressure differentials. The operable skylights atop the domes capture wind, driving a continuous stack effect for the rising hot air. Renzo Piano Building Workshop.

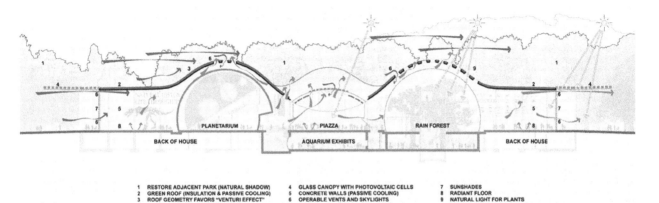

1	RESTORE ADJACENT PARK (NATURAL SHADOW)	4	GLASS CANOPY WITH PHOTOVOLTAIC CELLS	7	SUNSHADES
2	GREEN ROOF (INSULATION & PASSIVE COOLING)	5	CONCRETE WALLS (PASSIVE COOLING)	8	RADIANT FLOOR
3	ROOF GEOMETRY FAVORS "VENTURI EFFECT"	6	OPERABLE VENTS AND SKYLIGHTS	9	NATURAL LIGHT FOR PLANTS

Figure 9-4 Daylighting, views, and natural ventilation were achieved through excavation and grading outside the building. Exterior retractable sunshades allow for passive heating and cooling, depending on the season (and the resulting sun angles). Renzo Piano Building Workshop.

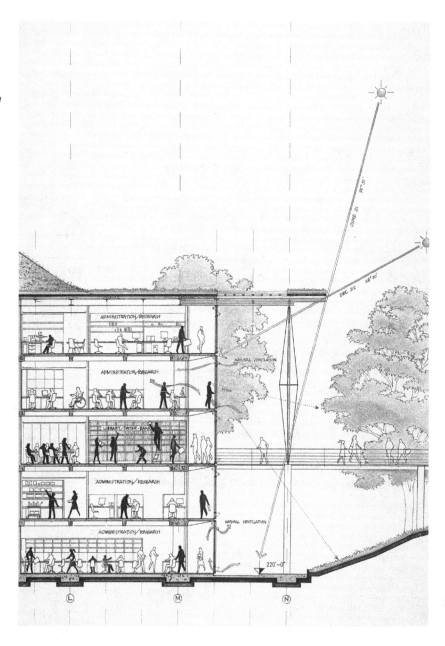

to the extent possible. Excavated soil was reused for adjacent landscaping, 9,000 tons of concrete debris was reused for roadway construction, and 12,000 tons of steel was recycled locally. All new concrete used a combination of 30 percent fly ash and 20 percent slag, by-products of coal-fired power plants and metal smelting, respectively. One hundred percent of the structural steel was composed of recycled material. The recycled denim fabric selected for acoustical insulation is a postindustrial product composed primarily of cotton, a rapidly renewable resource.

Water and Living Systems

The primarily subgrade life support system drives a range of aquatic habitats, from tropical to subarctic. Water from the Pacific Ocean is continuously pumped through a 2-mile pipeline to replenish the slowly evaporating water in the tanks. Before circulating through the extensive network of piping en route to the tanks, the water is carefully fil-tered and chemically balanced to meet the specific needs of each aquatic habitat. All water consumption systems and equipment are highly water efficient. The public bathrooms utilize waterless urinals and dual-flush toilets, while miniturbines in the low-flow faucets power activation sensors. Exhibit signage above fixtures encourages water conservation and, as a gesture toward waste reduction, all bottled water usage has been eliminated from the academy.

CHARTWELL SCHOOL: DESIGN TEACHES CHILDREN TO CELEBRATE WATER AND ENERGY

Douglas Atkins, executive director of Chartwell Elementary School, believes that an ideal learning environment is one that teaches students both inside and outside the classroom. When he set out to build a new campus for the school—founded to serve students with a wide range of language-related learning challenges—on the old army base at Fort Ord in Monterey, California, Atkins assembled the most innovative design team he could find, which included EHDD Architecture, GLS Landscape Architecture, and Sherwood Design Engineers, among others. The result of our work is the new Leadership in Energy and Environmental Design (LEED) Platinum–certified Chartwell School campus.

Recently named one of the American Institute of Architects Committee on the Environment's (AIA/COTE) Top Ten Green Projects, Chartwell School incorporates water features that teach students about their connection to natural resources. From a rainwater harvesting system to

Figure 9-5 Incorporating innovative water-saving features, among the many strategies employed, helps Chartwell School achieve educational and environmental success. Michael David Rose Photography.

Figure 9-6 Harvested rainwater is used to reduce potable water demands at Chartwell School and to educate children about environmental stewardship. Michael David Rose Photography.

dual-flush toilets and waterless urinals, Chartwell preserves water and energy while offering students a firsthand lesson in sustainability, in this way serving as both a model and a working laboratory for designing better-performing schools.

Water as a Teaching Tool

Monterey's water supply is severely constrained, so to maximize this valuable resource, our team installed a rainwater harvesting system that doubles as an educational tool for students.

The school's roof is a conventional standing metal seam roof, with gravity gutter downspouts that drain into a 1,000-gallon sump tank in the ground. That water is then pumped into an 8,000-gallon cistern right outside the classrooms. The tank has a measuring device showing the water level, which allows students to see how much the level increases each time it rains.

When the tank overflows, it automatically spills into an interactive water sluice that students can see and engage with. A weekend of heavy rain typically fills the tank to the brim, so the students get a real-time lesson in the importance of rainfall half a dozen times a season.

Atkins notes that dyslexic students often have relative strengths in visuospatial problem solving, so keeping systems exposed and letting students see the pipes and machinery helps their understanding of the world and their connection to it. Sherwood planned Chartwell's water features accordingly: overflow is used to water the science garden and the windowsill gardens outside each classroom. Math classes use the cistern to do calculations about precipitation rates, surface area, and volume.

The harvested rainwater is then filtered and used for nonpotable toilet flushing, which is the dominant use of water in the building. With one-third of the roof as a catchment area, Chartwell reduces its potable water demand by 60 to 70 percent.

Another innovative water feature at Chartwell are the fog catchers: specially designed nets that convert coastal fog to water droplets that collect in a tank. The units are part of a worldwide science project that collects data from fog catchers and is helping to demonstrate the viability of using fog to promote subsistence agriculture in places like the Atacama Desert in Chile.[2] All these features help students connect with water locally while broadening their perspective globally.

✒ For more information on this subject please see www.sherwoodinstitute.org/ideas.

Energy-Efficient Building Techniques

Using a U.S. Environmental Protection Agency (EPA) Design for Deconstruction research grant, the Chartwell School team explored building materials that could be easily disassembled for maintenance or reconstruction and thereby provide closed-loop material cycles.

Despite building on the site of the former officer's club, our team had to excavate and reengineer the land up to 17 feet deep in some places, including behind a substantial retaining wall. A major concern became the embodied energy of concrete, which is much higher than that of wood. So instead of pouring the long retaining wall from traditional concrete (which makes that energy much harder to recover), we used a tieback dry-stack retaining wall system. Each of the separate pieces can be unstacked and used again.

The team followed the same philosophy with numerous other components of the building, including windows and doors. We exposed electrical boxes and conduits, making them easier to access for maintenance and repair while helping the students understand how the building works. By building with fewer, bigger components—like large trusses spaced 4 feet apart—the team reduced material use, saving dozens of joists, hundreds of clips, and thousands of nails.

Design Informing Behavior

Cutting-edge facilities like Chartwell School are a blend of high-tech and human operation. Principal Atkins knows well that even good technology is only 70 percent of the battle. To truly "celebrate water," the students must learn how to use the buttons on the dual-flush toilets, while teachers must learn to control temperature and light by opening windows and drawing shades instead of flicking switches.

If Chartwell is proof that building higher-performing schools and workplaces begins with good design, it is also proof that it doesn't end there. Ultimately, these lessons apply to all green buildings.

"We're in a race to transform our building stock on a massive scale," says Scott Shell of EHDD Architecture. "We're trying to outpace climate change, and it's unclear who's going to win that race right now. In California, water has enormous embodied energy, so we hope our efforts toward water efficiency and rainwater collection at Chartwell help speed the transformation to a new model."

In seeking to design an optimal learning environment, our team developed a project that we continue to learn from, and that inspires others to do the same. As architects, designers, and engineers, we have as much to learn about how buildings and the environment work together as the students and teachers at Chartwell School.

Pearl Island, Panama: Designing Buildings for Energy Savings

Hart Howerton, Atelier Ten, and Sherwood Design Engineers

The Pearl Island project is covered more fully in chapter 8. This section concentrates on building-scale strategies that helped reduce energy use and were critical to the success of the project's vision for sustainable development. These elements, defined below, are helpful tools and design considerations for buildings in many of the places engineers work.

Well-designed, properly oriented buildings employ numerous built-in energy savings strategies. Enhanced building envelopes, high-efficiency appliances, and climate-responsive design are energy-efficiency features that can reduce residential and commercial electricity use by 40 to 60 percent over buildings where these steps are not taken.

Passive design strategies make use of a site's natural forces to provide warmth, light, and comfort. These strategies save energy throughout the life of a project, and include proper building orientation, appropriate glazing ratio, external shading, thermal zoning, insulation, and natural ventilation. High-performance walls and windows, as well as thermal massing and passive conditioning, can also be explored. These are fundamental passive design strategies for any climate.

Designers can greatly reduce the size of the energy production system by optimizing the performance of each building, calibrating energy production over the course of a day more closely to energy demand, and utilizing a series of intelligent systems to capitalize on the behavior of occupants and residents.

1. Trees and vegetation will shade buildings from morning heat gain.
2. Deep roof overhangs on the south and west facades shield interior spaces from afternoon heat gain, reducing the need for space cooling. Ceiling fans are included in these "transitional" spaces to complement natural breezes.
3. Fixed shading devices (trellises, shutters, landscape elements) shield interior spaces from direct gain.
4. Thin building masses combined with large window openings encourage natural ventilation to maximize "free" cooling.
5. Breezes blowing over water elements like pools, ponds, and fountains provide increased evaporative cooling in drier seasons or climates.

Shading and Orientation

Shading and building orientation can help to minimize a building's heating and cooling loads, thereby reducing energy use. By preventing direct solar radiation from landing on windows, building shading prevents heat buildup

Figure 9-7 In warmer climates, buildings set into the landscape can utilize the natural conditions of the site to reduce heat gain and provide passive cooling. Hart Howerton.

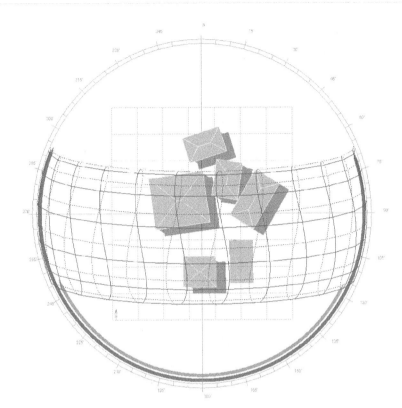

Figure 9-8 Sun-path diagram. The consideration of building orientation on a site-by-site basis can significantly reduce heat gain—and, consequently, energy demand—for a building. Atelier Ten.

inside the building. Shading also plays an important role in creating a visually comfortable interior environment, reducing glare and promoting even daylight distribution. Building orientation is the foundation for a successful shading strategy, facilitating control of solar gains and deployment of overhangs, louvers, shades, screens, and shutters. Effective shading and orientation strategies should be considered for each building type.

Design Recommendations for Effective Shading

- Provide external shading for all glazed areas. Shading type and geometry can be optimized as the building design progresses. Consider fixed versus movable shades and internal shades for supplementary glare control.
- Orient buildings north to south to reduce heating and cooling loads.

- Shading devices should be made of light and reflective materials to avoid absorption and reradiation of heat.
- Shading devices should be designed to prevent reflection onto any part of the buildings or openings and to prevent trapping hot air.

Thermal Zoning

One of the most effective ways to reduce energy use for air-conditioning is to define thermal zones within a building with different comfort requirements. These requirements change over the course of a day, in sometimes unpredictable ways. Zoning and partitioning buildings can prevent accidental energy waste, such as air-conditioning one area while windows are open in another. Figure 9-9 shows thermal zoning of a typical residence at Pearl Island.

Bedrooms are likely the most closely conditioned spaces, because occupants are sedentary and are sensitive to discomfort due to variations in temperature and humid-

Figure 9-9 Typical thermal zoning diagram. Thermal zoning in buildings on Pearl Island allows for a dramatic reduction in energy demands, cooling only the area necessary at any given time. Atelier Ten.

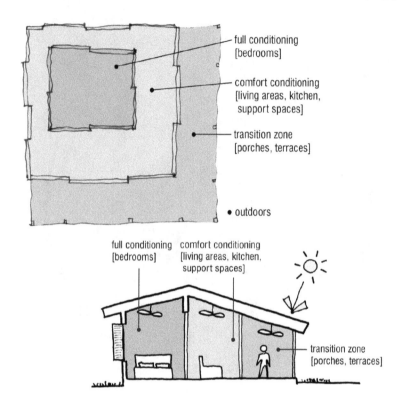

full conditioning
[bedrooms]

comfort conditioning
[living areas, kitchen,
    support spaces]

transition zone
[porches, terraces]

• outdoors

full conditioning   comfort conditioning
[bedrooms]   [living areas, kitchen,
        support spaces]

transition zone
[porches, terraces]

ity while sleeping. Work areas can be similarly restrictive. These areas can be partitioned so they can be closed off from the rest of the house.

Living areas, kitchens, and support areas can often be conditioned more loosely. These areas may be opened to the outdoors more often, using operable windows or doors. Occupants may be more active in these rooms and therefore tolerant of broader temperature ranges.

Outdoor living spaces can act as transition spaces, or buffers, between outside and indoor conditions. A gradual transition from outside to inside is usually more comfortable than an abrupt change. This transition zone can be open to the outdoors, or it can be open to the living areas, depending on preference and climate.

Natural Ventilation

The transitional areas, such as living rooms and outdoor spaces, have wider comfort ranges than bedrooms. These spaces can be naturally ventilated. In addition to providing fresh air, natural ventilation can augment air move-

ment, which increases evaporation off the skin and thereby cools the body, effectively widening the comfort zone.

Single-sided ventilation relies on windows on one side of the space for incoming and outgoing air. Ventilation air from a single side cannot penetrate into deep spaces, so this strategy is best suited to shallow rooms with large windows.

Cross-ventilation moves air from one facade to another and is effective with somewhat smaller windows and deeper spaces. Ideally, the design team should locate inlet openings to capture the prevailing wind direction. For the most effective cross-ventilation, inlet and outlet should be roughly similar in size; this will allow air to enter and exit through any opening if the wind changes direction. Windows should be placed so air crosses the narrowest dimension of the space. In taller spaces, such as stair shafts, stack ventilation may also be effective.

Stack ventilation relies on the natural convection of warm air to the top of a space, drawing cooler outside air in its wake. Stack effects are somewhat harder to predict, but rules of thumb for sizing windows and chimneys are at bottom left of each diagram.

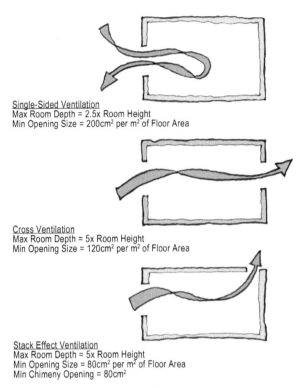

Single-Sided Ventilation
Max Room Depth = 2.5x Room Height
Min Opening Size = 200cm² per m² of Floor Area

Cross Ventilation
Max Room Depth = 5x Room Height
Min Opening Size = 120cm² per m² of Floor Area

Stack Effect Ventilation
Max Room Depth = 5x Room Height
Min Opening Size = 80cm² per m² of Floor Area
Min Chimeny Opening = 80cm²

Figure 9-10 Natural ventilation strategies. A variety of natural ventilation techniques can be applied, based on the specifics of the building design. Atelier Ten.

SUSTAINABLE SITES INITIATIVE

This sidebar contains both paraphrases and direct quotes from http://www.sustainablesites.org (accessed October 15, 2009).

There has been an enormous focus on green buildings over the last decade, with a proliferation of ratings standards, performance criteria, and policy initiatives focused on increasing the sustainability of the built environment. But buildings are only one piece of any site. The exterior environment is an equally important component—one that has received much less attention. The Sustainable Sites Initiative is an interdisciplinary effort led by the American Society of Landscape Architects (ASLA) to address that gap in our current practice of sustainability. In partnership with the Ladybird Johnson Wildflower Center and the United States Botanic Garden, the Sustainable Sites Initiative was created to promote sustainable land development and management practices for all sites, with and without buildings, including

- open spaces such as local, state, and national parks; conservation easements and buffer zones; and transportation rights-of-way;
- sites with buildings, including industrial, retail, and office parks; military complexes; airports; botanical gardens; streetscapes and plazas; residential and commercial developments; and public and private campuses.

The Sustainable Sites Initiative has created voluntary national guidelines and performance benchmarks for sustainable land design, construction, and maintenance practices. These are intended to provide tools for design professionals and policy makers who influence land development and management practices. The guidelines are meant to be used by a wide range of people who design, construct, operate, and maintain landscapes, including planners, landscape architects, engineers, developers, builders, maintenance crews, horticulturists, governments, land stewards, and organizations offering building standards.

A Steering Committee representing eleven stakeholder groups was selected to guide the initiative. More than thirty experts working on a range of technical subcommittees have developed sustainable benchmarks for soils, hydrology, vegetation, human health and well-being, and material selection. The U.S. Green Building Council (USGBC), a stakeholder in the initiative, anticipates incorporating these guidelines and performance benchmarks into future iterations of the LEED Green Building Rating System.

The Sustainable Sites Initiative guidelines and performance benchmarks can apply to all landscapes. The guidelines are designed to create voluntary standards that will

- elevate the value of landscapes by outlining the economic, environmental, and human well-being benefits of sustainable sites;
- connect buildings and landscapes to contribute to environmental and community health;
- provide performance benchmarks for site sustainability;
- link research and practice associated with the most sustainable materials and techniques for site development construction and maintenance;
- provide recognition for high performance in sustainable site design, development, and maintenance;
- encourage innovation.

For more information on the Sustainable Sites Initiative please see www.sherwoodinstitute.org/resources.

BRISBANE CITY HALL: GREEN SITE DESIGN

Kevin Perry and Ben Ngan, Nevue Ngan Associates

As part of the water pollution control measures taken in San Mateo County, California, a $4 vehicle registration fee was recently imposed on motor vehicles registered in the county. A portion of those funds was earmarked for demonstration projects that showcase the use of sustainable stormwater management facilities to reduce, capture, and treat runoff from roadways and parking lots. A prime example of such a project is the site design of the city hall in Brisbane, California, a small city in San Mateo County. Nevue Ngan Associates and Sherwood Design Engineers collaborated to redesign the city hall parking lot to achieve multiple site design objectives. Nevue Ngan Associates completed the conceptual design of the Brisbane City Hall improvements and worked closely with Sherwood to incorporate several key design principles throughout the design process.

Site Layout Strategy: Provide Efficient Site Design

One of the first questions designers or builders should ask themselves about their project is, has the impervious area from streets, parking lots, and/or buildings been minimized? From a design perspective, there are several effective strategies for minimizing these areas. What makes sense from a design perspective, however, may conflict with prevailing policy. Design and policy must work together in order to achieve site-specific stormwater goals. A carefully thought-out site plan will often yield the space for a stormwater facility that fits seamlessly with the other site uses. This holds true for new streets, parking lots, and buildings but is especially evident when designing street and parking lot retrofit projects.[3]

For Brisbane City Hall, our design team emphasized efficient site design in order to maximize potential landscape area and minimize impervious surface. The site was designed to drain stormwater runoff onto the landscape's surface and minimize underground piped infrastructure. The parking lot and overall site were greened by adding new drainage features, trees, and extensive stormwater-tolerant plantings.

Figure 9-11 Brisbane City Hall was an implementation opportunity for the San Mateo Green Streets program. Without losing any parking stalls, this retrofit project incorporates comprehensive stormwater management in areas that were previously used for parking. © Sherwood Design Engineers.

Figure 9-12 Brisbane City Hall. The improvements to the site include the transformation of asphalt parking into a large rain garden as well as vegetated bioswales throughout the site to treat stormwater runoff. © Sherwood Design Engineers.

Choose Stormwater Facilities

Designing stormwater facilities that actively capture and treat runoff from impervious surfaces is the first priority. The shape and slope of the site, as well as the rainfall char-acteristics, all help determine the type of facilities that are appropriate for a particular site. Vegetated swales, planters, rain gardens, and other stormwater facilities can be designed to match a site's land use and its various constraints.

Figure 9-13 Bioswales are a key component of green streets retrofit projects. They are often able to fit into long, linear spaces at the edges of streets and to provide infiltration and water quality benefits. This installation at Brisbane City Hall creatively weaves around utility obstacles and fits between the street and the building. © Sherwood Design Engineers.

Figure 9-14 From a report by Steven R. Hartsell, registered environmental health specialist, on April 23, 2009, percolation test results in the rain garden show an average percolation rate of 15.5 minutes per inch. This indicates that the soil in this planter now has a capacity to disperse water at rate of 0.8 gallons per square foot of infiltrative area per day. This is far better than the rate previously achieved in this area: 0.2 gallons per square foot of infiltrative area per day. Nevue Ngan Associates.

At Brisbane City Hall, the design team introduced a stepped rain garden that allows for sedimentation, treatment, and infiltration. Thus, each stage of the rain garden was designed to accomplish certain water treatment functions. Room for the large rain garden was created by redesigning the parking lot in a more efficient way to yield landscape space for stormwater management without losing any parking capacity. In turn, runoff from the parking lot is treated in the rain garden and a swale integrated into the landscape on the other side of the building. Runoff from the building's rooftop is also treated in these facilities prior to being discharged into the city's storm drain system.

🖱 For more information on this subject please see www.sherwoodinstitite.org/casestudy.

STANFORD UNIVERSITY GREEN DORM: A LIVING LABORATORY

Brad Jacobsen, project manager, EHDD Architecture

The Stanford Green Dorm project is unique in its conception in many ways: as a housing project overseen by the School of Engineering; as an engineering lab cohabitating with a forty-seven-student dorm; but most of all, as a living laboratory for ongoing research and education on sustainable building, engineering, and student living. The building provides a framework that supports both short- and long-term transformations. As building monitoring reveals the subtle workings of the building's ecosystem, refinements can be made to improve its performance. In the long term, as building technology continues to advance over the next several decades, equipment can be swapped out and tested in situ.

Sustainable buildings need to perform in the real world. Research by the New Buildings Institute indicates that actual building performance does not track very well to performance modeled during the design stage. The primary reason for this seems to be the difficulty in predicting actual usage and ensuring proper commissioning and operation. We need new models of design processes that embrace the full life cycle of buildings and enlarge the concept of integrated design to include the people who

Figure 9-15 A cross-section of the green dorm highlights strategies that transform this building into a "living laboratory." EHDD Architecture.

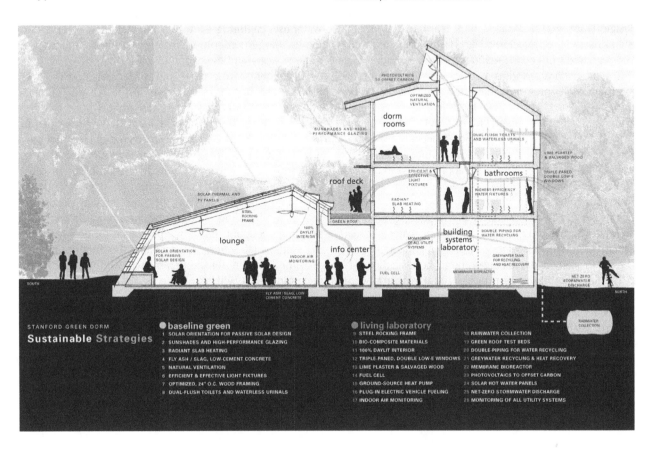

STANFORD GREEN DORM
Sustainable Strategies

● **baseline green**
1 SOLAR ORIENTATION FOR PASSIVE SOLAR DESIGN
2 SUNSHADES AND HIGH-PERFORMANCE GLAZING
3 RADIANT SLAB HEATING
4 FLY ASH / SLAG, LOW-CEMENT CONCRETE
5 NATURAL VENTILATION
6 EFFICIENT & EFFECTIVE LIGHT FIXTURES
7 OPTIMIZED, 24" O.C. WOOD FRAMING
8 DUAL-FLUSH TOILETS AND WATERLESS URINALS

● **living laboratory**
9 STEEL ROCKING FRAME
10 BIO-COMPOSITE MATERIALS
11 100% DAYLIT INTERIOR
12 TRIPLE-PANED, DOUBLE LOW-E WINDOWS
13 LIME PLASTER & SALVAGED WOOD
14 FUEL CELL
15 GROUND-SOURCE HEAT PUMP
16 PLUG-IN ELECTRIC VEHICLE FUELING
17 INDOOR AIR MONITORING

18 RAINWATER COLLECTION
19 GREEN ROOF TEST BEDS
20 DOUBLE-PIPING FOR WATER RECYCLING
21 GREYWATER RECYCLING & HEAT RECOVERY
22 MEMBRANE BIOREACTOR
23 PHOTOVOLTAICS TO OFFSET CARBON
24 SOLAR HOT WATER PANELS
25 NET-ZERO STORMWATER DISCHARGE
26 MONITORING OF ALL UTILITY SYSTEMS

Figure 9-16 Students conducted experiments in other dorm buildings to gather necessary data that helped shape the building system design response. Professor John Haymaker, Stanford University, Department of Civil and Environmental Engineering.

will operate and occupy projects over their lifetime. The defining feature of the Stanford Green Dorm project is the early engagement of the widest range of stakeholders, including students (users), faculty (researchers), and student housing staff (operators), and the centrality of life-cycle thinking to design goals. This expanded, integrated design team was led through a feasibility study that encompassed the project in all its phases, from conception to design and from construction through occupation.[4]

The project has served as a vehicle for learning from the very start. Many professors integrated the project into their curricula and used it as the basis for assignments. Student-led research projects contributed crucial data to the project and beyond. For example, one sophomore student tested a selection of ultra-low-flow showerheads in student dorms and found a few that met with student approval. Based on these results, the university swapped out 1,827 showerheads in the dorms during winter break. By reducing water flow from 2.5 gallons per minute to 1.3 gallons per minute, Stanford now saves an estimated 12 million gallons of water per year. Other research included shower water temperature research to assist in sizing and reducing domestic hot water loads.

Faculty members have structured research around the design process as well. For example, Professor John Haymaker led the development of a goal preferences survey and design option matrix dubbed MACDADI (multi-attribute collective decision analysis for design initiatives). This matrix ties potential design strategies directly to project goals, which are then weighted according to the values that various stakeholders assign. This process will continue through the design process to track the success of the design in meeting project goals.

The overarching design goal was to create a facility that supports ongoing learning and research, and that changes over time. Project team members expect that meeting performance goals requires participation and experimentation throughout the life of the building. One primary performance goal is to close the water cycle by reducing water use, capturing rainwater, and recycling water within the building in order to ultimately eliminate the import of potable water and the export of wastewater.

The extent of recycling and reuse will increase over time as sampling and testing confirms the quality of treated graywater and blackwater. Researchers hope that the results will not only convince local code authorities to allow the use of treated water on this project but that they might impact building codes throughout the state of California and beyond. Similarly, the goal of a zero-energy building will be met through experimentation both on the building systems side and the way occupants live in the building, recognizing the critical impact that building occupants have on energy use. An on-site building systems laboratory will facilitate this monitoring and provide flexibility for the deployment and testing of new technologies; it will also serve as a teaching lab for students and visitors.

The Stanford Green Dorm is a framework to be occupied and acted on by students and researchers. Attempting to achieve zero-energy and zero-water buildings requires a very different understanding of the relationship of design to building operation by design teams, owners, and users. Design sets up the potential for resource efficiency. Construction teams need to commission buildings to optimize performance on day one.

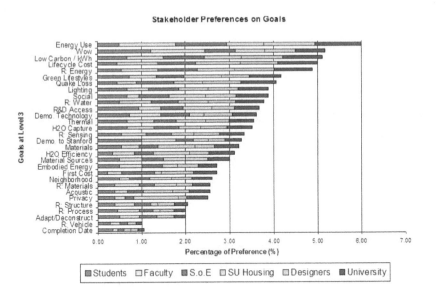

Figure 9-17 *The MACDADI survey polls stakeholders on preferences to create a values-based decision-making tool.[5] Professor John Haymaker, Stanford University, Department of Civil and Environmental Engineering.*

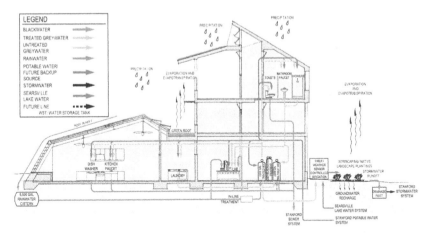

Figure 9-18 *Sherwood Design Engineers developed the water balance for the green dorm as a net-zero system. It is designed to phase in over time and eventually be fully independent of municipal water, recycling all of the water it consumes and augmenting the building's needs with rainwater collected from the roof. © Sherwood Design Engineers.*

Facility managers need to maintain and schedule buildings appropriately. Building users need to operate buildings effectively.

Finally, building performance data must be collected at a level of granularity that enables us to both understand how a project is performing compared to appropriate benchmarks and to troubleshoot areas of underperformance. In the near future, such data will be readily accessible to building users, operators, and designers via the Internet, ensuring a continued engagement with project performance after the pencils have been put down and the last hard hats have left the site.

PEARL RIVER TOWER, GUANGZHOU, CHINA

Project Context

The Pearl River Tower began as a response to an international design competition in which the Chicago office of Skidmore, Owings & Merrill (SOM) was invited to participate by the client, CMTC of China, a quasi-governmental entity. The design team created a concept through which both the passive and active energy strategies shape the form of the building, and the form of the building, in turn, optimizes their functionality.

Design

Roger Frechette, who headed SOM's engineering team for the Burj Khalifa in Dubai, the world's tallest building, also led the engineering design effort for the Pearl River Tower. The tower is a 71-story, 2.3-million-square-foot office building with an overall height of 309.6 meters. "Sustainability can often be nonspecific and confusing," says Frechette. He wanted to come up with something clear and understandable to the layperson. So his team decided to make it a zero-energy building.

The designers defined *zero energy* for this building as creating no net increase in demand on the city's power-generating infrastructure.

The building was designed based on the four following principles:

1. Reduction (using energy-efficient systems and passive design)
2. Reclamation (reusing energy once injected into a building)
3. Absorption (tapping into surrounding streams of energy, including wind, solar radiation, and groundwater heat exchange)
4. Generation (using microturbines to generate power)

Figure 9-19 The Pearl River Tower in Guangzhou, China, is an outstanding example of the confluence of art and engineering. The engineering form that harnesses the natural forces and optimizes the sustainable systems gracefully meets architectural expression. These elements combine and respond to each other, creating an outstanding, high-performance building. © Skidmore, Owings & Merrill LLP 2009. All rights reserved.

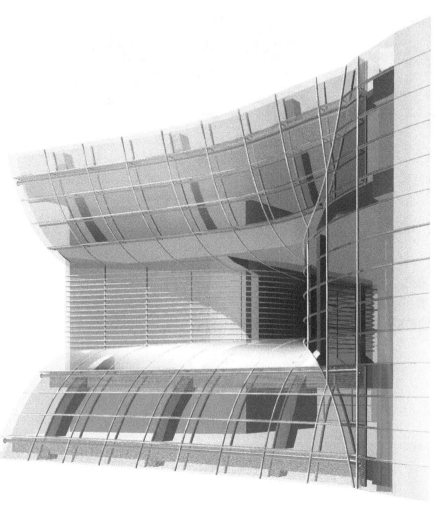

Figure 9-20 Wind turbine generators are positioned in the building's funnel-shaped recesses. These mechanical floors create power that runs the building systems. © Skidmore, Owings & Merrill LLP 2009. All rights reserved.

At one of the early competition meetings, the designers suggested that the team move past the half-hearted approach to sustainability common in the construction of high-rise towers at the time and pushed the team to embed and integrate sustainable elements into the building that could not be removed as breakaway components.

Buildings are often designed to ignore their environment. They become stoic elements constructed to withstand and defy their surroundings, from which they become insulated. SOM's team decided to turn that thinking inside out. They observed that the strongest force to be dealt with in the building's structural design was wind. (Seismic forces are less relevant for a building this tall;

designing to withstand wind forces is more important, since such buildings function as big sails.) The team suggested bringing the wind through the tower and harnessing its power rather than fighting it.

The engineers devised a building form that pulls the environment's energy into it and through it. The design outcome incorporates openings for wind turbines that funnel the wind on the building's two mechanical floors. The design maximizes the pressure differential from the front to the back of the building, drawing accelerated wind through the vortex openings. Not only do the openings provide power to the building, they also reduce the wind shear on the building, allowing the steel structure to perform better.

Figure 9-21 Two openings at each of the mechanical floors accelerate wind speeds two to three times, improving the building's power-generating potential exponentially. © Skidmore, Owings & Merrill LLP 2009. All rights reserved.

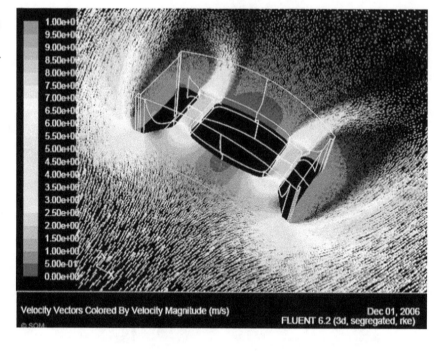

Figure 9-22 The building skin minimizes heat entering the building and ensures that glass temperatures remain low. Lower interior glass temperatures (as much as 20°F lower than those in comparable buildings), in turn, allow better use of the floor space adjacent to the glass perimeter. © Skidmore, Owings & Merrill LLP 2009. All rights reserved.

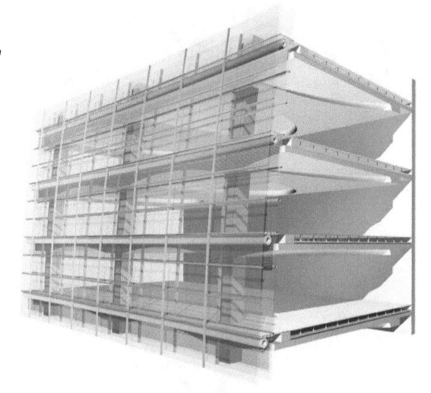

Additionally, SOM's team conceived of a design to optimize solar radiation and maximize generation from building-integrated photovoltaics (PVs). PV power is often impractical in high-rise applications; a major challenge is that PVs create direct current (DC) power, while most appliances and systems use alternating current (AC) power. In order to convert the energy from DC to AC, inverters, transformers, and rectifiers are usually needed. (Buildings typically can't use DC power because of the inefficiencies and line losses involved in moving DC power over a distance.) In Pearl River Tower, the double-wall ventilated cavity has operable blinds with eight positions between horizontal and vertical. The blinds have been designed to run off of DC power from the PVs immediately adjacent, solving the line-loss challenge. The blinds rotate into position to block the sun's rays and serve as sunshades run by DC motors when the sun is shining on the building.

The building's radiant cooling system will be the largest installation of its kind in the world, covering 2.2 million square feet. Typically, buildings of this kind are cooled by circulating large volumes of air through the building multiple times—and creating massive amounts of ductwork to handle it. With a radiant cooling system, the air is moved only for air circulation and only passes through the building once. Radiant systems work by circulating water through the building; this circulating water absorbs excess heat from occupants. Circulating water is far more efficient than circulating air because unlike air, it is noncompressible.

The Pearl River Tower has planted the seeds for change in southern China, seeds that are likely to bear fruit around the world. Rethinking the way we design buildings to become a functional extension of our infrastructure networks is fundamental to the sustainability of our cities.

Notes

1. "The Living Museum," *LIVE from the California Academy of Sciences*, 10 (fall 2008).
2. http://www.fogquest.org.
3. Nevue Ngan Associates and Sherwood Design Engineers, *San Mateo County Sustainable Green Streets and Parking Lots Design Guidebook* (2009), http://www.flowstobay.org/ms_sustainable_streets.php.
4. New Buildings Institute, http://www.newbuildings.org/measuredPerformance.htm.
5. Stanford University, "Lotus Living Laboratory," http://www.stanford.edu/group/greendorm/.

Conclusion

A movement that began with green buildings has been expanded to include green sites, green streets, and green cities. Integrated strategies for land use, infrastructure development, and the responsible management of natural resources are being developed on all continents, in dozens of countries, in hundreds of cities, and in thousands of projects all over the world. So this book ends back where it began—the beginning of a more comprehensive and integrated approach to sustainable design.

The next hundred years of urban development are poised to proceed in a radically different direction from the last hundred years. And what will make that new direction possible is the recognition that sustainable cities, like the sustainable systems they depend on, are held together by more than just a series of infrastructure projects. This book has aimed at demonstrating the value of ongoing collaboration among architects, planners, ecologists, engineers, and many others in service of this recognition. Likewise, the built environment itself is the result of a multitude of transformative agents, both technical and nontechnical. Watershed-scale thinking, life-cycle analyses, long-term sustainability planning, and forward-thinking policies are all playing a vital role in promoting responsible design. As this book has shown, engineers have a real role to play in bringing technical expertise to these nontraditional, nontechnical aspects of the field.

Sustainable design is not just about today; it is about creating the framework and laying the groundwork for a built environment that we can pass on with pride to future generations. In some cases, this means taking a long view and making a series of incremental changes so our inheritors will have sustainable societies to live in one hundred years from now. In other cases, it means making radical changes when new cities or neighborhoods are being built so that we don't repeat the unsuccessful patterns of the past.

Yet as we speed into the future, we must also delve into our history and reconnect with strategies that worked well for our ancestors. Methods used four thousand years ago to harvest water, turn waste into fertilizer and energy, or source renewable building materials must be remembered and maintained. We can embrace technology without thinking that new technologies are the only solution; passive building design and bike-friendly streets are a look both backward and forward in urban design. We must find tools and wisdom in the natural processes that are evident around us, and discover new methods for making them work in the modern environment.

It is with this understanding that we created the Sherwood Institute, a nonprofit research and policy group, established to further the advancements associated with Sherwood Design Engineers' project work. The focus of the Institute is to develop lasting solutions to implement sustainable infrastructure globally with an initial focus on the complexities surrounding our pressing issues related to water, energy and climate change.

Even as we write, rapid changes are occuring in this field. Every day new patents are filed, new projects begun, new laws passed, and new ideas discussed. There is far more to cover than could possibly be fit between these covers; with this in mind, we wish to extend the resources this book provides through an evolving, online resource we have dubbed Chapter 10. It is available online at http://www.sherwoodinstitute.org, offering greater depth into the projects featured here, as well as access to new technologies and breakthroughs in our practice. Like this book, Chapter 10 was established to advance the evolution and implementation of sustainable design, and to deepen the interdisciplinary collaboration necessary for finding solutions to complex design and engineering challenges.

Index

WILEY BOOKS ON Sustainable Design

For these and other Wiley books on sustainable design, visit www.wiley.com/go/sustainabledesign

Environmental Benefits Statement

This book is printed with soy-based inks on presses with VOC levels that are lower than the standard for the printing industry. The paper, Rolland Enviro 100, is manufactured by Cascades Fine Papers Group and is made from 100 percent post-consumer, de-inked fiber, without chlorine. According to the manufacturer, the use of every ton of Rolland Enviro100 Book paper, switched from virgin paper, helps the environment in the following ways:

Mature trees saved	Waterborne waste not created	Waterflow saved	Atmospheric emissions eliminated	Solid wastes reduced	Natural gas saved by using biogas
17	6.9 lbs.	10,196 gals.	2,098 lbs.	1,081 lbs.	2,478 cubic feet